my **revision** notes





## OCR A-level

# CHEMISTRY A

Mike Smith



HODDER
EDUCATION
AN HACHETTE UK COMPANY

Hachette UK's policy is to use papers that are natural, renewable and recyclable products and made from wood grown in sustainable forests. The logging and manufacturing processes are expected to conform to the environmental regulations of the country of origin.

Orders: please contact Bookpoint Ltd, 130 Park Drive, Milton Park, Abingdon, Oxon OX14 4SE. Telephone: (44) 01235 827720. Fax: (44) 01235 400454. Email education@bookpoint.co.uk

Lines are open from 9 a.m. to 5 p.m., Monday to Saturday, with a 24-hour message answering service. You can also order through our website: www.hoddereducation.co.uk

ISBN: 978 1 4718 4228 3



First published in 2016 by

Hodder Education,
An Hachette UK Company
Carmelite House
50 Victoria Embankment
London EC4Y 0DZ
www.hoddereducation.co.uk

Impression number 10 9 8 7 6 5 4 3 2 1

Year 2020 2019 2018 2017 2016



Cover photo reproduced by permission of Nnierda/Fotolia

Typeset in Bembo Std Regular, 11/13 pts. by Aptara, Inc.

Printed in Spain

A catalogue record for this title is available from the British Library.

# Get the most from this book

Everyone has to decide his or her own revision strategy, but it is essential to review your work, learn it and test your understanding. These Revision Notes will help you to do that in a planned way, topic by topic. Use this book as the cornerstone of your revision and don't hesitate to write in it — personalise your notes and check your progress by ticking off each section as you revise.

## Tick to track your progress

Use the revision planner on pages 4 and 5 to plan your revision, topic by topic. Tick each box when you have:

- revised and understood a topic
- tested yourself
- practised the exam questions and gone online to check your answers and complete the quick quizzes

You can also keep track of your revision by ticking off each topic heading in the book. You may find it helpful to add your own notes as you work through each topic.

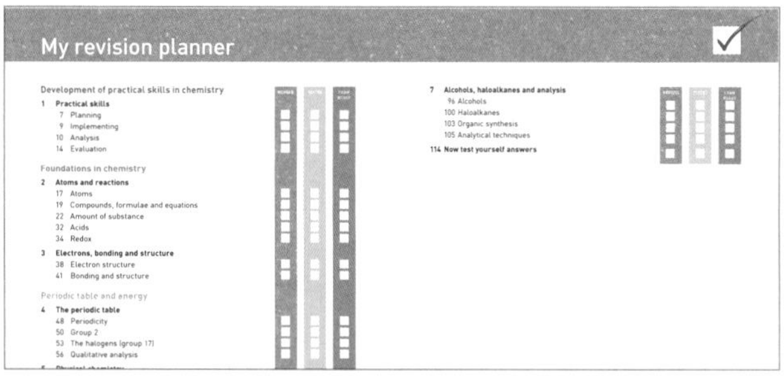


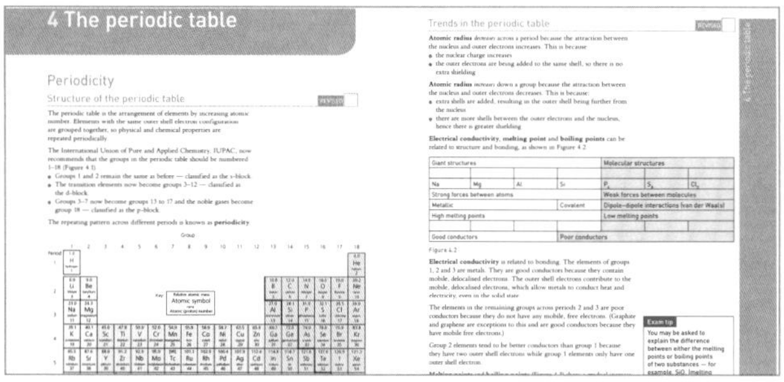


# Features to help you succeed

## Exam tips

Expert tips are given throughout the book to help you polish your exam technique in order to maximise your chances in the exam.

## Typical mistakes

The author identifies the typical mistakes candidates make and explain how you can avoid them.

## Now test yourself

These short, knowledge-based questions provide the first step in testing your learning. Answers are at the back of the book.

## Definitions and key words

Clear, concise definitions of essential key terms are provided where they first appear.

Key words from the specification are highlighted in bold throughout the book.

## Revision activities

These activities will help you to understand each topic in an interactive way.

## Exam practice

Practice exam questions are provided for each topic. Use them to consolidate your revision and practise your exam skills.

## Summaries

The summaries provide a quick-check bullet list for each topic.

## Online

Go online to check your answers to the exam questions and try out the extra quick quizzes at **www.hoddereducation.co.uk/myrevisionnotes**

087291
540SMI
TASC

# My revision planner

REVISED TESTED EXAM READY

# Countdown to my exams

## 6–8 weeks to go

- Start by looking at the specification — make sure you know exactly what material you need to revise and the style of the examination. Use the revision planner on pages 4 and 5 to familiarise yourself with the topics.
- Organise your notes, making sure you have covered everything on the specification. The revision planner will help you to group your notes into topics.
- Work out a realistic revision plan that will allow you time for relaxation. Set aside days and times for all the subjects that you need to study, and stick to your timetable.
- Set yourself sensible targets. Break your revision down into focused sessions of around 40 minutes, divided by breaks. These Revision Notes organise the basic facts into short, memorable sections to make revising easier.

REVISED ☐

## 2–5 weeks to go

- Read through the relevant sections of this book and refer to the exam tips, exam summaries, typical mistakes and key terms. Tick off the topics as you feel confident about them. Highlight those topics you find difficult and look at them again in detail.
- Test your understanding of each topic by working through the 'Now test yourself' questions in the book. Look up the answers at the back of the book.
- Make a note of any problem areas as you revise, and ask your teacher to go over these in class.
- Look at past papers. They are one of the best ways to revise and practise your exam skills. Write or prepare planned answers to the exam practice questions provided in this book. Check your answers online and try out the extra quick quizzes at **www.hoddereducation.co.uk/myrevisionnotes**
- Use the revision activities to try out different revision methods. For example, you can make notes using mind maps, spider diagrams or flash cards.
- Track your progress using the revision planner and give yourself a reward when you have achieved your target.

REVISED ☐

## 1 week to go

- Try to fit in at least one more timed practice of an entire past paper and seek feedback from your teacher, comparing your work closely with the mark scheme.
- Check the revision planner to make sure you haven't missed out any topics. Brush up on any areas of difficulty by talking them over with a friend or getting help from your teacher.
- Attend any revision classes put on by your teacher. Remember, he or she is an expert at preparing people for examinations.

REVISED ☐

## The day before the examination

- Flick through these Revision Notes for useful reminders, for example the exam tips, exam summaries, typical mistakes and key terms.
- Check the time and place of your examination.
- Make sure you have everything you need — extra pens and pencils, tissues, a watch, bottled water, sweets.
- Allow some time to relax and have an early night to ensure you are fresh and alert for the examinations.

REVISED ☐

## My exams

**A-level Chemistry A Paper 1**

Date:.................................................................

Time: .................................................................

Location: ...........................................................

**A-level Chemistry A Paper 2**

Date:.................................................................

Time: .................................................................

Location: ...........................................................

**A-level Chemistry A Paper 3**

Date:.................................................................

Time: .................................................................

Location: ...........................................................

# 1 Practical skills

Chemistry is a practical subject so the development of practical skills is essential. These skills will be assessed by your teachers, not under exam conditions. During the course you will be required to carry out a number of experiments, a minimum of 12, which are separately assessed. The experiments that you carry out will cover a range of technical skills and practical apparatus. Teachers will award a pass (or fail) to their students, and performance in this component will be integral to, and examined in, all components of the one-year and the full two-year course.

The assessment will cover four key areas: planning, implementing, analysis and evaluation.

Table 1.1 gives a brief outline of the sorts of experiments you might be expected to encounter.

**Table 1.1**

| Year 1 | Year 2 |
|---|---|
| Mole determination | Rates of reaction |
| Acid–base titration | pH measurement |
| Qualitative testing of ions | Electrochemical cells |
| Preparation of an organic liquid | Redox titrations |
| | A range of organic syntheses and organic analysis |
| You will be expected to develop your research skills throughout the course. | |

## Planning

Planning a scientific investigation is an essential skill and enables priorities to be dealt with in a controlled manner instead of simply reacting to things as they come along.

It is essential that you are able to identify the key stages in a scientific investigation and select the appropriate:

- reagents and conditions
- practical technique(s) and apparatus

When you have decided on the chemicals and apparatus that you will need you must carry out a **risk assessment** to ensure that appropriate precautions are put in place to allow the chemicals to be handled safely. Details of individual hazards can be obtained from **www.cleapss.org.uk/secondary/secondary-science/hazcards**. Whenever carrying out a chemical experiment it is usual to wear a laboratory coat and possibly protective gloves, but it is essential to *wear safety glasses at all times* when handling chemicals.

## Now test yourself

TESTED

1 Figure 1.1 shows a number of hazard warning labels. Use the internet or look up a chemical catalogue to help you identify which hazard is represented by each warning label.

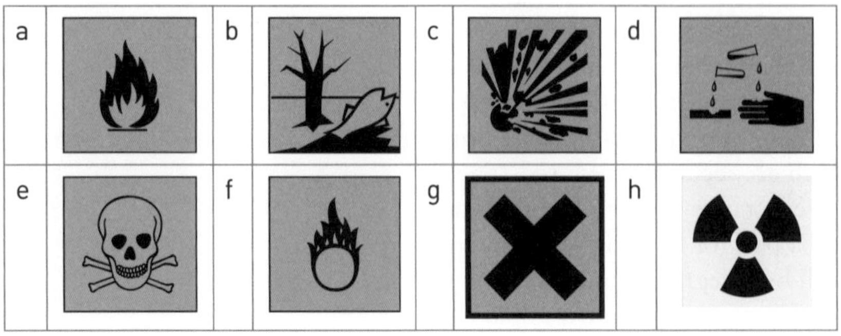


Figure 1.1

*Note*: Some chemicals are too hazardous to be used in schools, therefore not all of these warning labels will be found in your chemistry laboratory.

Answer on p. 211

### Revision activity

Use either your schools database (probably CLEAPSS) or the internet to decide on what safety precautions you would need to take if you were carrying out an experiment using:
(a) sodium hydroxide
(b) hydrogen peroxide
(c) ethanoyl chloride

## Identifying practical techniques and equipment

REVISED

A crucial stage in planning a scientific investigation is to identify the most appropriate practical technique to allow you to safely carry out your experiment.

## Now test yourself

TESTED

2 Match up the number of each laboratory technique in Table 1.2 to the ***letter*** of its most appropriate use.

Table 1.2

| | Technique | | Use |
|---|---|---|---|
| **1** | Filtration | **A** | Weighing out chemicals |
| **2** | Water bath | **B** | Determining the concentration of a solution |
| **3** | Distillation | **C** | Heating an aqueous solution rapidly to 60°C |
| **4** | Balance | **D** | Separating a mixture of liquids |
| **5** | Bunsen burner | **E** | Collecting a gas that is insoluble in water |
| **6** | Gas syringe | **F** | Separating a solid from a liquid |
| **7** | Titration | **G** | Heating a flammable liquid to 120°C |
| **8** | Collecting a gas over water | **H** | Maintaining a reaction at 50°C |
| **9** | Heating mantle | **I** | Collecting a water-soluble gas |

Answer on p. 211

Having identified the most appropriate technique for a particular scientific investigation, apparatus must then be selected to allow that technique to be carried out effectively and safely.

# Implementing

For most practicals that you carry out you will be provided with a set of instructions and it is essential that you follow these.

Chemical experiments are a bit like recipes, and for them to work you have to follow the recipe precisely. However, each piece of laboratory apparatus used to measure a quantity has a limit to its precision. For example, a fairly standard balance may give a measurement to 2 decimal places but as you are using it the second decimal place often fluctuates and may change. This indicates that the balance has an inbuilt error.

A useful rule of thumb for any apparatus is that the error range will be +/− half of the smallest digit. Table 1.3 shows an example.

**Table 1.3**

| Balance | Mass | Error range | Range |
|---|---|---|---|
| 1 decimal place | 2.4 g | +/− 0.05 | 2.35–2.45 g |
| 2 decimal places | 2.40 g | +/− 0.005 | 2.395–2.405 g |
| 3 decimal places | 2.400 g | +/− 0.0005 | 2.3995–2.4005 g |

For most measuring equipment, the manufacturer will give the maximum error that is inherent in using that piece of apparatus; this is sometimes etched onto the apparatus but, in other cases, will need to be looked up.

The **percentage error** for each balance is shown below:

1-decimal-point balance $\frac{0.05}{2.4} \times 100 = 2.08\%$

2-decimal-point-balance $\frac{0.005}{2.40} \times 100 = 0.208\%$

3-decimal-point balance $\frac{0.0005}{2.400} \times 100 = 0.0208\%$

The more accurate the apparatus, the lower the percentage error.

The maximum error is an inevitable part of using that piece of equipment and is distinct from the competence with which the experiment is carried out. Measuring a volume in an apparatus, such as a pipette, only requires one reading, so only one error is incurred (the error range, usually +/− 0.05 $cm^3$, is etched onto the pipette). However, measuring a volume in a burette requires two readings — the initial volume and the final volume, so the maximum error is doubled.

Important decisions are sometimes based on the results of experiments. For example, titrations are used in health care, in the food industry and in forensic science. It is crucial that the people making decisions based on the results obtained understand the extent to which they can rely on the data from their analysis.

**Percentage error** = $\frac{\text{maximum error}}{\text{actual value}} \times 100$

**Revision activity**

You have to measure 24 $cm^3$ of liquid using either a 10 $cm^3$ or a 25 $cm^3$ measuring cylinder. Check the glassware in your laboratory to find the error range and decide which would be the most accurate.

## Volumetric equipment

REVISED

It is important to stress that when using volumetric apparatus the correct position of the meniscus is essential. In Figure 1.2, (a) is the correct way to measure volume, taking account of the meniscus. All volumetric apparatus (pipettes, burettes and volumetric flasks) are manufactured such that the correct volume is obtained when the bottom of the meniscus sits exactly on the line.

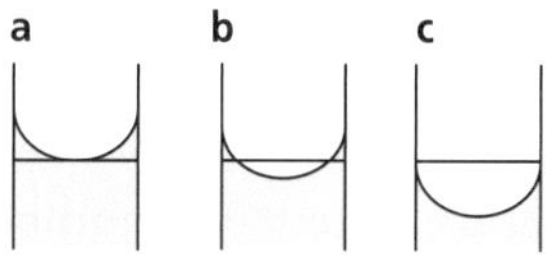


**Figure 1.2**

## Now test yourself

TESTED

3 (a) Calculate the percentage error in measuring 50 $cm^3$ of a solution using:
   (i) a 250 $cm^3$ measuring cylinder with a maximum error of 1 $cm^3$
   (ii) a 100 $cm^3$ measuring cylinder with a maximum error of 0.5 $cm^3$
   (iii) a 50 $cm^3$ pipette with a maximum error of 0.1 $cm^3$
   (iv) a 25 $cm^3$ pipette with a maximum error of 0.06 $cm^3$, used twice
   (v) a 50 $cm^3$ burette, where each reading has a maximum error of 0.05 $cm^3$
(b) Calculate the percentage error in measuring a temperature rise of 6°C using a thermometer with a maximum error of:
   (i) 0.5°C
   (ii) 0.1°C

Answer on p. 211

## Recording results

REVISED

When recording data, the precision should be indicated appropriately. For example, if you use a balance that reads to 2 decimal places, the masses recorded should indicate this. This may seem obvious for a mass of, for example, 24.79 g. However, you must remember that this applies equally for a mass of, for example, 24.80 g. Here the '0' should be included after the '8' to indicate that this mass is also precise to 2 decimal places. Recording the mass as 24.8 g is incorrect and will be penalised in an exam.

Burette readings are normally recorded to 0.05 $cm^3$ as this represents the appropriate maximum error. In Figure 1.3 a reading of 12.60 $cm^3$ or of 12.65 $cm^3$ is acceptable, but 12.64 $cm^3$ or 12.6 $cm^3$ are not.

The maximum error can be regarded as +/− one half of the smallest division, which for a standard burette is 0.10 $cm^3$, so the error is +/− 0.05 $cm^3$. The volume measured in a burette should always be recorded to 2 decimal places and the second decimal place must always be either '0' or '5'.

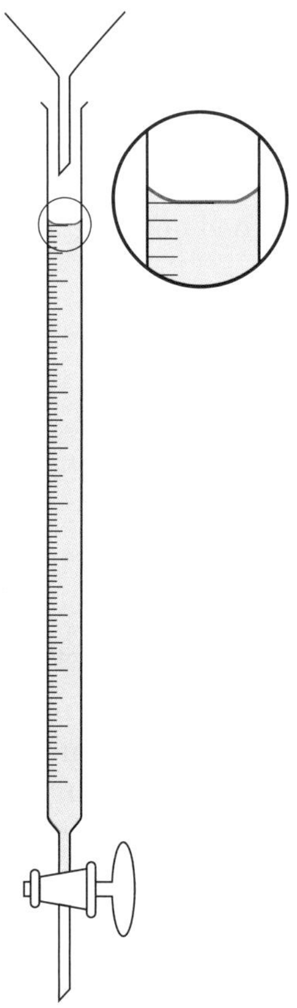

Figure 1.3

# Analysis

When carrying out experiments you will be expected to interpret both qualitative and quantitative data.

In the first year of the course the qualitative analysis that you are expected to know is listed in section 3.1.4 of the specification, which details a range of chemical tests for ions including: carbonate ($CO_3^{2-}$), sulfate ($SO_4^{2-}$), halides ( $Cl^-$, $Br^-$, $I^-$) and ammonium ($NH_4^+$).

You will encounter quantitative analysis when carrying out experiments involving moles (see pages 22–27) or enthalpy changes, which occur later in the course.

## Significant figures

REVISED

In some cases the number of significant figures is simply the number of digits in the answer. 72.67 has 4 significant figures, while 72.7 has 3 significant figures and 73 has just 2.

In other cases numbers may need rounding up or down before quoting the answer to a particular number of significant figures. 94.64 has 4 significant figures but to 3 significant figures this is 94.6 (as 94.64 is nearer to 94.6 than to 94.7). A number ending in a '5' is rather arbitrarily raised to the number above. So 11.5 must be written as 12 when quoted to 2 significant figures.

When a number such as 0.00461 has '0's *after* the decimal point these are not considered as 'significant'. 0.00461 therefore has 3 significant figures.

When a number has '0's *before* the decimal point they are significant, such that 7630.00 has 4 significant figures (Figure 1.4).

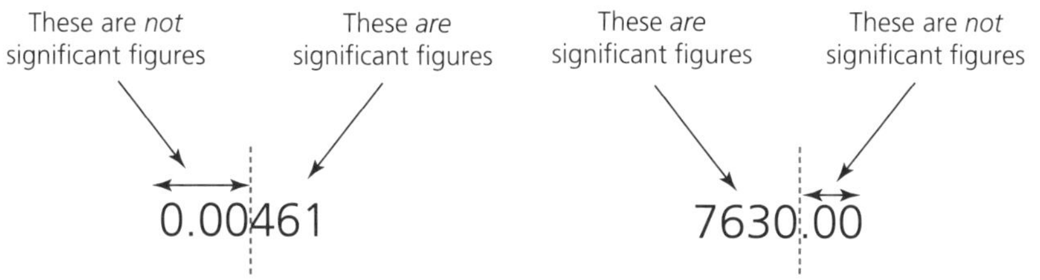
These are *not* significant figures
These *are* significant figures
These *are* significant figures
These are *not* significant figures
0.00461
7630.00

**Figure 1.4**

A number such as 1950 has 4 significant figures but if you are asked to quote this to 2 significant figures there is a temptation to quote this as '2000', which is incorrect as 2000 has 4 significant figures. The way round it is to write the number in standard (index) form i.e. $2.0 \times 10^3$. 1950 written in standard form would be $1.95 \times 10^3$, which is to 3 significant figures.

Often your calculator will display an answer containing more digits than you were given in the data.

Suppose you were asked to calculate the concentration of HCl(aq) when $24.2\,cm^3$ of the HCl(aq) was neutralised by $25.0\,cm^3$ of $0.500\,mol\,dm^{-3}$ NaOH(aq). If you did this calculation correctly your calculator would show the concentration to be $0.516528925\,mol\,dm^{-3}$. The concentration of the solution is not known to this degree of precision.

The accuracy should be limited to the precision of the data or, in an experiment, the accuracy of the apparatus. In the example above the data are given to 3 significant figures and so the answer should also be limited to 3 significant figures. The figures after the third are dropped and the number is *rounded*. 0.516528925 when rounded to 3 significant figures is 0.517.

When carrying out a calculation always quote your answer to the same number of significant figures as given in the data. If the number of significant figures in the data varies, the least accurate should be used.

**Exam tip**

When carrying out calculations it is essential that you do not round until the end of the calculation. If necessary use the 'memory' function on your calculator.

## Using numbers in standard (index) form

REVISED

Numbers can be written in different formats. A common way to write numbers is to use the decimal notation, for example 123642.78 and 0.0005432. When working with very large numbers (123642.78) or very small numbers (0.0005432) it is convenient to write these in **standard notation**. This means writing the number as a product of two factors:

- in the first factor the decimal point *always* comes after the first digit
- the second factor is *always* a multiple of 10

**Example**

| **Number** | 9874 | 987.4 | 98.74 | 9.874 | 0.9874 | 0.09874 | 0.009874 |
|---|---|---|---|---|---|---|---|
| **Standard form** | $9.874 \times 10^3$ | $9.874 \times 10^2$ | $9.874 \times 10^1$ | $9.874 \times 10^0$* | $9.874 \times 10^{-1}$ | $9.874 \times 10^{-2}$ | $9.874 \times 10^{-3}$ |

* Since $10^0 = 1$, it follows that $9.874 \times 10^0$ is normally written as 9.874.

## Now test yourself

4 (a) Write the following numbers to 3 significant figures.
  (i) 734.8
  (ii) 698.456
  (iii) 0.0003456
(b) Write the following numbers to 2 significant figures and in standard form.
  (i) 734.8
  (ii) 698.456
  (iii) 0.0003456

Answer on p. 211

**Exam tip**

It is always useful to estimate the answer to a calculation before doing the calculation on a calculator. It makes it easy to spot whether or not you have input the data into the calculator correctly.

## Drawing graphs

REVISED

Figure 1.5 shows a simple relationship between two variables.

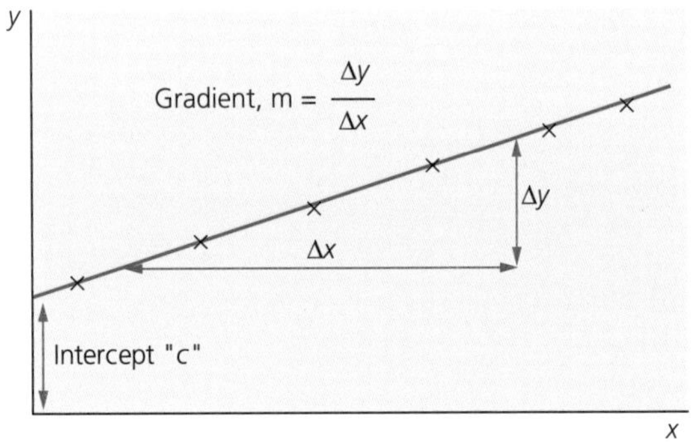


**Figure 1.5**

The relationship between $x$ and $y$ is $y = mx + c$ (where $m$ is the gradient and $c$ is the intercept). $\Delta x$ is the change in $x$ and $\Delta y$ is the change in $y$. The gradient, $m$, can be calculated by using $m = \Delta y/\Delta x$.

**Exam tip**

The symbol Δ is used to represent 'change in…', such that $\Delta T$ is change in temperature, $\Delta P$ is change in pressure and $\Delta V$ is change in volume.

When drawing graphs you should:

1 Choose a scale that will allow the graph to cover as much of the graph paper as possible. It is helpful to start both axes at zero but if all the points on one axis are between 90 and 100, to start at zero on that axis would cramp your graph into a small section of the paper (Figure 1.6a). In this case it is much better to truncate the $x$-axis so that the graph fills as much of the paper as possible (Figure 1.6b).

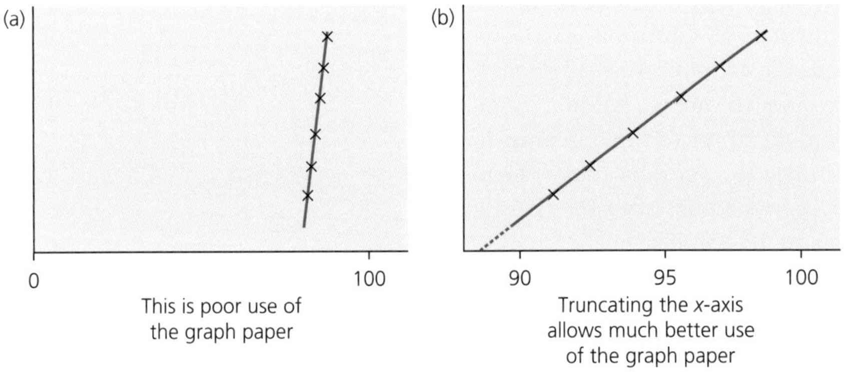


**Figure 1.6**

2 Label the axes with the dimensions and the units such as:
- ○ Volume/$cm^3$
- ○ Concentration/mol $dm^{-3}$

3 After plotting all the points on a graph often you may not get a perfect straight line or a curve that goes through all of the points. You have to draw a line of best fit for the points (Figure 1.7).

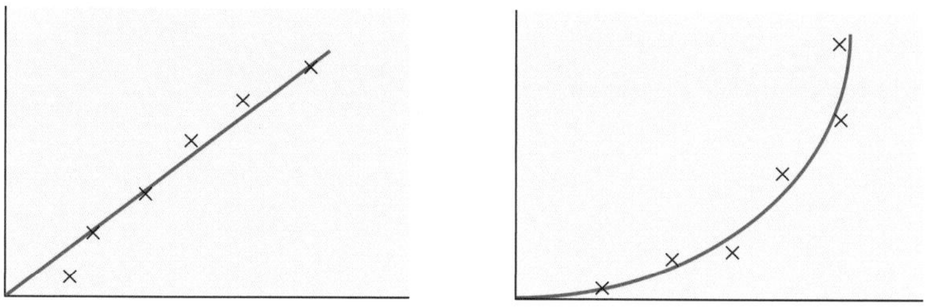

Figure 1.7

4 Figure 1.8 shows how to draw tangents to a curve.

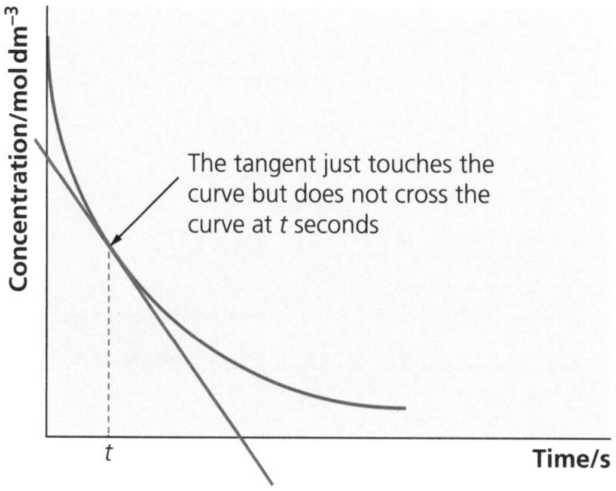
Concentration/mol dm⁻³
The tangent just touches the curve but does not cross the curve at t seconds
t
Time/s

Figure 1.8

By calculating the gradient of the tangent it is possible to work out how the concentration changes with respect to time after *t* seconds. This enables you to calculate the rate of reaction after *t* seconds. The units of rate are the units of *y*/*x*, which are mol $dm^{-3}$/s, which is written as mol $dm^{-3}\,s^{-1}$.

**Revision activity**

A student reacted 0.42 g sodium hydrogen carbonate, $NaHCO_3(s)$ with excess dilute HCl(aq) and measured the volume of $CO_2(g)$ evolved every minute.

$$NaHCO_3(s) + HCl(aq) \rightarrow NaCl(aq) + H_2O(l) + CO_2(g)$$

The results are recorded in Table 1.4.

Table 1.4

| Time/min | 0 | 1 | 2 | 3 | 4 | 5 | 6 | 7 | 8 |
|---|---|---|---|---|---|---|---|---|---|
| Volume of $CO_2$(g)/$cm^3$ | 0 | 40 | 71 | 96 | 105 | 114 | 118 | 120 | 120 |

Plot the results, label the axes, and deduce the rate of reaction after:
(a) 2 minutes
(b) 4 minutes

# Evaluation

You should be able use your knowledge and understanding to evaluate your results and use them to draw valid conclusions. You should be able to identify anomalies in experiment data.

## Now test yourself

TESTED

5 A student carries out a titration and records his results, as shown in Table 1.5.

Table 1.5

| Titration | Volume/$cm^3$ |
|---|---|
| Rough | 23 |
| 1 | 23.50 |
| 2 | 24.50 |
| 3 | 23.60 |

He wants to work out the average titre value. Which results in the table should he ignore? Calculate the average titre.

Answer on p. 211

## Limitations in experimental procedure

REVISED

Apart from the limitations imposed by apparatus, experiments also have errors caused by the procedure adopted. Such errors are difficult to quantify, but the following check list might help you to assess an experiment.

### Purity of chemicals

Can you be sure that the substances you are using are pure? Solids may be damp and if a damp solid is weighed, the absorbed moisture is included in the mass.

Does the experiment involve a reactant or a product that could react with the air? Remember that air contains carbon dioxide, which is acidic and reacts with alkalis. Some substances react with the oxygen present. Air is also always damp.

### Heating substances

If you need to heat a substance until it decomposes, you can only be sure that the decomposition is complete if you heat to constant mass.

Is it possible that heating is too strong and the product has decomposed further?

### Solutions

If an experiment is quantitative, can you guarantee that any solution used is exactly at the stated concentration?

### Gases

If a gas is collected during the experiment, can you be sure that none has escaped? If you collect a gas over water, are you sure it is not soluble?

If you collect the gas in a gas syringe the volume of the gas is temperature-dependent.

### Timing

If an experiment involves timing, are you sure that you can start and stop the timing exactly when required?

### Enthalpy experiments

Heat loss is always a problem in enthalpy experiments, particularly if the reaction is slow.

## Improving experimental design

REVISED

It is useful to look at all measurements and to calculate the percentage error in each. Is there any measurement whose percentage error is significantly larger than the others? If there is it is worth considering using more precise apparatus for that measurement.

It is a mistake to imagine that perfection can be achieved by using more complicated apparatus if the fault lies in the method that is being employed.

If the problem is that a gas to be collected over water is slightly soluble then a change in the method is appropriate. Using a gas syringe would be an effective remedy.

If the problem with an enthalpy reaction is that it is too slow, maybe using powders or a more concentrated solution would help.

## Exam practice

1 Two students were each provided with a small lump of impure magnesium carbonate and each student was asked to design an experiment to determine the percentage purity.

(a) One student decided to react the impure magnesium carbonate with hydrochloric acid and collect the carbon dioxide evolved by displacement of water.

$MgCO_3(s) + 2HCl \rightarrow MgCl_2(aq) + H_2O(l) + CO_2(g)$

(i) Sketch the apparatus that the student would use. [2]
(ii) Explain how the student would calculate the percentage purity. [4]
(iii) Identify a procedural error in the method adopted. [1]
(iv) Suggest an improvement. [1]

(b) The second student decided to decompose the magnesium carbonate and to weigh the magnesium oxide using a 2-decimal-point balance.

$MgCO_3(s) \rightarrow MgO(s) + CO_2(g)$

(i) Write a brief method for this experiment. [5]
(ii) If the final mass of MgO(s) was 0.20 g, calculate the percentage error in weighing this sample. [2]

2 Lithium reacts with water to produce a solution of lithium hydroxide and hydrogen gas.

**$2Li(s) + 2H_2O(l) \rightarrow 2LiOH(aq) + H_2(g)$**

The apparatus shown in Figure 1.9 was used to monitor the rate of reaction.

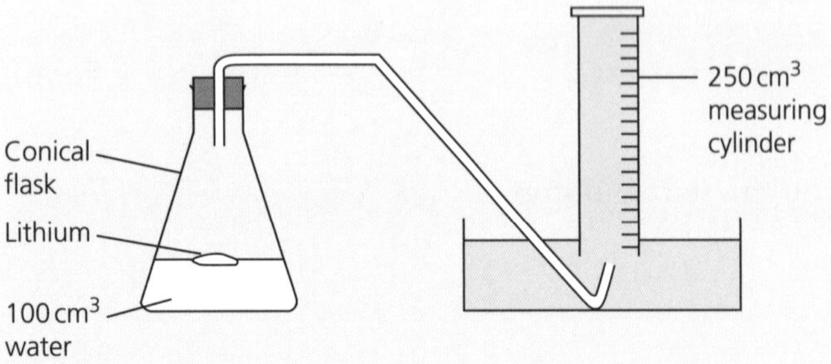


**Figure 1.9**

A small piece of lithium was weighed on a two decimal point balance and added to the conical flask and the bung quickly replaced. The volume of $H_2(g)$ collected was recorded every 30 seconds. The results are shown in Table 1.6.

**Table 1.6**

| | Error range |
|---|---|
| Mass of weighing boat = 12.56 g | +/– 0.005 g |
| Mass of weighing boat + lithium = 12.68 g | +/– 0.005 g |

| Time/s | 30 | 60 | 90 | 120 | 150 | 180 | 210 | 240 |
|---|---|---|---|---|---|---|---|---|
| Volume of $H_2(g)/cm^3$ | 60 | 110 | 150 | 180 | 195 | 203 | 208 | 208 |
| The error range in when reading the volume of the $H_2(g)$ is +/– 1.00 $cm^3$ | | | | | | | | |

(a) Plot the results. Draw a tangent at 60 seconds and deduce the rate of reaction after 60 seconds by finding the gradient of the tangent at 60 seconds. [4]

(b) Calculate the percentage error in:

(i) the mass of lithium

(ii) the volume of hydrogen after 240 seconds [4]

(c) Suggest an improvement to the method. Justify your suggestion. [3]

## Answers and quick quiz 1 online

ONLINE

## Summary

You should now have an understanding of:

- planning — experimental design and the need to ensure that safe practices are adopted
- implementing — how to use practical apparatus and techniques correctly
- recording — observations and results recorded appropriately
- analysis — interpreting experimental qualitative and quantitative data
- evaluation — how to draw conclusions, estimate errors and suggest valid improvements

# 2 Atoms and reactions

## Atoms

The protons, neutrons and electrons that make up atoms are described in Table 2.1.

**Table 2.1**

| Particle | Relative mass | Relative charge | Distribution |
|---|---|---|---|
| Proton, p | 1 | 1+ | Nucleus |
| Neutron, n | 1 | 0 | Nucleus |
| Electron, e | 1/1836 | 1− | Orbits/shells |

The **atomic number** and the **mass number** can be used to deduce the number of protons, neutrons and electrons in atoms and in ions.

Atoms are neutral and contain the same number of protons as electrons. Positive ions have lost electrons and hence have more protons than electrons; negative ions have gained electrons so they have fewer protons than electrons (Figure 2.1).

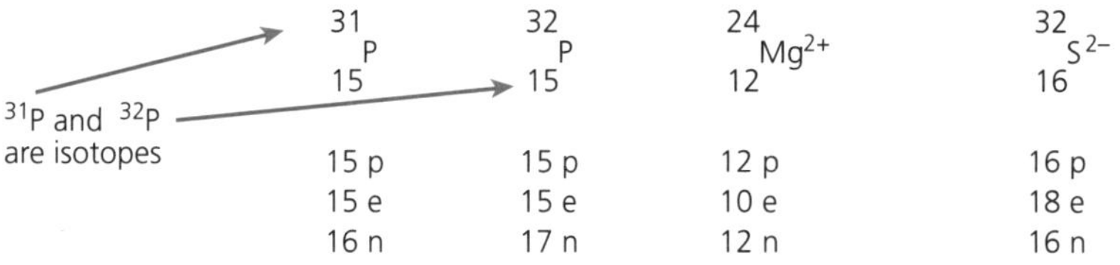


**Figure 2.1**

Chlorine has two **isotopes**: $^{35}Cl$ and $^{37}Cl$.

**Atomic number** is the number of protons in an atom or an ion of an element.

**Mass number** is the number of protons plus neutrons in the nucleus of an atom.

(Mass number minus atomic number) tells us the number of neutrons in an atom.

**Isotopes** are atoms of the same element with different masses — they have the same number of protons (and electrons) but different number of neutrons.

## Relative masses

REVISED

Most exam papers ask for at least one or two definitions, which might include definitions of **relative isotopic mass** or **relative atomic mass**.

It is possible to use the definition of relative atomic mass and amend it slightly to create definitions for:

- **relative molecular mass** which applies to all covalent molecules
- **relative formula mass** which applies to all compounds

**Relative molecular mass** is the weighted mean mass of a molecule compared with 1/12th of the mass of a $^{12}C$ atom.

**Relative formula mass** is the weighted mean mass of a formula unit compared with 1/12th of the mass of a $^{12}C$ atom.

The **relative isotopic mass** is the mass of an atom/isotope of the element compared with 1/12th of the mass of a $^{12}C$ atom whose mass is exactly 12.

The **relative atomic mass** of an element is the weighted mean mass of an atom of the element compared with 1/12th of the mass of a $^{12}C$ atom whose mass is exactly 12.

# Calculations

## Relative atomic mass

**Example 1**

A sample of iron contains three isotopes: $^{54}Fe$, $^{56}Fe$ and $^{57}Fe$. The relative abundance is 2 : 42 : 1 respectively. Calculate the relative atomic mass.

**Answer**

Three isotopes, therefore three brackets, each containing the mass number of the isotope, multiplied by the relative amount of each

Relative atomic mass

$$\frac{(54 \times 2) + (56 \times 42) + (57 \times 1)}{(2 + 42 + 1)} = \frac{(108 + 2352 + 57)}{45} = \frac{2517}{45} = 55.9$$

Sum of relative amounts

**Example 2**

Ne has two isotopes, $^{20}Ne$ and $^{22}Ne$, and the relative atomic mass is 20.18. Calculate the percentage of each isotope.

**Answer**

If the percentage of $^{20}Ne$ is $x$% then there must be $(100 - x)$% of $^{22}Ne$, such that:

$$\frac{20x + 22(100 - x)}{100} = 20.18$$

$$20x + 2200 - 22x = 2018$$

$$20x - 22x = 2018 - 2200$$

$$-2x = -182$$

$$x = 91\%$$

The sample contains 91% $^{20}Ne$ and 9% $^{22}Ne$.

## Relative molecular mass and relative formula mass

Relative molecular mass applies to covalent molecules only. Relative formula mass applies to all substances.

**Example 1**

Calculate the relative molecular mass of glucose, $C_6H_{12}O_6$.

**Answer**

$C_6H_{12}O_6 = (6 \times 12.0) + (12 \times 1.0) + (6 \times 16.0) = 72.0 + 12.0 + 96.0 = 180.0$

**Example 2**

Calculate the relative formula mass of sodium carbonate, $Na_2CO_3$.

**Answer**

$Na_2CO_3 = (23.0 \times 2) + 12.0 + (16.0 \times 3) = 46.0 + 12.0 + 48.0 = 106.0$

**Example 3**

Calculate the relative formula mass of barium chloride crystals, $BaCl_2.2H_2O$.

**Answer**

$BaCl_2.2H_2O = 137.3 + (2 \times 35.5) + 2(1.0 + 1.0 + 16.0) = 137.3 + 71.0 + 36.0 = 244.3$

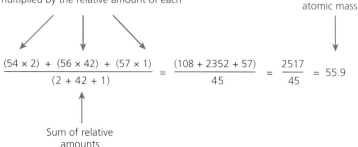

## Now test yourself

TESTED

1 Deduce the number of protons, neutrons and electrons present in each of the following:
(a) $^{16}O$
(b) $^{23}Na^{+}$
(c) $^{19}F^{-}$

2 Rubidium consists of two isotopes: $^{85}Rb$ has an abundance of 72.2% and $^{87}Rb$ has an abundance of 27.8%. Calculate the weighted mean atomic mass of rubidium.

3 A sample of boron was known to contain two different isotopes, $^{10}_{5}B$ and $^{11}_{5}B$. The relative atomic mass of the sample of boron was 10.8. Calculate the percentage of each isotope in the sample.

4 Calculate the relative formula mass of each of the following:
(a) magnesium hydroxide, $Mg(OH)_2$
(b) sodium carbonate crystals, $Na_2SO_4.10H_2O$

5 Lithium has two isotopes, $^{6}Li$ and $^{7}Li$.
(a) Define the key term *isotope*.
(b) Explain how the two isotopes of lithium differ.
(c) Use the mass spectrum below to calculate the $A_r$ of lithium. Quote your answer to 2 significant figures.

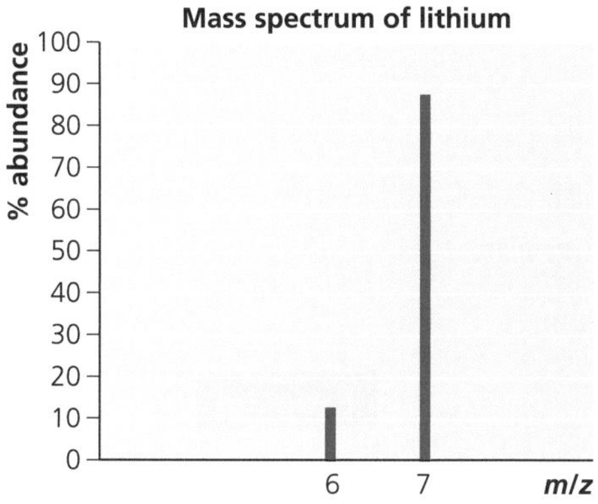


Answers on p. 211

**Exam tip**

Students often lose marks by careless use of words. For instance, sodium carbonate, $Na_2CO_3$, must *not* be described as a molecule — it is a giant lattice made up of millions of ions and does not exist as a single $Na_2CO_3$ molecule. The same applies to $BaCl_2.2H_2O$.

**Revision activity**

Select an element with atomic number between 21 and 30. Use the internet or a reference book to find the stable isotopes of that element. Calculate its relative atomic mass.

# Compounds, formulae and equations

## Chemical equations

REVISED

It is essential that you are able to write the formulae of a range of common chemicals and to write balanced equations.

The periodic table can be used to deduce the formula of most chemicals, although there are many exceptions (Table 2.2).

**Table 2.2**

| Group | 1 | 2 | 13 | 14 | 15 | 16 | 17 |
|---|---|---|---|---|---|---|---|
| Number of bonds (valency) | 1 | 2 | 3 | 4 | 3 | 2 | 1 |

When a group 1 element forms a compound with a group 16 element:

- the group 1 element (e.g. lithium, Li) forms one bond and the group 16 element (e.g. oxygen, O) forms two bonds. It follows that two lithiums are required for each oxygen. Hence, the formula of the compound is $Li_2O$.

When a group 13 element forms a compound with a group 16 element:

- the group 13 element (e.g. aluminium, Al) forms three bonds and the group 16 element (e.g. oxygen, O) forms two bonds. It follows that two aluminiums require three oxygens (each supply six bonds). Hence, the formula of the compound is $Al_2O_3$.

Another way of deducing formulae is to use the 'valency cross-over' technique. Using aluminium oxide as an example, follow these simple steps.

**Step 1** Write each of the symbols:

Al O

**Step 2** Write the valency at the top right-hand side of the symbol:

$Al^3$ $O^2$

**Step 3** Cross over the valencies:

**Step 4** Write the crossed-over valencies at the bottom right of the other symbol:

$Al_2O_3$

This is the formula of the compound.

You are expected to know the formulae of: hydrochloric acid, HCl; sulfuric acid, $H_2SO_4$; nitric acid, $HNO_3$; and their corresponding salts.

You should be able to use Table 2.3 to work out most formulae.

**Table 2.3 Valencies of elements and groups of elements**

| | | |
|---|---|---|
| **1** | All group 1 elements, hydrogen (H), silver (Ag) and ammonium ($NH_4$) | All group 17 elements, hydroxide (OH), nitrate ($NO_3$), hydrogencarbonate ($HCO_3$) |
| **2** | All group 2 elements, iron (Fe), copper (Cu), zinc (Zn), lead (Pb), tin (Sn) | Oxygen (O), sulfur (S), sulfate, ($SO_4$) carbonate, ($CO_3$) |
| **3** | All group 13 elements, iron (Fe) | |
| **4** | Carbon (C), silicon (Si), lead (Pb), tin, (Sn) | |

**Exam tip**

It is important that you learn all of these valencies — if you get a formula wrong it usually means you will get the equation wrong and also any subsequent calculations. Getting a formula right means you are less likely to lose marks in any calculation that follows.

## Writing equations

The importance of being able to provide the correct formulae for substances is that it enables you to write equations for chemical reactions that take place. An equation not only summarises the reactants used and the products obtained but it also indicates the numbers of particles of each substance that are required or produced.

A very simple case is the reaction of carbon and oxygen to make carbon dioxide. This is summarised in an equation as:

$$C + O_2 \rightarrow CO_2$$

It tells us that one atom of carbon reacts with one molecule of oxygen to make one molecule of carbon dioxide.

The reaction between carbon and hydrogen is:

$$C + 2H_2 \rightarrow CH_4$$

This means that two molecules of hydrogen are required for each atom of carbon in order to make one molecule of methane, $CH_4$.

In any equation all symbols must be balanced. You may be asked to include state symbols: (g), (l), (s) or (aq).

## Now test yourself

TESTED

6 Write the chemical formula of each of the following compounds:
  (a) magnesium chloride
  (b) aluminium sulfate
7 The formula of rubidium chloride is RbCl. What is the formula of rubidium sulfate?
8 The formula of manganese sulfate is $MnSO_4$. What is formula of manganese bromide?
9 Write an equation, including state symbols, for the reaction between:
  (a) zinc oxide solid and aqueous hydrochloric acid
  (b) methane, $CH_4$, and oxygen to form carbon dioxide and water

Answers on p. 211

You will also be expected to learn and recall the formula of various ions, including those listed in Table 2.4.

**Table 2.4** Common ions (cations and anions)

| Positive ions (cations) | | Negative ions (anions) | |
|---|---|---|---|
| $NH_4^+$ | Ammonium | $NO_3^-$ | Nitrate |
| $Zn^{2+}$ | Zinc | $CO_3^{2-}$ | Carbonate |
| $Ag^+$ | Silver | $SO_4^{2-}$ | Sulfate |
| $Fe^{2+}$ | Iron(II) | $OH^-$ | Hydroxide |
| $Fe^{3+}$ | Iron(III) | $Cl^-$, $Br^-$, $I^-$ | Halides |

All ionic compounds are neutral and the charges of the separate ions have to balance.

- The ammonium ion has a charge of 1+ and the hydroxide ion has a charge of 1− so the formula of ammonium hydroxide is $NH_4OH$.
- The iron(II) ion has a charge of 2+ and the hydroxide ion has a charge of 1− so the formula of iron(II) hydroxide is $Fe(OH)_2$.
- The iron(III) ion has a charge of 3+ and the hydroxide ion has a charge of 1− so the formula of iron(III) hydroxide is $Fe(OH)_3$.

## Now test yourself

TESTED

10 What are the formulae of the following ionic compounds:
  (a) silver sulfate
  (b) aluminium nitrate
  (c) iron(III) nitrate

Answer on p. 211

# Amount of substance

## The mole

REVISED

The mass of 1 mol of substance = relative formula mass in grams = **molar mass**. The units of molar mass are $g\,mol^{-1}$.

The amount of substance in moles is given the symbol ***n***.

The **mole** is defined as the amount of substance that contains as many particles as there are atoms in 12 g of the carbon-12 ($^{12}C$) isotope and is equal to the **Avogadro constant,** $N_A = 6.02 \times 10^{23}\,mol^{-1}$.

**Molar mass** is defined as the mass per mole of a substance and is given the symbol ***M***.

**Revision activity**

A sweet has the dimensions shown in Figure 2.2.

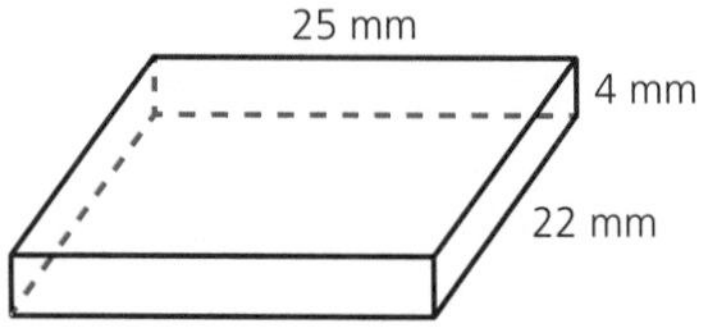


**Figure 2.2**

**(a)** Calculate the volume of 1 sweet in (i) $mm^3$, (ii) $m^3$, (iii) $km^3$.
**(b)** Calculate the volume of 1 mole of the sweets in $km^3$.
**(c)** The UK has an area of approximately 243 610 $km^2$. If 1 mole of the sweets were placed on the UK, calculate the depth of the sweets.

## Empirical and molecular formulae

REVISED

It is important to understand the difference between an **empirical** and a **molecular formula**.

The **empirical formula** is the simplest whole number ratio of atoms of each element in a compound.

The **molecular formula** is the actual number of atoms of each element in a molecule of a compound.

**Example**

Compound **A** has a relative molecular mass of 90 and has a composition by mass of carbon, 26.8%; hydrogen, 2.2%; oxygen, 71.0%. Calculate the empirical formula and the molecular formula.

Divide the % of each element by its own relative atomic mass:

| C | : | H | : | O |
|---|---|---|---|---|
| $\frac{26.8}{12.0}$ | : | $\frac{2.2}{1.0}$ | : | $\frac{71.0}{16.0}$ |
| 2.2 | : | 2.2 | : | 4.4 |

Divide each by the smallest:

$\frac{2.2}{2.2} = 1$ $\quad \frac{2.2}{2.2} = 1$ $\quad \frac{4.4}{2.2} = 2$

Ratio is 1:1:2, hence the empirical formula is $C_1H_1O_2 = CHO_2$.

Deduce how many empirical units are needed to make up the **molecular mass:**

$$CHO_2 = 12.0 + 1.0 + 32.0 = 45.0$$

$$\frac{\text{molecular mass}}{\text{empirical mass}} = \frac{90.0}{45.0} = 2.0$$

Therefore, the molecular formula is made up of *two* empirical units. Hence the molecular formula is $C_2H_2O_4$.

**Typical mistake**

When carrying out calculations, students often round numbers in the middle of the calculation instead of at the end. This often leads to an incorrect answer. This is illustrated below in an empirical formula calculation.

A compound contains 40.7% carbon, 5.1% hydrogen and 54.2% oxygen by mass.

Typical mistake

| C | : | H | : | O |
|---|---|---|---|---|
| $\frac{40.7}{12.0}$ | : | $\frac{5.1}{1.0}$ | : | $\frac{54.1}{16.0}$ |
| 3.4 | : | 5.1 | : | 3.4 |
| 1 | : | **1.5** | : | 1 |
| 1 | : | **2** | : | 1 |

Hence, empirical formula is $CH_2O$

Correct method

| C | : | H | : | O |
|---|---|---|---|---|
| $\frac{40.7}{12.0}$ | : | $\frac{5.1}{1.0}$ | : | $\frac{54.1}{16.0}$ |
| 3.4 | : | 5.1 | : | 3.4 |
| 1 | : | 1.5 | : | 1 |
| 2 | : | 3 | : | 2 |

Hence, empirical formula is $C_2H_3O_2$

The mistake occurs here when 1.5 is rounded up to 2. You should always look to see if a simple multiple can lead to a set of whole numbers. In this case they should all have been multiplied by 2.

## Anhydrous and hydrated salts

REVISED

Most salts exist in the solid state either as a pure substance or as crystals that have water molecules embedded into their structure. The pure substance is described as **anhydrous,** which means that it contains no water. The crystals containing water are said to possess water of crystallisation and are described as **hydrated**.

The water present in hydrated salts is indicated by writing the formula of the substance followed by a full stop and the number of molecules of water — for example, iron(II) sulfate crystals have the formula $FeSO_4.7H_2O$.

You should be able to calculate the water of crystallisation.

**Example 1**

A sample of copper sulfate crystals has a mass of 6.80 g. When heated, until all the water of crystallisation has been driven off, the mass is reduced to 4.35 g. Calculate the formula of the copper sulfate crystals.

Answer

mass of water driven off by heating = 6.80 – 4.35 = 2.45 g

moles of water of crystallisation = $\frac{2.45}{18.0}$ = 0.136 mol

molar mass of anhydrous copper sulfate = 63.5 + 32.1 + (4 × 16.0)

= 159.6 g mol$^{-1}$

moles of copper sulfate = $\frac{4.35}{159.6}$ = 0.02726 mol

mole ratio of copper sulfate to water = 0.02726 : 0.136 or 1:5

Therefore, the formula of hydrated copper sulfate is $CuSO_4.5H_2O$.

**Exam tip**

The methodology for calculating water of crystallisation is exactly the same as for calculating empirical formula.

Step 1 — find the ratio of the moles of anhydrous salt to moles of water.

Step 2 — divide each by the smallest, and find the simplest whole number ratio.

The ratio should always be 1 mol anhydrous salt:whole number of moles of water.

**Example 2**

A sample of magnesium sulfate crystals contains 9.78% Mg, 38.69% $SO_4^{2-}$ and 51.53% $H_2O$ by mass. Determine the formula of the crystals.

**Answer**

amount (in moles) of magnesium = $\frac{9.78}{24.3}$ = 0.4025 mol

amount (in moles) of sulfate = $\frac{38.69}{96.1}$ = 0.4026 mol

amount (in moles) of water = $\frac{51.53}{18.0}$ = 2.863 mol

ratio = 0.4025:0.4026:2.863 or 1:1:7

Therefore, the formula of magnesium sulfate crystals is $MgSO_4.7H_2O$.

## Calculating moles from mass

REVISED

$$\text{amount of substance in moles, } n = \frac{\text{mass of substance in grams } (m)}{\text{molar mass of substance } (M)}$$

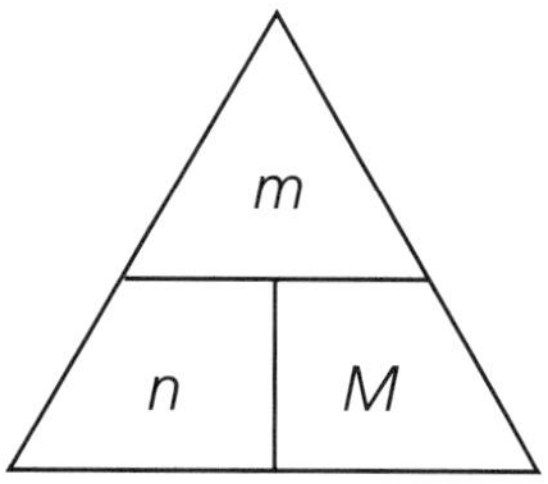


Therefore,

$$n = \frac{m}{M}$$

This applies to atoms and to compounds. The examples below illustrate the sort of questions that you may be asked. The triangle can be used to help you rearrange the equation.

**Example 1**

Calculate the amount in moles present in 1.49 g of $Li_2O$.

**Answer**

mass, $m$ (in grams) = 1.49 g

Using the formula $Li_2O$, it is possible to deduce the molar mass of $Li_2O$. Molar mass ($M$) is calculated by adding together the relative atomic mass of each individual element in the compound.

$A_r$ data: Li = 6.9; O = 16.0

molar mass, $M$ = 6.9 + 6.9 + 16.0 = 29.8

$$n = \frac{m}{M}$$

$$n = \frac{1.49}{29.8} = 0.050\text{ mol}$$

**Example 2**

Calculate the mass of 0.25 moles of $NiSO_4$.

**Answer**

number of moles, $n$ = 0.25 mol

Using the formula $NiSO_4$, it is possible to deduce the molar mass of $NiSO_4$. Molar mass is calculated by adding together the relative atomic mass of each individual element in the compound.

$A_r$ data: Ni = 58.7; S =32.1; O = 16.0

Note that there are four oxygen atoms ($4 \times 16.0 = 64.0$).

**molar mass, *M*, of $NiSO_4$ = 58.7 + 32.1 + 64.0 = 154.8**

$$n = \frac{m}{M}$$

Rearranging gives:

$$m = nM$$

$$m = 0.25 \times 154.8 = 38.7\,g$$

## Now test yourself

TESTED

11 Determine the amount, in moles, present in each of the following:
 (a) 8.0 g of sulfur
 (b) 1.68 g of calcium oxide

12 Calculate the mass in grams of each of the following:
 (a) 0.04 mol of aluminium chloride
 (b) 0.45 mol of aluminium hydroxide

13 Calculate the molar mass of an element when 2.60 g is equivalent to 0.05 mol of that element. Identify the element.

14 A compound contains a group 2 metal, X. 0.02 mol of the hydroxide of X has a mass of 2.432 g. Identify the metal X. Show all your working.

Answers on p. 211

## Calculating moles from gases

REVISED

It is difficult to measure the mass of a gas but easy to measure the volume. Avogadro deduced that all gases, under the same conditions of temperature and pressure, occupy the same volume and that at room temperature and pressure the volume of 1 mol of a gas is equal to $24\,dm^3$. It follows that the amount in moles of a gas can be calculated using:

$$n = \frac{V\ (\text{in } dm^3)}{24} \quad \text{or} \quad n = \frac{V\ (\text{in } cm^3)}{24000}$$

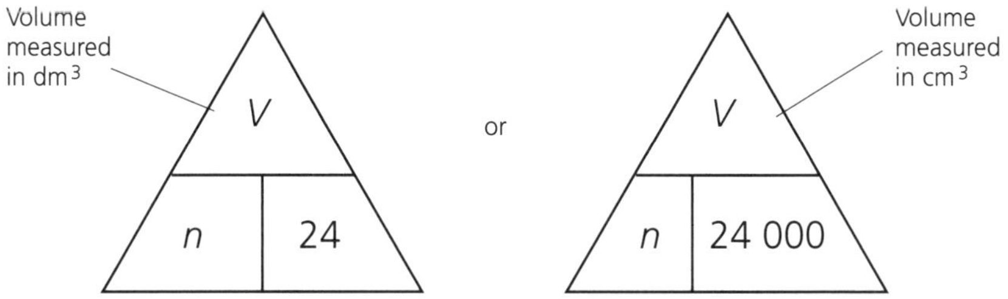


### Example

Calculate the amount in moles present in $120\,cm^3$ of hydrogen at room temperature and pressure.

**Answer**

The volume of gas is given in $cm^3$, so use $n = \frac{V}{24000}$.

$$n = \frac{120}{24000} = 0.0050 = 5.0 \times 10^{-3}$$

## Now test yourself

TESTED

15 When heated, dinitrogen monoxide decomposes to nitrogen and oxygen. The equation for the reaction is:

$$2N_2O(g) \rightarrow 2N_2(g) + O_2(g)$$

What volumes of oxygen and nitrogen are obtained when 50 $cm^3$ of dinitrogen monoxide decomposes?

16 Calculate the mass of each of the following volumes (1 mol of gas has a volume of 24 $dm^3$).

(a) 4 $dm^3$ of carbon dioxide

(b) 500 $cm^3$ of ethane

Answers on p. 211

### Revision activity

Calculate the approximate volume of you bedroom in $cm^3$. Assume that your room contains 80% nitrogen and 20% oxygen. Calculate the mass of gas in your bedroom.

## Calculating moles from solutions

REVISED

Many reactions are carried out in solution. The amount of chemical present is best described by using concentration, *c*, of the solution in mol $dm^{-3}$ and the volume, *V*, of the solution.

The units of concentration are nearly always measured in mol $dm^{-3}$; it follows that *V* is the volume of the solution measured in $dm^3$.

Amount (in moles) in a solution can be calculated using:

$$n = c \times V$$

If *V* is given in $cm^3$ then use:

$$n = c \times \frac{V\,(cm^3)}{1000}$$

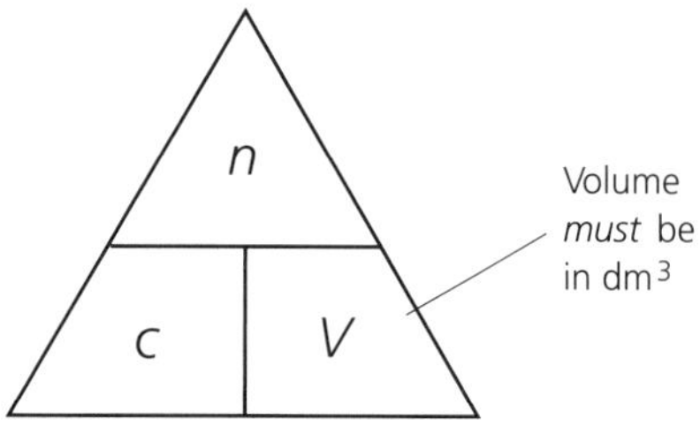


The examples below illustrate the sort of questions that you may be asked.

### Example 1

Calculate the amount in moles present in 250 $cm^3$ of a 0.50 mol $dm^{-3}$ solution.

**Answer**

concentration, $c = 0.50\ mol\ dm^{-3}$

volume, $V = 250\ cm^3$

The volume must be converted into $dm^3$:

$$V = \frac{250}{1000} = 0.250\ dm^3$$

$$n = cV$$

So,

$$n = 0.50 \times 0.250 = 0.125\ mol$$

**Example 2**

Calculate the concentration of a NaOH solution when 4.0 g NaOH is dissolved in 250 $cm^3$.

**Answer**

This is slightly more complicated. You first have to calculate the amount in moles of NaOH used by using the mass (4.0 g) and the formula, NaOH to deduce the molar mass (23.0 + 16.0 + 1.0 = 40.0):

$$n = \frac{m}{M} = \frac{4.0}{40.0} = 0.10\,\text{mol}$$

Concentration is calculated thus:

$$c = \frac{n}{V} = \frac{0.10}{250/1000} = \frac{0.10}{0.250} = 0.40\,\text{mol dm}^{-3}$$

Mole calculations appear on almost every exam paper. It is important that you are able to:

- write and balance full equations
- calculate reacting masses
- calculate reacting gas volumes
- calculate reacting volumes of solutions
- calculate concentrations from titrations

## The ideal gas equation

REVISED

The particles that make up a gas move in all directions at great speeds. They are so widely spaced that any forces of attraction between the gas particles are insignificant. Table 2.5 compares gases with other states of matter.

**Table 2.5**

| States of matter | Solid | Liquid | Gas |
|---|---|---|---|
| |  | 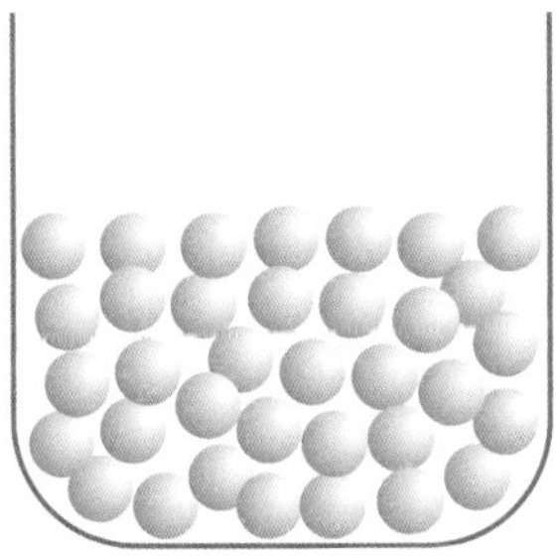 | 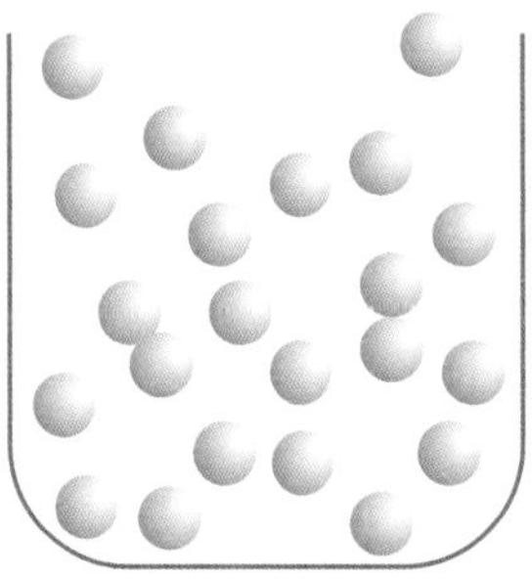 |
| Movement of particles | Vibrate about a fixed position | Slow random movement | Fast random movement |
| Packing of particles | Close packed | Close packed | Widely spaced |
| Volume | Fixed | Fixed | Not fixed — the volume changes if temperature or pressure changes |
| Shape | Fixed | Not fixed — takes on shape of container | Not fixed — takes on shape of container |

If the temperature of a gas increases so does the volume, but if the pressure on the gas increases the volume will decrease. The relationship between the volume of a gas and the temperature and the pressure can be expressed in the form of an equation known as the ideal gas equation:

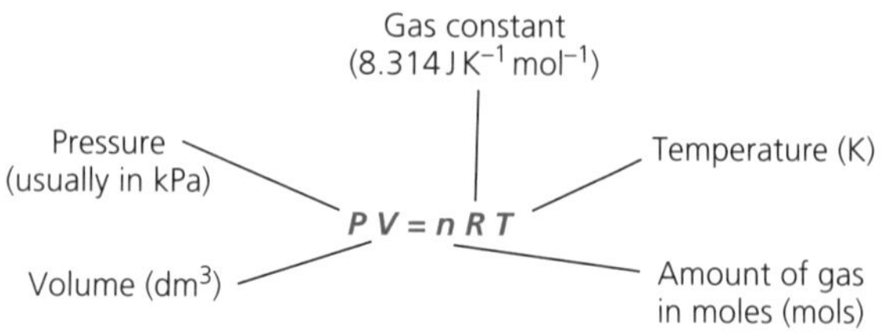


For a given amount of gas:

$$\frac{PV}{T} = \text{constant}$$

The value of the constant is $nR$, where $n$ is the amount of the gas in moles and $R$ is the gas constant.

It follows that:

$$\frac{P_1V_1}{T_1} = \frac{P_2V_2}{T_2}$$

$P_1$, $V_1$, and $T_1$ are the initial pressure, volume and temperature, and $P_2$, $V_2$ and $T_2$ are the final pressure, volume and temperature.

Real gases deviate from ideal gases, but real gases approach ideal behaviour at very high temperatures and at very low pressures.

**Exam tip**

The value and units of the gas constant will be on the data sheet, which will be supplied in all examinations.

**Example 1**

If the volume of a gas collected at 50°C and 110 kPa is 75 cm$^3$, what would the volume be at STP?

For calculations of this type it is best to use the equation:

$$\frac{P_1V_1}{T_1} = \frac{P_2V_2}{T_2}$$

The only unknown is $V_2$ so the equation can be rearranged to give:

$$\frac{P_1V_1T_2}{P_2T_1} = V_2$$

Pressure is in kPa. Standard pressure is 101 kPa.

Temperatures must be in K:

$T_1 = 50°C + 273 = 323\text{ K}$

standard temperature = 0°C = 273 K

The units of volume used for $V_1$ will also be the units of the calculated volume $V_2$.

$$\frac{110 \times 75 \times 273}{101 \times 323} = \frac{2\,252\,250}{32\,623} = 69\text{ cm}^3$$

**Example 2**

2.63 g of a noble gas occupies a volume of 500 cm³ at RTP. Identify the noble gas.

**Answer**

Use the ideal gas equation, $PV = nRT$. Because we are using RTP, the only unknown is the amount in moles, $n$.

The ideal gas equation can be rearranged to give:

$$n = \frac{PV}{RT}$$

$$n = \frac{101 \times 0.5}{8.314 \times 298} = 0.02 \, \text{mol}$$

We now know that 0.02 mols of the noble gas has a mass = 2.63 g, so the atomic mass of the noble gas is:

$$A_r = \frac{m}{n} = \frac{2.63}{0.02} = 131.5$$

Therefore the noble gas is xenon (atomic mass of xenon = 131.3 g mol⁻¹).

## Now test yourself

TESTED ☐

17  At standard pressure and a temperature of 37°C, 3.81 g of a halogen gas occupies a volume of 610 cm³. Identify the halogen gas.

Answer on p. 211

## Stoichiometric relationships in calculations

REVISED ☐

The example below shows how reacting masses, reacting gas volumes and reacting volumes of solutions could all be tested in a single equation.

**Exam tip**

It is essential that you learn to read like a chemist. Units are important and give clues as to which equation to use:
- mol dm⁻³ indicates concentration and therefore you are likely to use $n = cV$.
- g mol⁻¹ indicates molar mass and therefore you are likely to use $n = m/M$.

**Example**

Zinc reacts with dilute hydrochloric acid to produce zinc chloride and hydrogen gas. Write a balanced equation for this reaction and calculate the mass of zinc required to react with 50 cm³ of a 0.10 mol dm⁻³ solution of dilute hydrochloric acid. Deduce the volume (cm³) of hydrogen produced in this reaction and calculate the concentration of the zinc chloride solution that would be formed.

**Answer**

**Equation**   $Zn + 2HCl \rightarrow ZnCl_2 + H_2$

The numbers in front of each formula in the balanced equation tells us the number of moles used and gives the ratio of the reacting moles, i.e. the mole ratio.

| Equation | Zn | + | 2HCl | → | ZnCl₂ | + | H₂ |
|----------|-----|---|------|---|-------|---|-----|
| Mole ratio | 1 mol | : | 2 mol | : | 1 mol | : | 1 mol |

You can calculate $n$ for HCl since we are given both $c$ and $V$:

$$n = 0.10 \times \frac{50}{1000} = 0.0050 = 5.0 \times 10^{-3}$$

You can now work out the number of moles of all the other chemicals in the equation by using the mole ratios in the balanced equation:

| | | | | | | | |
|---|---|---|---|---|---|---|---|
| Equation | $Zn$ | + | $2HCl$ | $\rightarrow$ | $ZnCl_2$ | + | $H_2$ |
| Mole ratio | 1 mol | : | 2 mol | : | 1 mol | : | 1 mol |
| Actual moles | $\frac{5 \times 10^{-3}}{2}$ | | $5.0 \times 10^{-3}$ | | $\frac{5 \times 10^{-3}}{2}$ | | $\frac{5 \times 10^{-3}}{2}$ |
| | $2.5 \times 10^{-3}$ | | | | $2.5 \times 10^{-3}$ | | $2.5 \times 10^{-3}$ |

We can use $n = \frac{m}{M}$ to find the mass of Zn required:

$m = nM$

$m = 2.5 \times 10^{-3} \times 65.4$

$m = 0.16\,g$

We can use $n = cV$ to find the concentration of $ZnCl_2(aq)$:

$c = \frac{n}{V}$

$c = \frac{2.5 \times 10^{-3}}{50/1000}$

$c = 0.050\,mol\,dm^{-3}$

We can use $n = \frac{V}{24000}$ to find the volume of $H_2$ produced:

$V = n \times 24000$

$V = 2.5 \times 10^{-3} \times 24000$

$V = 60\,cm^3$

## Now test yourself

TESTED

18 How many moles are there in each of the following?
 (a) $200\,cm^3$ of $0.5\,mol\,dm^{-3}$ sulfuric acid
 (b) $25\,cm^3$ of $0.1\,mol\,dm^{-3}$ hydrochloric acid

19 Calculate the mass of solid sodium hydroxide which, when dissolved, would make $250\,cm^3$ of $0.2\,mol\,dm^{-3}$ solution of sodium hydroxide.

20 What is the concentration obtained by diluting $50\,cm^3$ of $2\,mol\,dm^{-3}$ sodium carbonate with water to make:
 (a) $500\,cm^3$ of solution
 (b) $250\,cm^3$ of solution

21 A solution of potassium carbonate has a concentration of $0.04\,mol\,dm^{-3}$. $25.0\,cm^3$ of this solution is neutralised by $28.10\,cm^3$ of hydrochloric acid.
 (a) Write a balanced equation for the reaction between potassium carbonate and hydrochloric acid.
 (b) How many moles of potassium carbonate are contained in $25.0\,cm^3$ of solution?
 (c) How many moles of hydrochloric acid are needed to neutralise the number of moles of potassium carbonate in $25.0\,cm^3$?
 (d) What is the concentration of the hydrochloric acid in $mol\,dm^{-3}$?

Answers on pp. 211–212

## Percentage yield calculations

REVISED



Percentage yield calculations involve mole calculations and are often used when preparing organic compounds. Reactions of organic molecules will be covered fully in Module 4 (AS) and Module 6 (A level). A typical calculation is shown below.

**Example**

Ethanol, $C_2H_5OH$, can be oxidised to form ethanal, $CH_3CHO$. If 2.30 g of ethanol are oxidised to produce 1.32 g of ethanal, calculate the percentage yield.

**Answer**

Any mole calculations require a balanced equation, so it is essential that you are able to write suitable balanced equations and to use the mole ratios from the equation. [O] can be used to represent the oxidising agent.

| | | | | | | | |
|---|---|---|---|---|---|---|---|
| Equation | $C_2H_5OH$ | + | [O] | $\rightarrow$ | $CH_3CHO$ | + | $H_2O$ |
| Mole ratio | 1 mol | | 1 mol | | 1 mol | | 1 mol |

The equation shows that 1 mole of ethanol produces 1 mole of ethanal.

**Step 1:** calculate the number of moles of ethanol used:

$$\text{amount of ethanol used} = n = \frac{\text{mass (in g)}}{\text{molar mass}}$$

$$n = \frac{m}{M}$$

$$\text{amount of ethanol used} = n = \frac{2.3}{46} = 0.05\text{ mol}$$

Since the mole ratio is 1:1, the amount of ethanal that could be made is also 0.05 mol.

**Step 2**: Calculate the number of moles of ethanal actually produced:

$$\text{amount of ethanal produced} = n = \frac{m}{M}$$

$$= \frac{1.32}{44} = 0.03\text{ mol}$$

**Step 3:** Calculate the percentage yield by using:

$$\text{percentage yield} = \frac{\text{actual yield} \times 100}{\text{maximum yield}}$$

$$= 0.03 \times \frac{100}{0.05}$$

$$= 60\%$$

## Now test yourself

TESTED

22 A student reacted 4.60 g of ethanol ($C_2H_5OH$) with an excess of methanoic acid (HCOOH) and made 5.92 g of ethyl methanoate ($HCOOC_2H_5$). Calculate the student's percentage yield. The equation for the reaction is:

$$C_2H_5OH + HCOOH \rightleftharpoons HCOOC_2H_5 + H_2O$$

Answer on p. 212

## Atom economy calculations

REVISED

$$\text{atom economy} = \frac{\text{molar mass of desired product}}{\text{molar mass of all products}} \times 100$$

The reaction between ethanol, $C_2H_5OH$, and ethanoic acid, $CH_3COOH$, is used to make the ester ethyl ethanoate, $CH_3COOC_2H_5$.

$$CH_3COOH + C_2H_5OH \rightarrow CH_3COOC_2H_5 + H_2O$$

The desired product is the ester, but water is also produced.

molar mass of $CH_3COOC_2H_5$ = 88 g

molar mass of $H_2O$ = 18 g

$$\text{atom economy} = \frac{88}{88 + 18} \times 100$$

$$= \frac{88}{106} \times 100 = 83\%$$

A high atom economy is good, since that would indicate a low level of waste. Atom economy can be greatly enhanced if a use can be found for the by-product.

**Exam tip**

If asked to define atom economy, simply use this equation.

**Exam tip**

When carrying out calculations do not round numbers during the calculation. Keep the number in your calculator and only round when you have finished the entire calculation.

### Now test yourself

TESTED

23 A student prepared a sample of methanol, $CH_3OH$, by reacting bromomethane with potassium hydroxide.

$$CH_3Br + KOH \rightarrow CH_3OH + KBr$$

Calculate the atom economy for the preparation of methanol.

Answer on p. 212

# Acids

## Acids and bases

REVISED

The release of a proton, $H^+$, by an **acid** can only occur in aqueous solution. Pure HCl is a covalent gas and it is only when it comes into contact with water that it can release a $H^+$ (proton):

$$HCl(g) + H_2O(l) \rightarrow H_3O^+(aq) + Cl^-(aq)$$

An **acid** is a proton donor.

$H_3O^+(aq)$ is usually written as $H^+(aq)$ and the above equation shown as:

$$HCl(aq) \rightarrow H^+(aq) + Cl^-(aq)$$

You are expected to know the formulae of some common acids: hydrochloric acid, HCl; sulfuric acid, $H_2SO_4$; nitric acid, $HNO_3$; and ethanoic acid, $CH_3COOH$. The acidic proton in ethanoic acid is $CH_3COO$**H**.

Acids have a pH below 7, and the stronger acids have lower pHs. Acids can be sub-divided into strong acids and weak acids.

- Strong acids include HCl, $H_2SO_4$ and $HNO_3$. They are regarded as strong acids because in solution they totally dissociate into their ions. The equation always includes the '$\rightarrow$' symbol.

  $$HCl(aq) \rightarrow H^+(aq) + Cl^-(aq)$$

- Weak acids include organic acids such as ethanoic acid, $CH_3COOH$. They are weak acids because in solution they only partially dissociate into their ions. The equation always includes the '⇌' symbol.

  $CH_3COOH(aq) \rightleftharpoons CH_3COO^-(aq) + H^+(aq)$

Common **bases** include metal oxides (e.g. $Na_2O$, MgO, CuO), metal hydroxides (e.g. NaOH, KOH, $Cu(OH)_2$), ammonium hydroxide ($NH_4OH$) and metal carbonates (e.g. $K_2CO_3$, $ZnCO_3$). Hydroxides, such as NaOH(aq), are strong bases and completely dissociate, whereas $NH_4OH(aq)$ is a weak base and only partially dissociates:

$NaOH(aq) \rightarrow Na^+(aq) + OH^-(aq)$

$NH_4OH(aq) \rightleftharpoons NH_4^+(aq) + OH^-(aq)$

Common **alkalis** include group 1 hydroxides, such as LiOH and NaOH, and some group 2 hydroxides, for example $Ca(OH)_2$.

**Revision activity**

There are very many naturally occurring organic acids. Find the formulae of: lactic acid, malic acid, tartaric acid, ascorbic acid and citric acid. What do they all have in common?

A **base** is a proton acceptor.

An **alkali** is a soluble base that releases hydroxide ions, $OH^-$ when in aqueous solution.

## Salts

REVISED

A **salt** is formed when an acid reacts with a metal, a carbonate, a base or an alkali, as in the following examples. Acids react in aqueous solution and all reactions can be represented with either a balanced equation or an ionic equation:

Acid and metal:

| | |
|---|---|
| Balanced equation | $2HCl(aq) + Mg(s) \rightarrow MgCl_2(aq) + H_2(g)$ |
| Ionic equation | $2H^+(aq) + Mg(s) \rightarrow Mg^{2+}(aq) + H_2(g)$ |

Acid and carbonate:

| | |
|---|---|
| Balanced equation | $2HCl(aq) + K_2CO_3(aq) \rightarrow 2KCl(aq) + H_2O(l) + CO_2(g)$ |
| Ionic equation | $2H^+(aq) + CO_3^{2-}(aq) \rightarrow H_2O(l) + CO_2(g)$ |

Acid and base:

| | |
|---|---|
| Balanced equation | $2HCl(aq) + CuO(s) \rightarrow CuCl_2(aq) + H_2O(l)$ |
| Ionic equation | $2H^+(aq) + CuO(s) \rightarrow Cu^{2+}(aq) + H_2O(l)$ |

Acid and an alkali:

| | |
|---|---|
| Balanced equation | $HCl(aq) + NaOH(aq) \rightarrow NaCl(aq) + H_2O(l)$ |
| Ionic equation | $H^+(aq) + OH^-(aq) \rightarrow H_2O(l)$ |

Bases such as ammonia react with acids to produce a salt. Ammonium sulfate, $(NH_4)_2SO_4$, is used as a fertiliser and is manufactured by reacting ammonia with sulfuric acid:

| | |
|---|---|
| Balanced equation | $2NH_3(aq) + H_2SO_4(aq) \rightarrow (NH_4)_2SO_4(aq)$ |

You are expected to do acid–base titrations in the laboratory and then carry out calculations. A titration is a process whereby a precise volume of one solution is added to another solution until the exact volume required to complete the reaction has been found. You are expected to obtain results accurate to within $0.10\,cm^3$. Practical skills will be examined in all exams.

A **salt** is formed when an acid has one or more of its hydrogen ions replaced by either a metal ion or an ammonium ion, $NH_4^+$.

**Typical mistakes**

Examiners often use unfamiliar acids such as phosphoric acid, $H_3PO_4$, and expect students to be able to work out the formulae of salts formed from the acid. Statistics show that the majority of students find this difficult. The way to work it out is to use the clue in $H_3PO_4$. The phosphate ion combines with three hydrogens, so it must be valency 3. Therefore, if it forms a salt with a group 1 metal, for example sodium, the formula is $Na_3PO_4$; with a group 2 metal, for example magnesium, the formula is $Mg_3(PO_4)_2$.

**Exam tip**

Organic acids such as ethanoic acid contain –COOH, and when they react the H in the –COOH is replaced by a metal ion or an ammonium ion.

**Example**

It was found that 18.60 $cm^3$ HCl(aq) neutralised exactly 25.0 $cm^3$ 0.100 mol $dm^{-3}$ NaOH(aq). Calculate the concentration of the HCl(aq) solution.

Answer

**Step 1** Work out how many moles, *n*, of sodium hydroxide were used. This is possible because the concentration, *c*, and the volume, *V*, are known.

The concentration of the sodium hydroxide is 0.100 mol $dm^{-3}$ of solution and 25.0 $cm^3$ was used.

$$n = cV = 0.100 \times \frac{25.0}{1000} = 0.00250\,\text{mol}$$

**Step 2** Refer to the balanced equation to see how many moles of hydrochloric acid are needed to react with this number of moles of sodium hydroxide.

| | | | | | | | | |
|---|---|---|---|---|---|---|---|---|
| The equation for the reaction is: | NaOH | + | HCl | → | NaCl | + | $H_2O$ |
| The mole ratio is: | 1 | : | 1 | : | 1 | : | 1 |

Therefore, 1 mol of NaOH reacts with 1 mol of HCl.

As 0.00250 mol of NaOH were used, 0.00250 mol of HCl must be required to react completely.

Since 18.60 $cm^3$ of HCl were added from the burette, 18.60 $cm^3$ of HCl must contain 0.00250 mol.

**Step 3** Convert the information obtained about the hydrochloric acid into its concentration in mol $dm^{-3}$.

$$c = \frac{n}{V} = \frac{0.00250}{18.6/1000} = \frac{0.00250}{0.0186} = 0.134\,\text{mol dm}^{-3}$$

**Exam tip**

All ions have the state symbol (aq). When balancing an ionic equation, you must balance charge as well as symbols.

## Now test yourself

TESTED

24 Write the formulae of the following salts.
(a) calcium nitrate
(b) aluminium sulfate
(c) magnesium ethanoate

25 Write full and ionic equations for each of the following reactions:
(a) aqueous solutions of ethanoic acid and sodium hydroxide
(b) solid $CaCO_3$ and aqueous nitric acid

Answers on p. 212

# Redox

A species is said to be **oxidised** if it loses electrons. The converse is true for **reduction**. One way of remembering this is the acronym OILRIG:

**O**xidation **I**s **L**oss **R**eduction **I**s **G**ain

**Oxidation** involves the loss of electrons or an increase in the oxidation number.

**Reduction** involves the gain of electrons or a decrease in the oxidation number.

**Redox reactions** are reactions in which electrons are transferred from one substance to another.

# Oxidation number





Oxidation number is a convenient way of identifying whether or not a substance has undergone either **oxidation** or **reduction**. In order to work out the oxidation number you must learn a few simple rules (Table 2.6).

**Table 2.6 Rules for determining oxidation numbers**

| Rule | Example |
|---|---|
| All elements in their natural state have the oxidation number zero | Hydrogen, $H_2$; oxidation number = 0 |
| Oxidation numbers of the atoms of any compound always add up to zero | Carbon dioxide, $CO_2$; sum of oxidation numbers = 0 |
| Oxidation numbers of the components of any ion always add up to the charge of the ion | Nitrate, $NO_3^-$; sum of oxidation numbers = −1 |

There are certain elements whose oxidation numbers never change but some other elements have variable oxidation numbers and these have to be deduced.

When calculating the oxidation numbers of elements in either a compound or an ion you should apply the following order of priority:

1 The oxidation numbers of elements in groups 1, 2 and 3 are always +1, +2 and +3 respectively.
2 The oxidation number of fluorine is always −1.
3 The oxidation number of hydrogen is usually +1.
4 The oxidation number of oxygen is usually −2.
5 The oxidation number of chlorine is usually −1.

By applying these rules *in sequence*, it is possible to deduce any oxidation number.

**Example 1**

Deduce the oxidation number of Mn in $KMnO_4$.

**Answer**

$KMnO_4$ is a compound and therefore the oxidation numbers must add up to zero.

In order of priority K comes first and its oxidation number is +1; O is second and its oxidation number is −2 *but* there are 4 oxygens hence a total of −8.

In order for the oxidation numbers to add up to zero, the oxidation number of Mn in $KMnO_4$ must be +7.

**Example 2**

Deduce the oxidation number of I in $IO_3^-$.

**Answer**

$IO_3^-$ is an ion and therefore the oxidation numbers must add up to the charge on the ion, i.e. they must add up to −1.

In order of priority, O comes first and its oxidation number is −2. However, there are three oxygens in $IO_3^-$, so the total for oxygen is −6.

In order for the oxidation numbers to add up to the charge of the ion (−1) the oxidation number of I in $IO_3^-$ must be +5.

When magnesium reacts with steam, magnesium oxide and hydrogen are formed:

$$Mg(s) + H_2O(g) \rightarrow MgO(s) + H_2(g)$$

It is easy to see that magnesium has been oxidised (it has gained oxygen) and that water has been reduced (it has lost oxygen). The oxidation numbers for this reaction are shown in Figure 2.3.

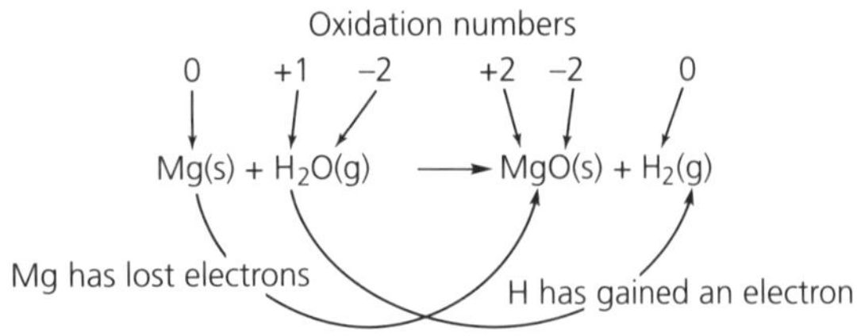


**Figure 2.3**

An increase in oxidation number is due to oxidation.

A decrease in oxidation number is due to reduction.

Electron transfer can be shown by using ionic half-equations, for example:

| | |
|---|---|
| $Mg \rightarrow Mg^{2+} + 2e^-$ | (*loss* of electrons = oxidation) |
| $2H^+ + 2e^- \rightarrow H_2$ | (*gain* of electrons = reduction) |

## Now test yourself

TESTED

26 Deduce the oxidation numbers in each of the following:

(a) $H_2O$, NaOH, $KNO_3$, $NH_3$, $N_2O$

(b) $SO_4^{2-}$, $CO_3^{2-}$, $NH_4^+$, $MnO_4^-$, $Cr_2O_7^{2-}$

Answer on p. 212

## Redox reactions

REVISED

Metals generally react by losing electrons (oxidation is loss), so the oxidation number increases, for example:

| | Mg | → | $Mg^{2+}$ | + | $2e^-$ |
|---|---|---|---|---|---|
| **Oxidation numbers:** | 0 | | +2 | | |

Non-metals generally react by gaining electrons (reduction is gain), so the oxidation number decreases, for example:

| | $F_2$ | + | $2e^-$ | → | $2F^-$ |
|---|---|---|---|---|---|
| **Oxidation numbers:** | 0 | | | | −1 |

## Now test yourself

TESTED

27 Use oxidation numbers to identify what has been oxidised in the following reaction:

$$Zn + CuSO_4 \rightarrow Cu + ZnSO_4$$

Answer on p. 212

**Exam tip**

Redox reactions occur throughout the A-level course, so it is essential that you can work out oxidation numbers. This becomes more important in the second year of the course when studying redox titrations and electrode potentials. Make sure that you know the rules and can apply the order of priority for working out oxidation numbers: groups 1, 2 and 3, followed by F, H, O and Cl.

## Exam practice

1 (a) A chemist reacted oxygen separately with magnesium and with sulfur to form magnesium oxide and sulfur dioxide respectively. Write an equation for each reaction. [1]

(b) The reactions in (a) are both redox reactions in which reduction and oxidation take place. Explain, using the changes in oxidation number for sulfur, whether sulfur has undergone oxidation or reduction. [2]

(c) The chemist added water to magnesium oxide and to sulfur dioxide, forming two aqueous solutions. Write equations for the reactions that took place. [2]

2 10.00 g of sodium carbonate crystals $Na_2CO_3.xH_2O$ are dissolved to make 1.00 $dm^3$ of solution. 25.0 $cm^3$ of this solution are neutralised by 17.50 $cm^3$ of 0.100 mol $dm^{-3}$ hydrochloric acid.

(a) Calculate the amount, in moles, of hydrochloric acid present in 17.50 $cm^3$. [1]

(b) Deduce the number of moles of sodium carbonate present in 25.0 $cm^3$. [2]

(c) Calculate the number of moles and mass of sodium carbonate in 1.0 $dm^{-3}$ of the solution. [2]

(d) Use your answer to (c) to deduce the mass of water in the crystals. [2]

(e) Deduce the value of $x$ in $Na_2CO_3.xH_2O$. [2]

### Answers and quick quiz 2 online

ONLINE

## Summary

You should now have an understanding of:

- atomic structure, isotopes, relative masses, mass spectra
- how to deduce formulae and write equations
- mole calculations using the equations: $n = m/M$, $n = V/24$ and $n = cV$
- the ideal gas equation
- acids, bases and the formation of salts and be able to calculate the formulae of hydrated salts
- titrations
- oxidation and reduction in terms of oxidation numbers

# 3 Electrons, bonding and structure

## Electron structure

### Ionisation energy

REVISED

Ionisation energy gives evidence for the existence of shells and subshells of electrons.

The **first ionisation energy** can be represented by the equation:

$X(g) \rightarrow X^{+}(g) + e^{-}$

It is important to include the state symbols (g).

For elements that have more than one electron, it is possible to remove each electron stepwise.

The **second ionisation energy** is represented by the equation:

$X^{+}(g) \rightarrow X^{2+}(g) + e^{-}$

The second ionisation energy results in the formation of a 2+ ion and starts with a 1+ ion. It follows that the ***n*th ionisation energy** is:

$X^{(n-1)+}(g) \rightarrow X^{n+}(g) + e^{-}$

**Typical mistakes**

When asked to write an equation to illustrate the third ionisation energy many students write: $X(g) \rightarrow X^{3+}(g) + 3e^{-}$. This is incorrect as it represents the first, second and third ionisation energies combined.

The correct response is $X^{2+}(g) \rightarrow X^{3+}(g) + e^{-}$. It is worth remembering that there is always just one $e^{-}$ on the right-hand side of the equation and that the charges on both sides have to balance.

The **first ionisation energy** of an element is the energy required to remove one electron from each atom in one mole of gaseous atoms to form one mole of gaseous ions of charge 1+.

The **second ionisation energy** is the energy required to remove one electron from each ion in one mole of gaseous ions of charge 1+ to form one mole of gaseous ions of charge 2+.

The ***n*th ionisation energy** is the energy required to remove one electron from each ion in one mole of gaseous ions of charge $(n-1)^{+}$ ions to form one mole of gaseous $n^{+}$ ions.

### Trends in ionisation energies

REVISED

There are *three* factors that influence ionisation energy.

Factor 1 — distance of the outermost electron from the nucleus (atomic radius)

Factor 2 — electron shielding (the number of inner shells)

Factor 3 — nuclear charge (the number of protons in the nucleus)

Down a group:

Factor 1 — atomic radii increases, which should make it easier to remove an electron

Factor 2 — shielding increases, which should make it easier to remove an electron

Factor 3 — nuclear charge increases, which should make it more difficult to remove an electron

Factors 1 and 2 outweigh factor 3, so ionisation energy *decreases* down a group.

Across a period:

Factor 1 — atomic radii decreases, which should make it more difficult to remove an electron

Factor 2 — shielding remains the same, which has no effect on the ease of removing an electron

Factor 3 — nuclear charge increases, which should make it more difficult to remove an electron

Factors 1 and 3 mean that ionisation energy *increases* across a period.

It is possible to remove electrons stepwise from an atom and to measure the size of successive ionisation energies. When the successive energies are plotted, the graph provides evidence for the existence of shells. Phosphorus has 15 electrons, which are arranged 2,8,5. The evidence for this is the plot of successive ionisation energies shown (Figure 3.1).

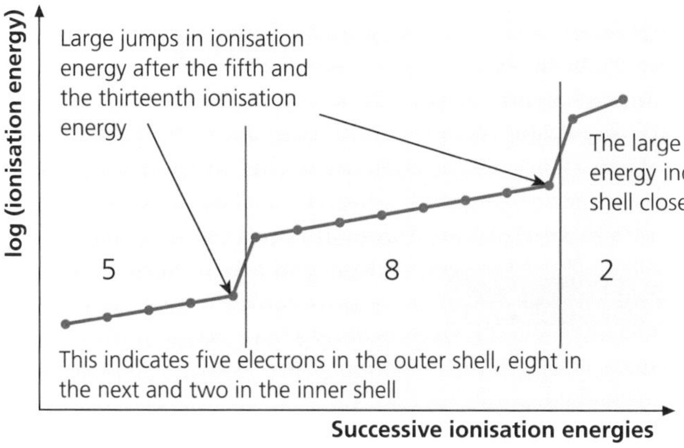


**Figure 3.1** Successive ionisation energies of $_{15}P$

Plotting successive ionisation energies confirms what you learnt at GCSE. It shows that the first shell contains a maximum of two electrons and the second shell contains a maximum of eight electrons.

There is further experimental evidence to suggest that each shell is made of smaller subshells.

**Exam tip**

This is how to sketch a plot of successive ionisation energies of an element — for example $_{13}Al$. The atomic number 13 tells you that aluminium has 13 protons and 13 electrons. Use your GCSE knowledge to work out that the electrons are arranged 2, 8, 3. When sketching the successive ionisation energies, remember that the electrons in the outer shell are removed first. In this case, therefore, you draw the ionisation energies of the three outer shell electrons followed by a big increase, then the ionisation energies for the next shell, which contains eight electrons, followed by another big jump, and finally the ionisation energies for the inner two electrons.

## Now test yourself

TESTED

1 Element X is in period 3. The first seven successive ionisation energies are shown below:
1012, 1903, 2912, 4957, 6274, 21 269, 25 398
  (a) Use these ionisation energies to identify element X. Explain your reasoning.
  (b) Write an equation to represent the third ionisation energy of element X.

Answer on p. 212

By studying the first ionisation energies of the first 20 elements we obtain evidence for the existence of subshells (Figure 3.2).

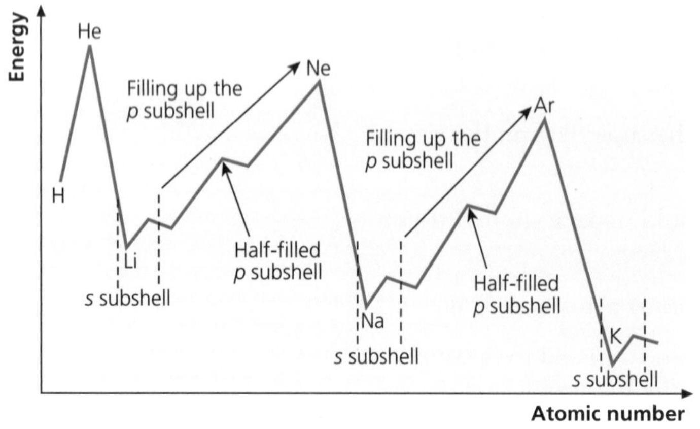


Figure 3.2 **Evidence for the existence of subshells**

> **Exam tip**
>
> The specification does not require you to explain why the ionisation energy drops immediately after a half-filled *p* subshell.

The graph shows that there is a gradual increase in ionisation energies across a period, and it also reveals several small peaks and troughs. These peaks and troughs are repeated in each period. They provide evidence for the existence of subshells (*s*, *p* and *d*). There is a periodic variation throughout all of the elements and there is evidence for several shells and subshells.

> **Typical mistake**
>
> Questions often ask students to complete or to state the number of electrons in a *p*-orbital or a *d* subshell or the third shell and it is essential to differentiate between *orbitals, subshells and shells*. All orbitals contain a maximum of two electrons, subshells are made up orbitals and shells consist of subshells. Table 3.1 demonstrates this.

Table 3.1 **Shells and subshells**

| Shell | Subshells | | | | Total number of electrons | | | | Total |
|---|---|---|---|---|---|---|---|---|---|
| 1st | 1s | | | | 2 | | | | 2 |
| 2nd | 2s | 2p | | | 2 | 6 | | | 8 |
| 3rd | 3s | 3p | 3d | | 2 | 6 | 10 | | 18 |
| 4th | 4s | 4p | 4d | 4f | 2 | 6 | 10 | 14 | 32 |

We now know that the subshells are made up of orbitals.

## Now test yourself

TESTED

2 Explain why the first ionisation energy of potassium is less than that of sodium.

Answer on p. 212

## Electron configuration

REVISED

The concept of an orbital is difficult and if you are asked to define an orbital, the simplest definition is:

**An orbital is a region around the nucleus that can hold up to two electrons with opposite spin.**

You should be able to describe, with the aid of a diagram, the shape of the *s*- and the *p*-orbitals.

There are three $p$-orbitals, one along each of the $x$, $y$ and $z$ axes (Figure 3.3).

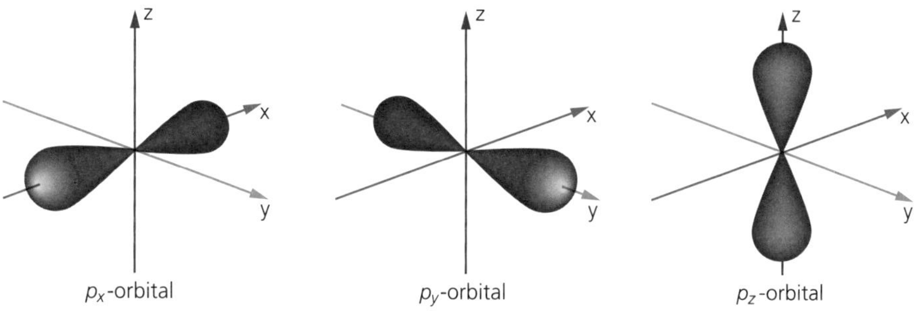


**Figure 3.3**

The sequence in which electrons fill the orbitals is shown in Figure 3.4.

Remember that, within an orbital, the electrons have opposite spins. The lowest energy level is occupied first; orbitals at the same energy level are occupied singly before pairing of electrons.

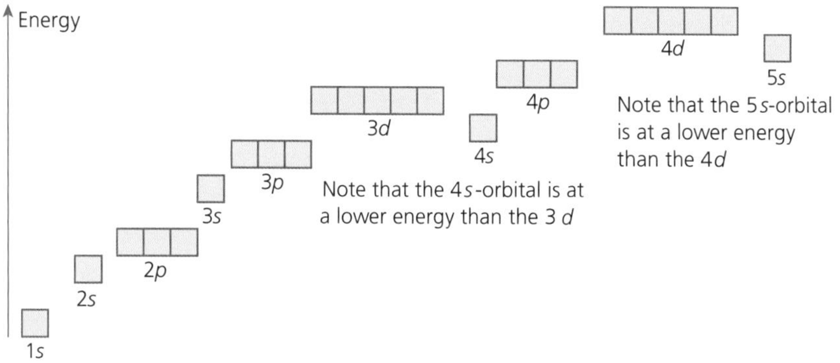


**Figure 3.4 Sequence in which the orbitals are filled by electrons**

You should be able to write the full electron configuration of the first 36 elements. For example:

**$_{15}$P is $1s^22s^22p^63s^23p^3$ or [$_{10}$Ne] $3s^23p^3$**

**$_{25}$Mn is $1s^22s^22p^63s^23p^63d^54s^2$ or [$_{18}$Ar] $3d^54s^2$**

**Exam tip**

Most students remember that the 4*s* fills before the 3*d*. However, when metals lose electrons to form ions, the 4*s* is also lost before the 3*d*. So, for example, the electron configuration of $_{22}Ti^{2+}$ is $1s^22s^22p^63s^23p^63d^2$ and *not* $1s^22s^22p^63s^23p^64s^2$ (the Ti atom is $1s^22s^22p^63s^23p^63d^24s^2$).

## Now test yourself

TESTED

3 Write the electron configuration of each of: N, $Al^{3+}$, $P^{3-}$, $Fe^{3+}$.

Answer on p. 212

# Bonding and structure

## Types of bond

REVISED

There are three main types of bond: **ionic**, **covalent** and **metallic**. Table 3.2 summarises each type.

An **ionic bond** is the electrostatic attraction between oppositely charged ions.

A **covalent bond** is the strong electrostatic attraction between a shared pair of electrons and the nuclei of the bonded atoms. Each atom provides one of the shared pair.

A **metallic bond** is the electrostatic attraction between positive metal ions in the lattice and the delocalised electrons.

Table 3.2 Properties of the three types of bond

| | Ionic | Covalent | Metallic |
|---|---|---|---|
| **Formation** | Formed by electron transfer from metal atom (X) to non-metal atom (Y) to produce oppositely charged ions $X^+$ and $Y^-$ | Formed when electrons are shared rather than transferred | The positive ions occupy fixed positions in a lattice and the delocalised electrons can move freely throughout the lattice |
| **Direction** | An ionic bond is directional acting between adjacent ions | A covalent bond is directional, acting solely between the two atoms involved in the bond | A metallic bond is non-directional because the delocalised electrons can move anywhere in the lattice |
| **Examples** | KBr, CuO | $O_2$, $C_2H_6$ | Ni, Mg |
| **Melting and boiling points** | High melting point and boiling point due to strong electrostatic forces between ions throughout the lattice | Low melting point and boiling point due to the simple molecular structure being held together by weak forces between molecules | High melting point and boiling point due to strong metallic bonds between the positive ions and negative electrons throughout the lattice |
| **Conductivity** | Non-conductor of electricity in solid state, but conducts when molten or dissolved in water because the ionic lattice breaks down and ions are free to move as mobile charge carriers | Non-conductors of electricity — no free or mobile charged particles | Good thermal and electrical conductors due to mobile, delocalised electrons that conduct heat and electricity, even in the solid state |
| **Solubility** | The ionic lattice dissolves in polar solvents (e.g. water) because polar water molecules attract ions in the lattice and surround each ion (hydration) | Simple molecular structures soluble in non-polar solvents (e.g. hexane) but usually insoluble in water | Insoluble in polar and non-polar solvents<br>Some metals react with water |

In addition to covalent bonding, **dative covalent** or coordinate bonds exist. These are also the result of two shared electrons but in this case one of the atoms supplies both shared electrons.

**Typical mistake**

When asked to describe bonding and properties students often lose marks by careless use of technical terms — for example, by describing an ionic bond as the attraction between oppositely charged atoms, rather than between oppositely charged ions.

**Revision exercise**

Look up the conductivity of aluminium, copper, silver, gold, platinum. Put them in order of conductivity. Which is the best conductor? Why is the best conductor not used for electrical wiring?

## Dot-and-cross diagrams

REVISED

Dot-and-cross diagrams are a simple visual way to illustrate both ionic and covalent bonding Figure 3.5.

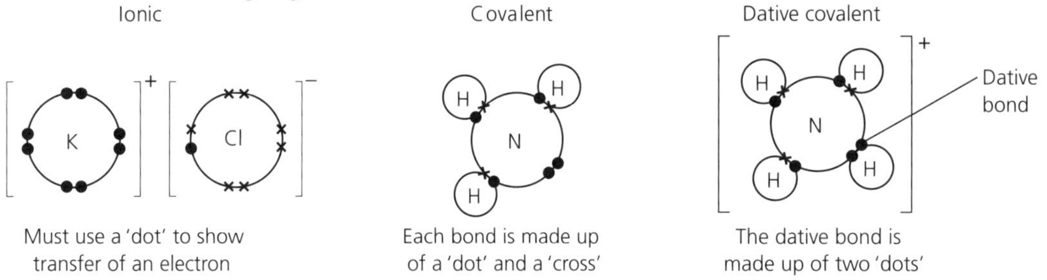


**Figure 3.5** Bonding in potassium chloride, ammonia and the ammonium ion

**Typical mistake**

Exam questions may ask students to draw a dot-and-cross diagram of a compound such as magnesium oxide, MgO. A common incorrect response is shown in Figure 3.6.

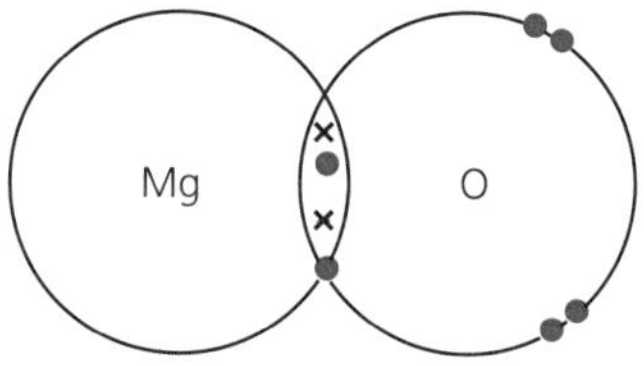


**Figure 3.6**

Here, magnesium oxide is shown as covalent (sharing electrons), when it is ionic. The two outer electrons of magnesium should be transferred to oxygen, resulting in the formation of $Mg^{2+}$ and $O^{2-}$ ions. A good guide is to look at the mark allocation — 1 mark usually indicates that a covalent structure is required, 2 marks usually indicates ionic.

## Shapes of molecules

REVISED

The main points of the **electron pair repulsion theory** are:

- Electron pairs repel one another as far apart as possible.
- The shape depends upon the number and type of electron pairs surrounding the central atom.
- Lone pairs of electrons are more 'repelling' than bonded pairs of electrons.
- The order of repulsion is: lone pair–lone pair > lone pair–bonded pair > bonded pair–bonded pair.

You should be able to draw a dot-and-cross diagram of a molecule and use it to determine the number and type of electron pairs around the central atom. Then use Table 3.3 to predict the shape, the bond angle and whether or not it is symmetrical.

**Table 3.3** Shapes of molecules

| Number of bonded pairs of electrons | Number of lone pairs of electrons | Shape | Approximate bond angle | Symmetry |
|---|---|---|---|---|
| 2 | 0 | Linear | 180° | Yes |
| 3 | 0 | Trigonal planar | 120° | Yes |
| 4 | 0 | Tetrahedral | 109.5° | Yes |
| 5 | 0 | Trigonal bipyramidal | 90° and 120° | Yes |
| 6 | 0 | Octahedral | 90° | Yes |
| 3 | 1 | Pyramidal | 107° | No |
| 2 | 2 | Angular | 104° | No |

The **electron-pair repulsion theory** states that electron pairs repel each other and the shape of a covalent molecule is determined by the number (and type) of electron pairs around the central atom.

**Exam tip**

In exams, questions asking for an explanation of the electron pair repulsion theory are often answered badly. Learn the key definition above and the bullet points. If you know these, you will score 3 or 4 easy marks.

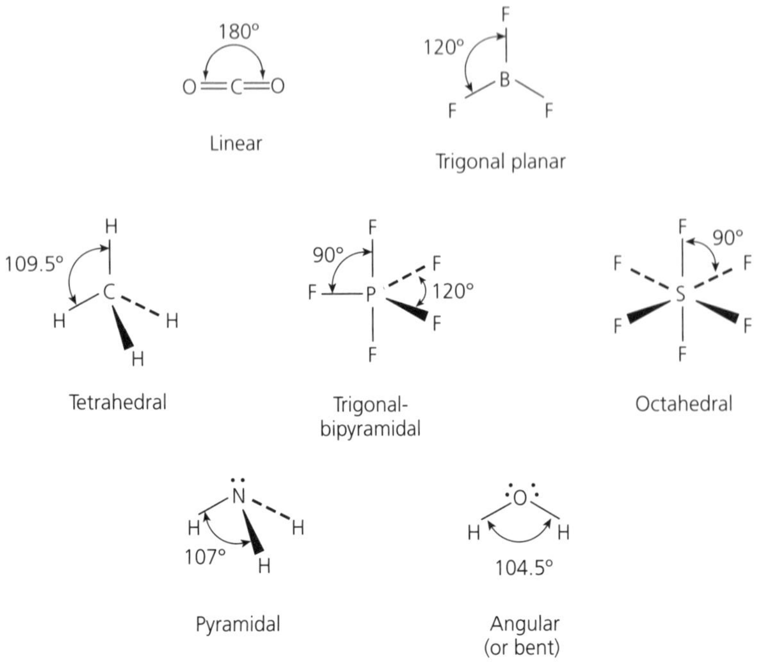


**Figure 3.7**

> **Exam tip**
>
> If the central atom in a molecule contains only bonded pairs of electrons any dipoles usually cancel, so the molecule is non-polar.

## Now test yourself

TESTED

4 Determine the shape of each of the following molecules and ions. You may find it helpful to refer to the periodic table to establish the number of outer shell electrons.

(a) $H_2S$
(b) $PH_3$
(c) $SCl_2$
(d) $CH_2Cl_2$
(e) $CH_3^+$
(f) $H_3O^+$

Answers on p. 212

## Electronegativity

REVISED

Ionic and covalent bonds are extremes — most bonds are neither 100% ionic nor 100% covalent but somewhere in-between.

When a covalent bond forms between two different elements it is likely that the elements will attract the covalent bonded pair of electrons unequally. The ability of an atom to attract the bonding electrons in a covalent bond is known as the **electronegativity**.

> **Electronegativity** is the attraction that each bonded atom has for the pair of electrons in the gaseous covalent bond.

Electronegativity increases across a period but decreases down a group such that fluorine is the most electronegative element.

**Table 3.4 Electronegativity**

| | | | | | | |
|---|---|---|---|---|---|---|
| Li<br>1.0 | Be<br>1.5 | B<br>2.0 | C<br>2.5 | N<br>3.0 | O<br>3.5 | F<br>4.0 |
| Na<br>0.9 | | | | | | Cl<br>3.0 |
| K<br>0.8 | | | | | | Br<br>2.8 |

In molecules like HCl the two electrons in the covalent bond are shared unequally. Chlorine has a higher electronegativity than hydrogen, so the two shared electrons are pulled towards the chlorine atom resulting in the formation of a permanent dipole.

The bond in HCl consists of two shared electrons (essentially covalent) but also contains δ+ and δ− charges (hence the ionic character).

- The greater the difference between electronegativities, the greater the ionic character of the bond.
- The greater the similarity in electronegativities, the greater the covalent character of the bond.

## Bond polarity

REVISED

In general, a compound made of two or more different non-metals will be a **polar molecule** unless the molecule is symmetrical, in which case any dipoles due to **polar bonds** cancel out.

Common examples include HCl, $H_2O$ and $NH_3$ (Figure 3.8).

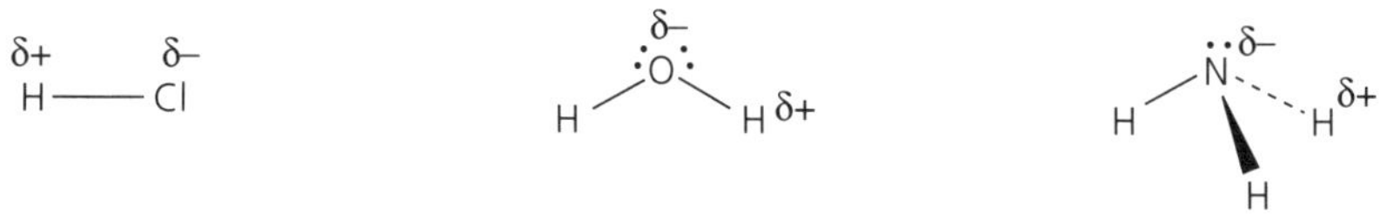


**Figure 3.8 Some polar molecules**

If a molecule is formed from two different elements the dipoles usually cancel if the molecule is trigonal planar, tetrahedral, trigonal bipyramidal or octahedral. Molecules with these shapes tend to be non-polar.

A **polar bond** is a covalent bond between two atoms with different electronegativities in which the bonded electron pair is drawn closer to the more electronegative atom.

A **polar molecule** is a molecule in which the electron density is not equally distributed resulting in areas of high electron density (δ−) and areas of low electron density (δ+)

## Intermolecular forces

REVISED

Ionic, covalent and metallic bonds are all strong bonds with bond enthalpies from 200–600 kJ mol$^{-1}$. There are three other types of bond that are much weaker, having enthalpies from 2–40 kJ mol$^{-1}$. These bonds are formed *between* molecules and are collectively known as **intermolecular** forces.

**Permanent dipole–dipole** interactions (van der Waals forces) are usually found between polar molecules such as HCl. Dipole–dipole interactions are weak intermolecular forces between the permanent dipoles of different molecules (Figure 3.9).

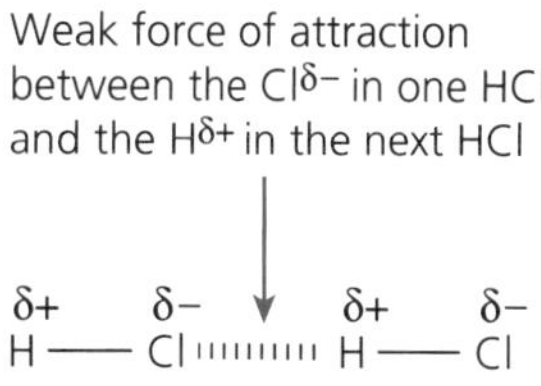


**Figure 3.9**

**Induced dipole–dipole interactions** (van der Waals forces or London dispersion forces) are the weakest of the forces and act between all molecules, polar or non-polar. They are caused by the movement of electrons. The strength of the induced dipole–dipole interactions depends on the number of electrons in the molecule. The more electrons present in an atom or molecule, the greater are the forces.

If you are asked to explain or define an induced dipole–dipole interaction (van der Waals force) there are three key features that you must include:

- the movement of electrons generates an instantaneous dipole
- this instantaneous dipole induces another dipole in neighbouring atoms or molecules
- the attraction between the temporary induced dipoles results in the dipole–dipole interaction

**Hydrogen bonds** (Figure 3.10) exist between molecules that contain hydrogen atoms bonded to nitrogen, oxygen or fluorine. They are comparatively strong dipole–dipole interactions. Hydrogen bonds exist, for example, between molecules in $NH_3$, $H_2O$ and HF. The lone pairs of electrons on the nitrogen, oxygen and fluorine play an essential role in the formation of hydrogen bonds. Hydrogen bonds are also found in alcohols.

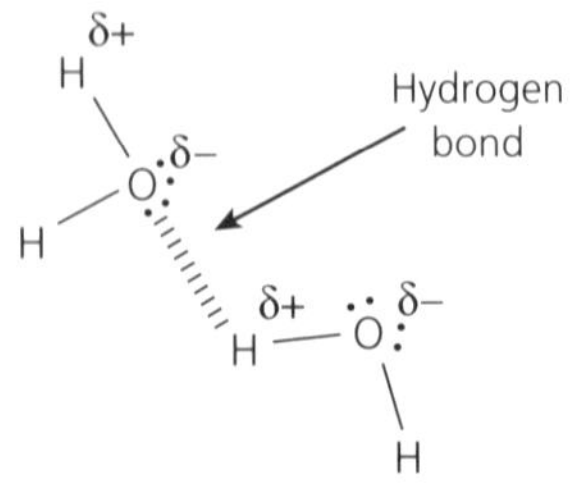


Figure 3.10

**Typical mistake**

Alcohols, such as methanol ($CH_3OH$), also form hydrogen bonds. If asked to draw two molecules of methanol and show how hydrogen bonds are formed, students often draw the hydrogen bond in the wrong position, as shown in Figure 3.12a. Figure 3.12b shows the correct response.

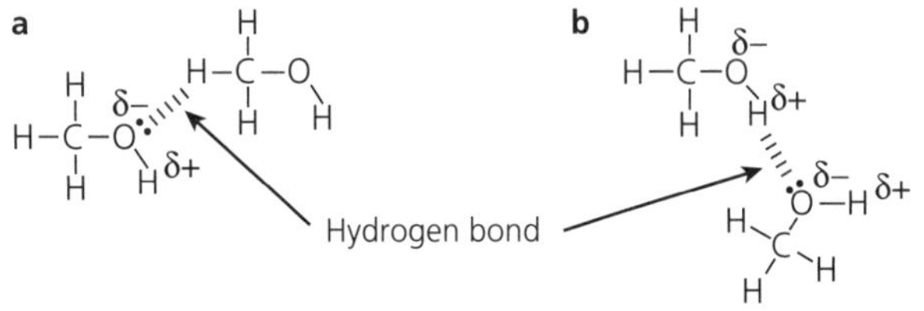


Figure 3.12

**Exam tip**

When asked to show how a hydrogen bond is formed between two water molecules, most students score the marks. However, when asked to show how a hydrogen bond is formed between two ammonia molecules, most students fail to score. You need to practise this. The correct diagram is shown in Figure 3.11.

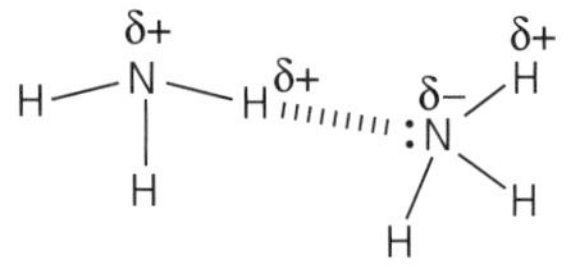

Figure 3.11

Special properties of water arising from hydrogen bonding are:

Solid (ice) is less dense than liquid (water) because the hydrogen bonds in ice hold the $H_2O$ molecules further apart, creating an open lattice structure.

The melting point and boiling point of water are higher than expected owing to the additional energy required to break the hydrogen bonds.

**Typical mistake**

When asked to explain the special properties of water many students state that water has a high melting point. We all know that water melts at 0°C — which is *not* very high. Water has a higher *than expected* melting point. The evidence for this is found by comparing the melting point of $H_2O$ with those of $H_2S$, $H_2Se$ and $H_2Te$, all of which are group 6 hydrides.

## Bonding and physical properties

REVISED

**Giant ionic structures** are held together by strong electrostatic attractions between the ions throughout the lattice. Properties include the following:

- They have high melting points and boiling points.
- They are good conductors when molten or aqueous because they only have mobile charged particles(ions) when molten or when dissolved in water.
- They are soluble in polar solvents such as water.

**Simple covalent structures** are molecular; the molecules are held together by weak intermolecular forces. However, some covalent molecules, such as water and iodine, also form **simple molecular lattices**. The molecules are held in position in the lattice by intermolecular forces that are comparatively easy to break. Properties include the following:

- They have lower melting points and boiling points.
- They are poor conductors because they do not have any mobile charged particles (electrons or ions).
- They are soluble in non-polar solvents such as water.

## Exam practice

1 (a) Explain what is meant by the term *electronegativity*. [2]
(b) Draw a diagram to show hydrogen bonding between two molecules of water. Your diagram must include the bond angle, the dipoles and relevant lone pairs of electrons. [4]
(c) State and explain two properties of ice that are a direct result of hydrogen bonding. [4]

2 The electron-pair repulsion theory can be used to predict the shape of covalent molecules. State what is meant by the term *electron pair repulsion theory* and use it to determine the shapes of four molecules of your choice. Choose molecules that illustrate four different shapes. State the bond angle in each shape. [11]

3 Magnesium oxide is a solid with melting point 2852°C; the melting point of sulfur dioxide is −73°C. Explain, in terms of structure and bonding, why there is such a large difference between the melting points of these two oxides. [6]

4 Chlorine reacts with sodium to form sodium chloride.
(a) Describe the bonding in $Cl_2$, Na and NaCl. [8]
(b) Relate the physical properties of $Cl_2$ and NaCl to their structure and bonding. [8]

### Answers and quick quiz 3 online

ONLINE

## Summary

You should now have an understanding of:

- ionisation energies
- electron configuration using $1s^22s^2$... notation
- ionic, covalent and metallic bonding
- shapes of covalent molecules and ions
- electronegativity and bond polarity
- intermolecular forces including hydrogen bonding and van der Waals forces

# 4 The periodic table

## Periodicity

### Structure of the periodic table

REVISED

The periodic table is the arrangement of elements by increasing atomic number. Elements with the same outer shell electron configuration are grouped together, so physical and chemical properties are repeated periodically.

The International Union of Pure and Applied Chemistry, IUPAC, now recommends that the groups in the periodic table should be numbered 1–18 (Figure 4.1).

- Groups 1 and 2 remain the same as before — classified as the s-block.
- The transition elements now become groups 3–12 — classified as the d-block.
- Groups 3–7 now become groups 13 to 17 and the noble gases become group 18 — classified as the p-block.

The repeating pattern across different periods is known as **periodicity**.

Key: Relative atomic mass / Atomic symbol / name / Atomic (proton) number

| Period \ Group | 1 | 2 | 3 | 4 | 5 | 6 | 7 | 8 | 9 | 10 | 11 | 12 | 13 | 14 | 15 | 16 | 17 | 18 |
|---|---|---|---|---|---|---|---|---|---|---|---|---|---|---|---|---|---|---|
| 1 | 1.0 H hydrogen 1 | | | | | | | | | | | | | | | | | 4.0 He helium 2 |
| 2 | 6.9 Li lithium 3 | 9.0 Be beryllium 4 | | | | | | | | | | | 10.8 B boron 5 | 12.0 C carbon 6 | 14.0 N nitrogen 7 | 16.0 O oxygen 8 | 19.0 F fluorine 9 | 20.2 Ne neon 10 |
| 3 | 23.0 Na sodium 11 | 24.3 Mg magnesium 12 | | | | | | | | | | | 27.0 Al aluminium 13 | 28.1 Si silicon 14 | 31.0 P phosphorus 15 | 32.1 S sulfur 16 | 35.5 Cl chlorine 17 | 39.9 Ar argon 18 |
| 4 | 39.1 K potassium 19 | 40.1 Ca calcium 20 | 45.0 Sc scandium 21 | 47.9 Ti titanium 22 | 50.9 V vanadium 23 | 52.0 Cr chromium 24 | 54.9 Mn manganese 25 | 55.8 Fe iron 26 | 58.9 Co cobalt 27 | 58.7 Ni nickel 28 | 63.5 Cu copper 29 | 65.4 Zn zinc 30 | 69.7 Ga gallium 31 | 72.6 Ge germanium 32 | 74.9 As arsenic 33 | 79.0 Se selenium 34 | 79.9 Br bromine 35 | 83.8 Kr krypton 36 |
| 5 | 85.5 Rb rubidium 37 | 87.6 Sr strontium 38 | 88.9 Y yttrium 39 | 91.2 Zr zirconium 40 | 92.9 Nb niobium 41 | 95.9 Mo molybdenum 42 | [98] Tc technetium 43 | 101.1 Ru ruthenium 44 | 102.9 Rh rhodium 45 | 106.4 Pd palladium 46 | 107.9 Ag silver 47 | 112.4 Cd cadmium 48 | 114.8 In indium 49 | 118.7 Sn tin 50 | 121.8 Sb antimony 51 | 127.6 Te tellurium 52 | 126.9 I iodine 53 | 131.3 Xe xenon 54 |
| 6 | 132.9 Cs caesium 55 | 137.3 Ba barium 56 | 138.9 La lanthanum 57 | 178.5 Hf hafnium 72 | 180.9 Ta tantalum 73 | 183.8 W tungsten 74 | 186.2 Re rhenium 75 | 190.2 Os osmium 76 | 192.2 Ir iridium 77 | 195.1 Pt platinum 78 | 197.0 Au gold 79 | 200.6 Hg mercury 80 | 204.4 Tl thallium 81 | 207.2 Pb lead 82 | 209.0 Bi bismuth 83 | [209] Po polonium 84 | [210] At astatine 85 | [222] Rn radon 86 |
| 7 | [223] Fr francium 87 | [226] Ra radium 88 | [227] Ac actinium 89 | [261] Rf rutherfordium 104 | [262] Db dubnium 105 | [266] Sg seaborgium 106 | [264] Bh bohrium 107 | [277] Hs hassium 108 | [268] Mt meitnerium 109 | [271] Ds darmstadtium 110 | [272] Rg roentgenium 111 | Elements with atomic numbers 112–116 have been reported but not fully authenticated | | | | | | |
| | | | | 140.1 Ce cerium 58 | 140.9 Pr praseodymium 59 | 144.2 Nd neodymium 60 | 144.9 Pm promethium 61 | 150.4 Sm samarium 62 | 152.0 Eu europium 63 | 157.2 Gd gadolinium 64 | 158.9 Tb terbium 65 | 162.5 Dy dysprosium 66 | 164.9 Ho holmium 67 | 167.3 Er erbium 68 | 168.9 Tm thulium 69 | 173.0 Yb ytterbium 70 | 175.0 Lu lutetium 71 | |
| | | | | 232 Th thorium 90 | [231] Pa protactinium 91 | 238.1 U uranium 92 | [237] Np neptunium 93 | [242] Pu plutonium 94 | [243] Am americium 95 | [247] Cm curium 96 | [245] Bk berkelium 97 | [251] Cf californium 98 | [254] Es einsteinium 99 | [253] Fm fermium 100 | [256] Md mendelevium 101 | [254] No nobelium 102 | [257] Lr lawrencium 103 | |

**Figure 4.1** The periodic table

## Trends in the periodic table

REVISED

**Atomic radius** *decreases* across a period because the attraction between the nucleus and outer electrons increases. This is because:

- the nuclear charge increases
- the outer electrons are being added to the same shell, so there is no extra shielding

**Atomic radius** *increases* down a group because the attraction between the nucleus and outer electrons decreases. This is because:

- extra shells are added, resulting in the outer shell being further from the nucleus
- there are more shells between the outer electrons and the nucleus, hence there is greater shielding

**Electrical conductivity**, **melting point** and **boiling points** can be related to structure and bonding, as shown in Figure 4.2.

| Giant structures | | | | Molecular structures | | |
|---|---|---|---|---|---|---|
| | | | | | | |
| Na | Mg | Al | Si | $P_4$ | $S_8$ | $Cl_2$ |
| Strong forces between atoms | | | | Weak forces between molecules | | |
| Metallic | | | Covalent | Dipole–dipole interactions (van der Waals) | | |
| High melting points | | | | Low melting points | | |
| | | | | | | |
| Good conductors | | | Poor conductors | | | |

Figure 4.2

**Electrical conductivity** is related to bonding. The elements of groups 1, 2 and 3 are metals. They are good conductors because they contain mobile, delocalised electrons. The outer shell electrons contribute to the mobile, delocalised electrons, which allow metals to conduct heat and electricity, even in the solid state.

The elements in the remaining groups across periods 2 and 3 are poor conductors because they do not have any mobile, free electrons. (Graphite and graphene are exceptions to this and are good conductors because they have mobile free electrons.)

Group 2 elements tend to be better conductors than group 1 because they have two outer shell electrons while group 1 elements only have one outer shell electron.

**Melting points** and **boiling points** (Figure 4.3) show a gradual increase from group 1 to group 14 followed by a sharp drop to groups 15, 16 and 17. This drop signifies the move from giant structures in groups 1, 2, 3 and 14 to simple molecular structures in groups 15 to 17.

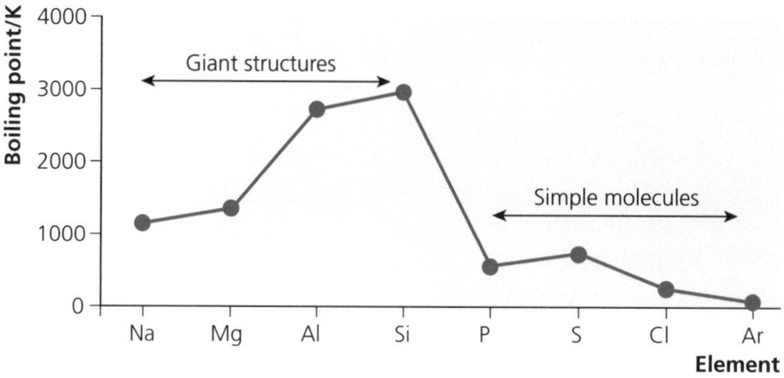


**Figure 4.3 Boiling points of the elements across period 3**

**Exam tip**

You may be asked to explain the difference between either the melting points or boiling points of two substances — for example, $SiO_2$ (melting point = 2200°C) and $SiCl_4$ (melting point = −70°C). This is straightforward. If a compound has a high melting point ($SiO_2$), it is usually because it exists as a giant lattice with strong bonds throughout. If a compound has a low melting point ($SiCl_4$), it is usually because it exists as simple molecules with weak intermolecular forces.

**Ionisation energy** *decreases* down a group because:

- Factor 1 — the outer electrons are further from the nucleus, therefore it is easier to remove an electron.
- Factor 2 — shielding increases because of additional inner shells, therefore it is easier to remove an electron.
- Factor 3 — there are more protons in the nucleus, making it harder to remove an electron.

This results in a decrease in the effective nuclear charge because factors 1 and 2 outweigh factor 3.

**Ionisation energy** *increases* across a period because:

- Factor 1 — the outer electrons are closer to the nucleus, therefore it is harder to remove an electron.
- Factor 2 — shielding is by the same number of inner shells, so it has no effect.
- Factor 3 — there are more protons in the nucleus, making it harder to remove an electron.

This results in an increase in the effective nuclear charge.

## Now test yourself

TESTED

1 For each of the following pairs of elements, state which element has the higher first ionisation energy and explain your answer.
 (a) Mg and Na
 (b) Mg and Ca
 (c) Ne and Na

2 The first seven successive ionisation energies of an element, M, are shown in Table 4.1.

Table 4.1

| | 1 | 2 | 3 | 4 | 5 | 6 | 7 |
|---|---|---|---|---|---|---|---|
| Successive IE/kJ mol$^{-1}$ | 790 | 1600 | 3200 | 4400 | 16 100 | 19 800 | 23 800 |

Suggest in which group of the periodic table you would expect to find element M. Explain your reasoning.

Answers on p. 212

# Group 2

## Redox reactions of group 2 metals

REVISED

### Electron configuration

Each group 2 element has two electrons in its outer shell and readily forms a 2+ ion that has the same electron configuration as a noble gas. It follows that group 2 elements are oxidised when they react. You should be able to use **oxidation number** to illustrate the redox reactions that occur when group 2 elements react with oxygen and with water. Redox is covered on pages 34–36.

### Physical properties

Group 2 elements are metals and are, therefore, good conductors. They have reasonably high melting and boiling points. They generally form ionic compounds that are good conductors when molten or aqueous, but poor conductors when solid.

## Reaction with $O_2$

Magnesium, calcium, strontium and barium all react with oxygen to produce an oxide. Reactivity increases down the group, which is because of the increasing ease in which the group 2 element forms the corresponding 2+ ion.

| | |
|---|---|
| $Mg(s) + \frac{1}{2}O_2(g) \rightarrow MgO(s)$ | Burns with a bright white light |
| $Ca(s) + \frac{1}{2}O_2(g) \rightarrow CaO(s)$ | Burns with a brick red colour |
| $Sr(s) + \frac{1}{2}O_2(g) \rightarrow SrO(s)$ | Burns with a crimson colour |
| $Ba(s) + \frac{1}{2}O_2(g) \rightarrow BaO(s)$ | Burns with a light green colour |

Each of the above reactions is a redox reaction in which the oxidation number of the group 2 element increases from 0 to +2 and the oxidation number of oxygen decreases from 0 to −2.

## Reaction with water

Group 2 elements also undergo redox reactions with water. The oxidation number of the group 2 element increases from 0 to +2 and the oxidation number of hydrogen decreases from +1 to 0:

| | | | | | | | |
|---|---|---|---|---|---|---|---|
| | $Mg(s)$ | + | $2H_2O(g)$ | $\rightarrow$ | $Mg(OH)_2(s)$ | + | $H_2(g)$ |
| Oxidation numbers | 0 | | +1 −2 | | +2 −2+1 | | 0 |

$Mg(s) + 2H_2O(l) \rightarrow Mg(OH)_2(s) + H_2(g)$

$Ca(s) + 2H_2O(l) \rightarrow Ca(OH)_2(aq) + H_2(g)$

$Sr(s) + 2H_2O(l) \rightarrow Sr(OH)_2(aq) + H_2(g)$

$Ba(s) + 2H_2O(l) \rightarrow Ba(OH)_2(aq) + H_2(g)$

The rate of reaction increases down the group, largely due to the ease of cation ($M^{2+}$ ion) formation.

The reaction between magnesium and water is slow. The resultant $Mg(OH)_2$ is barely soluble in water and forms a white suspension.

Magnesium reacts with steam to produce magnesium oxide and hydrogen:

$Mg(s) + H_2O(g) \rightarrow MgO(s) + H_2(g)$

## Reaction with dilute acids

Group 2 elements react readily with dilute acids to form a salt and hydrogen. The reactivity again increases down the group. The equation for the reaction varies depending on the acid:

$Mg(s) + 2HCl(aq) \rightarrow MgCl_2(aq) + H_2(g)$

$Mg(s) + H_2SO_4(aq) \rightarrow MgSO_4(aq) + H_2(g)$

But the ionic equation is the same irrespective of the acid:

$Mg(s) + 2H^+(aq) \rightarrow Mg^{2+}(aq) + H_2(g)$

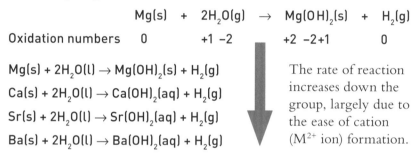

## Now test yourself

TESTED

3 With the aid of equations, identify two redox reactions of calcium. State what has been oxidised in each.

4 Group 2 metals react with aqueous acids to form a salt and hydrogen. Give the formula of the salt formed when:

(a) barium reacts with nitric acid

(b) strontium react with ethanoic acid

(c) calcium reacts with phosphoric acid, $H_3PO_4$

Answers on p. 212

# Reactions of group 2 compounds

REVISED

## Reaction of the oxides with water

All group 2 metal oxides react with water to form hydroxides:

| | |
|---|---|
| $MgO(s) + H_2O(l) \rightarrow Mg(OH)_2(s)$ | A suspension is formed |
| $CaO(s) + H_2O(l) \rightarrow Ca(OH)_2(aq)$ | $Ca(OH)_2(aq)$ is known as limewater |
| $SrO(s) + H_2O(l) \rightarrow Sr(OH)_2(aq)$ | |
| $BaO(s) + H_2O(l) \rightarrow Ba(OH)_2(aq)$ | |

These are *not* redox reactions. The oxidation numbers of all the elements are unaltered, for example:

| | | | | | |
|---|---|---|---|---|---|
| | $MgO(s)$ | + | $2H_2O(g)$ | $\rightarrow$ | $Mg(OH)_2(s)$ |
| Oxidation numbers | +2 −2 | | +1 −2 | | +2 −2+1 |

The resulting hydroxide solutions are alkaline and have pH values in the region 8–12. The pH varies depending on the concentration of the solution. Calcium hydroxide is used in agriculture to neutralise acidic soils; magnesium hydroxide is used in some indigestion tablets as an antacid.

**Exam tip**

A question may ask what you would observe when a certain reaction occurs. Use the state symbols as a guide and remember that you will only see effervescence (bubbles) if a gas is produced.

## Thermal decomposition of group 2 carbonates

The carbonates are all decomposed to form oxides and carbon dioxide:

| | |
|---|---|
| $MgCO_3 \rightarrow MgO + CO_2$ | Easy to decompose |
| $CaCO_3 \rightarrow CaO + CO_2$ | |
| $SrCO_3 \rightarrow SrO + CO_2$ | |
| $BaCO_3 \rightarrow BaO + CO_2$ | Hard to decompose |

These are *not* redox reactions. The oxidation numbers of all the elements are unaltered, for example:

| | | | | |
|---|---|---|---|---|
| | $MgCO_3(s)$ | $\rightarrow$ | $MgO(s)$ + | $CO_2(g)$ |
| Oxidation numbers | +2 +4−2 | | +2 −2 | +4−2 |

**Exam tip**

The easiest way to ensure that decomposition is complete is to heat to constant mass.

**Revision activity**

On a postcard write a summary of the reactions of group 2 metals and their compounds.

## Now test yourself

TESTED

5 Write an equation, including state symbols, for the reaction between strontium carbonate and nitric acid.

Answer on p. 212

# The halogens (group 17)

The halogens are elements that have seven electrons in their outer shells and are in group 17 (formerly group 7) of the periodic table. The halogens exist as simple diatomic molecules.

## Electron configuration

REVISED

Each group 17 element has seven electrons in its outer shell and readily forms a 1– ion (an anion) that has the same electron configuration as a noble gas.

$_{9}F$ $1s^2 2s^2 2p^5$

$_{17}Cl$ $1s^2 2s^2 2p^6 3s^2 3p^5$

$_{35}Br$ $1s^2 2s^2 2p^6 3s^2 3p^6 3d^{10} 4s^2 4p^5$

$_{53}I$ $1s^2 2s^2 2p^6 3s^2 3p^6 3d^{10} 4s^2 4p^6 4d^{10} 5s^2 5p^5$

## Physical properties

REVISED

**Table 4.2 Physical properties of the group 17 elements**

| Element | State at room temperature | Colour | Volatility |
|---|---|---|---|
| Fluorine, $F_2$ | Gas | Yellow | Down the group there is an increase in induced dipole–dipole interactions, which corresponds to the increased number of electrons in the halogen molecules. This increase reduces the volatility and, therefore, increases the melting and boiling point |
| Chlorine, $Cl_2$ | Gas | Green | |
| Bromine, $Br_2$ | Liquid | Orange/ brown | |
| Iodine, $I_2$ | Solid | Grey/ black | |
| All are non-metallic, so are poor conductors | | | |

## Redox reactions and trends in reactivity

REVISED

The reactivity of the halogens decreases down the group. This is opposite to the reactivity of the group 2 elements. Group 2 metals react by losing electrons and on descending the group it becomes easier to lose electrons. Halogens react by gaining electrons to form halide anions. The ease of gaining the electron decreases down group 17. This is because atomic radius and shielding increase down the group, and this reduces the effective nuclear attraction for electrons.

Fluorine is a powerful oxidising agent and readily gains electrons. →

$F_2 + 2e^- \rightarrow 2F^-$ **Most reactive**

$Cl_2 + 2e^- \rightarrow 2Cl^-$

$Br_2 + 2e^- \rightarrow 2Br^-$

$I_2 + 2e^- \rightarrow 2I^-$ **Least reactive**

**Exam tip**

It is important to make sure that you know the difference between a halogen and a halide. In exams, many students confuse chloride with chlorine.

## Displacement reactions

REVISED

A halogen ($F_2$, $Cl_2$ and $Br_2$) can displace a halide ion ($Cl^-$, $Br^-$ and $I^-$) from one of its salts, as shown in Table 4.3.

**Table 4.3 Displacement reactions**

| | Fluoride, $F^-$ | Chloride, $Cl^-$ | Bromide, $Br^-$ | Iodide, $I^-$ |
|---|---|---|---|---|
| **Fluorine, $F_2$** | | Yes | Yes | Yes |
| **Chlorine, $Cl_2$** | No | | Yes | Yes |
| **Bromine, $Br_2$** | No | No | | Yes |
| **Iodine, $I_2$** | No | No | No | |

Displacement reactions illustrate the decrease in oxidising power down group 7.

Chlorine oxidises both bromide and iodide ions. The ionic equation for the oxidation of bromide is:

$$Cl_2(aq) + 2Br^-(aq) \rightarrow 2Cl^-(aq) + Br_2(aq)$$

During the reaction, the orange-brown colour of bromine appears.

The ionic equation for the oxidation of iodide is:

$$Cl_2(aq) + 2I^-(aq) \rightarrow 2Cl^-(aq) + I_2(aq)$$

During the reaction, the brown-black colour of iodine appears. On adding an organic solvent, the solution turns a distinctive violet-purple colour.

Bromine oxidises $I^-$ only:

$$Br_2(aq) + 2I^-(aq) \rightarrow 2Br^-(aq) + I_2(aq)$$

Iodine does *not* oxidise either chloride or bromide.

Each of the displacement reactions is a redox reaction. In each case, the halogen higher in the group gains electrons (is reduced) to form the corresponding halide ion (Figure 4.4).

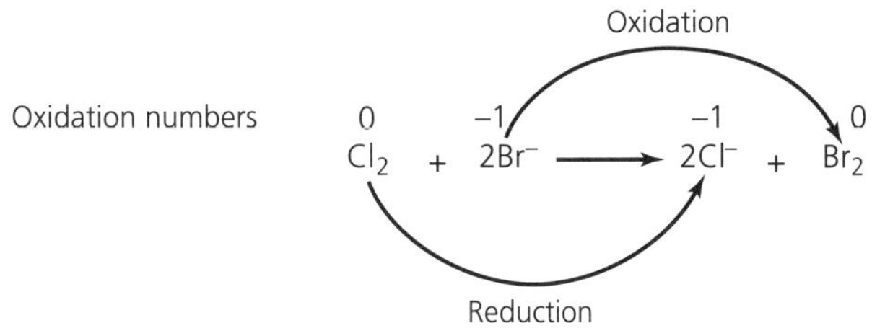


**Figure 4.4**

## Uses of chlorine

Chlorine is used in the treatment of water. Chlorine reacts with water in a reversible reaction and the resultant mixture kills bacteria:

$$Cl_2(aq) + H_2O(l) \rightleftharpoons HCl(aq) + HClO(aq)$$

The reaction is a redox reaction, but it is unusual in that chlorine undergoes both **oxidation** and **reduction** (Figure 4.5).

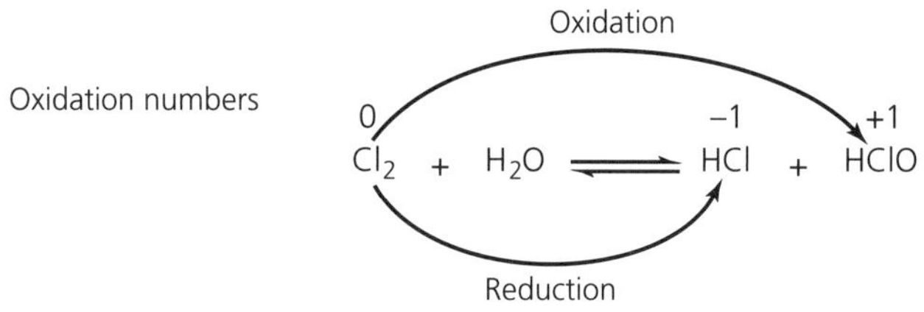


**Figure 4.5**

One chlorine atom in the $Cl_2$ molecule is oxidised. Its oxidation number changes from 0 to +1. The other chlorine atom is reduced. Its oxidation number changes from 0 to −1. This type of reaction is called **disproportionation**.

**Disproportionation** is the simultaneous oxidation and reduction of an element such that during a reaction its oxidation number both increases and decreases.

Chlorine is used in water treatment to kill bacteria and make the water safe to drink. This has to be weighed against the possible risks because chlorine is toxic and reacts with substances such as hydrocarbons to form chlorinated hydrocarbons. If drinking water contained hydrocarbons this could present a risk to health.

Chlorine also reacts with sodium hydroxide to form bleach, which is a mixture of sodium chloride and sodium chlorate(I). This is also a disproportionation reaction of chlorine (Figure 4.6):

$$Cl_2(g) + NaOH(aq) \rightarrow NaCl(aq) + NaClO(aq)$$

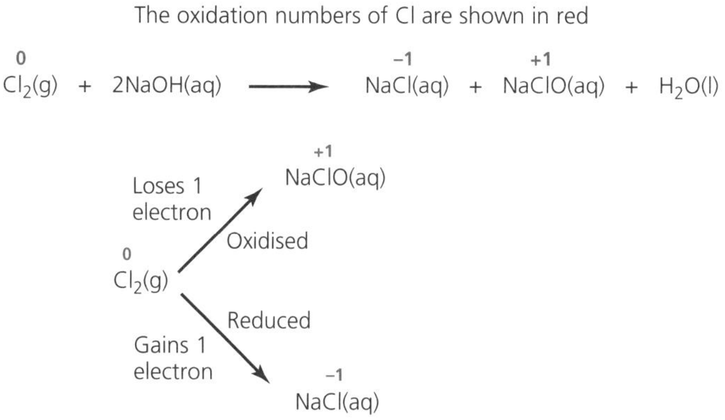


**Figure 4.6**

Chlorine reacts with NaOH(aq) to form a number of different chlorates, including sodium chlorate(I), NaClO; sodium chlorate(III), $NaClO_2$; and sodium chlorate(V), $NaClO_3$. In each of these reactions NaCl and water are also formed. Each reaction is a disproportionation reaction.

**Example**

When chlorine reacts with a hot concentrated solution of NaOH(aq), sodium chlorate(V), $NaClO_3$(aq), is formed. Construct an equation for this reaction.

**Answer**

We know that NaCl(aq) will be formed along with $NaClO_3$(aq). The oxidation changes in Cl are −1 in NaCl and +5 in $NaClO_3$ (Figure 4.7).

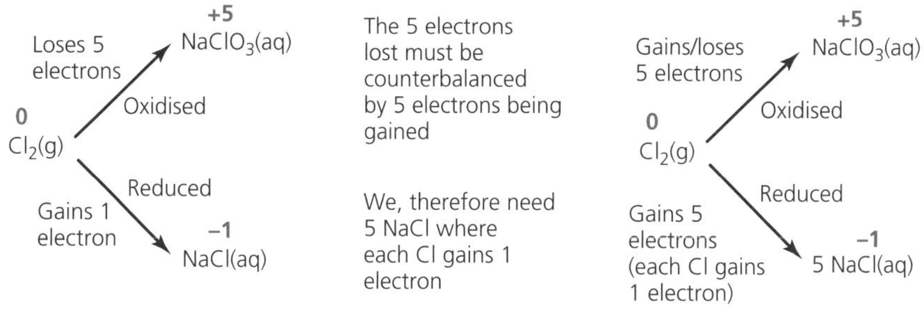


Figure 4.7

We now know that the products will contain $1NaClO_3$(aq), 5NaCl(aq) and $H_2O$(l). So that the balanced equation can be constructed to give:

$$3Cl_2(g) + 6NaOH(aq) \rightarrow NaClO(aq) + 5NaCl(aq) + 3H_2O(l)$$

It is important to remember that oxidation number changes have to be balanced as well as balancing symbols.

## Now test yourself

TESTED

6 Write an equation for the reaction between chlorine and NaOH to produce $NaClO_2$, NaCl and $H_2O$.

Answer on p. 212

## Reactions of halide ions

REVISED

Silver chloride, silver bromide and silver iodide are insoluble in water. Therefore, the presence of chloride, bromide or iodide ions in a solution can be detected by the addition of a solution of silver nitrate ($AgNO_3$(aq)). Each of the silver halides forms a different coloured precipitate. Each of the precipitates can be distinguished by their solubility in ammonia.

$$Ag^+(aq) + Cl^-(aq) \rightarrow AgCl(s)$$

AgCl is a white precipitate, which is soluble in dilute $NH_3$.

$$Ag^+(aq) + Br^-(aq) \rightarrow AgBr(s)$$

AgBr is a cream precipitate, which is soluble in concentrated $NH_3$.

$$Ag^+(aq) + I^-(aq) \rightarrow AgI(s)$$

AgI is a yellow precipitate, which is insoluble in concentrated $NH_3$.

**Revision activity**

On a postcard write a summary of the reactions of group 17 the halogens and their compounds.

## Now test yourself

TESTED

7 Chlorine reacts explosively with ethyne, $C_2H_2$, to form carbon and hydrogen chloride.
(a) Construct an equation, including state symbols, for this reaction.
(b) Using oxidation numbers, explain the role of chlorine.
(c) If chlorine is replaced by fluorine, would the reaction be more or less explosive? Explain your answer.

Answer on p. 212

# Qualitative analysis

You will be expected to analyse and detect a range of ions by a series of test tube reactions. Table 4.4 details qualitative tests for a range of ions.

**Table 4.4**

| Ion | Test | Equation | Observation |
|---|---|---|---|
| $CO_3^{2-}$ | Add an acid, $H^+$(aq) | $CO_3^{2-}(aq) + 2H^+(aq) \rightarrow CO_2(g) + H_2O(l)$ | Effervescence, bubbles |
| $SO_4^{2-}$ | Add aqueous $BaCl_2$(aq) | $SO_4^{2-}(aq) + Ba^{2+}(aq) \rightarrow BaSO_4(s)$ | White precipitate |
| $Cl^-$ | Add $AgNO_3$(aq) | $Cl^-(aq) + Ag^+(aq) \rightarrow AgCl(s)$ | White precipitate* |
| $Br^-$ | | $Br^-(aq) + Ag^+(aq) \rightarrow AgBr(s)$ | Cream precipitate* |
| $I^-$ | | $I^-(aq) + Ag^+(aq) \rightarrow AgI(s)$ | Yellow precipitate* |
| $NH_4^+$ | Warm with NaOH(aq) | $NH_4^+ + OH^-(aq) \rightarrow NH_3(g) + H_2O(l)$ | $NH_3$(g) is evolved which turns moist red litmus blue |

*The silver halide precipitates can be further distinguished by adding ammonia to the precipitates. See above.

## Now test yourself

TESTED

8 Barium carbonate, barium chloride and barium sulfate are all white solids. Suggest a series of reactions that could be used to distinguish which is which. Write ionic equations for each reaction.

Answer on p. 212

**Revision activity**

On a postcard write a summary of the observations that you would see when testing for anions and cations.

## Exam practice

1 (a) Chlorine bleach is made by the reaction of chlorine with aqueous sodium hydroxide. In this reaction the oxidation number of $Cl_2$ changes and $Cl_2$ is said to undergo disproportionation.

$$Cl_2(g) + 2NaOH(aq) \rightarrow NaClO(aq) + NaCl(aq) + H_2O(l)$$

(i) Determine the oxidation number of chlorine in $Cl_2$, NaClO and NaCl. [1]

(ii) State what is meant by the term *disproportionation*. [1]

(iii) The bleaching agent is the $ClO^-$ ion. In the presence of sunlight, this ion decomposes to release oxygen gas. Construct an equation for this reaction. [2]

(b) The sea contains a low concentration of bromide ions. Bromine can be extracted from seawater by first concentrating the seawater and then bubbling chlorine through this solution.

(i) Suggest how the seawater could be concentrated [1]

(ii) The chlorine oxidises bromide ions to bromine. Construct a balanced ionic equation for this reaction. [1]

(c) Vinyl chloride is a compound of chlorine, carbon and hydrogen. It is used to make polyvinylchloride (PVC). Vinyl chloride has the percentage composition by mass: chlorine, 56.8%; carbon, 38.4 %; hydrogen, 4.8%.

(i) Show that the empirical formula of vinyl chloride is $ClC_2H_3$. Show your working. [2]

(ii) The molecular formula of vinyl chloride is the same as its empirical formula. Draw a possible structure, including bond angles, for a molecule of vinyl chloride. [2]

2 (a) Barium is a group 2 element. It reacts with oxygen to form compound **A** and with water to form compound **B** and gas **C**. With the aid of suitable equations, identify, **A**, **B** and **C**. [3]

(b) (i) Write an equation, including state symbols, for the thermal decomposition of barium carbonate. [2]

(ii) Calculate the minimum volume of 0.05 mol $dm^{-3}$ HCl(aq) that is needed to react with 1.00 g of barium carbonate. Show all your working. [4]

(iii) Explain why *more* 0.05 mol $dm^{-3}$ HCl(aq) would be needed to react with 1.00 g of magnesium carbonate than with 1.00 g of barium carbonate. Show all your working. [2]

### Answers and quick quiz 4 online

ONLINE

## Summary

You should now have an understanding of:

- trends in atomic radii
- trends in melting points and boiling points
- trends in ionisation energies
- reactions of group 2 elements with oxygen and with water
- reactions of group 2 oxides with water
- decomposition of group 2 carbonates
- physical properties of group 17 elements
- displacement reactions of the halogens and the halides
- reactions of halides with $Ag^+$ and $NH_3$
- disproportionation reactions of chlorine
- qualitative analysis for carbonate, sulfate, halides and ammonium ions

# 5 Physical chemistry

## Enthalpy changes

### $\Delta H$ of reaction, formation, combustion and neutralisation

REVISED

Enthalpy change, $\Delta H$, is the exchange of energy between a reaction mixture and its surroundings. It is measured at constant temperature and constant pressure. The units are $kJ\,mol^{-1}$.

$\Delta H$ can be calculated using the equation:

**$\Delta H$ = enthalpy of products – enthalpy of reactants**

Enthalpy changes can be represented by simple enthalpy profile diagrams.

For an exothermic reaction, the enthalpy profile diagram shows the products at a lower energy than the reactants. For an endothermic reaction the enthalpy profile diagram shows the products at a higher energy than the reactants. The difference in the enthalpy is $\Delta H$. $E_a$ is the **activation energy** (Figure 5.1).

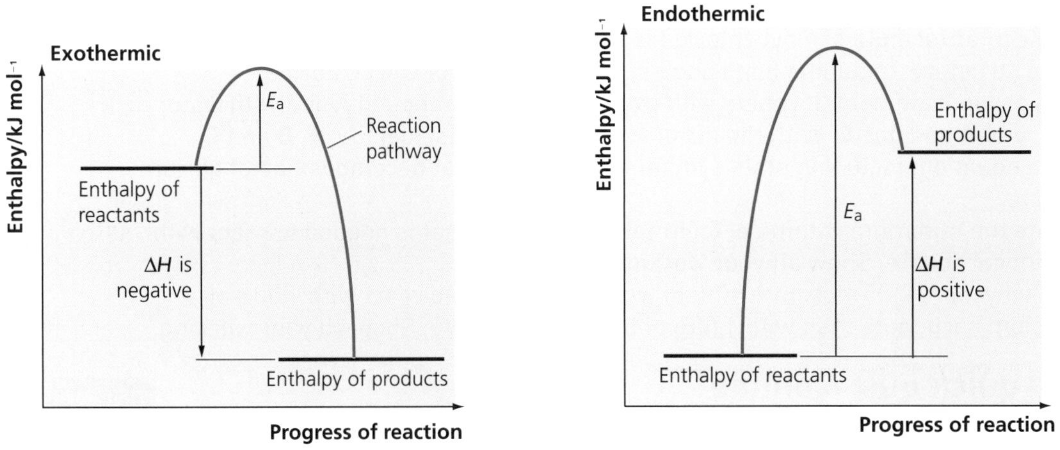


**Figure 5.1 Enthalpy profiles for an exothermic and an endothermic reaction**

Oxidation reactions such as the combustion of fuels are exothermic and release energy to the surroundings. This results in an increase in temperature of the surroundings. The enthalpy profile in Figure 5.2 illustrates the combustion of methane.

**Activation energy** is the *minimum* amount of energy required to start the reaction.

**Standard state** is the physical state of a substance at 298 K and 101 kPa.

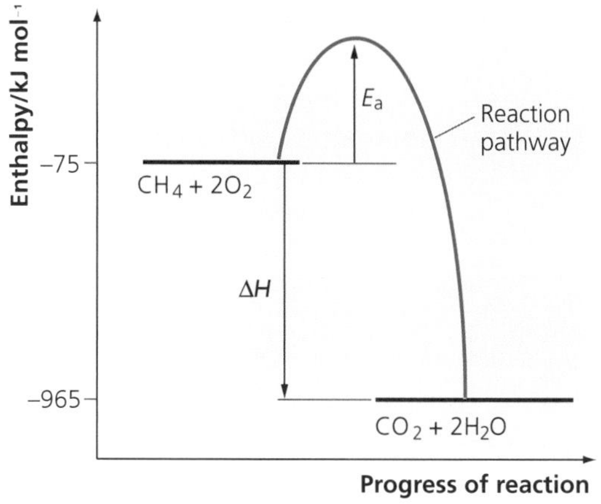


**Figure 5.2 Enthalpy profile for the combustion of methane**

The activation energy is the minimum energy needed for colliding particles to react. In any chemical reaction bonds are broken and new bonds are formed. Breaking bonds is an endothermic process that requires energy. This energy requirement contributes to the activation energy of a reaction.

## Standard enthalpy changes

REVISED

All **standard enthalpy changes** relate to substances in their **standard states** and are, therefore, measured under standard conditions. The standard temperature is 298 K (25°C) and the standard pressure is 101 kPa (for exam purposes 100 kPa is acceptable). Standard temperature and pressure are abbreviated to s.t.p.

Examinations often ask for a definition of an enthalpy change. It is advisable to learn the definitions on this page.

You may also have to show your understanding by writing equations that illustrate the standard enthalpy changes of reaction, formation and combustion.

Rules for writing equations to illustrate standard enthalpies of formation and combustion are shown in Table 5.1.

**Table 5.1**

| Standard enthalpy of formation | Standard enthalpy of combustion |
|---|---|
| Show the elements as the reactants<br>Produce **1** mol of the substance, even if this means having fractions in the equation<br>Show the state symbols | React **1** mol of the substance with excess oxygen, even if this means having fractions in the equation<br>Show the state symbols |
| Example:<br>$2C(s) + 3H_2(g) + ½O_2(g) \rightarrow CH_3CH_2OH(l)$ | Example:<br>$C_2H_6(g) + 3½O_2 \rightarrow 2CO_2(g) + 3H_2O(l)$ |

The **standard enthalpy of neutralisation** is the enthalpy change when 1 mol of water is formed from the reaction of an acid and base under standard conditions of 298 K and 101 kPa. The equation for the standard enthalpy of neutralisation of dilute hydrochloric acid by sodium hydroxide solution is:

$$HCl(aq) + NaOH(aq) \rightarrow NaCl(aq) + H_2O(l)$$

**Standard enthalpy change of reaction, $\Delta_rH^\ominus$**, is the enthalpy change when the number of moles of the substances in the balanced equation react under standard conditions of 298 K and 101 kPa.

**Standard enthalpy change of formation $\Delta_fH^\ominus$**, is the enthalpy change when 1 mol of a substance is formed from its elements, in their natural state, under standard conditions of 298 K and 101 kPa.

**Standard enthalpy change of combustion, $\Delta_cH^\ominus$**, is the enthalpy change when 1 mol of a substance is burnt completely, in an excess of oxygen, under standard conditions of 298 K and 101 kPa.

**Standard enthalpy change of neutralisation, $\Delta_{neut}H^\ominus$**, is the enthalpy change when 1 mol of water is formed in a neutralisation reaction (a reaction between an acid and a base) under standard conditions of 298 K and 101 kPa.

**Standard state** is the physical state of a substance at 298 K and 101 kPa.

An ionic equation can also be used to show the standard enthalpy of neutralisation:

$$H^+(aq) + OH^-(aq) \rightarrow H_2O(l)$$

**Revision activity**

On a postcard write definitions for the enthalpies of: reaction, formation, combustion and neutralisation. Illustrate each with a suitable equation.

### Typical mistake

If you are asked to write an equation to illustrate the enthalpy of neutralisation using sulfuric acid and sodium hydroxide, do *not* write: $H_2SO_4(aq) + 2NaOH(aq) \rightarrow Na_2SO_4(aq) + 2H_2O(l)$, because this equation shows the formation of two moles of water and by definition the enthalpy of neutralisation forms one mole of water. The correct equation is:

$$\tfrac{1}{2}H_2SO_4(aq) + NaOH(aq) \rightarrow \tfrac{1}{2}Na_2SO_4(aq) + H_2O(l)$$

## Now test yourself

TESTED ☐

1 Define *standard enthalpy change of formation*. Write an equation to illustrate the standard enthalpy change of formation of propanal, $CH_3CH_2CHO(l)$.
2 Define *standard enthalpy change of combustion*. Write an equation to illustrate the standard enthalpy change of combustion of propanone, $CH_3COCH_3(l)$.

Answer on p. 213

## Enthalpy changes using experimental data

REVISED ☐

The standard enthalpy change, $\Delta_r H^\ominus$, for reactions that take place in solution can usually be measured directly using the simple apparatus shown in Figure 5.3. The result obtained is only approximate because there will be heat losses to the surroundings.

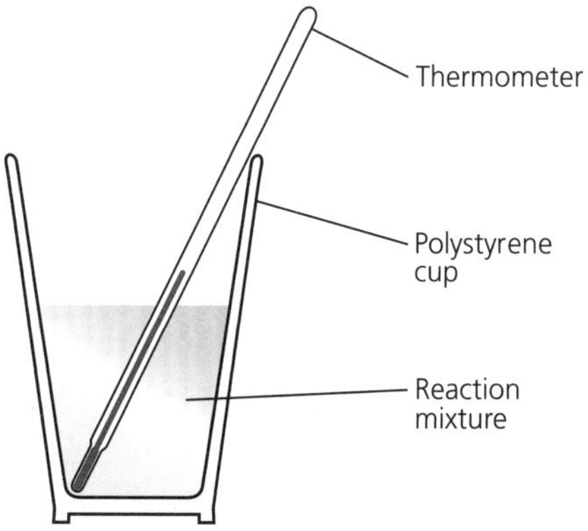

The energy transfer for the reaction mixture is given the symbol $q$ and can be calculated using the equation:

$$q = mc\Delta T$$

where $m$ is the mass of the reaction mixture, $c$ is the specific heat capacity of the reaction mixture and $\Delta T$ is the change in temperature.

The enthalpy change for the reaction mixture, $q$, has a value in either J (joules) or kJ (kilojoules) depending on the units of specific heat capacity. It is usual to adjust this value so that $\Delta H$ can be quoted for 1 mol of reactant with the units of $kJ\,mol^{-1}$. The standard enthalpy change, $\Delta H_r$, for the reaction is calculated by dividing the energy transferred by the number of moles, $n$, of reactant used:

$$\Delta_r H^\ominus = \frac{q}{n} = \frac{mc\Delta T}{n}$$

Thermometer

Polystyrene cup

Reaction mixture

**Figure 5.3**

### Example

When 50.0 cm³ of 2.00 mol dm⁻³ hydrochloric acid is mixed with 50.0 cm³ of 2.00 mol dm⁻³ sodium hydroxide solution, the temperature increased by 13.7°C.

Calculate the standard enthalpy change of neutralisation of hydrochloric acid. Assume that the specific heat capacity, $c$, = 4.20 J g⁻¹ K⁻¹ and that the density of both the hydrochloric acid and sodium hydroxide solution is both 1.00 g cm⁻³.

Answer

Step 1: calculate the energy transferred in the reaction by using:

$q = mc\Delta T$

$m$ = mass of the two solutions = 50.0 + 50.0 = 100.0 g

$q = mc\Delta T = 100.0 \times 4.20 \times 13.7 = 5754\,J = 5.754\,kJ$

Step 2: convert the answer to $kJ\,mol^{-1}$ by dividing by the number of moles used:

amount, $n$, in moles of HCl $= cV = 2.00 \times \frac{50}{1000} = 0.1\,mol$

$\Delta_{neut}H = \frac{q}{n} = \frac{5.754}{0.1} = 57.54 = = 57.5\,kJ\,mol^{-1}$

Remember that because the temperature went up it is an exothermic reaction. Therefore:

$\Delta_{neut}H = -57.5\,kJ\,mol^{-1}$

**Typical mistake**

In a question such as '2.30 g ethanol was burnt and raised the temperature of 300 $cm^3$ of water by 12.5°C. Calculate $\Delta_cH^\ominus$ for ethanol', the density of water and the specific heat capacity, $c$, of the apparatus would be given. In the first step, when using $q = mc\Delta T$, many students make the mistake of using 2.30 g as the mass. The mass used should be the mass of water.

## Now test yourself

TESTED

3 When 25.0 $cm^3$ of 1.00 $mol\,dm^{-3}$ nitric acid was mixed with 50.0 $cm^3$ of 0.50 $mol\,dm^{-3}$ sodium hydroxide solution the temperature increased by 4.6°C. Calculate the enthalpy change of neutralisation of nitric acid. Assume that the specific heat capacity, $c = 4.20\,J\,g^{-1}\,K^{-1}$ and that the density of both nitric acid and sodium hydroxide solution is 1.00 $g\,cm^{-3}$.

Answer on p. 213

## Enthalpy changes using average bond enthalpy data

REVISED

Breaking a bond requires energy; forming a bond releases energy. The energy required to break a bond has the same numerical value as the energy released when the bond is formed.

**Bond enthalpies** are the *average* (mean) values and do *not* take into account the specific chemical environment. Some average bond enthalpies are shown in Table 5.2.

**Bond enthalpy** is the enthalpy change required to break the same bond in all the molecules in 1 mol of a gas and to separate the resulting gaseous (neutral) particles/atoms/radicals so they exert no forces on each other. It is best reinforced by a simple equation such as:

$Cl{-}Cl(g) \rightarrow Cl\bullet(g) + Cl\bullet(g)$

**Table 5.2 Some average bond enthalpies**

| **Bond** | C–H | C=O | O=O | O–H | C–N | C=C | C–C | H–H |
|---|---|---|---|---|---|---|---|---|
| **$\Delta H$/kJ $mol^{-1}$** | +413 | +805 | +498 | +464 | +286 | +612 | +347 | +436 |

## Calculations involving average bond enthalpy

REVISED

Calculations are straightforward. In order for a reaction to take place existing bonds have first to be broken (energy is required, so endothermic) and then new bonds have to be formed (energy is given out, so exothermic).

The enthalpy of combustion of methane can be calculated using average bond enthalpies. The equation is:

$CH_4 + 2O_2 \rightarrow CO_2 + 2H_2O$

It is useful to draw out the reaction using displayed formulae so that all the bonds broken and formed can be seen clearly (Figure 5.4).

**Figure 5.4**

Bonds broken:

$4 \times (C{-}H) = 4 \times +413 = +1652\,kJ\,mol^{-1}$

$2 \times (O{=}O) = 2 \times +498 = +996\,kJ\,mol^{-1}$

**total energy needed to *break* all bonds = +2648 kJ mol$^{-1}$**

Bonds formed:

$2 \times (C{=}O) = 2 \times -805 = -1610\,kJ\,mol^{-1}$

$4 \times (O{-}H) = 4 \times -464 = -1856\,kJ\,mol^{-1}$

**total energy released to *form* all bonds = −3466 kJ mol$^{-1}$**

Enthalpy change for the reaction:

$\Delta H = +2648 - 3466 = -818\,kJ\,mol^{-1}$

The accepted value for this reaction is −890 kJ mol$^{-1}$, which differs substantially from −818 kJ mol$^{-1}$. This is largely explained by using average bond enthalpies for the C–H, C=O and O–H bonds in the calculation and not specific bond enthalpies.

## Enthalpy changes using Hess's law

REVISED

For energetic (the activation energy is very high) or kinetic (the reaction rate is very slow) reasons, the enthalpy changes for many chemical reactions cannot be measured directly by experiment, but they can be calculated using **Hess's law**.

**Hess's law** states that if a reaction can take place by more than one route, the overall enthalpy change for the reaction is the same irrespective of the route taken, provided that the initial and final conditions are the same.

The enthalpy of formation of CO(g) cannot be measured directly but it can be calculated using Hess's law.

The enthalpy change for the following reactions can be measured experimentally:

$C(s) + O_2(g) \rightarrow CO_2(g) \qquad \Delta H = -394\,kJ\,mol^{-1}$

$CO(g) + \frac{1}{2}O_2(g) \rightarrow CO_2(g) \qquad \Delta H = -284\,kJ\,mol^{-1}$

When applying Hess's law it is helpful to construct an enthalpy triangle.

Step 1: start with the enthalpy change that has to be calculated. Call it $\Delta H_1$. Write an equation for the reaction. This is the top line of the triangle.

$C(s) + \frac{1}{2}O_2(g) \xrightarrow{\Delta H_1} CO(g)$

Step 2: construct a cycle with two alternative routes:

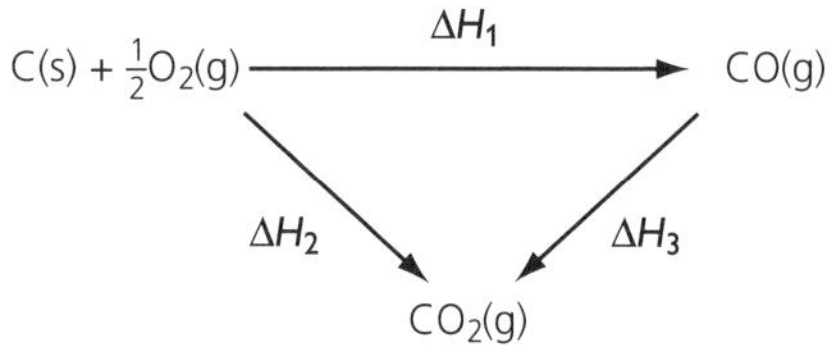

Step 3: apply Hess's law to the triangle:

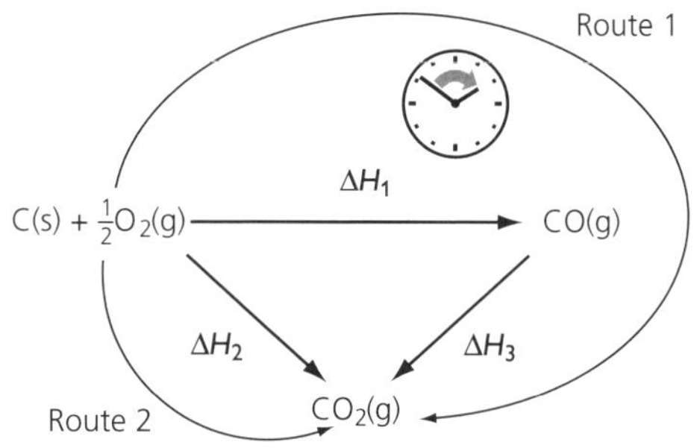


Look at the direction of the arrows. Route 1 has arrows that point in the clockwise direction; route 2 has arrows that point in the anti-clockwise direction.

**route 1 = route 2**

$\Delta H_1 + \Delta H_3 = \Delta H_2$

$\Delta H_1 = \Delta H_2 - \Delta H_3$

$= -394 - (-284) = -394 + 284 = -110\,\text{kJ mol}^{-1}$

**So, for** $C(s) + \frac{1}{2}O_2(g) \rightarrow CO(g)$, $\Delta H = -110\,\text{kJ mol}^{-1}$

The enthalpy of formation of carbon monoxide is $-110\,\text{kJ mol}^{-1}$.

## Enthalpy of formation from enthalpies of combustion

If you are asked to calculate the enthalpy change of formation using enthalpies of combustion, it is best to construct a cycle with the combustion products at the bottom. The arrows always point downwards to the combustion products (Figure 5.5).

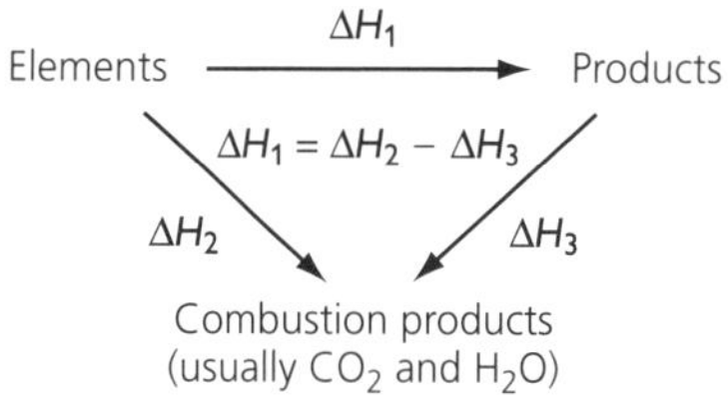


**Figure 5.5**

If Hess's law is applied to the cycle:

$\Delta H_1 + \Delta H_3 = \Delta H_2$ hence $\Delta H_1 = \Delta H_2 - \Delta H_3$

## Enthalpy of combustion from enthalpies of formation

If you are asked to calculate the enthalpy change of combustion from enthalpy of formation data, it is best to construct a cycle with the elements at the bottom. The arrows always point upwards (Figure 5.6).

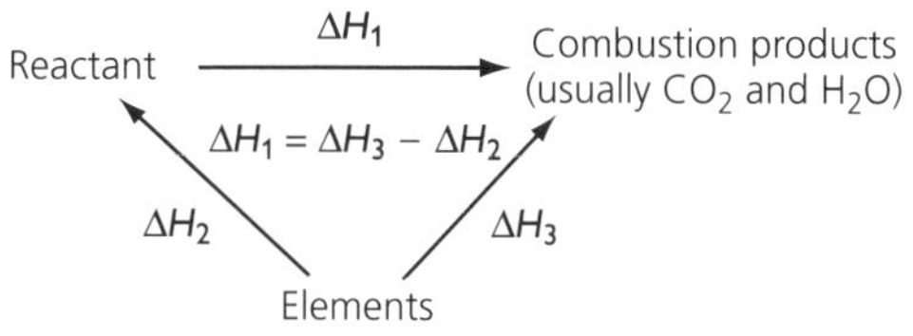


**Figure 5.6**

If Hess's law is applied to the cycle:

$\Delta H_1 + \Delta H_2 = \Delta H_3$ hence $\Delta H_1 = \Delta H_3 - \Delta H_2$

## Enthalpy of reaction from enthalpies of formation

If you are asked to calculate the enthalpy change of reaction from enthalpy of formation data, it is best to construct a cycle with the elements at the bottom. The arrows always point upwards.

**Example**

Use the enthalpy of formation data to calculate the enthalpy of reaction for:

$CH_3COCl(l) + C_2H_5OH(l) \rightarrow CH_3COOC_2H_5(l) + HCl(g)$

| | $CH_3COCl(l)$ | $C_2H_5OH(l)$ | $CH_3COOC_2H_5(l)$ | $HCl(g)$ |
|---|---|---|---|---|
| $\Delta H_f$/kJ mol$^{-1}$ | –272.9 | –277.1 | –479.3 | –92.3 |

**Answer**

Construct a simple triangle with the 'elements' at the bottom (Figure 5.7).

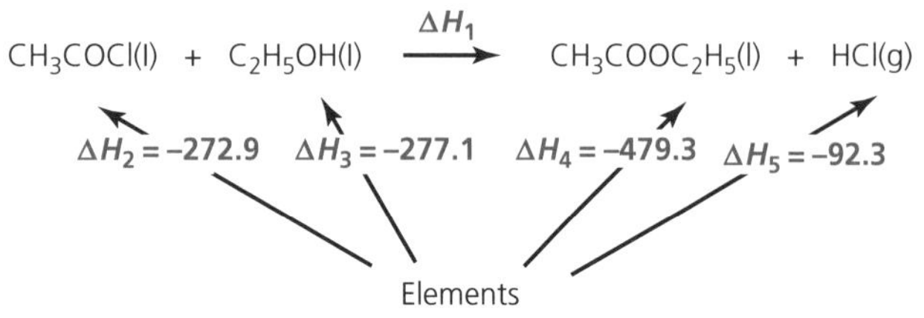


**Figure 5.7**

Clockwise steps will balance anti-clockwise steps such that:

$\Delta H_1 + \Delta H_2 + \Delta H_3 = \Delta H_4 + \Delta H_5$ which can be rearranged to give

$\Delta H_1 = \Delta H_4 + \Delta H_5 - \Delta H_2 - \Delta H_3 = -479.3 - 92.3 + 272.9 + 277.1 = -21.6\,\text{kJ mol}^{-1}$

**Exam tip**

Most exam papers contain at least one question using Hess's law. The data provided will have to be either enthalpies of combustion or enthalpies of formation. If the data provided are:

- standard enthalpies of combustion, the cycle will have combustion products at the bottom and the arrows will point down
- standard enthalpies of formation, the cycle will have elements at the bottom and the arrows will point up

## Now test yourself

TESTED

4 Use the data in the table below to calculate the standard enthalpy of formation for propane.

| Substance | $\Delta H_c^{\ominus}$/kJ mol$^{-1}$ |
|---|---|
| C(s) | –394 |
| $H_2(g)$ | –286 |
| $C_3H_8(g)$ | –2219 |

Answer on p. 213

# Reaction rates

Experimental observations show that the rate of a reaction is influenced by temperature, concentration and the use of a catalyst.

## Simple collision theory

REVISED

The collision theory of reactivity helps to provide explanations for these observations. A reaction cannot take place unless a collision occurs between reacting particles. Increasing temperature or concentration increases the chance of a collision occurring.

However, not all collisions lead to a successful reaction. The energy of a collision between reacting particles must exceed the minimum energy required for the reaction to occur. This minimum energy is known as the activation energy, $E_a$. Increasing the temperature affects the number of collisions with energy that exceeds the activation energy. A catalyst effectively lowers the activation energy.

## Calculation of reaction rates

REVISED

Take for example the reaction between calcium carbonate and hydrochloric acid:

$$CaCO_3(s) + 2HCl(aq) \rightarrow CaCl_2(aq) + CO_2(g) + H_2O(l)$$

In an experiment, the volume of carbon dioxide being produced could be measured as the reaction proceeds in a syringe, as shown in Figure 5.8.

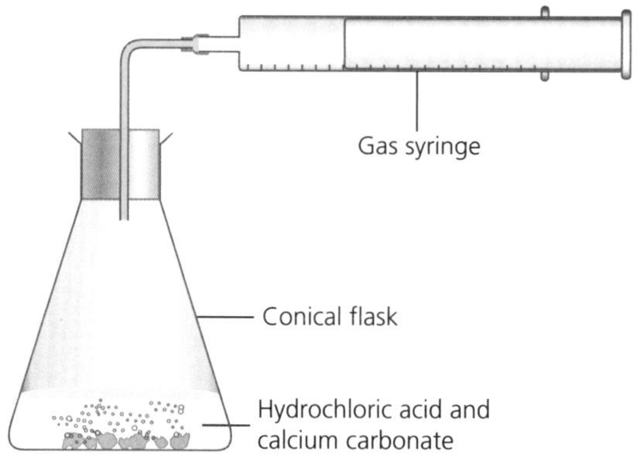


**Figure 5.8 Collection of gas using a gas syringe**

Carbon dioxide would initially be produced quickly but, as the reaction proceeded, it would gradually slow down as the reactants were used up. Eventually, once one or both of the reactants had been used up, the production of carbon dioxide would cease. A graph of the volume of carbon dioxide produced against time would appear as shown in Figure 5.9.

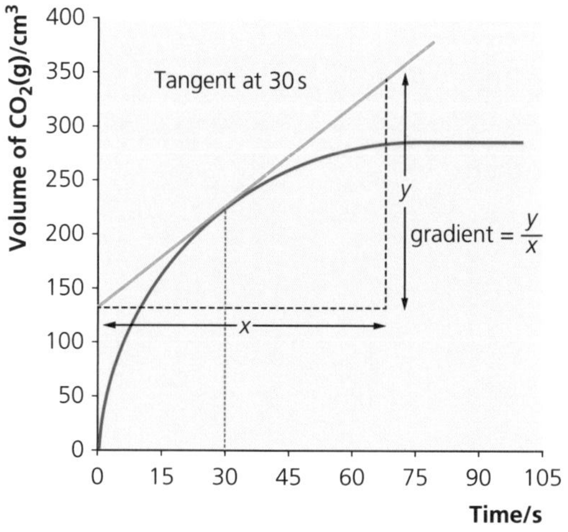


**Figure 5.9 Volume of carbon dioxide collected against time**

The rate is not constant but can be given a numerical value at any particular time by drawing a tangent to the curve and measuring its gradient. For example, in Figure 5.9 the rate at which the reaction is proceeding at 30 s is given by the gradient of the tangent at that point on the curve. In this case its value is $(350 - 130)\,cm^3/70\,s = 1.7\,cm^3\,s^{-1}$.

## Boltzmann's distribution of molecular energies

REVISED

Energy is directly proportional to absolute temperature. When collisions occur, the particles involved in the collision exchange (gain or lose) energy, even if a reaction does not occur. It follows that for any given mass of gaseous reactants at constant temperature; there will be a distribution of energies with some particles having more energy than others. Figure 5.10 shows a typical distribution of energies at constant temperature.

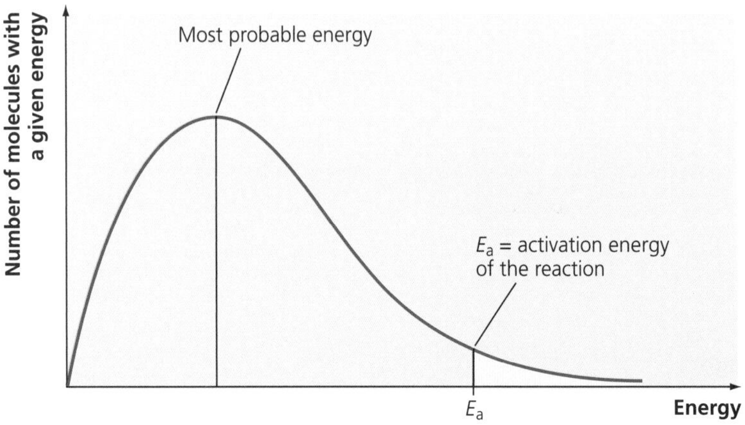


**Figure 5.10**

- The distribution always goes through the origin.
- The distribution is asymptotic to the horizontal axis at high energy, showing that there is no maximum energy. (Asymptotic means that the curve approaches the axis but will only meet it at infinity.)
- $E_a$ represents the activation energy — the minimum energy required to start the reaction.
- The area under the curve represents the total number of particles.
- The yellow shaded area represents the number of particles with sufficient energy to react. These are particles with energy greater than or equal to the activation energy, $E \geq E_a$ (Figure 5.11).

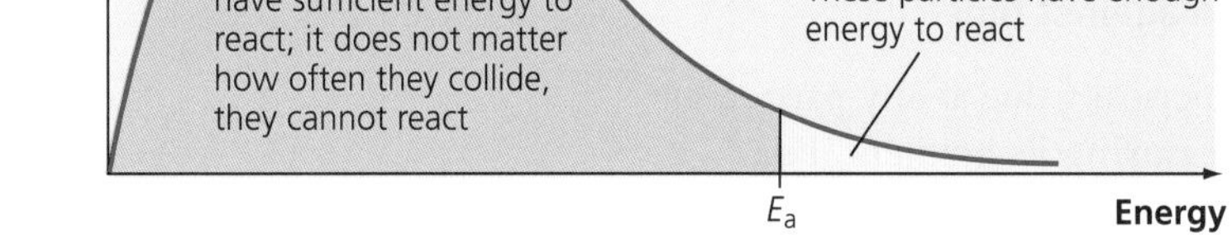

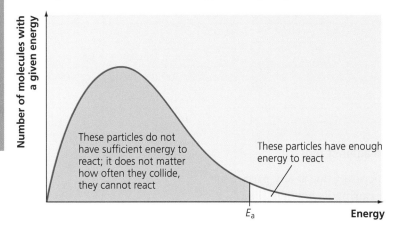

**Figure 5.11**

## Now test yourself

TESTED

5 Define the term *activation energy*, $E_a$.

Answer on p. 213

# Effects of concentration, temperature and using a catalyst on the rate of reaction

REVISED

## Effect of concentration

A useful analogy is to imagine your first driving lesson. The one thing you want to avoid is a collision! It follows that your first lesson is likely to be early on a Sunday morning on a quiet country lane, rather than at 5.00 p.m. on a Friday evening in the city centre. It is obvious that the high concentration of cars at rush hour increases the chance of a collision. The same is true for a chemical reaction. Increasing concentration simply increases the chance of a collision. The more collisions there are, the faster the reaction will be.

For a gaseous reaction, increasing pressure has the same effect as increasing concentration. When gases react they react faster at high pressure because as the pressure increases so does the concentration and hence there is an increased chance of a collision.

## Now test yourself

TESTED

6 Explain how increasing the pressure on a gaseous reaction affects the rate of reaction.

Answer on p. 213

## Effect of temperature

An increase in temperature (to $T_2$ in Figure 5.12) has a dramatic effect on the distribution of energies.

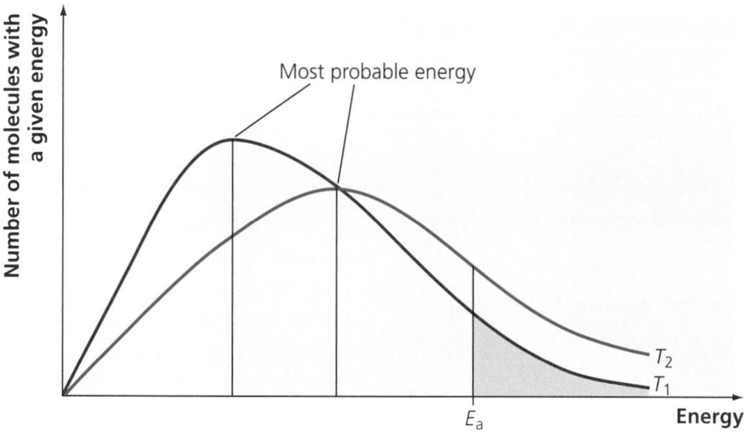


**Figure 5.12**

Only the temperature has changed. The number of particles is constant, so the area under both curves remains the same.

At higher temperature the distribution flattens and shifts to the right. This shows that increasing temperature increases the number of particles with energy greater than or equal to the activation energy, $E \geq E_a$, which means that at high temperature there are more particles with sufficient energy to react. Therefore, the reaction is faster. Decreasing the temperature has the opposite effect.

**Exam tip**

For a Boltzmann distribution curve at a higher temperature the marking points are for the following:

- The curve goes through the origin and there are fewer particles with low energy.
- The most probable energy moves to right (higher energy), but the height of the peak is lower.
- There are more particles with high energy, so a greater proportion of particles have energy that exceed the activation energy.

## Effect of a catalyst

Catalysts speed up reactions without themselves being changed permanently. Catalysts work by providing an alternative route for the reaction, which has a lower activation energy. This is illustrated in Figure 5.13.

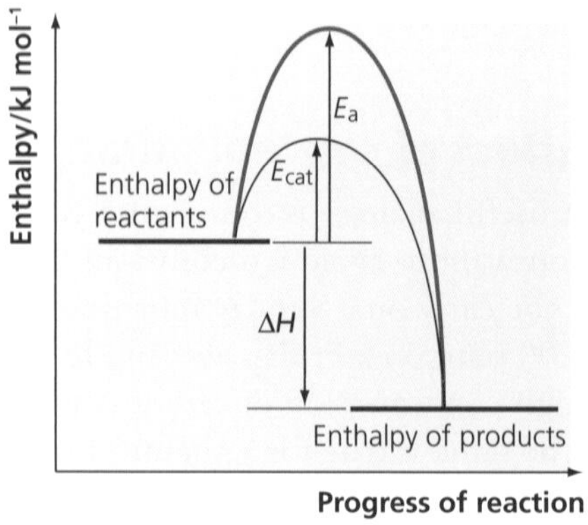


**Figure 5.13 Effect of a catalyst on activation energy**

$E_a$ is the activation energy of the uncatalysed reaction, $E_{cat}$ is the activation energy of the catalysed reaction. $E_{cat}$ is lower than $E_a$.

A catalyst lowers the activation energy but does not alter the Boltzmann distribution (Figure 5.14). It increases the number of particles with energy greater than or equal to the new activation energy, $E_{cat}$.

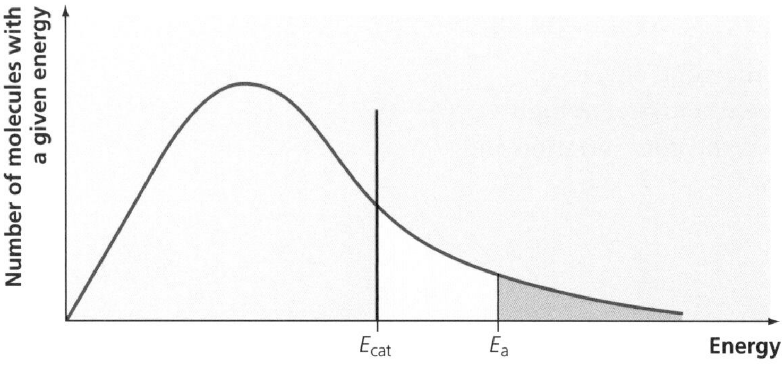


**Figure 5.14 Effect of a catalyst on Boltzmann distribution**

### Now test yourself

TESTED

7 Draw an enthalpy profile diagram and a Boltzmann distribution to show how a catalyst works.

Answer on p. 213

## Types of catalyst

REVISED

### Homogeneous catalysts

A suitable example involves the oxidation of iodide ions using persulfate ions (peroxosulfate ions).

Iodide ions, $I^-$(aq), are easily oxidised and the persulfate ion, $S_2O_8^{2-}$(aq), is a powerful oxidising agent, but surprisingly the reaction between them in water is slow. The equation for the reaction is:

$$S_2O_8^{2-} + 2I^- \rightarrow 2SO_4^{2-} + I_2$$

For the reaction to occur the two ions must collide, however, the rate of collision is slow because both ions are negative and repel each other.

The reaction can be catalysed by adding aqueous solutions of either $Fe^{2+}$(aq) ions or $Fe^{3+}$(aq) ions.

The transition metal ions catalyse the reaction by providing an alternate mechanism (Table 5.3).

A **homogeneous catalyst** is in the same phase (gas, liquid or solid) as the reactants. The most common type of homogeneous catalysis involves reactions in aqueous solutions.

**Table 5.3**

| Catalyst | $Fe^{2+}(aq)$ | $Fe^{3+}(aq)$ |
|---|---|---|
| **Step 1** | $S_2O_8^{2-} + 2Fe^{2+} \rightarrow 2SO_4^{2-} + 2Fe^{3+}$ | $2Fe^{3+} + 2I^- \rightarrow 2Fe^{2+} + I_2$ |
| **Step 2** | $2Fe^{3+} + 2I^- \rightarrow 2Fe^{2+} + I_2$ | $S_2O_8^{2-} + 2Fe^{2+} \rightarrow 2SO_4^{2-} + 2Fe^{3+}$ |
| | $Fe^{2+}$ is reformed and acts as a catalyst | $Fe^{3+}$ is reformed and acts as a catalyst |
| **Net reaction** | $S_2O_8^{2-} + 2I^- \rightarrow 2SO_4^{2-} + I_2$ | $S_2O_8^{2-} + 2I^- \rightarrow 2SO_4^{2-} + I_2$ |

The $Fe^{2+}$ and the $Fe^{3+}$ ions provide an alternative mechanism that involves an intermediate step of lower activation energy. The activation energy is lowered because both steps in either mechanism involve ions of opposite charge. The iron ions from the catalyst take part in the reaction, but are released at the end of the reaction, so the final amount of the catalyst is the same as when the reagents were mixed.

Another example of a homogeneous catalyst occurs in the loss of ozone from the upper atmosphere (stratosphere). This is a gas phase reaction in which chlorine radicals act catalytically.

## Heterogeneous catalysts

A heterogeneous catalyst works by adsorbing the gases onto its solid surface. This adsorption weakens bonds within the reactant molecules, which lowers the activation energy of the reaction. Bonds are broken and new bonds are formed. The product molecules are desorbed from the solid surface of the catalyst.

Iron is used as the catalyst in the Haber process for the production of ammonia (Figure 5.15).

$$N_2(g) + 3H_2(g) \xrightarrow[\text{as catalyst}]{Fe(s)} 2NH_3(g)$$

**Figure 5.15**

The internal combustion engine discharges pollutants into the atmosphere. Modern cars are fitted with catalytic converters (made from platinum, rhodium and palladium) that reduce the emission of unburnt hydrocarbons, carbon monoxide and oxides of nitrogen.

Removal of unburnt hydrocarbons:

$$C_8H_{18}(g) + 12\tfrac{1}{2}O_2(g) \rightarrow 8CO_2(g) + 9H_2O(g)$$

Removal of carbon monoxide and nitrogen monoxide:

$$2NO(g) + 2CO(g) \rightarrow N_2(g) + 2CO_2(g)$$

Removal of oxides of nitrogen:

$$2NO_2(g) + 4CO(g) \rightarrow N_2(g) + 4CO_2(g)$$

All of the above reactions are in the gas phase. The catalytic converter is a solid mounted on a fine aluminium mesh.

A **heterogeneous catalyst** is in a different phase from the reactants. The most common type of heterogeneous catalysis involves reactions of gases in the presence of a solid catalyst.

**Exam tip**

If you are asked how a heterogeneous catalyst works, look at the marks allocation. If there is more than 1 mark, the explanation required is usually:

- The catalyst works by adsorbing gases onto its surface.
- This weakens the bonds, which lowers the activation energy and leads to a chemical reaction.
- The products of the reaction are desorbed from the surface of the catalyst.

## Now test yourself

TESTED

8 Explain what is meant by *heterogeneous catalysis* and by *homogeneous catalysis*. Give an example of each type.

Answer on p. 213

### Economic importance of catalysts

Catalysts are of great economic importance. They often allow reactions to be carried out at lower temperatures and/or pressures, which reduce costs. They also enable the use of different reactions with lower atom economies. This also reduces waste. Enzymes are being used increasingly to generate specific products and to enable reactions to be carried out close to room temperature and pressure.

# Chemical equilibrium

## Reversible reactions

REVISED

There are many everyday examples of reversible reactions or processes, the most common being the changes between the physical states of water. If the temperature of water falls below 0°C, the water freezes and ice forms. When the temperature rises above 0°C, the ice melts and water forms again. This process can be represented as:

$$H_2O(s) \rightleftharpoons H_2O(l)$$

The $\rightleftharpoons$ symbol indicates that a reaction is reversible.

Esterification is an example of a reversible chemical reaction. Esterification is covered in full in Module 6 of the A level course.

### Dynamic equilibrium

In a reversible reaction (Figure 5.15), the reaction from left to right is called the forward reaction; the reaction from right to left is the reverse reaction.

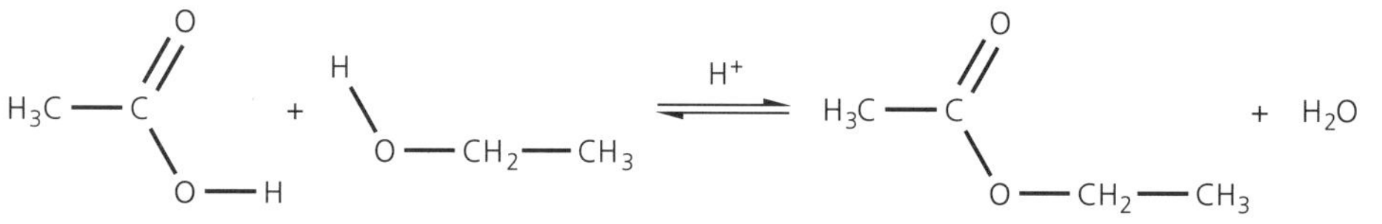


**Figure 5.15**

When ethanoic acid and ethanol are refluxed in the presence of an acid catalyst, the forward reaction, $r_1$, is initially fast because the concentration of both reagents is high. However, as they react, the concentration of each decreases, lowering the rate of the forward reaction.

The reverse reaction, $r_2$, is initially very slow because the amounts of ethyl ethanoate and water present are very small. However, as time progresses, the concentration of ethyl ethanoate and water gradually increases, as does the rate of the reverse reaction.

In summary, the forward reaction, $r_1$, starts off fast but slows down, while the reverse reaction, $r_2$, starts slowly and speeds up. It follows that they will reach a point when the rate of the forward reaction exactly equals the rate of the reverse reaction:

$$r_1 = r_2$$

When this happens the system is said to be in **dynamic equilibrium**. It is dynamic because the reagents and the products are constantly interchanging. It is in equilibrium because the amount of each chemical

A **dynamic equilibrium** is reached when the rate of the forward reaction equals the rate of the reverse reaction. The concentration of the reagents and products remain constant; the reagent and the product molecules react continuously.

in the system remains constant. Dynamic equilibrium can only be reached if the system is closed.

## Now test yourself

TESTED

9 Explain what is meant by the terms *reversible reaction* and *dynamic equilibrium*.

Answer on p. 214

## Le Chatelier's principle

REVISED

**Le Chatelier's principle** is used to predict the effect of changes in conditions on the position of equilibrium.

**Le Chatelier's principle** states that if a closed system at equilibrium is subject to a change, the system will move to *minimise* the effect of that change.

The factors that can be readily changed are concentration, temperature and pressure:

- If the concentration is increased, the system will move to decrease the concentration.
- If the temperature is increased, the system will move to decrease the temperature.
- If the pressure is increased, the system will move to decrease the pressure.

### Effect of changing pressure on the position of equilibrium

The pressure of a gas mixture depends on the number of gas molecules in the mixture. The greater the number of gas molecules in the equilibrium mixture, the greater is the pressure in the mixture. If the pressure is increased, a system at equilibrium alters to decrease the pressure by reducing the number of gas molecules in the system.

In a system such as $2SO_2(g) + O_2(g) \rightleftharpoons 2SO_3(g)$, if the pressure is increased, the position of the equilibrium moves to the *right*, so that the number of gas molecules is reduced from 3 to 2. This has the effect of reducing the pressure.

If the pressure is increased on a system such as $N_2O_4(g) \rightleftharpoons 2NO_2(g)$, the position of the equilibrium moves to the *left*, so that the number of gas molecules is reduced from 2 to 1. This has the effect of reducing the pressure.

If the pressure is increased on a system such as $2HI(g) \rightleftharpoons H_2(g) + I_2(g)$, the position of the equilibrium does not move, because there are the same number of gas molecules on each side of the equilibrium. A change in the equilibrium position has no effect on the pressure.

### Effect of changing temperature on the position of equilibrium

Temperature not only influences the rate of the reaction it also plays an important role in determining the equilibrium position. The effect of temperature can only be predicted if the $\Delta H$ value of the reaction is known.

Consider the reaction:

$$2A(g) + B(g) \rightleftharpoons C(g) + D(g) \qquad \Delta H = -100\,kJ\,mol^{-1}$$

It follows that:

- the forward reaction: $2A(g) + B(g) \rightarrow C(g) + D(g)$ is exothermic ($\Delta H = -100\,kJ\,mol^{-1}$)
- the reverse reaction: $C(g) + D(g) \rightarrow 2A(g) + B(g)$ is endothermic ($\Delta H = +100\,kJ\,mol^{-1}$)

According to le Chatelier's principle, if we increase the temperature of the reaction mixture, the system alters to decrease the temperature. This is achieved by the system favouring the reverse reaction, which is endothermic. This, therefore, helps to remove the additional enthalpy caused by increasing the temperature. The position of the equilibrium moves to the left.

Decomposition of hydrogen iodide is an endothermic reaction:

$$2HI(g) \rightleftharpoons H_2(g) + I_2(g)$$

- If the temperature is increased, the equilibrium moves to the right.
- If the temperature is decreased, the equilibrium moves to the left.

Oxidation of sulfur dioxide is an exothermic reaction:

$$SO_2(g) + O_2(g) \rightleftharpoons 2SO_3(g)$$

- If the temperature is increased, the equilibrium moves to the left.
- If the temperature is decreased, the equilibrium moves to the right.

## Now test yourself

TESTED

10 State le Chatelier's principle.

11 Use le Chatelier's principle to deduce what happens to the following equilibrium when it is subjected to the stated changes:

$$2NO_2(g) \rightleftharpoons N_2O_4(g) \quad \Delta H = -57.2\,kJ\,mol^{-1}$$

(a) the temperature is increased
(b) the pressure is decreased
(c) the $N_2O_4(g)$ is removed

Answers on p. 214

### Effect of a catalyst on the position of equilibrium

A catalyst is a substance that speeds up the rate of reaction by providing an alternative route, or mechanism, that has a lower activation energy. A catalyst does *not* alter the amount of product.

In a system at equilibrium, a catalyst speeds up the forward and the reverse reactions equally. Therefore, a catalyst has no effect on the *position* of the equilibrium but it reduces the time taken for equilibrium to be reached.

## Compromise conditions — the Haber process

REVISED

Large quantities of nitrogenous compounds, particularly fertilisers, are needed by humans. Atmospheric nitrogen is in plentiful supply but cannot be used directly. The Haber process is used to 'fix' atmospheric nitrogen and convert it into ammonia:

$$N_2(g) + 3H_2(g) \rightleftharpoons 2NH_3(g) \qquad \Delta H = -93\,kJ\,mol^{-1}$$

Le Chatelier's principle allows the optimum conditions for this industrial process to be determined.

The enthalpy change is $-93\,kJ\,mol^{-1}$, so the forward reaction is exothermic. Therefore, if the temperature is decreased the equilibrium moves to the right, so a low temperature is best (optimum) for the formation of ammonia.

If the pressure is increased on the system $N_2(g) + 3H_2(g) \rightleftharpoons 2NH_3(g)$, the equilibrium position moves to the right to reduce the number of molecules. This has the effect of reducing the pressure. Therefore, high pressure is optimum for the formation of ammonia.

The optimum conditions for the maximum yield of ammonia are low temperature and high pressure. However, the operating conditions of a modern plant are:

- a temperature of around 700 K (427°C)
- a pressure of around 100 atm

The conditions are a compromise. The temperature is a compromise between yield and rate — low temperature gives a high yield but the reaction is too slow.

The pressure is a compromise between yield and cost/safety — high pressure gives a high yield but it is both costly and dangerous (hydrogen gas is highly explosive).

The rate of reaction is improved by using a catalyst of finely divided iron or iron in a porous form that incorporates metal oxide promoters.

Table 5.4 gives the boiling points of the gases involved in the Haber process.

**Table 5.4 Boiling points of the gases involved in the Haber process**

| Gas | $N_2(g)$ | $H_2(g)$ | $NH_3(g)$ |
|---|---|---|---|
| Boiling point | 77 K (−196°C) | 20 K (−253°C) | 240 K (−33°C) |

If the equilibrium mixture is cooled to about −40°C the ammonia gas liquefies, so ammonia gas is lost from the equilibrium mixture. The system moves to minimise the effect of this loss. The reagents react to produce more ammonia gas to replace the ammonia gas that was liquefied. Any unreacted nitrogen and hydrogen is recycled and used again in a continuous process.

## The equilibrium constant, $K_c$

REVISED

For any reversible reaction that has reached dynamic equilibrium the concentrations of the reactants and products remain unchanged and it is possible to use these concentrations to calculate a numerical value for an important constant, $K_c$, known as the equilibrium constant. The equilibrium constant varies with temperature but its value is the same for any other change in condition.

In general terms for the reaction:

$$aA + bB \rightleftharpoons cC + dD$$

the equilibrium constant,

$$K_c = \frac{[C]^c[D]^d}{[A]^a[B]^b}$$

In the expression for $K_c$ the square brackets '[ ]' indicate that the concentrations of the reactants and products are expressed in units of $mol\,dm^{-3}$.

The concentrations of the chemicals on the right-hand side of the equation appear on the top line of the expression. The concentrations of reactants on the left appear on the bottom line. Each concentration term is raised to the power of the number in front of its formula in the balanced equation.

For the equilibrium:

$$3H_2(g) + N_2(g) \rightleftharpoons 2NH_3(g)$$

$$K_c = \frac{[NH_3(g)]^2}{[H_2(g)]^3[N_2(g)]}$$

If there is a solid reactant or product in the equilibrium then it is not included in the expression for $K_c$.

For the equilibrium:

$$H_2O(g) + C(s) \rightleftharpoons H_2(g) + CO(g)$$

$$K_c = \frac{[H_2(g)][CO(g)]}{[H_2O(g)]}$$

The value of $K_c$ is important because it gives an indication of the balance of reactants and products present in the equilibrium mixture. If $K_c$ has a large value it will mean that there are more of the products present than the reactants, if $K_c$ is small then it is the reactants that must be present in larger quantity. The values of $K_c$ do, in fact, vary enormously from large values down to values that are very small.

For example in the equilibrium:

$$CH_3COOH(l) + C_2H_5OH(l) \rightleftharpoons CH_3COOC_2H_5(l) + H_2O(l)$$

$$K_c = \frac{[CH_3COOC_2H_5(l)][H_2O(l)]}{[CH_3COOH(l)][C_2H_5OH(l)]}$$

The value of $K_c$ is approximately 4 at room temperature so there is approximately four times as much product as there are reactants. $K_c$ will not have any units because the concentrations of each component will cancel out in the equilibrium expression.

For the equilibrium between sulfur dioxide, oxygen and sulfur trioxide:

$$2SO_2(g) + O_2(g) \rightleftharpoons 2SO_3(g)$$

the equilibrium constant

$$K_c = \frac{[SO_3(g)]^2}{[SO_2(g)]^2[O_2(g)]}$$

has a size of approximately $1.0 \times 10^{12}$ at 230°C so in this case the equilibrium mixture has vastly more of the product, $SO_3$, than the reactants. In this case $K_c$ will have units of $1/\text{mol dm}^{-3}$ or $\text{dm}^{+3}\text{mol}^{-1}$ because the concentrations do not completely cancel in the equilibrium expression.

**Exam tip**

You will not be expected to supply units for equilibrium constants in the AS exam.

## The effect on $K_c$ of a change in temperature

The effect of a change in temperature on the value of $K_c$ is best explained using an example.

The equilibrium:

$$2SO_2(g) + O_2(g) \rightleftharpoons 2SO_3(g) \quad \Delta H = -197\,\text{kJ mol}^{-1}$$

is exothermic. An increase in temperature moves the equilibrium to the left and less $SO_3$ is produced. It must therefore follow that the value of the equilibrium constant will decrease as the temperature rises.

## Calculating an equilibrium constant

REVISED

If the equilibrium concentration of each component of an equilibrium mixture is known, the equilibrium constant can be calculated by substituting these values into the expression for the equilibrium constant.



**Example**

At 450°C, hydrogen and gaseous iodine form an equilibrium mixture with hydrogen iodide:

$$H_2(g) + I_2(g) \rightleftharpoons 2HI(g)$$

When an equilibrium mixture is analysed it is found to contain 0.015 mol dm$^{-3}$ of HI, 0.0012 mol dm$^{-3}$ of $I_2$ and 0.0038 mol dm$^{-3}$ of $H_2$.

Calculate the value of the equilibrium constant to 2 significant figures.

**Answer**

$$K_c = \frac{[HI(g)]^2}{[H_2(g)][I_2(g)]}$$

Therefore:

$$K_c = \frac{(0.015)^2}{(0.0012)(0.0038)} = 49$$

## Now test yourself

TESTED

12 Write the equilibrium constant for the equilibrium:

$$2NO_2(g) \rightleftharpoons N_2O_4(g)$$

(a) At a certain temperature the equilibrium constant for this reaction has a value of 0.0025. What does this indicate about the position of the equilibrium?
(b) If the concentration of $NO_2$ is 1.0 mol dm$^{-3}$, calculate the concentration of the $N_2O_4$ at this temperature.

13 When the equilibrium $2NOCl(g) \rightleftharpoons 2NO(g) + Cl_2(g)$ is analysed it is found that the equilibrium concentrations of the gases are NOCl = 3.42 mol dm$^{-3}$, NO = 0.32 mol dm$^{-3}$, $Cl_2$ = 0.16 mol dm$^{-3}$. Calculate $K_c$ for the equilibrium.

Answers on p. 214

## Exam practice

1 Bond enthalpies can provide information about the energy changes that accompany a chemical reaction.
(a) What do you understand by the term *bond enthalpy*? [2]
(b) (i) Write an equation, including state symbols, to illustrate the bond enthalpy of hydrogen chloride. [1]
(ii) Write an equation to illustrate the bond enthalpy of methane. [2]
(c) (i) The table below shows some average bond enthalpies.

| Bond | Average bond enthalpy/kJ mol$^{-1}$ |
|---|---|
| C–C | 350 |
| C=C | 610 |
| H–H | 436 |
| C–H | 410 |

Use the information in the table to calculate the enthalpy change for the hydrogenation of ethene (Figure 5.16). [3]

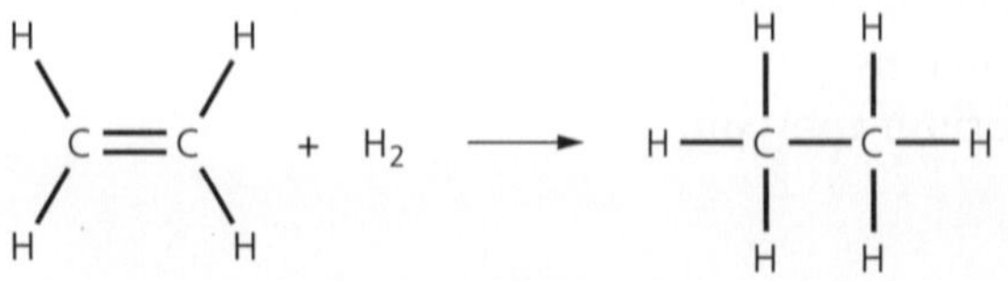


**Figure 5.16**

(ii) The enthalpy change of this reaction is found by experiment to be –136 kJ mol⁻¹. Explain why this value is different from that calculated in (i). [2]

(d) In the hydrogenation of ethane, nickel is used as a catalyst. Explain the mode of action of nickel in this reaction. [3]

2 When a mixture of hydrogen and oxygen is ignited by a spark, water is produced:

$2H_2(g) + O_2(g) \rightarrow 2H_2O(l) \quad \Delta H = -571.6\,kJ\,mol^{-1}$

$2H_2(g) + O_2(g) \rightarrow 2H_2O(g) \quad \Delta H = -483.6\,kJ\,mol^{-1}$

(a) On the same diagram, draw the enthalpy profiles for the formation of water and steam. [2]

(b) Use the enthalpy profile diagram to deduce the enthalpy change: [2]

$H_2O(l) \rightarrow H_2O(g)$

3 Octane, $C_8H_{18}$, is one of the hydrocarbons present in petrol.

(a) Define the term standard enthalpy change of combustion. [3]

(b) Use the data below to calculate the standard enthalpy change of combustion of octane. [3]

$C_8H_{18}(l) + 12\tfrac{1}{2}O_2(g) \rightarrow 8CO_2(g) + 9H_2O(l)$

| Compound | $\Delta_f H^\ominus$/kJ mol⁻¹ |
|---|---|
| $C_8H_{18}(l)$ | –250.0 |
| $CO_2(g)$ | –393.5 |
| $H_2O(l)$ | –285.9 |

(c) Combustion in car engines produces polluting gases, mainly carbon monoxide, unburnt hydrocarbons and oxides of nitrogen such as nitrogen(II) oxide, NO. Explain, with the aid of equations, how carbon monoxide and nitrogen(II) oxide are produced in a car engine. [2]

(d) (i) The catalytic converter removes much of this pollution in a series of reactions. Write an equation to show the removal of carbon monoxide and nitrogen(II) oxide gases. [1]

(ii) The removal of carbon monoxide and nitrogen(II) oxide gases involves a redox reaction. Use your answer to d(i) to identify the element being reduced and state the change in its oxidation number. [2]

4 Sulfuric acid, $H_2SO_4$, is made industrially by the contact process. This is an example of a dynamic equilibrium:

$2SO_2(g) + O_2(g) \rightleftharpoons 2SO_3(g) \qquad \Delta H = -98\,kJ\,mol^{-1}$

(a) State *two* features of a reaction with a *dynamic equilibrium*. [2]

(b) State and explain what happens to the equilibrium position of the above reaction when:

(i) the temperature is raised

(ii) the pressure is increased

(iii) Suggest the optimum conditions for the contact process. [6]

(c) (i) The conditions used for the contact process are a temperature of between 450°C and 600°C and a pressure of about 10 atm. Explain why the optimum conditions are not used. [3]

(ii) Vanadium(V) oxide is used as a catalyst. What effect does this have on the conversion of $SO_2(g)$ into $SO_3(g)$? [2]

(iii) At least three catalyst chambers are used to ensure maximum conversion of $SO_2(g)$. The conversion yield can exceed 98%. State two advantages of this high conversion rate. [2]

5 In the Haber process, hydrogen is reacted with nitrogen in the presence of a catalyst to produce ammonia:

$N_2(g) + 3H_2(g) \rightleftharpoons 2NH_3(g)$

The activation energy for the forward reaction is $+68\,kJ\,mol^{-1}$.
The activation energy for the reverse reaction is $+160\,kJ\,mol^{-1}$.

(a) (i) Use this information to sketch the energy profile diagram. Label clearly the activation energy for the forward reaction, $E_f$, and the activation energy for the reverse reaction, $E_r$. [2]
(ii) Explain what is meant by activation energy. [1]
(iii) Calculate the enthalpy change for the forward reaction. [1]

(b) Much of the ammonia produced is oxidised into nitric acid using the Ostwald process, which involves three stages:

| | | |
|---|---|---|
| Stage 1 | $4NH_3(g) + 5O_2(g) \rightleftharpoons 4NO(g) + 6H_2O(g)$ | $\Delta H = -950\,kJ\,mol^{-1}$ |
| Stage 2 | $2NO(g) + O_2(g) \rightleftharpoons 2NO_2(g)$ | $\Delta H = -114\,kJ\,mol^{-1}$ |
| Stage 3 | $3NO_2(g) + H_2O(g) \rightleftharpoons 2HNO_3(g) + NO(g)$ | $\Delta H = -117\,kJ\,mol^{-1}$ |

(i) With reference to the oxidation number of the nitrogen in $NH_3(g)$ (Stage 1) and in $HNO_3$ (Stage 3) show that this is an oxidation process. [3]
(ii) State le Chatelier's principle. [1]
(iii) Use le Chatelier's principle to predict and explain the temperature and the pressure that would give the maximum yield at equilibrium in Stage 1. [4]
(iv) Suggest what happens to the NO(g) produced in Stage 3. [1]

(c) The nitric acid produced in Stage 3 is a strong acid. Explain, with the aid of an equation, what is meant by the term *strong acid*. [2]

6 In an investigation to find the enthalpy change of combustion of ethanol, $C_2H_5OH$, a student found that 1.60 g of ethanol could heat 150 g of water from 22.0°C to 71.0°C. The specific heat capacity of ethanol is $4.2\,J\,g^{-1}\,K^{-1}$.

(a) Use the results to calculate a value for the enthalpy change of combustion of ethanol. [6]
(b) The theoretical value of the standard enthalpy change of combustion of ethanol is $-1367.3\,kJ\,mol^{-1}$. Give two reasons for the difference between the theoretical and experimental values. Suggest an improvement that could be made to the experiment to minimise the most significant error. [3]
(c) Catalysts are of great economic importance. Give an example of a catalyst that is in the same state as the reactants and an example of a catalyst that is in a different state from the reactants. State why the reactions you have chosen are important and explain how a catalyst increases the rate of reaction. [6]

7 When the indicator methyl orange is dissolved in water the following dynamic equilibrium is set up.

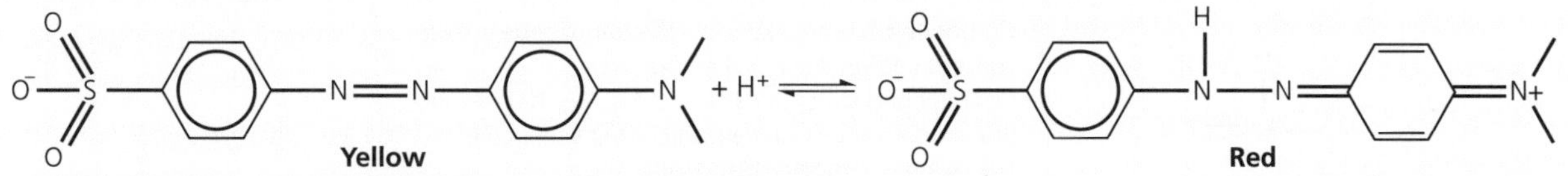


(a) Hydrochloric acid is added to the equilibrium mixture. State the colour change you would see. Explain your answer.
(b) Aqueous potassium hydroxide solution is added dropwise to the solution in **a** until no further colour change occurs. Suggest all the colour changes you would see. Explain your answer. [6]

## Answers and quick quiz 5 online

ONLINE

## Summary

You should now have an understanding of:

- exothermic and endothermic reactions
- enthalpies of reaction, formation and combustion
- bond enthalpies
- Hess's law and calculations using enthalpy cycles
- Boltzmann distributions and how temperature and catalysts affect rate
- catalysts
- le Chatelier's principle
- the equilibrium constant, $K_c$.

# 6 Basic concepts and hydrocarbons

## Naming and formulae of organic compounds

### Homologous series

REVISED

Organic compounds are grouped together in families called **homologous series**.

You are expected to be able to recognise and name alkanes, alkenes, alcohols and haloalkanes.

A **homologous series** is a group of compounds that have the same general formula and contain the same functional group (and therefore have similar chemical properties). Each member of the series differs from the next by $CH_2$.

**Table 6.1** Formulae and names of hydrocarbons

| | General formula | Naming |
|---|---|---|
| **Alkanes** | $C_nH_{2n+2}$ | Name always ends '-ane' |
| **Alkenes** | $C_nH_{2n}$ | Name always ends '-ene |
| **Alcohols** | $C_nH_{2n+1}OH$ | Name always ends '-ol' |
| **Haloalkanes** | $C_nH_{2n+1}X$ where X = Cl, Br, I | Name always starts 'chloro-', 'bromo-' or 'iodo-' |

Figure 6.1 shows how to name organic compounds.

A

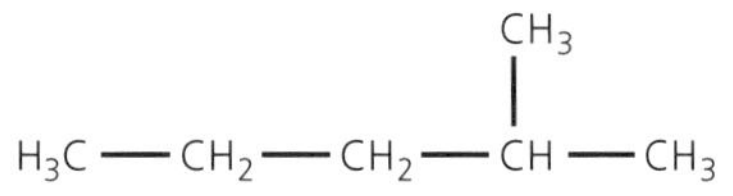

Compound A is an alkane — the name ends in *-ane*
Longest carbon chain is 5 — *pentane*
Branch on the second carbon contains one carbon — hence *2-methyl*
Full name is **2-methylpentane**

B

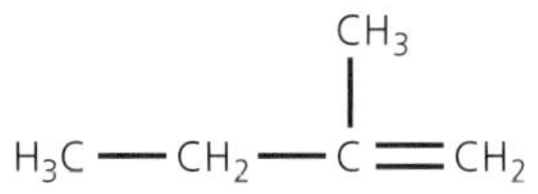

Compound **B** is an alkene — the name ends in *-ene*
Longest carbon chain is 4 — *butene*
Double bond starts at carbon atom 1 — but-*1*-ene
Branch on the second carbon contains one carbon — hence *2-methyl*
Full name is **2-methylbut-1-ene**

C

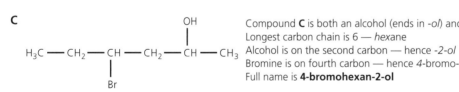

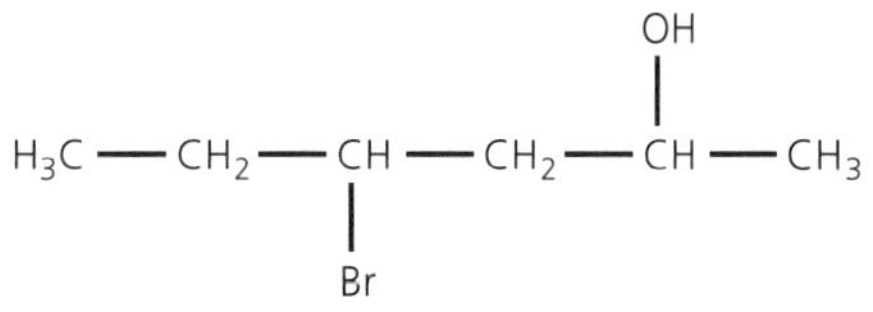

Compound **C** is both an alcohol (ends in *-ol*) and a bromoalkane (starts *bromo-*)
Longest carbon chain is 6 — *hexane*
Alcohol is on the second carbon — hence *-2-ol*
Bromine is on fourth carbon — hence *4*-bromo-
Full name is **4-bromohexan-2-ol**

**Figure 6.1** Naming organic compounds

### Representing organic formulae

REVISED

You are expected to draw and represent compounds in a number of different ways:

- A **structural formula** is accepted as the minimal detail, using conventional groups, for an unambiguous structure. The structural formula for butane, $C_4H_{10}$, is $CH_3CH_2CH_2CH_3$.

- A **displayed formula** shows both the relative placing of atoms and the number of bonds between them. The displayed formula of methylpropane is shown in Figure 6.2.

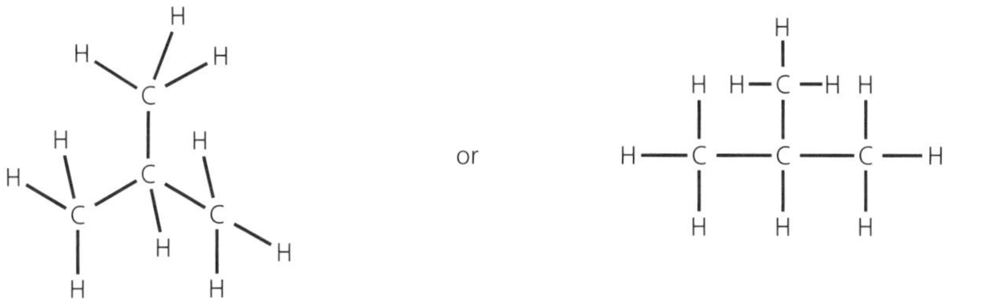

Figure 6.2

- A **skeletal formula** is a simplified organic formula. The hydrogen atoms in alkyl chains are not shown, leaving only the carbon skeleton and associated functional groups. The skeletal formulae for butane, methylpropane, pentan-2-ol and but-1-ene are shown in Figure 6.3.

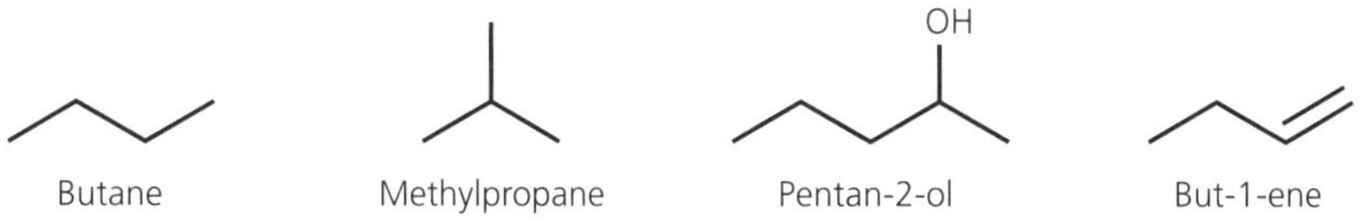


Figure 6.3

Figure 6.4 shows how cyclic compounds such as cyclohexane and benzene are represented.

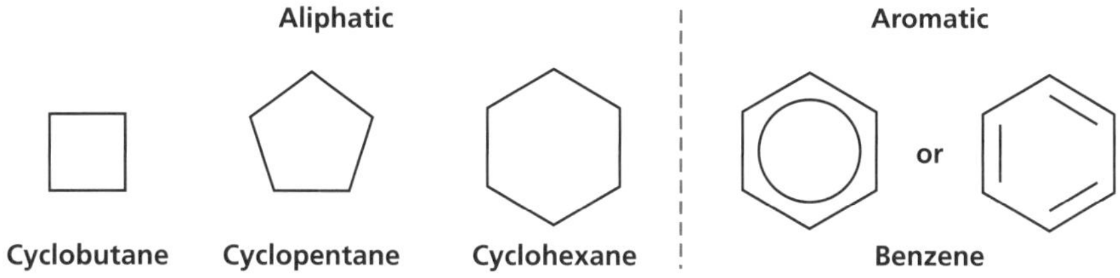


Figure 6.4

Compounds that contain a benzene ring are **aromatic** compounds whilst compounds that contain a non-aromatic ring are **alicyclic** compounds (Figure 6.5).

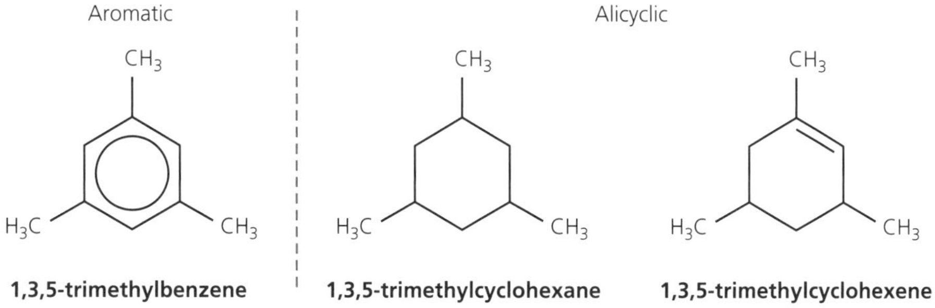


Figure 6.5

## Now test yourself

TESTED

1 Draw the displayed formula for each of the following molecules:
 (a) 2-chloropropane
 (b) 1-chloropropane
 (c) butan-2-ol
 (d) 2-methylpentane
 (e) 3-methylbut-1-ene

2 Name each of the following:

(a)

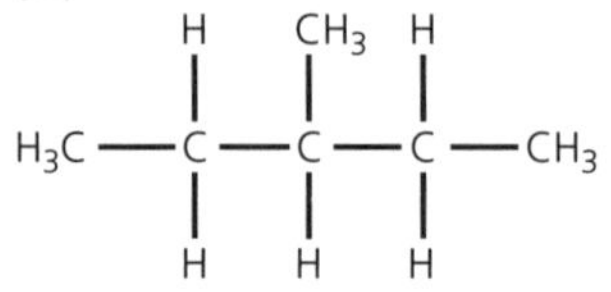

(b)

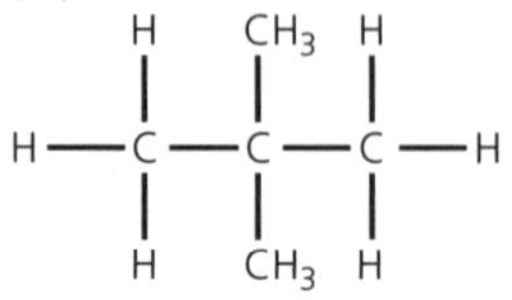

(c)

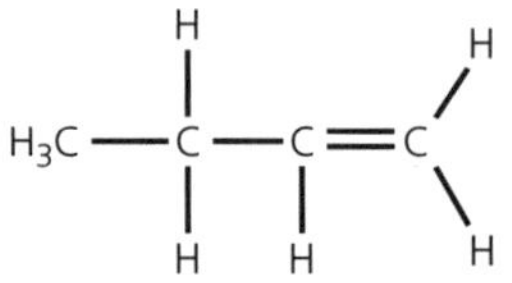

(d)

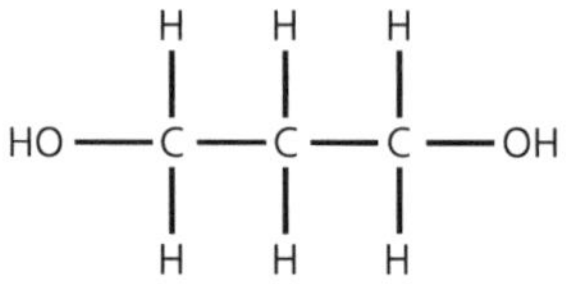

3 Name the following:
 (a) $CH_3CHBrCH_3$
 (b) $CH_3CHCHCH_3$
 (c) $(CH_3)_4C$
 (d) $CH_3CH_2CH(CH_3)CH_2CH_3$

Answers on p. 214

# Isomerism

## Structural isomerism

REVISED

**Structural isomers** with molecular formula $C_4H_{10}O$ are shown in Figure 6.6.

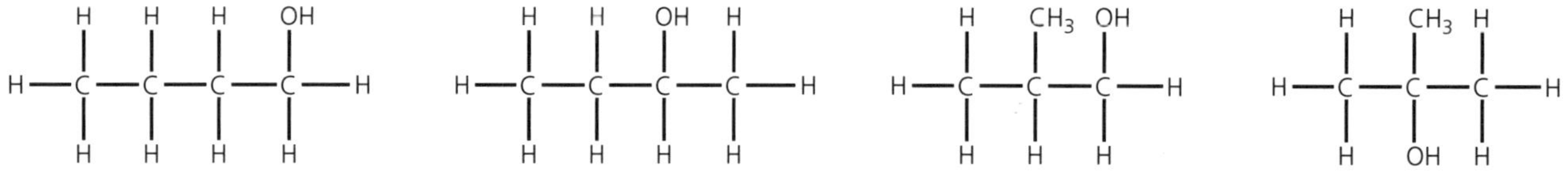

**Figure 6.6 Structural isomers of $C_4H_{10}O$**

> **Structural isomers** are compounds that have the same molecular formula but different structural formulae.

**Typical mistakes**

Questions are sometimes of the following form:

There are five isomers of $C_6H_{14}$. Three are drawn for you (Figure 6.7). Draw the other two.

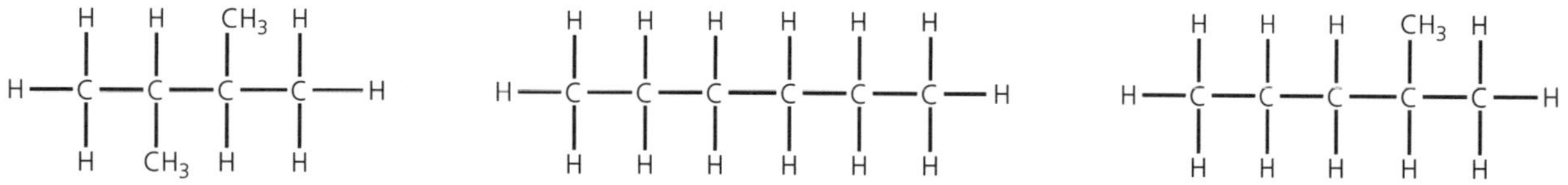

**Figure 6.7**

Few students gain both marks. Most redraw at least one of the above three isomers, but in a different orientation.

Skeletal isomers also cause problems — for example, when asked to draw isomers such as 1-chloropropane.

Many draw the carbon skeleton first as:

which correctly represents propane.

Most then add Cl to give:

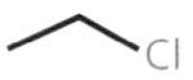


which changes it to chloroethane.

The correct skeletal formula for 1-chloropropane is:

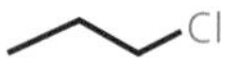


## *E/Z* isomerism (geometric isomerism)

REVISED

***E/Z* isomerism** is found in alkenes. The key features to look for are:

- the C=C double bond
- each carbon atom in the C=C double bond being bonded to two different atoms or groups

*E/Z* isomerism is explained fully in the section on alkenes.

***E/Z* isomers** have the same structural formula but the atoms are arranged differently in space around a C=C double bond.

## Reactions of functional groups

REVISED

When describing the reactions of any functional group you are expected to know the reagents, the conditions and to be able to write both a balanced equation and the mechanism.

**Reagents** These are the chemicals involved in the reaction.

**Conditions** These normally describe the temperature, pressure and/or the use of a catalyst,

**Mechanism** The overall reaction is broken down into separate steps. It is usual to identify the attacking species. This can be a **radical**, an **electrophile** or a **nucleophile**.

A **nucleophile** is a molecule or ion with a lone pair of electrons that can form a new covalent bond. A nucleophile is an **electron-pair donor**. Examples include $OH^-$, $:NH_3$.

A **radical** is a reactive particle with an unpaired electron. The symbol for a radical shows the unpaired electron as a dot, e.g. Cl•, $CH_3$•.

An **electrophile** is a reactive ion or molecule that attacks an electron-rich part of a molecule to form a new covalent bond. An electrophile is an **electron-pair acceptor**. Examples include $H^+$, $NO_2^+$.

The covalent bonds within organic compounds can be broken by either **homolytic fission** or by **heterolytic fission**.

**Homolytic fission** occurs when a covalent bond is broken and each bonding atom receives one electron from the bonding pair of electrons, forming two **radicals**:

$Cl{-}Cl \rightarrow Cl\cdot + \cdot Cl$

**Heterolytic fission** occurs when a covalent bond is broken and one bonding atom receives both electrons from the bonding pair of electrons, forming a **nucleophile** and an **electrophile**:

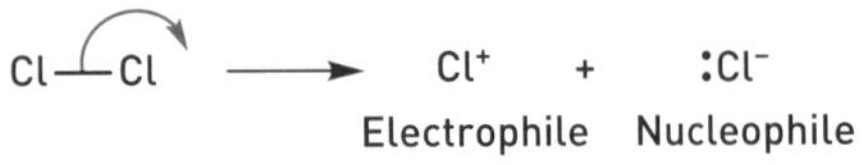


The curly arrow shows the movement of an electron pair, and shows heterolytic fission and formation of a covalent bond.

**Exam tip**

Words that end with '-phile' indicate a liking for — for example, a 'bibliophile' is someone who likes books. However, when explaining key terms such as 'electrophile' you will *not* score any marks for writing that 'it loves electrons'. Stick to the scientific definitions given above.

# Alkanes

## Physical properties of alkanes

REVISED

Hydrocarbons are compounds that contain hydrogen and carbon only. Alkanes and cycloalkanes are saturated hydrocarbons, as all of the C–C bonds are single bonds. This results in a tetrahedral shape, with bond angles 109.5°, around each carbon atom.

Different alkanes have different boiling points. The variation in boiling points depends on the amount of intermolecular forces. Alkanes have very low bond polarity and so the only type of intermolecular force is induced dipole–dipole interactions (van der Waals forces). There are two important trends in the variation of boiling points. First, as the relative molecular mass increases, the boiling point increases. This is due to

- an increase in chain length
- an increase in the number of electrons

Both of the above result in an increase in the number of induced dipole–dipole interactions. Second, for isomers with the same relative molecular mass, the boiling points decrease with an increase in the amount of branching. This can be explained by the fact that straight chains pack closer together, creating more intermolecular forces. This can be illustrated by the three isomers of pentane, $C_5H_{12}$ (Figure 6.8).

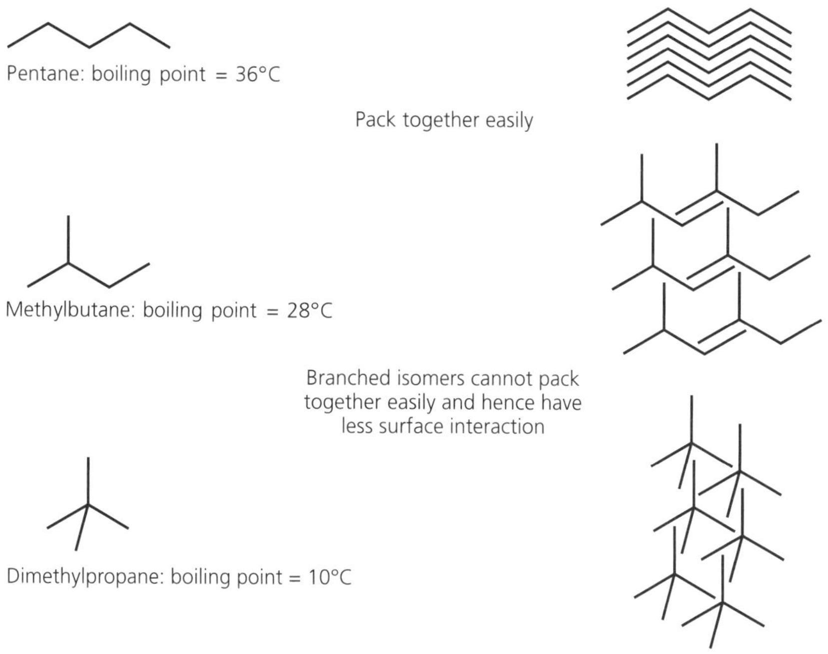


**Figure 6.8**

## Chemical properties of alkanes

REVISED

Alkanes are relatively unreactive because:

- they have very low bond polarity
- the C–C and the C–H bonds are strong bonds

### Combustion of alkanes

Alkanes burn easily, releasing energy (exothermic). They are used as fuels in industry, the home and in transport.

Complete combustion of alkanes in an excess of oxygen produces carbon dioxide and water.

$$C_2H_6 + 3\tfrac{1}{2}O_2 \rightarrow 2CO_2 + 3H_2O$$

Incomplete combustion of alkanes in a limited supply of oxygen produces carbon monoxide and water.

$$C_2H_6 + 2\tfrac{1}{2}O_2 \rightarrow 2CO + 3H_2O$$

Carbon monoxide is poisonous, so it is essential that hydrocarbon fuels are burnt in a plentiful supply of oxygen. Cars are fitted with catalytic converters to ensure that the amount of carbon monoxide emitted is reduced.

## Reactions of alkanes

REVISED

When describing the reactions of any functional group you are expected to know the reagents, the conditions and to be able to write both a balanced equation and the mechanism.

### Reaction between methane and bromine

Reagent: bromine

Conditions: ultraviolet light

Equation: $CH_4 + Br_2 \rightarrow CH_3Br + HBr$

Mechanism: radical substitution

Initiation: $Br_2 \rightarrow 2Br\bullet$

Propagation 1: $CH_4 + Br\bullet \rightarrow HBr + \bullet CH_3$

Propagation 2: $\bullet CH_3 + Br_2 \rightarrow CH_3Br + Br\bullet$

Termination: $\bullet CH_3 + \bullet CH_3 \rightarrow C_2H_6$ *or* $\bullet CH_3 + Br\bullet \rightarrow CH_3Br$

There are three distinct stages to the mechanism:

1 **Initiation** — radicals are generated. The ultraviolet light provides sufficient energy to break the Br–Br bond **homolytically** and generates radicals:

$Br_2 \rightarrow 2Br\bullet$

2 **Propagation** — involves two steps, each of which maintains the radical concentration. Usually a chlorine or bromine radical is swapped for an alkyl radical or vice versa (Figure 6.9).

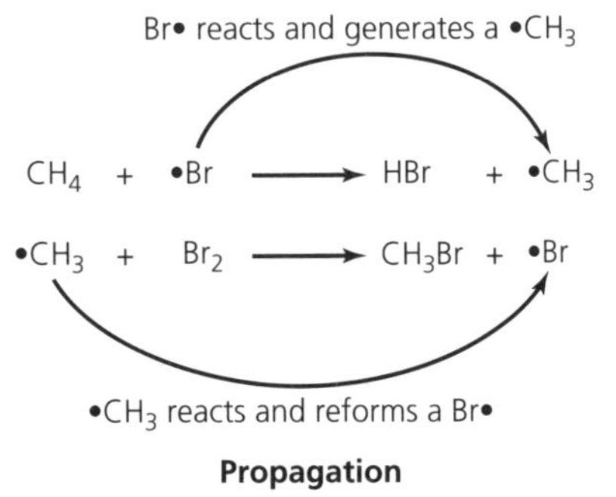


**Figure 6.9**

3 **Termination** — involves the loss of radicals:

$\bullet CH_3 + \bullet CH_3 \rightarrow C_2H_6$

Radical reactions have limitations. It is almost impossible to produce a single product because radicals are very reactive and it is difficult to avoid multiple substitutions of the hydrogen atoms in the alkane. For the reaction between $CH_4$ and $Cl_2$ the product would typically contain $CH_3Cl$, $CH_2Cl_2$, $CHCl_3$ and $CCl_4$. This makes separation difficult and costly.

**Typical mistake**

Students often get the first propagation step incorrect, which in turn means they will also lose a mark for the second propagation step. When asked to describe the mechanism for the reaction between butane and bromine, typical mistakes include:

1st propagation step $Br\bullet + C_4H_{10} \rightarrow C_4H_9Br + H\bullet$

2nd propagation step $H\bullet + Br_2 \rightarrow HBr + Br\bullet$

The first step should always produce HBr and the second should always make the product and regenerate the halide radical. The correct equations are:

1st propagation step $Br\bullet + C_4H_{10} \rightarrow HBr + C_4H_9\bullet$

2nd propagation step $C_4H_9\bullet + Br_2 \rightarrow C_4H_9Br + Br\bullet$

**Exam tip**

Remember that the first propagation step *always* produces a hydrocarbon radical ($\bullet C_nH_{2n+1}$) and HBr (or HCl).

**Homolysis** or **homolytic fission** occurs when a covalent bond is broken (fission) and each atom involved in the covalent bond takes one of the electrons from the bonded pair. This results in the formation of two radicals, for example:

$Cl\text{–}Cl \rightarrow Cl\bullet + Cl\bullet$

**Exam tip**

There are three mechanisms in the specification and each exam usually tests at least two. Make sure that you know them well.

**Revision activity**

On a postcard write a summary of the reactions of alkanes. Use pentane to illustrate the reactions/mechanisms.

## Now test yourself

TESTED

4 Calculate the formulae of alkanes A and B.
   (a) 100 cm$^3$ of alkane A was burnt in excess $O_2(g)$. It produced 300 cm$^3$ $CO_2(g)$ and 400 cm$^3$ $H_2O(g)$.
   (b) When burnt in excess $O_2(g)$, 0.1 mol of alkane B produced 10.8 g $H_2O(l)$.
5 Write the balanced equation and the mechanism for the reaction between cyclobutane and chlorine. Explain each of the following terms: radical; homolytic fission; initiation; propagation; termination and substitution.

Answers on p. 214

# Alkenes

Alkenes and cycloalkenes are unsaturated hydrocarbons and contain at least one C=C double bond. The double bond is made up of σ-bonds and a π-bond.

A **σ-bond** is a single covalent bond made up of two shared electrons with the electron density concentrated between the two nuclei.

A **π-bond** is formed by the sideways overlap of two adjacent *p*-orbitals (Figure 6.10).

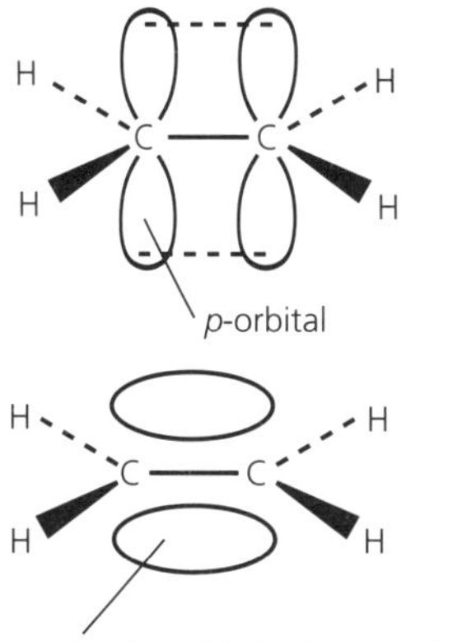


π molecular orbitals above and below the plane of the molecule

**Figure 6.10**

### Typical mistake

When asked to describe, with the aid of a diagram, how the π-bond is formed in an alkene, students often draw the following, which shows a treble (not double) bond between the two carbons:

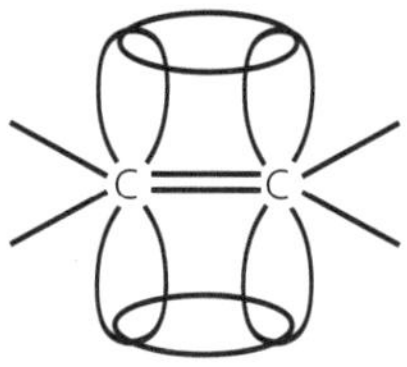


The correct response is:

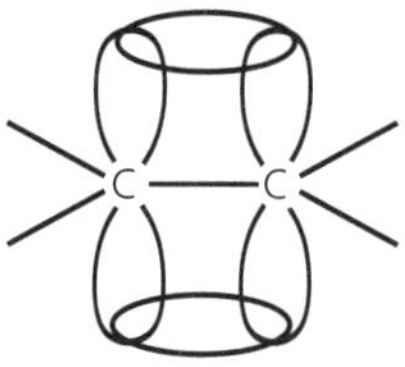


The bond angle on each side of the C=C double bond is approximately 120° (usually in the region 116–124°) which results in a trigonal planar structure (Figure 6.11).

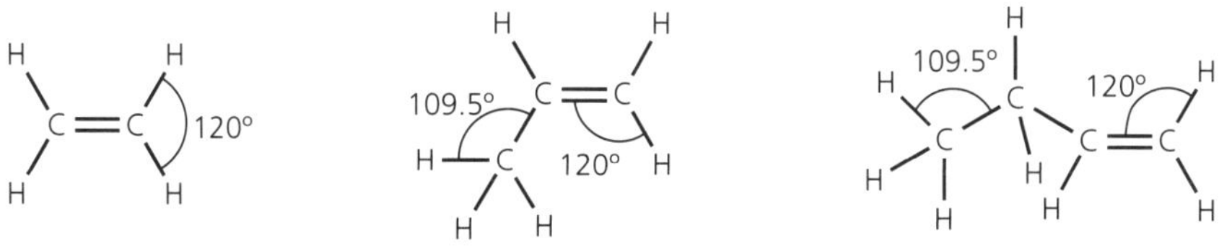


**Figure 6.11**

The C=C double bond prevents freedom of rotation, which under certain circumstances can lead to the existence of *E*/*Z* isomers.

The C=C double bond ensures that there is restricted rotation about the bond and the different atoms or groups attached to each carbon atom ensure that there is no symmetry around the carbon atoms in the C=C double bond (Figure 6.12).

But-1-ene and but-2-ene both have a C=C double bond but the right-hand carbon atom in the C=C double bond in but-1-ene is bonded to two hydrogen atoms and therefore does not exhibit *E*/*Z* isomerism. But-2-ene possesses both essential key features and hence has a *Z*- and an *E*-isomer (Figure 6.13).

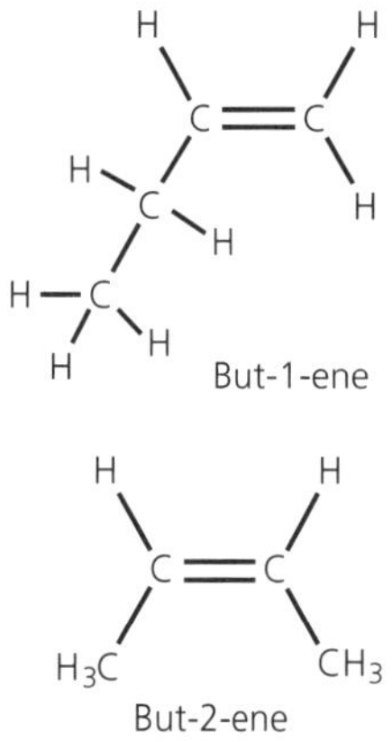


**Figure 6.12**

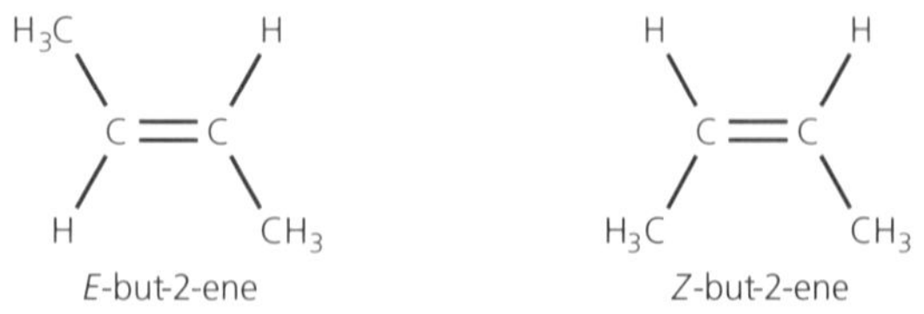
E-but-2-ene
Z-but-2-ene

*E/Z* isomers have a different geometry or 3D shape: this can be seen clearly when they are drawn as skeletal formulae

E-but-2-ene
Z-but-2-ene

**Figure 6.13**

> **Exam tip**
>
> To recognise *E/Z* isomers, ask yourself two simple questions:
> - Is the substance an alkene?
> - Is each carbon atom in the C=C double bond bonded to two different atoms or groups?

## Cahn, Ingold and Prelog rules

REVISED

The Cahn, Ingold and Prelog (CIP) rules enable you to decide whether you should name each isomer as an *E*-isomer or *a Z*-isomer. The atomic number of each atom bonded to the C in the C=C double bond determines whether or not it is an *E* isomer or a *Z* isomer:

- If the two attached atoms with the highest atomic numbers are on the diagonally opposite sides of the double bonds it is an *E*-isomer.
- If the two attached atoms with the highest atomic numbers are *not* diagonally opposite each other across the double bonds it is a *Z*-isomer.

**Example**

In a compound like $CH_3(Cl)C{=}CHOH$ (Figure 6.14), the C on the left-hand side of the C=C double bond is bonded to a Cl (atomic number 17) and a C (atomic number 6), while the C on the right-hand side is bonded to an H (atomic number 1) and an O (atomic number 8).

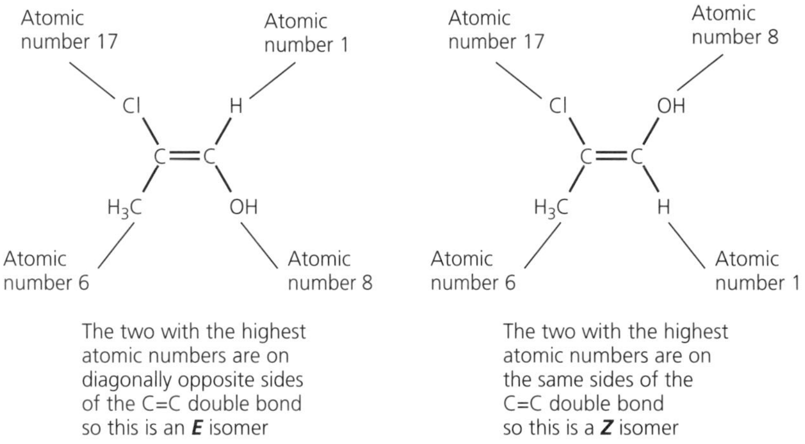
Atomic number 17
Atomic number 1
Atomic number 6
Atomic number 8
The two with the highest atomic numbers are on diagonally opposite sides of the C=C double bond so this is an E isomer
Atomic number 17
Atomic number 8
Atomic number 6
Atomic number 1
The two with the highest atomic numbers are on the same sides of the C=C double bond so this is a Z isomer

Figure 6.14

- If two attached atoms have the same atomic number then the adjacent atoms with the highest atomic number are taken into account. This occurs with attached alkyl groups such that $CH_3CH_2CH_2 >$ $CH_3CH_2 > CH_3$.

**Example**

In Figure 6.15 the C atom on the right of the C=C bond is bonded to two carbon atoms, each with atomic number 6. It is still possible to have *E/Z* isomers by considering the adjacent atoms: $CH_3$ has a mass of 15 and $CH_3CH_2$ has a mass of 29. It follows that the isomer on the left is the *Z*-stereoisomer and the isomer on the right is the *E*-isomer.

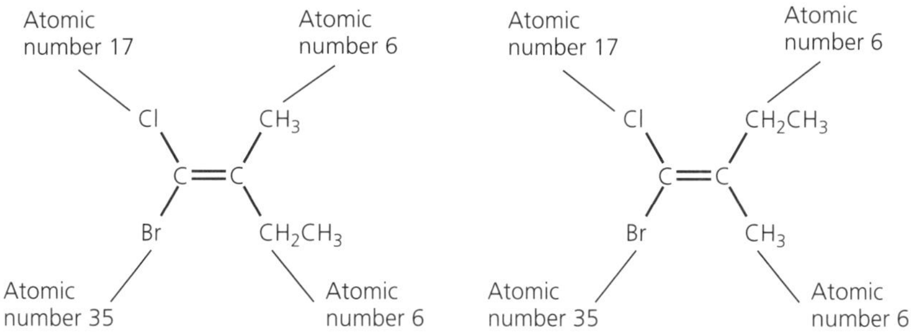


Figure 6.15

*Cis-trans* isomerism is a special case of *E/Z* isomerism in which two of the substituent groups attached to each carbon atom of the C=C group are the same.

## Now test yourself

TESTED

6 Draw and name the isomers of $C_6H_{14}$. Explain which isomers have the lowest boiling point.
7 Explain, using compounds of $C_4H_8$, what is meant by isomerism. Include in your answer structural isomerism and *E/Z* isomerism.

Answers on p. 214

## Addition reactions of alkenes

REVISED

The C=C double bond is an unsaturated bond and therefore undergoes addition reactions. Essentially, the double bond opens and an atom or group adds to each of the carbons. The general reaction can be summarised as shown in Figure 6.16.

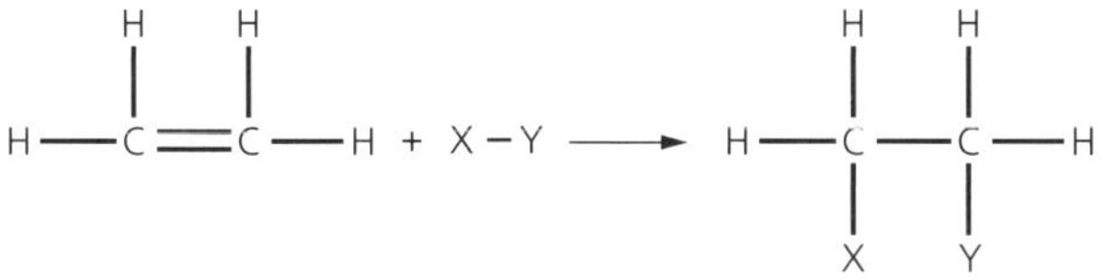


**Figure 6.16**

When preparing for examinations it is good practice to try to stick to a routine. For most organic reactions it is useful to know:

- reagents
- conditions (if any)
- observations (if any)
- balanced equations

The reactions of ethene are summarised in Figure 6.17.

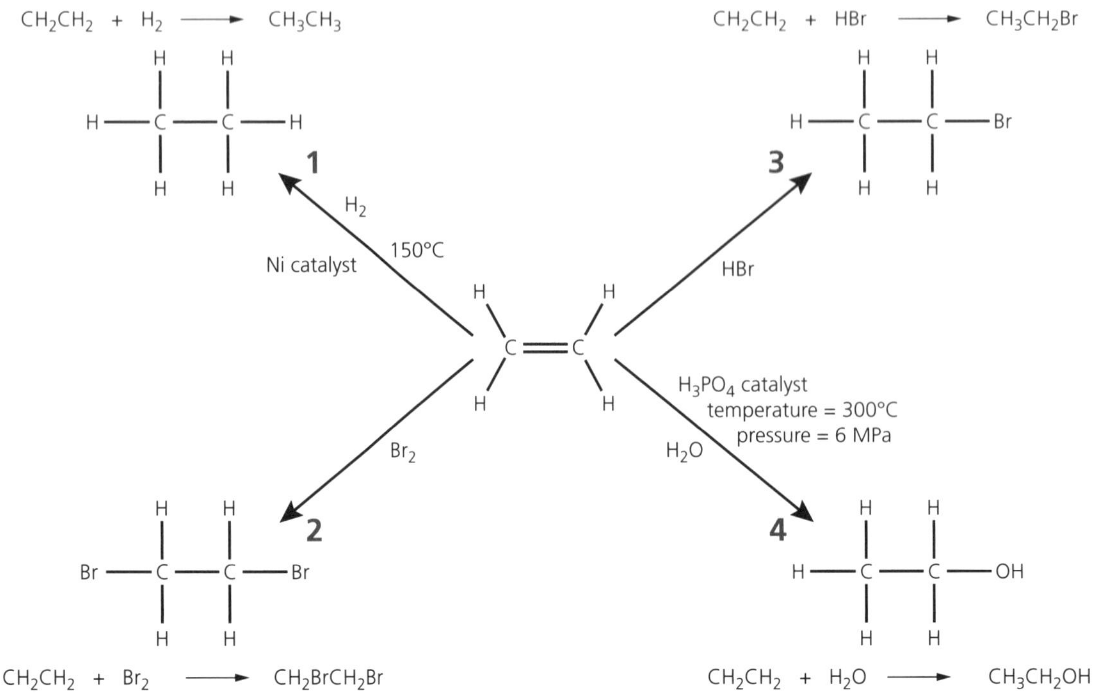


**Figure 6.17**

In the flow diagram:

- Reaction 1 is **hydrogenation**. It is used to produce margarine by reacting polyunsaturated vegetable oils, derived from plants, with hydrogen.
- Reaction 2 is **bromination**. It is used as a test for alkenes. The brown colour of the bromine fades and the reaction mixture becomes colourless.
- Reaction 3 is the **formation of haloalkanes**. The HBr is made *in situ* from NaBr + $H_2SO_4$.
- Reaction 4 is **hydration**. Ethene reacts with steam in the presence of a suitable acid catalyst to produce ethanol.

All other alkenes undergo similar reactions under similar conditions.

**Typical mistake**

When asked to describe what you would see when bromine reacts with an alkene, many students lose the mark by stating that the bromine would go 'clear'. Clear is the wrong word — bromine is already clear, it is a clear red-brown liquid. When it reacts it loses its colour (becomes decolorised).

**Typical mistake**

When drawing alcohols you have to be careful how you draw the bond to the hydroxyl (OH) group. It is easy to lose the mark, as shown in Figure 6.18a and 6.18b. Figure 6.18c shows how it should be drawn.

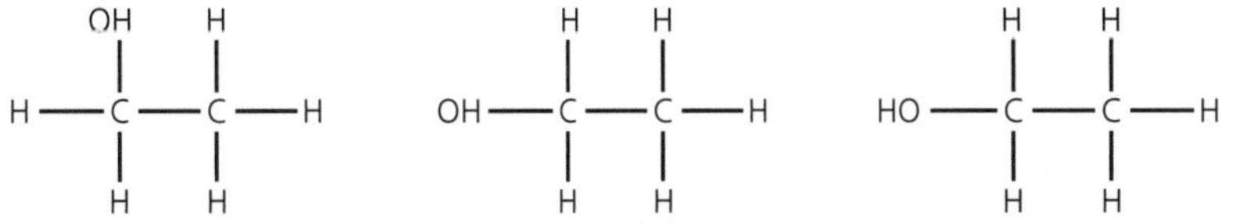

a b c

**Figure 6.18**

## Now test yourself

TESTED

8 (a) Write a balanced equation for each of the following:
 (i) the *complete* combustion of propene
 (ii) the reaction between but-1-ene and hydrogen
 (iii) hydration of but-2-ene
(b) Write an equation for the reaction between buta-1,3-diene and bromine. State what you would observe and name the organic product.
(c) Explain why the hydration of but-2-ene gives only one organic product but the hydration of but-1-ene gives two organic products.

Answer on p. 215

## Electrophilic addition

REVISED

Mechanisms involving electrophiles and nucleophiles involve the movement of electron pairs. This movement is shown by the use of curly arrows. The curly arrow always points from an area that is electron rich to an area that is electron deficient.

When describing mechanisms it is essential that you show:

- relevant dipoles
- lone pairs
- curly arrows

Alkenes, such as ethene, undergo electrophilic addition reactions. An electrophile is an electron pair acceptor that results in the formation of a covalent bond.

The mechanism of the reaction between ethene and bromine is shown in Figure 6.19.

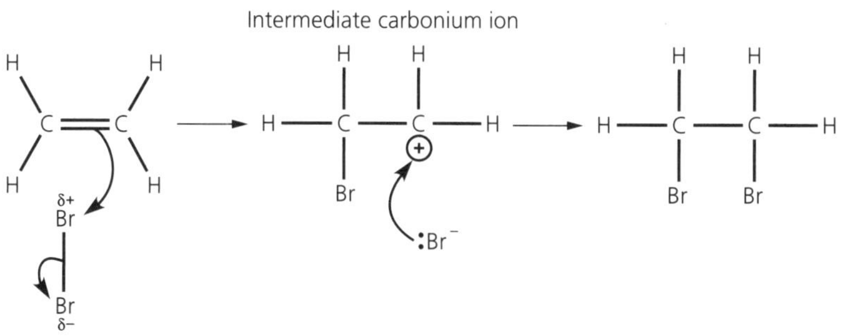


**Figure 6.19**

The key features of the mechanism are:

1 When the Br–Br approaches the ethene a temporary induced dipole is formed resulting in $Br^{\delta+}$–$Br^{\delta-}$.
2 The initial curly arrow starts at the π-bond (within the C=C double bond) and points to the $Br^{\delta+}$.
3 The second curly arrow shows the movement of the bonded pair of electrons in the Br–Br to the $Br^{\delta-}$ resulting in **heterolytic fission** of the Br–Br bond.
4 The formation of an intermediate carbonium ion (also called a carbocation) and a $:Br^-$ ion that now has the pair of electrons that were in the Br–Br bond occurs.
5 The third curly arrow from the $:Br^-$ to the positively charged carbonium ion results in the formation of 1,2-dibromoethane.

**Heterolysis** or **heterolytic fission** occurs when a covalent bond is broken (fission). One of the atoms receives both of the electrons from the covalent bond. This results in the formation of two oppositely charged ions. An example is $Cl{-}Cl \rightarrow Cl^+ + Cl^-$

## Now test yourself

TESTED

9 (a) Explain what is meant by an *electrophile*.
(b) Write a balanced equation for the reaction between $Br_2$ and cyclohexene and give the mechanism. Use curly arrows to show the movement of electrons. Show any relevant dipoles and lone pairs of electrons.
(c) When bromine reacts with an alkene, the Br–Br bond undergoes heterolytic fission (Figure 6.20).

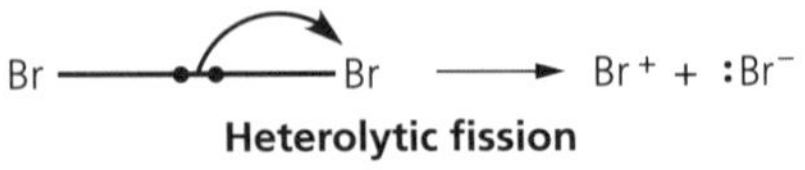


Figure 6.20

Compare this with the way the Br–Br bond is broken when bromine reacts with an alkane.

Answer on p. 215

### Exam tip

Mechanisms are generally well understood, but it is easy to lose marks by rushing and/or being careless. Look at the mechanism for the reaction between propene and bromine (Figure 6.21). At first glance it looks good, but there are *seven* errors or omissions. Can you spot all seven?

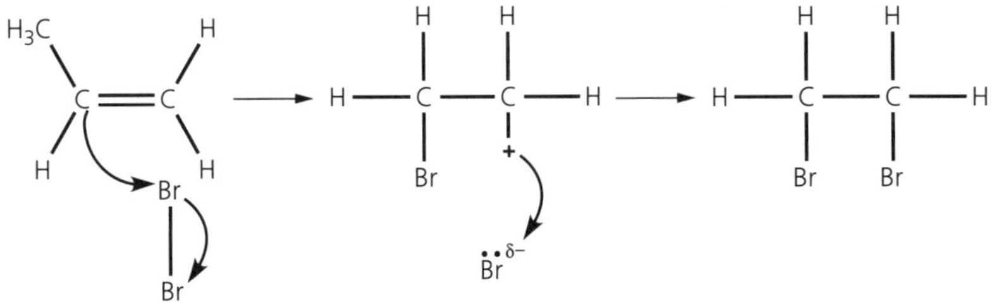


**Figure 6.21**

If you spot the mistakes made by others, it should prevent you from making the same mistakes.

When reacted with either HBr or $H_2O$, **unsymmetrical** alkenes, for example propene, produce a mixture of two isomers:

- Reaction of propene with HBr:

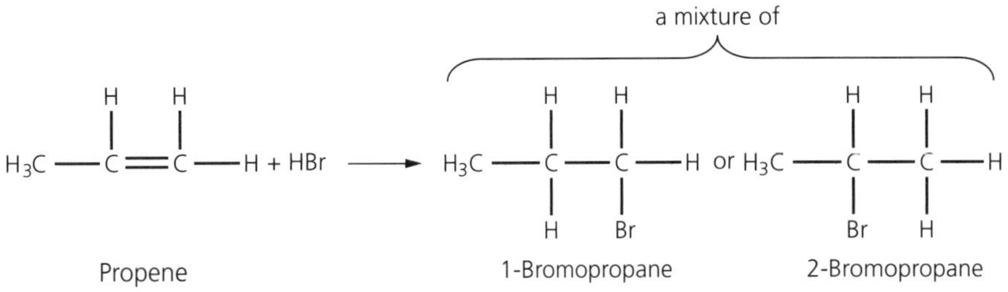


- Reaction of propene with $H_2O$:

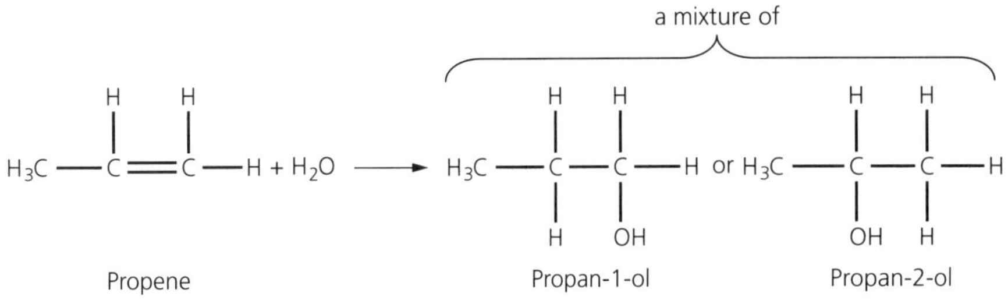

When either HBr or $H_2O$ reacts with an unsymmetrical alkene, the major product can be predicted using **Markownikoff's rule**.

For example, if propene, $CH_3CH{=}CH_2$, reacts with HBr, the *addent other than hydrogen* is Br and this will bond to the C in the C=C double bond with the lowest number of Hs. The Br will therefore bond to the CH (it only has one H) and not the $CH_2$ (Figure 6.22).

**Markownikoff's rule** states that the addent other than hydrogen goes to the least hydrogenated carbon.

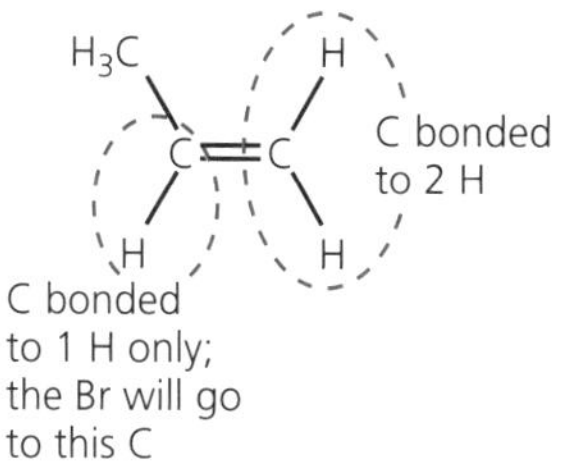


**Figure 6.22**

Considering the mechanism in detail, there are two alternatives (Figure 6.23).

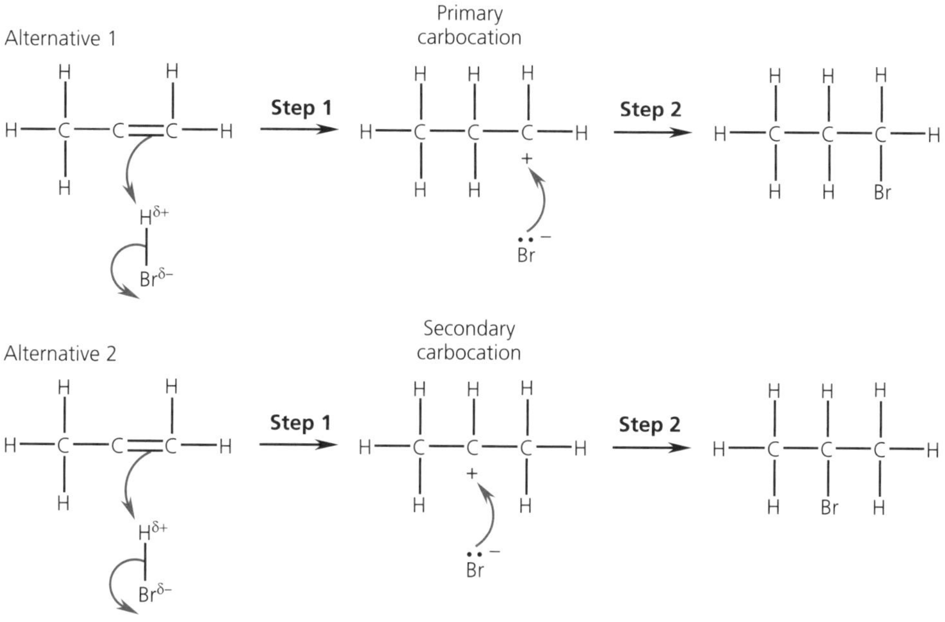


**Figure 6.23**

The product depends on the relative stabilities of the carbocation intermediates in the mechanism:

| | | | | | | |
|---|---|---|---|---|---|---|
| **Most stable** | **tertiary carbocation** | > | **secondary carbocation** | > | **primary carbocation** | **Least stable** |

The more stable the carbocation intermediate, the more likely it will result in the product such that 'alternative 2' in Figure 6.23 is the favoured mechanism, forming 2-bromopropane.

**Revision activity**

On two postcards use but-2-ene and but-1-ene to devise two spider diagrams for the reactions of alkenes.

## Addition polymerisation of alkenes

REVISED

Alkenes can undergo an addition reaction in which one alkene molecule joins to others and a long molecular chain is built up. The individual alkene molecule is a **monomer** and the long-chain molecule is called a **polymer**.

Some common monomers and their reactions are shown in Figure 6.24. $n$ represents a large number and can be as big as 10 000.

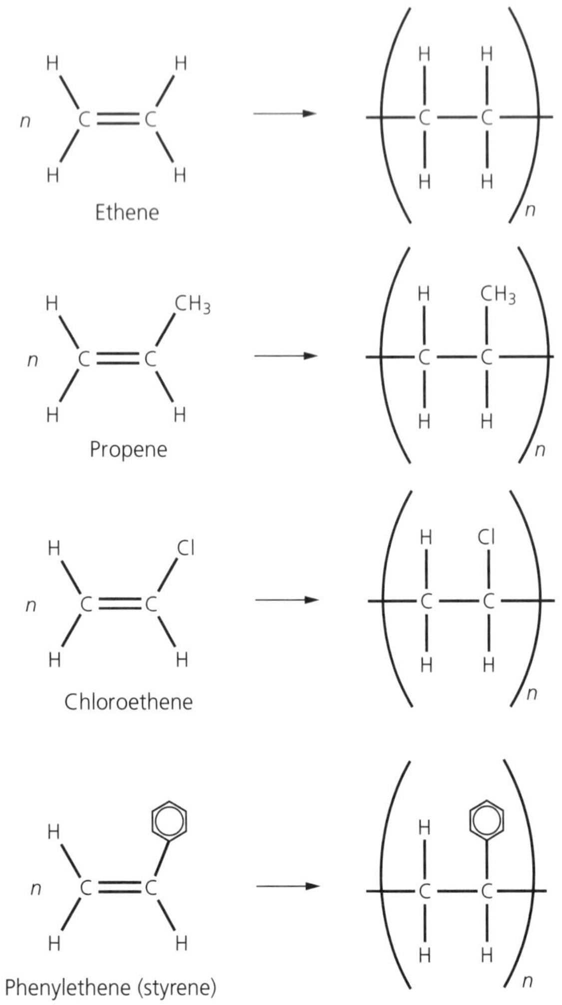


**Figure 6.24**

It is possible to deduce the repeat unit of an addition polymer and identify the monomer from which the polymer was produced (Figure 6.25).

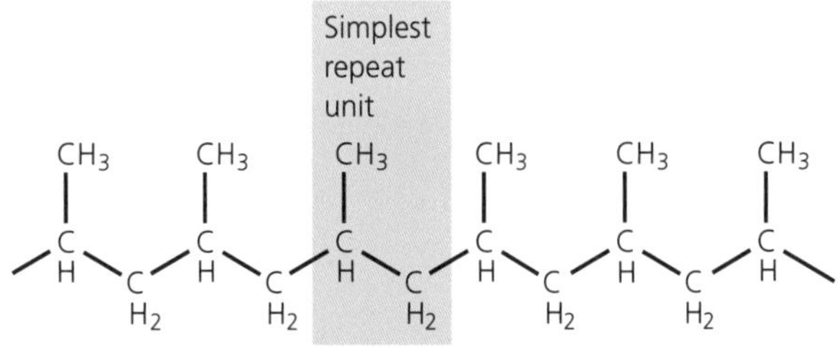


**Figure 6.25**

**Typical mistake**

When asked to draw two repeat units of the polymer formed from propene, a common incorrect response is:

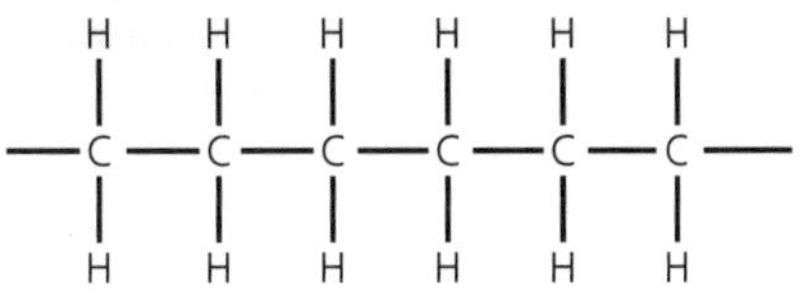

when it should be

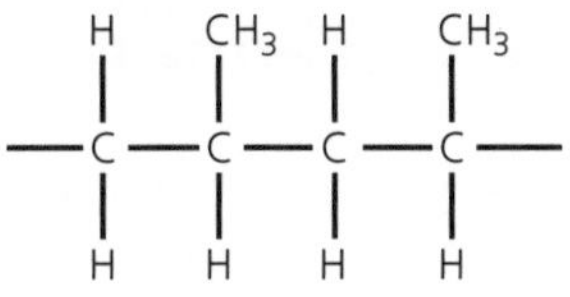

It is worth remembering that two repeat units of any addition polymer will always have a central backbone containing four carbon atoms.

## Now test yourself

TESTED

10 Alkenes can undergo addition polymerisation. Write an equation to show the polymerisation of but-1-ene. Draw two repeat units of the polymer.

Answer on p. 215

Polymers are an essential part of everyday life and have a wide variety of uses.

**Table 6.2** Uses of polymers

| Polymer | Uses |
|---|---|
| Poly(ethene) | Bags, insulation of electrical cables, bottles |
| Poly(propene) | Food boxes, clothing, ropes, carpets |
| Poly(chloroethene) — unplasticised | Water pipes, credit cards, window frames |
| Poly(chloroethene) — plasticised | Raincoats, shower curtains, packaging films |
| Poly(phenylethene) | Styrofoam cups, fast-food containers, refrigerator insulation, packaging, telephones, flowerpots |

The widespread use of these polymers has created a major disposal problem. The bonds in addition polymers are strong, non-polar covalent bonds, making most polymers resistant to chemical attack. As they are not broken down by bacteria, they are often referred to as being **non-biodegradable**.

Plastic waste is usually buried in landfill sites where it remains unchanged for decades. This means that local authorities have to find more and more landfill sites.

Alternatives to using landfill sites include:

- **incineration** Polymers are hydrocarbon based and are therefore potentially good fuels. When burnt, they release useful energy. Some plastics, such as PVC, also produce toxic gases (e.g. HCl) and the incinerators have to be fitted with gas-scrubbers.
- **recycling** Polymers can be recycled and used as feedstock for the production of new polymers. Different types of polymers have to be separated because recycling a mixture of polymers would produce an inferior plastic product.

**Biodegradable** polymers offer a better solution. Chemists are working to try and develop new polymers that have suitable properties. The aim is to create a polymer that contains an active functional group that can be attacked by bacteria. Other options are based on condensation polymers, which you will meet if you study chemistry at A2.

## Exam practice

1 (a) Ethane, $C_2H_6$, reacts with $Cl_2$ in the presence of sunlight to form a mixture of chlorinated products. One possible product is $C_2H_4Cl_2$.

(i) State the type of mechanism involved in this reaction. [1]

(ii) The initiation step involves the homolytic fission of the Cl–Cl bond. What is meant by the term *homolytic fission*? [1]

(iii) Name the two possible isomers of $C_2H_4Cl_2$. [2]

(b) When $C_2H_4Cl_2$ is treated with aqueous NaOH, it undergoes substitution reactions to form both $C_2H_4(OH)Cl$ and $C_2H_4(OH)_2$.

(i) State, and explain, the role of the $OH^-(aq)$ in these reactions. [2]

(ii) Draw two possible isomers of $C_2H_4(OH)_2$ [2]

2 (a) Steroids are compounds that contain four rings. Cholesterol is a steroid and it has the following percentage composition by mass: C, 83.93%; H, 11.92%; O, 4.15%.

Show that this is consistent with the molecular formula $C_{27}H_{46}O$ and that cholesterol has a relative molecular mass of 386. [3]

(b) Cholesterol has the structure shown in Figure 6.26. **R** represents an alkyl group.

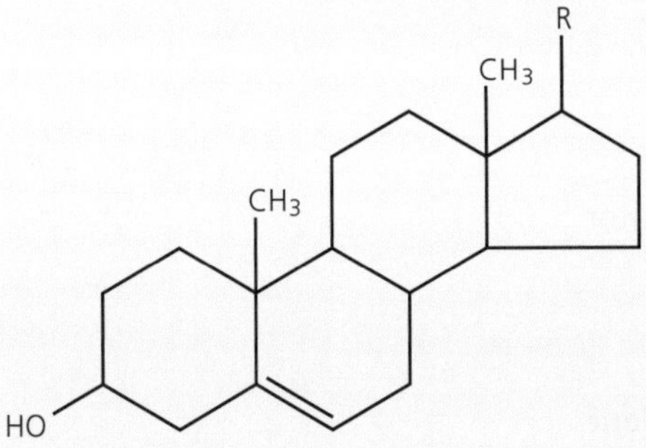


**Figure 6.26**

Identify the *two* functional groups present in cholesterol. [2]

(c) All of the compounds shown in Figure 6.27 have similar structures to cholesterol.

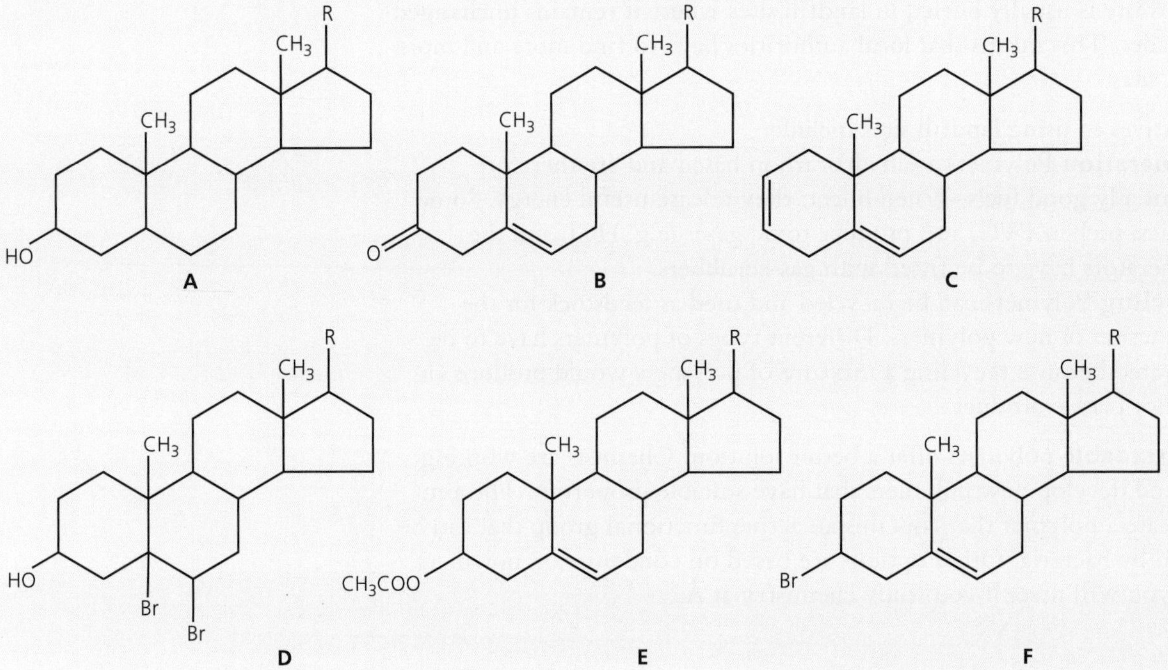


**Figure 6.27**

Suggest, by letter, which compound(s) might be made by reacting cholesterol with each of the following. Each letter may be used once, more than once or not at all.

(i) bromine
(ii) ethanoic acid
(iii) hydrogen
(iv) acidified dichromate(VI) ions
(v) concentrated sulfuric acid at about 170°C [5]

3 (a) The hydrocarbons in crude oil can be separated by fractional distillation. Explain what is meant by the terms:

(i) hydrocarbons [1]
(ii) fractional distillation [1]

(b) Dodecane, $C_{12}H_{26}$, can be isolated by fractional distillation.

(i) Calculate the percentage composition by mass of carbon in dodecane. [2]
(ii) Dodecane can be cracked into octane and ethene only. Write a balanced equation for this reaction. [1]

(c) Isomerisation of octane produces a mixture of isomers.

(i) Name the isomers of $C_8H_{18}$.

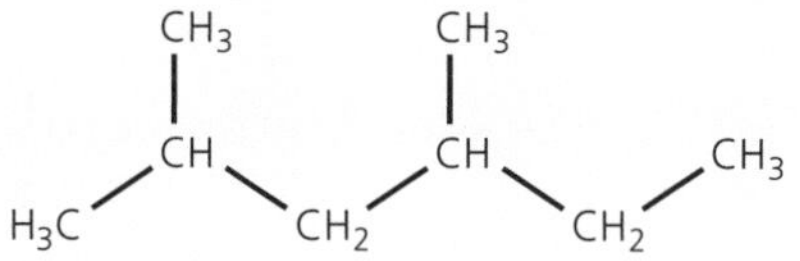


**A**

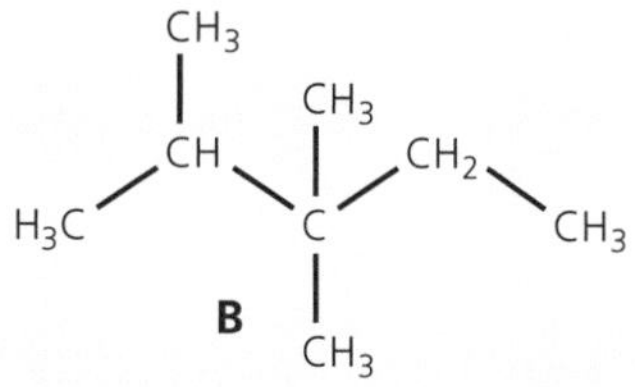


**B**

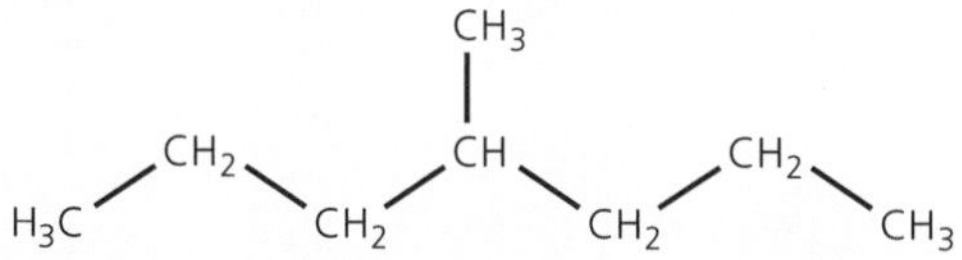


**C**

(ii) Isomers, **A**, **B** and **C** can be separated by fractional distillation. State the order, lowest boiling point first, in which they would distil. [1]
(iii) Justify the order stated in c(ii). [2]
(iv) Write a balanced equation for the *complete* combustion of octane, $C_8H_{18}$. [2]
(v) Why do oil companies isomerise alkanes such as octane? [1]

4 The fractions from crude oil are processed further by cracking, reforming and isomerisation. Outline, with the aid of suitable examples and equations, each of these processes. Explain the industrial importance of each process. [7]

## Answers and quick quiz 6 online

ONLINE

## Summary

You should now have an understanding of:

- the various ways in which organic formulae can be represented
- isomerism
- calculations used in organic chemistry
- key terms used in organic chemistry
- bonding, shape and boiling points of alkanes
- hydrocarbons as fuels including fractional distillation, cracking, isomerisation and reforming
- reactions of alkanes
- radical substitution mechanism
- bonding and shape of alkenes
- isomerism, including *E*/*Z* isomers
- addition reactions
- electrophilic addition mechanism
- Markownikoff addition
- polymerisation and the environmental aspects of disposal of waste polymers

# 7 Alcohols, haloalkanes and analysis

## Alcohols

### Classes of alcohol

REVISED

Alcohols all contain the hydroxy group, −OH, and all end in '-ol'. Alcohols can be classified as primary, secondary or tertiary.

Using 'R' to represent any other attachment, we can identify the nature of the alcohol:

Primary alcohols all contain:

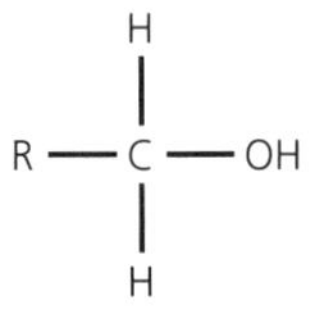

Secondary alcohols all contain:

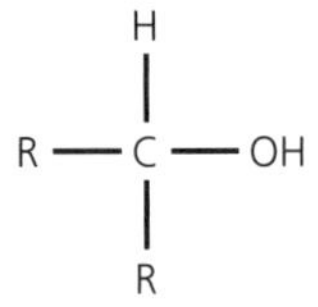

Tertiary alcohols all contain:

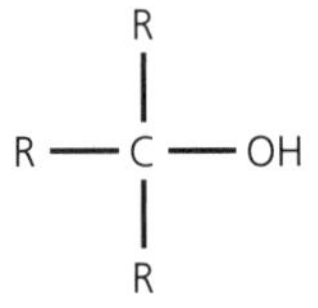

Examples of each type of alcohol are shown in Figure 7.1.

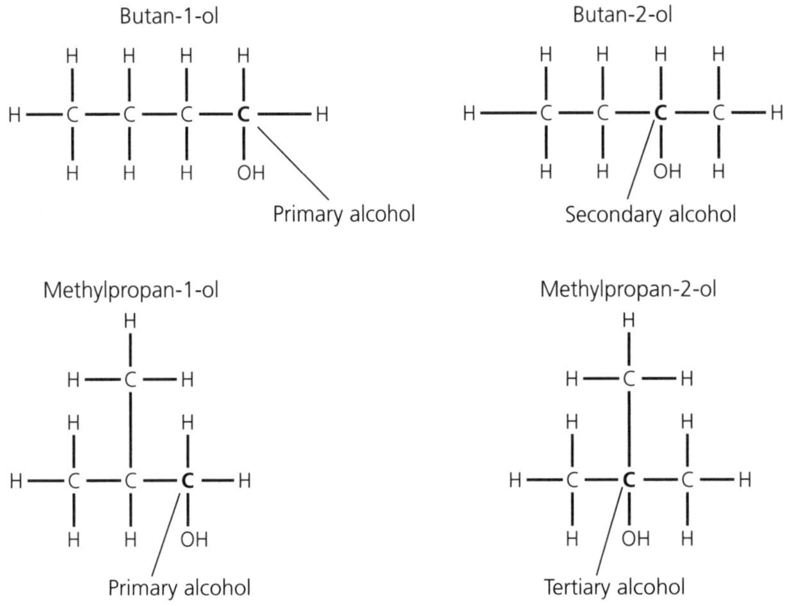


**Figure 7.1**

## Properties of alcohols

REVISED

Alcohols have relatively high boiling points. Hydrogen bonding decreases the volatility and, therefore, results in an increase in boiling point.

Methanol and ethanol are freely miscible with water. When mixed, some of the hydrogen bonds in the individual liquids are broken, but they are then replaced by new hydrogen bonds between the alcohol and water. Miscibility with water decreases with increasing relative molecular mass of the alcohol (Figure 7.2).

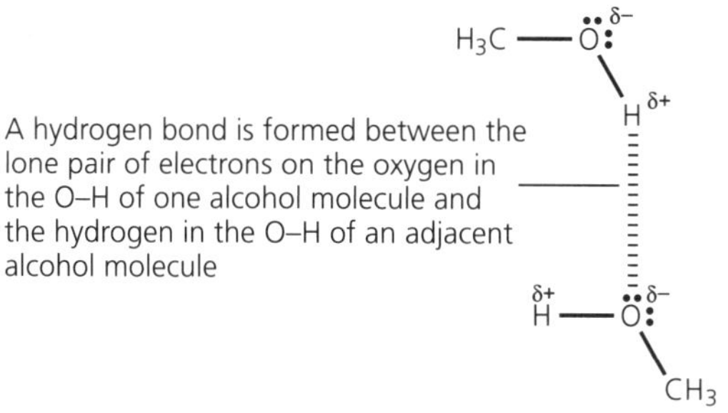


Figure 7.2

**Exam tip**

All alcohols can be represented by the formula R–OH, where R is the alkyl group. It follows that hydrogen bonding in any alcohol can be shown by drawing:

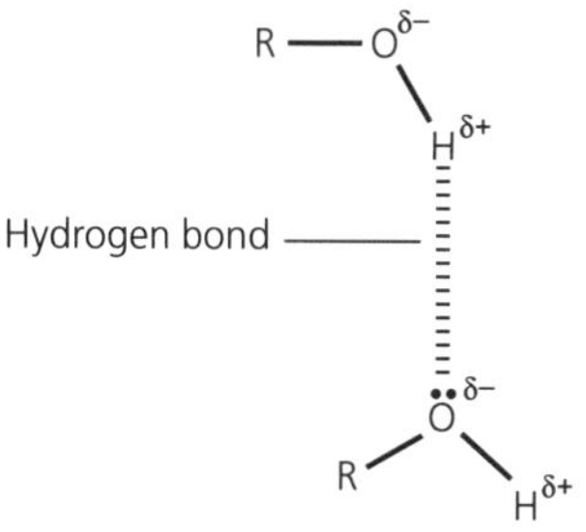


### Now test yourself

TESTED

1 Name each of the alcohols in Figure 7.3.

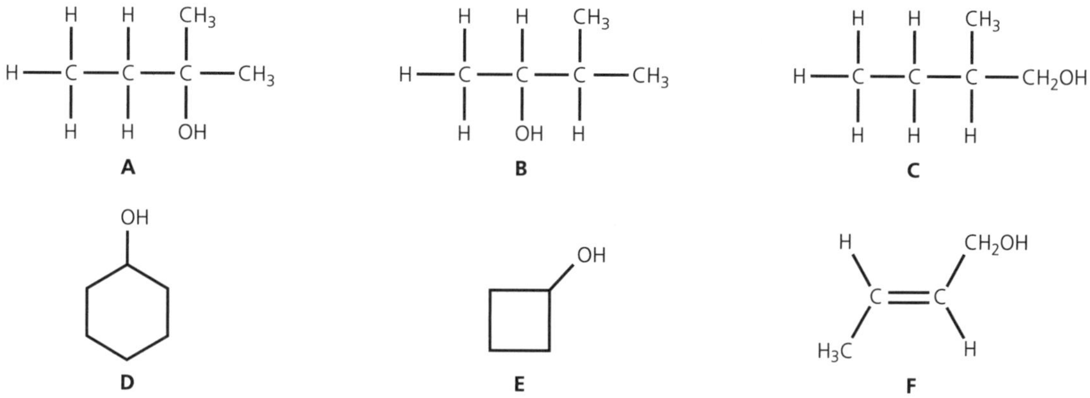


Figure 7.3

Answer on p. 215

## Reactions of alcohols

REVISED

### Combustion

Alcohols burn to produce carbon dioxide and water:

$$C_2H_5OH + 3O_2 \rightarrow 2CO_2 + 3H_2O$$

### Oxidation

Alcohols are oxidised using the oxidising mixture $Cr_2O_7^{2-}/H^+$ (e.g. $K_2Cr_2O_7/H_2SO_4$). Oxidation reactions differ depending on the classification of the alcohol.

Each oxidation reaction is accompanied by a distinctive colour change from orange to green. Balanced equations for the oxidation reactions are

**Exam tip**

When writing equations for the combustion of alcohols many students forget about the O in the alcohol and write the equation for ethanol as:

$$C_2H_5OH + 3\tfrac{1}{2}O_2 \rightarrow 2CO_2 + 3H_2O$$

rather than:

$$C_2H_5OH + 3O_2 \rightarrow 2CO_2 + 3H_2O$$

written using [O] to represent the oxidising agent. Water is always formed as a co-product.

When oxidising a primary alcohol, the choice of apparatus is important. **Refluxing** produces a carboxylic acid; **distillation** produces an aldehyde.

**Oxidation of a primary alcohol to an aldehyde** — the more volatile aldehyde is separated out during the distillation process. An example is:

$CH_3OH + [O] \rightarrow HCHO + H_2O$

**Methanol** **Methanal**

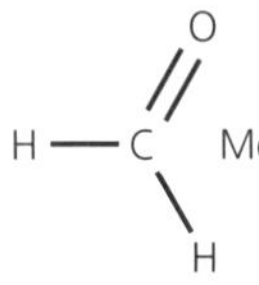

Methanal

**Oxidation of a primary alcohol to a carboxylic acid** — refluxing is used to ensure that volatile components (such as the aldehyde) do not escape and to ensure complete oxidation. An example is:

$CH_3CH_2OH + 2[O] \rightarrow CH_3COOH + H_2O$

**Ethanol** **Ethanoic acid**

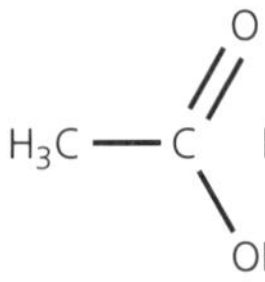

Ethanoic acid

Oxidation of a secondary alcohol to a ketone — either reflux or distillation can be used because a ketone is the only product, for example:

$CH_3CHOHCH_3 + [O] \rightarrow CH_3COCH_3 + H_2O$

**Propan-2-ol** **Propan-2-one**

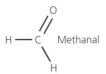

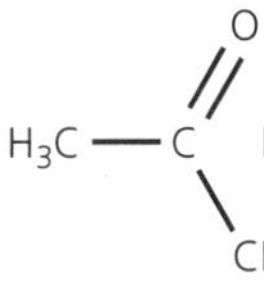

Propanone

**Typical mistake**

Oxidation of a primary alcohol to form a carboxylic acid is often incorrectly shown as:

$CH_3CH_2OH + [O] \rightarrow CH_3COOH + H_2$

which looks good as the symbols balance, *but* it is important to remember that water is *always* formed and the equation should be:

$CH_3CH_2OH + 2[O] \rightarrow CH_3COOH + H_2O$

## Dehydration (or elimination)

An alcohol reacts with hot concentrated sulfuric acid or hot pumice/ $Al_2O_3$ to form an alkene and water (Figure 7.4).

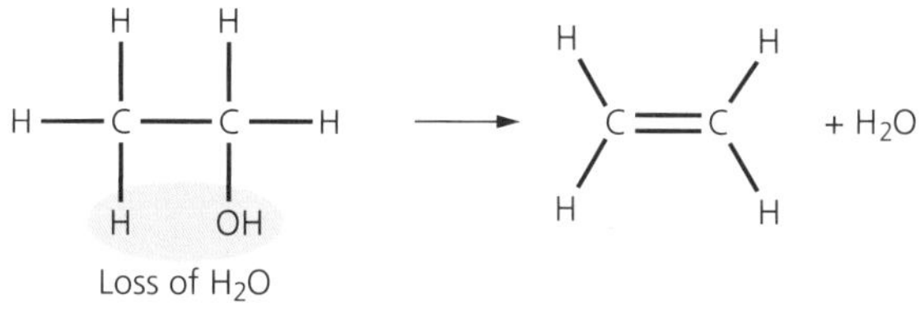


For alcohols like butan-2-ol it is possible to lose water in two ways:

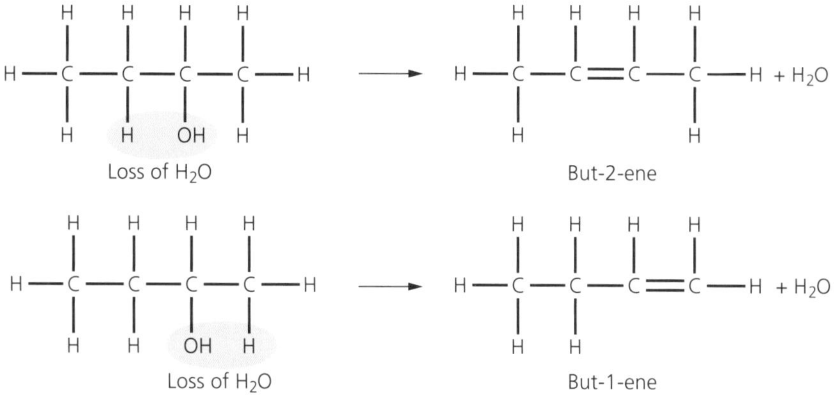


**Figure 7.4**

## Substitution with halide ions

An alcohol reacts with halide ions ($Cl^-$, $Br^-$ or $I^-$) in the presence of an acid to form haloalkanes:

$$H_3C\text{-}OH \xrightarrow[H_2SO_4]{NaBr} H_3C\text{-}Br$$

This can be represented by the equation:

$$H_3C\text{-}OH + Br^- \rightarrow H_3C\text{-}Br + H_2O$$

**Revision activity**

On three postcards use propan-1-ol, propan-2-ol and 2-methylpropan-2-ol and devise spider diagrams of the reactions of alcohols.

There is one other important reaction of alcohols. All alcohols — primary, secondary and tertiary — can react with carboxylic acids to form esters. This is covered fully in the second year of the A-level course. The equation for the formation of an ester is given in Figure 7.5.

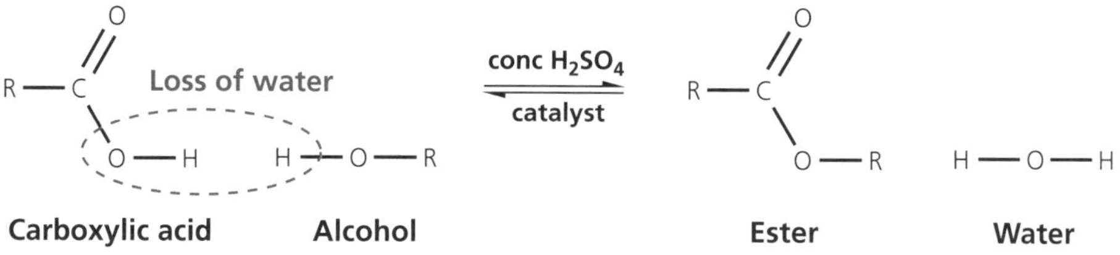


**Figure 7.5**

## Now test yourself

TESTED

2 Write a balanced equation for each of the following:
 (a) the complete combustion of propan-1-ol
 (b) the dehydration of pentan-3-ol
 (c) the oxidation of butan-2-ol (use [O] to represent the oxidising agent)
3 Explain what is meant by the terms *reflux* and *distillation*.
4 Explain, with the aid of equations, why the dehydration of pentan-3-ol gives one alkene but the dehydration of pentan-2-ol gives a mixture of three alkenes.

Answers on p. 215

# Haloalkanes

## Classification of haloalkanes

REVISED

Like alcohols, haloalkanes are subdivided into primary, secondary and tertiary. The rules for classification are the same. If the carbon atom that is bonded to the halogen (X) is bonded to one other carbon atom only, then the compound is a primary haloalkane. If the carbon atom in the C–X bond is bonded to two other carbon atoms, the compound is a secondary haloalkane. In a tertiary haloalkane, the carbon atom in the C–X bond is bonded to three other carbon atoms.

A **haloalkane** is a compound in which one or more hydrogen atoms of an alkane is replaced by a halogen. If one hydrogen is replaced the general formula is $C_nH_{2n+1}X$ (where X = Cl, Br or I).

The carbon–halogen bond is polar, which results in the carbon atom being susceptible to attack by a **nucleophile**. A nucleophile is an electron-pair donor.

## Hydrolysis of haloalkanes

REVISED

When a primary haloalkane is heated under reflux with an aqueous solution of an alkali, the haloalkane is oxidised to a primary alcohol.

Reagent: NaOH or KOH

Conditions: The solvent must be water and the reaction mixture must be heated under reflux.

Equation: $CH_3CH_2Br + NaOH \rightarrow CH_3CH_2OH + NaBr$

The hydrolysis takes place by nucleophilic substitution. When describing the mechanism, it is essential to show relevant dipoles, lone pairs of electrons and curly arrows (Figure 7.6).

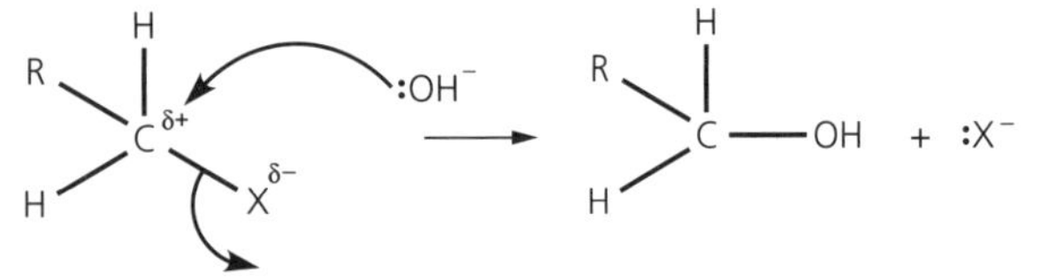


(R represents an alkyl group such as $CH_3$–, $C_2H_5$– etc.)

**Figure 7.6**

## Rate of hydrolysis

REVISED

When equal amounts of 1-chlorobutane, 1-bromobutane and 1-iodobutane are reacted under identical conditions with a hot aqueous solution containing a small amount of aqueous ethanolic silver nitrate, 1-iodobutane reacts the fastest and 1-chlorobutane reacts the slowest. The reaction can be monitored as the substituted halide ion reacts with the $Ag^+$ ion to produce a precipitate of white AgCl(s), cream AgBr(s) or yellow AgI(s).

The rate of hydrolysis can be explained by comparing the carbon–halogen bond enthalpies.

**Table 7.1 Bond enthalpies of carbon–halogen bonds**

| Bond | Bond enthalpy/kJ $mol^{-1}$ |
|---|---|
| C–F | 467 |
| C–Cl | 340 |
| C–Br | 280 |
| C–I | 240 |

The C–I bond is the weakest and the least energy is required to break it. The C–F is so strong that it rarely undergoes hydrolysis.

If a comparison is made of the rate of hydrolysis of primary, secondary and tertiary haloalkanes, the tertiary haloalkanes react fastest and the primary haloalkanes are the slowest. This can again be explained by the bond enthalpies: primary C–Cl bonds are the strongest and therefore the slowest, while tertiary C–Cl bonds are the weakest and therefore react the fastest.

**Typical mistake**

When asked to compare the rates of hydrolysis, many students lose marks by using incorrect language or technical terms. Students know that the iodo-compounds react fastest but often say that the difference in rate is due to the strength of the iodine bond, rather than the strength of the carbon–iodide (C–I) bond. The formula of iodine is $I_2$ and the strength of the I–I bond is irrelevant to this reaction.

## Now test yourself

TESTED

5

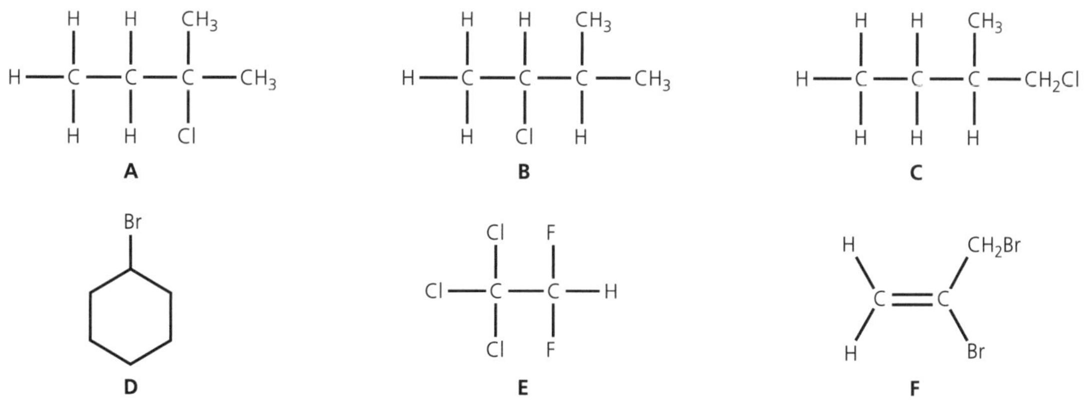


Figure 7.7

(a) Name the compounds A to F in Figure 7.7.
(b) Classify compounds A, B and C as either primary, secondary or tertiary.
(c) Write a balanced equation, and the mechanism, for the reaction of compound D with $OH^-$.
(d) When compound E is exposed to UV light it forms radicals. State what is meant by a *radical* and explain which radicals are most likely to be formed.

Answers on pp. 215–216

## Uses of haloalkanes

REVISED

Haloalkanes are used in the preparation of a wide range of products including pharmaceuticals (such as ibuprofen) and polymers such as PVC (made from $CH_2{=}CHCl$) and PTFE (made from $F_2C{=}CF_2$).

### CFCs

Haloalkanes were used to produce CFCs such as dichlorodifluoromethane, $CCl_2F_2$, and trichlorofluoromethane, $CCl_3F$. CFCs were developed for use in air conditioning, refrigeration units and aerosols because they are unreactive, non-flammable and non-toxic liquids of low volatility that can be readily evaporated and re-condensed. At the time of their introduction, the dangerous effect they would have on the stratosphere was not understood. It is thought that when CFCs reach the upper atmosphere they undergo photodissociation and generate chlorine radicals, Cl•:

$$CCl_2F_2 \xrightarrow{\text{ultraviolet}} \bullet CClF_2 + Cl\bullet$$

These are extremely reactive and react with the ozone in the presence of ultraviolet light. The chlorine radical is involved in the propagation steps:

$$Cl\bullet + O_3 \rightarrow ClO\bullet + O_2$$

$$ClO\bullet + O \rightarrow Cl\bullet + O_2$$

The net reaction is:

$$O_3 + O \rightleftharpoons 2O_2$$

Chemists are working to minimise damage to the environment by researching alternatives to CFCs. Initially these centred on the use of HCFCs, such as 1,1,1,2-tetrafluoroethane, that include a C–H bond that makes them more degradable in the atmosphere. Currently hydrocarbons are used as alternative propellants in aerosols. Carbon dioxide has been found to be a suitable alternative blowing agent in the manufacture of expanded polystyrene.

Ozone can also be broken down by other radicals, such as nitrogen monoxide, •NO, which is formed by reacting $N_2$ and $O_2$ at high temperature and pressure:

$$\tfrac{1}{2}N_2 + \tfrac{1}{2}O_2 \rightarrow \bullet NO$$

Nitrogen monoxide is found in the exhaust fumes of aircraft and can also react with the ozone by a series of reactions:

$$\bullet NO + O_3 \rightarrow \bullet NO_2 + O_2$$

$$\bullet NO_2 + O \rightarrow \bullet NO + O_2$$

The net reaction is $O_3 + O \rightleftharpoons 2O_2$ and •NO catalyses the breakdown of ozone.

**Exam tip**

All chemistry exams have to test 'How science works'. The way in which CFCs interact with ozone has a significant environmental impact. Make sure you know the equations.

# Organic synthesis

## Practical skills

REVISED

Figure 7.8 details how an organic synthesis might be planned, carried out and the product analysed.

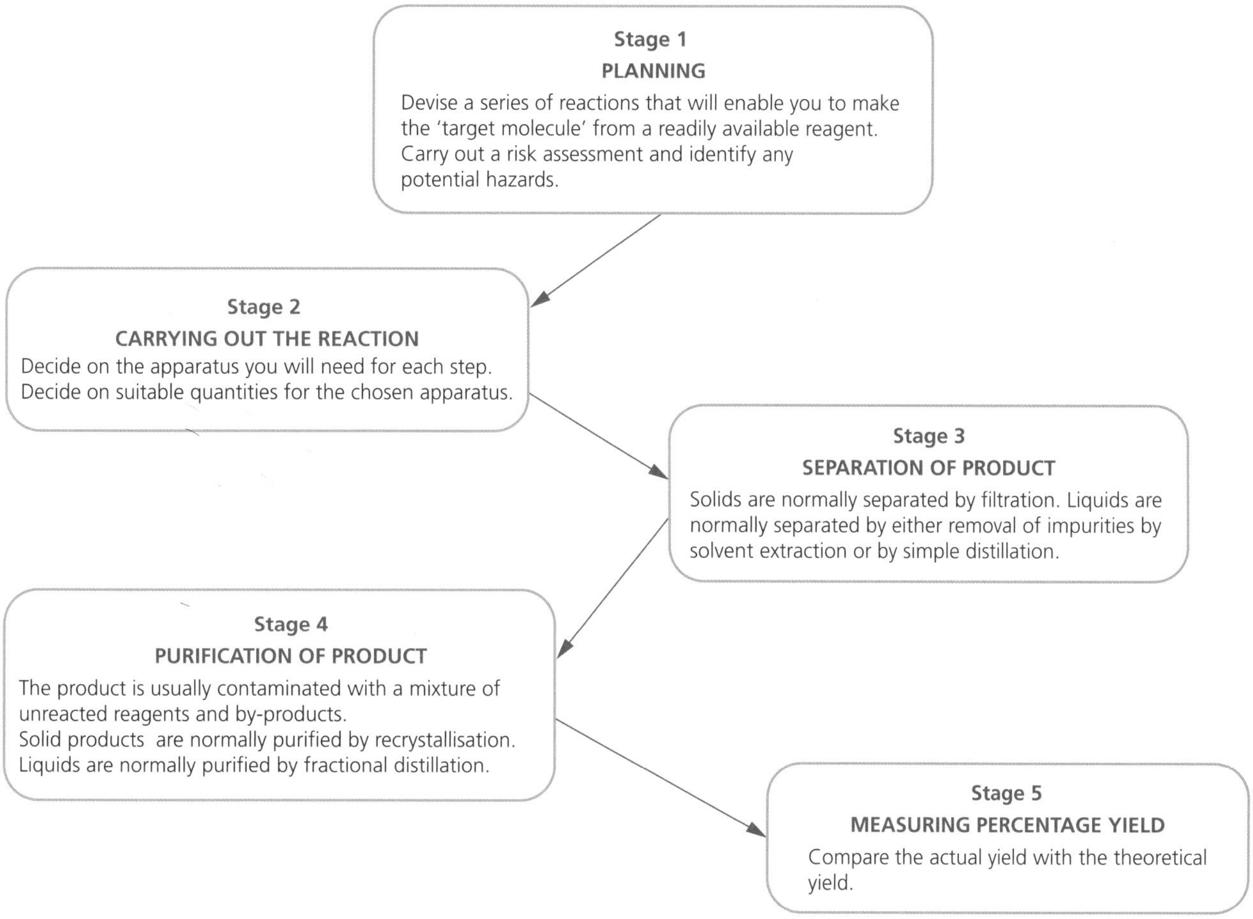

Stage 1
PLANNING
Devise a series of reactions that will enable you to make the 'target molecule' from a readily available reagent. Carry out a risk assessment and identify any potential hazards.
Stage 2
CARRYING OUT THE REACTION
Decide on the apparatus you will need for each step. Decide on suitable quantities for the chosen apparatus.
Stage 3
SEPARATION OF PRODUCT
Solids are normally separated by filtration. Liquids are normally separated by either removal of impurities by solvent extraction or by simple distillation.
Stage 4
PURIFICATION OF PRODUCT
The product is usually contaminated with a mixture of unreacted reagents and by-products.
Solid products are normally purified by recrystallisation.
Liquids are normally purified by fractional distillation.
Stage 5
MEASURING PERCENTAGE YIELD
Compare the actual yield with the theoretical yield.


**Figure 7.8** Preparation of an organic compound

## Synthetic routes

REVISED

Functional groups provide the key to organic molecules. Knowledge of the properties and reactions of a limited number of functional groups enables the preparation of a wide variety of organic compounds.

Table 7.2 summarises the reactions of these groups.

**Table 7.2**

| Functional group | | | |
|---|---|---|---|
| **Name** | **General formula** | **Type of reactions** | **Reagents that react** |
| Alkane | $C_nH_{2n+2}$ | Radical substitution | $Cl_2$, $Br_2$ |
| Alkene | $C_nH_{2n}$ | Electrophilic addition | $H_2$, HCl, HBr, $Cl_2$, $Br_2$ $H_2O(g)$ |

| Functional group | | | |
|---|---|---|---|
| **Name** | **General formula** | **Type of reactions** | **Reagents that react** |
| Alcohol | R–OH | Oxidation<br>Esterification*<br>Elimination<br>Halogenation | $H^+/Cr_2O_7^{2-}$<br>RCOOH (carboxylic acids)<br>$H_2SO_4$<br>$NaBr/H_2SO_4$ |
| Haloalkane | R–Cl | Nucleophilic substitution<br>Hydrolysis | Common nucleophiles include: $:OH^-$, $*:NH_3$, $*:CN^-$ |

*Only likely to be tested after the second year of the A-level course

Organic chemists often start by examining the 'target molecule'. Then they work backwards through a series of steps to find suitable starting chemicals that are available and cheap enough (Table 7.3).

**Table 7.3**

| Functional group | Reagent | Target functional group |
|---|---|---|
| Alkane | Halogen | Haloalkane |
| Alkene | Hydrogen halides | Haloalkanes |
| | Halogens | Di-haloalkanes |
| | Steam | Alcohol |
| | Hydrogen | Alkanes |
| Alcohols | Carboxylic acids* | Esters |
| | $H^+/Cr_2O_7^{2-}$ | Aldehyde, ketone or carboxylic acid |
| | Hot concentrated $H_2SO_4$ | Alkene |
| | NaBr in presence of $H_2SO_4$ | Haloalkane |
| Haloalkane | NaOH(aq) | Alcohol |
| | $NH_3$ (ethanol)* | Amine |
| | Cyanide, –C≡N* | Nitrile |

*Only likely to be tested after the second year of the A-level course

**Example**

**Preparation of propanone starting from propene**

In this case, the 'target molecule' is propanone and the 'starting molecule', propene, is an alkene.

**Step 1** Start with the target molecule and identify the compounds that could readily be converted directly into the target — concentrate on the functional group.

Propanone is a ketone that can be made from the oxidation of a secondary alcohol, propan-2-ol.

**Step 2** Look at your starting molecule, propene. What reactions of alkenes do you know?

You should now see a possible two-stage synthetic route from your starting molecule to the target molecule. In this case, the route can go via the alcohol.

| | | | | |
|---|---|---|---|---|
| $H_2C{=}CHCH_3$ | → | $H_3CCH(OH)CH_3$ | → | $H_3CCOCH_3$ |
| starting molecule | | intermediate molecule | | target molecule |

You will need to know the reagents and conditions for each step (Figure 7.9).

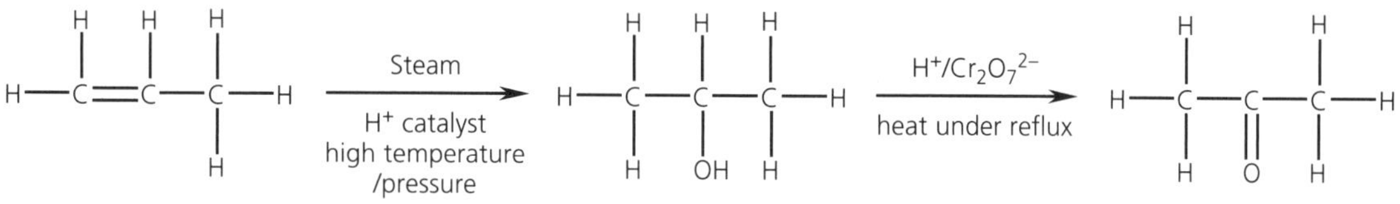


Figure 7.9

You may have to write equations for each step:

Step 1 $CH_2{=}CHCH_3 + H_2O \rightarrow CH_3CH(OH)CH_3$

Step 2 $CH_3CH(OH)CH_3 + [O] \rightarrow CH_3COCH_3 + H_2O$

Chemists normally seek a synthetic route that has the least number of stages and which, therefore, produces a higher yield of the product. It is rare for any one reaction to be 100% efficient; normally the percentage yield is significantly below the theoretical yield.

## Now test yourself

TESTED

6 Compound A decolorises bromine and when heated with acidified dichromate the dichromate turns from orange to green. Which of the three compounds is compound A most likely to be:

**$CH_3CH_2CH_2OH$**  **$CH_3CH{=}CHCOOH$**  **$CH_3CHCHCH_2OH$**

Explain your answer.

7 Devise a two-stage synthesis for converting:
(a) methane to methanol
(b) propene into propanone
State the reagents and conditions needed for each conversion.

Answers on p. 216

# Analytical techniques

## Infrared spectroscopy

REVISED

Infrared spectra can be used to identify key absorptions of alcohol, carbonyl, carboxylic acid and amine functional groups.

### Absorption of infrared radiation by atmospheric gases — the greenhouse effect

The Earth is warmed mostly by the energy transmitted from the Sun. This consists largely of visible light, but there is also some ultraviolet and some infrared radiation. Most ultraviolet radiation is removed in the upper parts of the atmosphere (the stratosphere) by the ozone layer.

Over time, the surface temperature of the Earth has remained more or less constant because an equilibrium has been established between arriving and departing energy. The departing energy is almost wholly infrared radiation. Many gases in the atmosphere absorb some of this infrared energy and the absorbed infrared radiation is later released and re-emitted back to the Earth's surface.

Carbon dioxide, methane and water molecules absorb infrared radiation, as do many other gases. Any compound that contains C=O, C–H and O–H bonds will absorb infrared radiation. A wide range of gases contribute to the overall **greenhouse effect**.

The contribution of an individual gas to the greenhouse effect depends on three factors:

- its ability to absorb infrared — methane is 25 more times effective in absorbing infrared than carbon dioxide
- its atmospheric concentration — carbon dioxide is over 200 times more abundant than methane
- its residence time — CFCs can stay in the atmosphere for very many years

If the concentration of these gases is allowed to rise, the average temperature at the Earth's surface will increase.

> **Exam tip**
>
> All chemistry exams have to incorporate different aspects of 'How science works', and over recent years this area of the specification has been examined extensively. It is important that you take time to learn the relevant detail. Just because things like the 'greenhouse effect' and 'global warming' appear almost daily in the news, do not assume that you know it all. Look at the mark schemes and find out exactly what the examiner expects you to write.

## Now test yourself

TESTED

8 State what happens to the bonds in a carbon dioxide molecule when it absorbs infrared radiation.

9 State *three* factors that influence the contribution of a gas to the greenhouse effect.

Answers on p. 216

The role of carbon dioxide as a contributor to **global warming** is the focus of much attention. This is because it is produced in huge quantities by the burning of fossil fuels.

The difficulty of providing a reliable prediction emphasises the complex nature of the chemistry of the atmosphere. Animals release carbon dioxide as they respire; plants absorb carbon dioxide during photosynthesis. Much carbon dioxide is absorbed as it dissolves into surface waters. In addition, it is not possible to predict how long an individual molecule may stay in the atmosphere — only average figures (residence time) are available. These factors make it difficult to predict the likely outcome of increasing pollution levels.

However, there is now a general acceptance of the scientific evidence explaining global warming which has prompted many governments to promote the use of renewable energy sources such as wind, solar and tidal.

> **Exam tip**
>
> Datasheets are supplied in exams so there is no need to learn the absorptions.

## Using infrared spectra to identify organic compounds

The absorptions in infrared spectra can be roughly divided into three distinct sections (Figure 7.10).

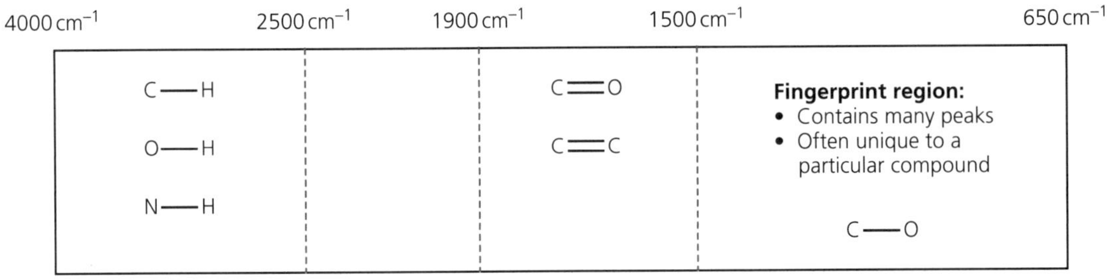


**Figure 7.10**

The infrared spectrum of ethanoyl chloride, $CH_3COCl$, shown in Figure 7.11, has an absorption due to the C–Cl bond, which occurs in the fingerprint region.

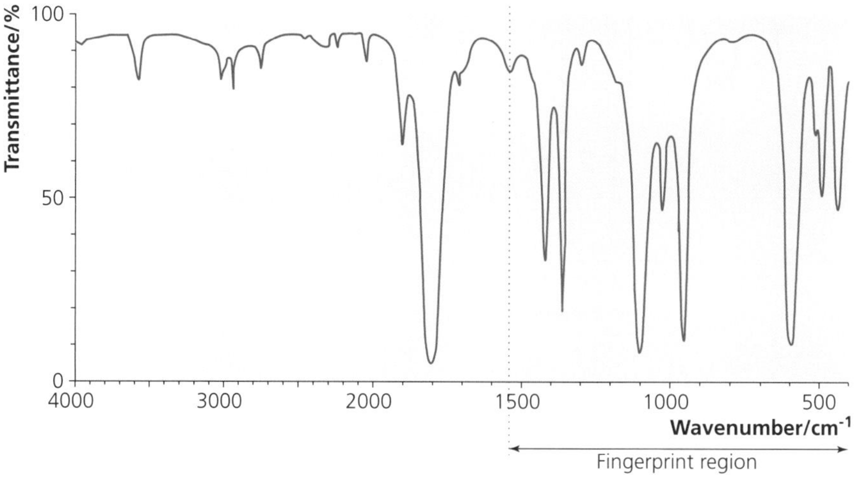


**Figure 7.11**

However, because there are so many peaks in the fingerprint region they are difficult to assign and it is almost impossible to tell, at a glance, which peak is due to the C–Cl bond.

The key absorptions that you may be expected to identify are given in Table 7.4.

**Table 7.4 Key infrared absorptions**

| Bond | Location | Wavenumber range/$cm^{-1}$ |
|---|---|---|
| *C–X | Haloalkanes (X = Cl, Br or I) | 500–800 |
| *C–F | Fluoroalkanes | 1000–1350 |
| *C–O | Alcohols, esters, carboxylic acids | 1000–1300 |
| C=C | Alkenes | 1620–1680 |
| C=O | Aldehydes, ketones, carboxylic acids, esters, amides | 1640–1750 |
| C–H | Any organic compound with a C–H bond | 2850–3100 |
| O–H | Carboxylic acids | 2500–3300 (very broad) |
| O–H | Alcohols | 3200–3600 (broad) |
| *These occur in the fingerprint regions and are difficult to assign | | |

You might be expected to distinguish between the infrared spectra of an alcohol and its oxidation products: aldehyde, ketone and carboxylic acid.

For an alcohol you need to identify *two* peaks (Figure 7.12):

- 1000–1300 $cm^{-1}$ — all alcohols contain a C–O bond but they are difficult to assign as they are in the fingerprint region.
- 3200–3500 $cm^{-1}$ — all alcohols contain a O–H bond, which gives rise to a broad peak and should not be confused with the small sharp peaks due to C–H bonds.

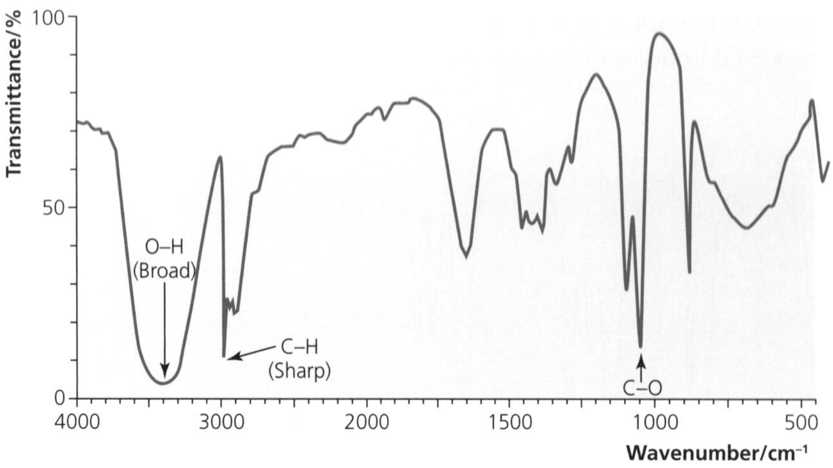


**Figure 7.12 Infrared spectrum of an alcohol**

For an aldehyde or a ketone you need to identify *one* peak:

- 1640–1750 $cm^{-1}$ — all aldehydes and ketones contain a C=O bond (Figure 7.13).

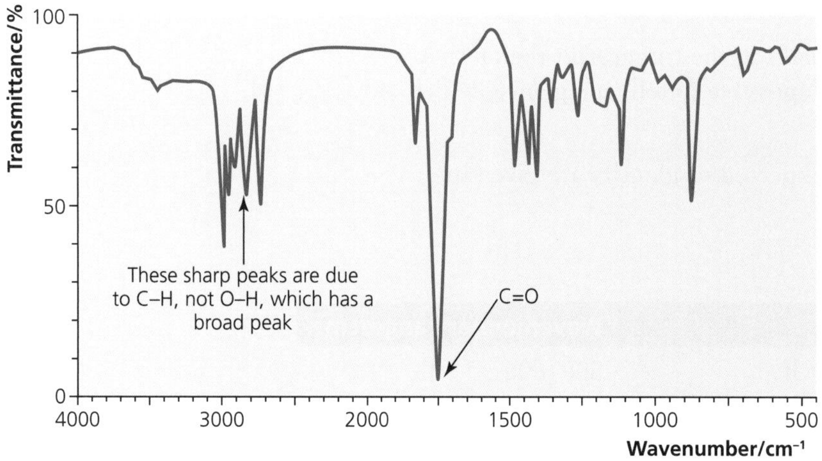


**Figure 7.13 Infrared spectrum of a ketone**

For a carboxylic acid you need to identify *two* (possibly three) peaks (Figure 7.14):

- 1640–1750 $cm^{-1}$ — all carboxylic acids contain a C=O bond.
- 2500–3300 $cm^{-1}$ — all carboxylic acids contain a O–H bond which is a very broad peak.
- 1000–1300 $cm^{-1}$ — all carboxylic acids contain a C–O bond but they are difficult to assign as they are in the fingerprint region.

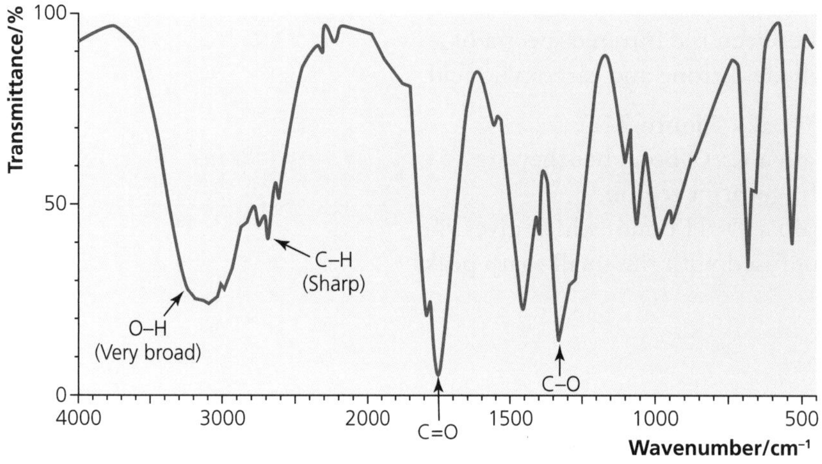


**Figure 7.14 Infrared spectrum of a carboxylic acid**

Infrared spectroscopy is a powerful tool in identifying a particular functional group. When identifying a specific chemical, it is usually used in conjunction with other analytical techniques such as mass spectrometry, chromatography and nuclear magnetic resonance (NMR) spectroscopy. At AS you are expected to be able to link together information obtained from an infrared spectrum and a mass spectrum.

Infrared spectrometry is also used:

- to monitor air pollution and can detect gases such as CO and NO
- in breathalysers to measure ethanol in breath

## Mass spectrometry

REVISED

Mass spectrometry provides evidence for the existence of isotopes. For an atom, a typical print-out from the detector looks like a 'stick-diagram'. Each stick represents an ion (isotope); the taller the 'stick' the more abundant the ion (isotope).

The mass spectrum of boron is shown in Figure 7.15.

The *x*-axis is labelled '*m/z*', which means mass/charge. However, since the charge is 1+ it is effectively the relative mass of the ions that is recorded.

The mass spectrum of boron shows two lines, indicating there are two isotopes with mass 10 and 11.

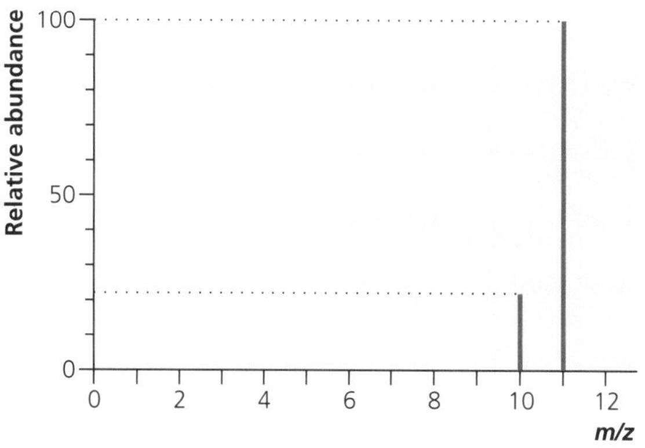

**Figure 7.15** Mass spectrum of boron

The mass spectrometer is also used to analyse compounds, although the number of lines obtained may be large. This is because bombardment by electrons causes the molecule to break up and each of the fragments obtained registers on the detector. This can be an advantage as it is sometimes possible to obtain details of the molecule's structure, as well as its overall molecular mass.

The mass spectrum of propane ($C_3H_8$) is shown in Figure 7.16.

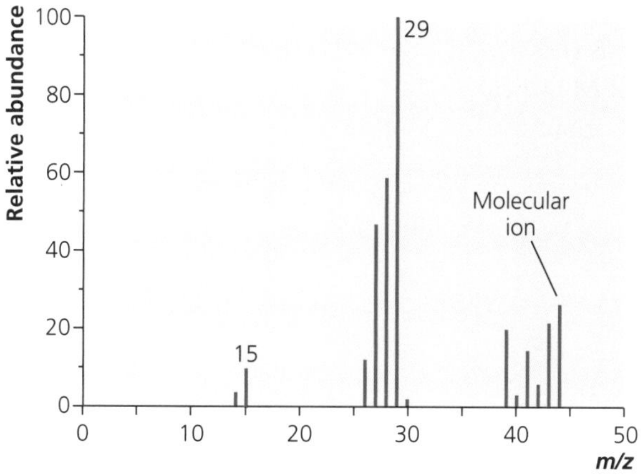

**Figure 7.16** Mass spectrum of propane

Propane has relative molecular mass of 44.0 and, as expected, the peak furthest to the right of the spectrum represents the ion $C_3H_8^+$. This is called the **molecular ion peak** (or the **M** peak). However, the molecular ion is unstable and breaks down to ion fragments of the molecule, which are also detected. Some examples are labelled on the spectrum.

The peak at *m/z* 29 occurs because a $CH_3$ unit has been broken from the $CH_3CH_2CH_3$ chain and the ion $CH_3CH_2^+$ has been detected (Figure 7.17).

$$\left(H_3C \longrightarrow CH_2 - \vert - CH_3\right)^+(g) \longrightarrow \left(H_3C \longrightarrow CH_2\right)^+(g) \quad + \quad CH_3(g)$$

The C–C bond breaks and produces two fragments

One fragment has a + charge and the other is neutral

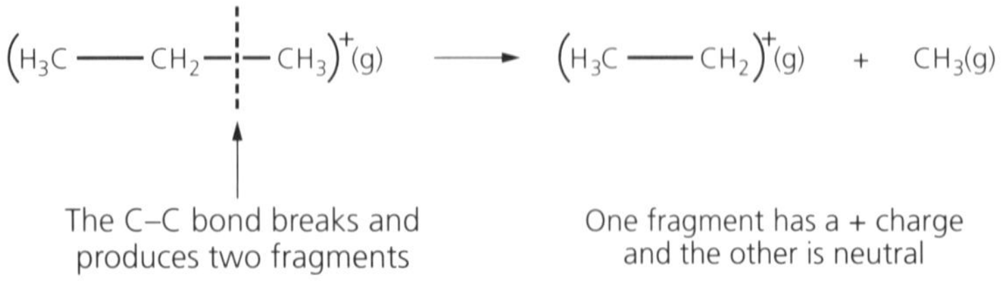

Figure 7.17

The peak at $m/z$ 15 represents a $CH_3^+$ ion, and it is possible to suggest the identity of all other peaks in the spectrum (Figure 7.18).

$$\left(H_3C \longrightarrow CH_2 - \vert - CH_3\right)^+(g) \longrightarrow CH_3^+(g) \quad + \quad \left(H_3C \longrightarrow CH_2\right)(g)$$

The C–C bond breaks and produces two fragments

One fragment has a + charge and the other is neutral

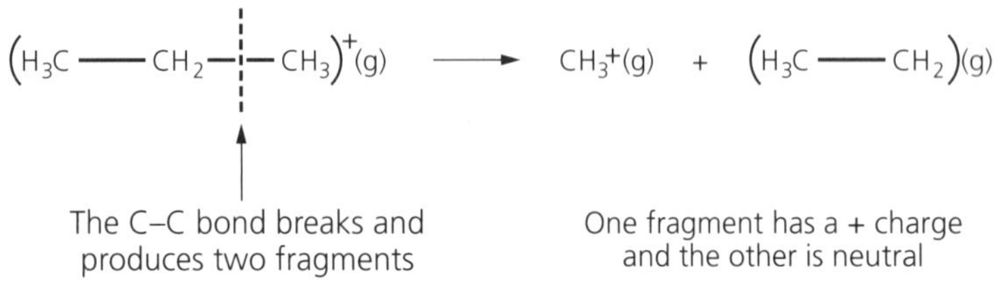

Figure 7.18

Fragmentation leads to a large number of peaks, giving a 'fingerprint' of the molecule. In conjunction with a computer using a spectral database, this enables a particular chemical to be identified.

For the exam you may be expected to identify a few common fragment ions, such as those in Table 7.5.

Table 7.5

| $m/z$ value | Ion responsible |
|---|---|
| 15 | $CH_3^+(g)$ |
| 29 | $CH_3CH_2^+(g)$ |
| 43 | $CH_3CH_2CH_2^+(g)$ |
| Alkyl chains extend by $CH_2$ so it is possible that you will get peaks at 57, 71 etc. | |
| 31 | $CH_2OH^+(g)$ (primary alcohol) |

You should be aware that the mass spectra of many compounds show not only the M peak (the molecular ion peak) but also a small M+1 peak due to the presence of the isotope $^{13}C$, which is present in all organic substances (Figure 7.19).

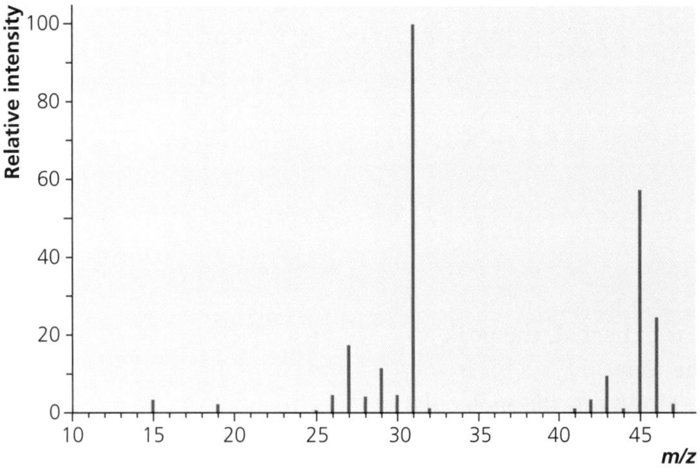

Figure 7.19

## Now test yourself

TESTED

10 The infrared spectrum and the mass spectrum of compound A are shown in Figures 7.20 and 7.21.

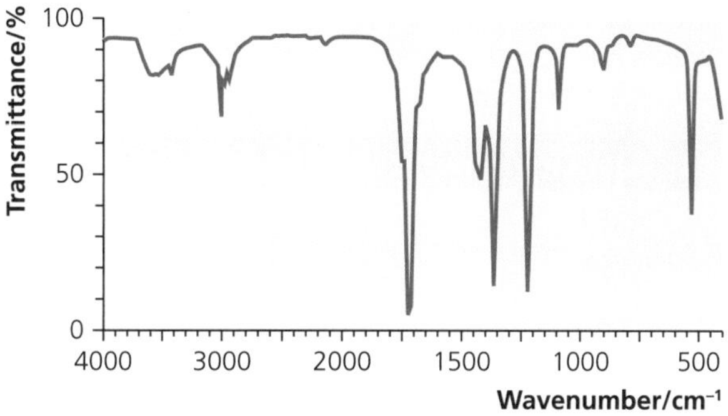


Figure 7.20 **Infrared spectrum of compound A**

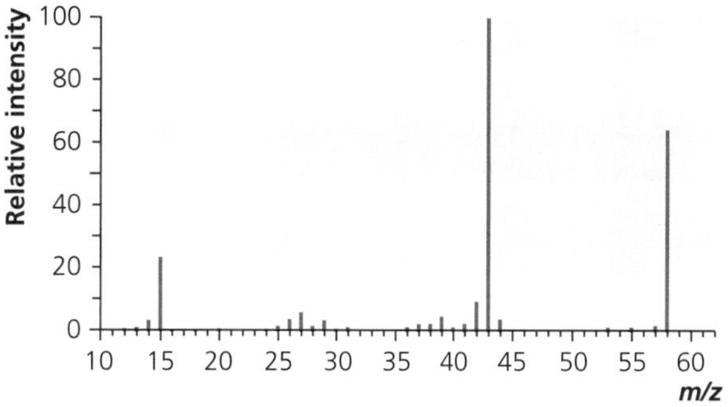


Figure 7.21 **Mass spectrum of compound A**

(a) Use the infrared spectrum to determine whether compound A contains:
   (i) O–H
   (ii) C=O
(b) Use the mass spectrum to determine the molar mass of compound A.
(c) Show that the molecular formula of compound A is $C_3H_6O$. Show *all* your working.
(d) Draw and name isomers of $C_3H_6O$.
(e) Use the fragmentation pattern in the mass spectrum to identify compound A. Show *all* your working.

Answers on p. 216

**Revision activity**

Look up the formulae of aspirin and paracetamol and suggest the *m*/*z* values of the molecular ion peaks of each. From the structures of aspirin and paracetamol state the range (cm$^{-1}$) of two absorptions that you would expect in each spectrum. Explain how you could distinguish between aspirin and paracetamol.

## Exam practice

1 Compound **A** in Figure 7.22 contains two functional groups. Compound **A** can be oxidised to produce a mixture of Compound **B**, molecular formula $C_3H_4O_2$ and compound **C**, molecular formula $C_3H_4O_3$.

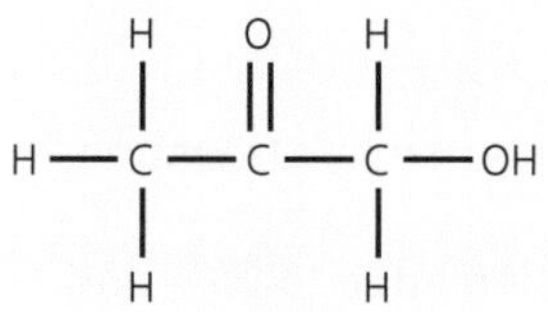


Compound **A**

**Figure 7.22**

(a) Identify the functional groups in compound **A**. [3]
(b) (i) State the molecular formula of compound **A**. [1]
   (ii) Identify which of the functional groups could be oxidised. [1]
   (iii) Suggest a suitable oxidising mixture [2]
   (iv) State what you would observe during the oxidation [1]
   (v) Identify compound **B**. [1]
   (vi) Write a balanced equation for the formation of compound **C** from compound **A**. Use [O] to represent the oxidising agent. [2]

2 Alcohols can be converted into chloroalkanes by reaction with hydrochloric acid, HCl. 2-chloro-2-methylbutane can be prepared by shaking together 5.3 $cm^3$ (4.4 g) of 2-methylbutan-2-ol with 20 $cm^3$ of concentrated HCl. After 10 minutes, two separate layers begin to form.

(a) (i) What is the molecular formula of 2-methylbutan-2-ol? [1]

(ii) Write a balanced equation for the reaction between 2-methylbutan-2-ol and HCl. [1]

(b) Use the data in the table below to answer the questions that follow.

| Compound | Relative molecular mass | Density/g $cm^{-3}$ | Boiling point/°C |
|---|---|---|---|
| 2-methylbutan-2-ol | 88.0 | 0.81 | 102 |
| 2-chloro-2-methylbutane | 106.5 | 0.87 | 86 |
| Water | 18.0 | 1.00 | 100 |

One of the layers is aqueous and the other contains the organic product. Suggest whether the upper or lower layer is likely to contain the organic product. Explain your reasoning. [1]

(c) The organic layer was shaken with a dilute solution of sodium hydrogencarbonate, $NaHCO_3$. A gas was given off. Identify the gas. Suggest the chemical that could have reacted with the $NaHCO_3$ to form the gas. [2]

(d) The resulting impure organic liquid was dried with anhydrous calcium chloride and then distilled. 3.73 g of pure 2-chloro-2-methylbutane were produced.

(i) At what temperature would you expect the *pure* organic product to distil? [1]

(ii) Calculate the percentage yield of 2-chloro-2-methylbutane in this experiment. [3]

(iii) Calculate the atom economy of the reaction. [2]

3 At one time, CFCs were used widely. They are now banned from production because of their damaging effect on the ozone layer.

(a) One of the reasons CFCs used to be manufactured was for use as propellants in aerosols. Give *three* properties of CFCs that made them suitable for this purpose. [3]

(b) CFCs damage the ozone layer by upsetting the equilibrium between oxygen and ozone in the stratosphere.

(i) Write an equation for the equilibrium [1]

(ii) Explain how this equilibrium is maintained in the stratosphere. [2]

(iii) By using appropriate equations, explain how the CFC of formula $CF_3Cl$ could deplete ozone. [3]

(iv) Explain why a single molecule of $CF_3Cl$ can cause the destruction of many molecules of ozone. [2]

(c) The use of CFCs is now widely banned. However, it is expected that destruction of the ozone layer will continue for many more years. Explain why this is the case. [2]

## Answers and quick quiz 7 online

ONLINE

## Summary

You should now have an understanding of:

- reactions of alcohols including combustion, oxidation, elimination and esterification
- hydrolysis of haloalkanes
- nucleophilic substitution mechanism
- CFCs and ozone
- how to devise a two-stage synthesis
- absorption of infrared radiation by atmospheric gases
- how to recognise absorptions due to O–H and C=O bonds in infrared spectra
- how to determine the molar mass of a molecule by using the molecular ion peak in a mass spectrum

# 8 Rates, equilibria and pH

## How fast?

This topic builds on your understanding of the AS reaction rates chemistry. It involves measuring and calculating reaction rates using rate equations.

### Orders, rate equations and rate constants

REVISED

The rate of a reaction is usually measured as the change in concentration of a reaction species with time. The units of rate are $mol\,dm^{-3}\,s^{-1}$ (Figure 8.1).

The units of rate = $mol\,dm^{-3}$ $s^{-1}$

concentration → $mol\,dm^{-3}$; per time → $s^{-1}$

**Figure 8.1 Equation for reaction rate**

#### Measuring rates from graphs

Consider the reaction:

A + B → C + D

It is possible to measure the rate of disappearance of either A or B or the appearance of one of the products, C or D. The data can be plotted on a concentration–time graph. The gradient of the tangent is a measure of the reaction rate (Figure 8.2).

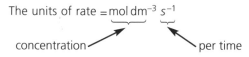

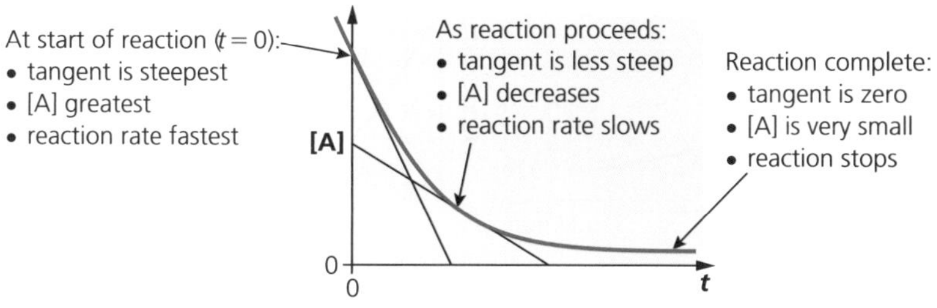


**Figure 8.2 Concentration–time graph**

### The rate equation

REVISED

#### Orders of reaction

The rate equation of a reaction shows how the rate is affected by the concentration of each reactant. It can only be determined by experiment.

In general, for the reaction A + B → C + D, the reaction rate is given by:

$rate = k[A]^m[B]^n$

- $k$ is the rate constant of the reaction.
- $m$ and $n$ are the **orders of reaction** with respect to A and B.

The overall order of reaction is $(m + n)$.

You know from 'Reaction rates' in Module 3 that increasing concentration usually results in an increased rate of reaction. However, different reagents can behave in a different manner. If we double the concentration of a reagent and the rate increases proportionately (i.e. the rate also doubles) then the reaction is said to be **first order** with respect to that reagent. If doubling the concentration of a reagent results in a four-fold increase in reaction rate, the reaction is said to **second order** with respect to that reagent. If increasing the concentration of a reagent has no effect, the reaction is said to be **zero order** with respect to that reagent.

### The rate constant

The rate constant *k* indicates the rate of the reaction:

- A large value of *k* means a fast rate of reaction.
- A small value of *k* means a slow rate of reaction.

An increase in temperature speeds up the rate of most reactions by increasing the rate constant *k*.

## Rate graphs and orders

REVISED

### Concentration–time graphs

During a reaction the concentrations of the reagent(s) and product(s) change. Measuring the concentration of a reactant or a product at regular time intervals produces data that can be plotted on a graph. The shape of the resultant graph can be used to predict the order of reaction. If the graph is not a straight line the order can be determined by measuring the **half-life** of a reactant. The half-life of a reactant is the time taken for its concentration to halve during the reaction. See Table 8.1.

**Table 8.1**

| Zero order | First order | Second order |
|---|---|---|
| 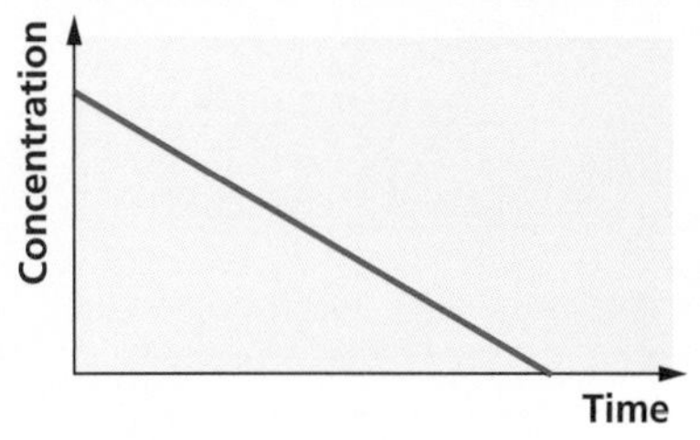 | 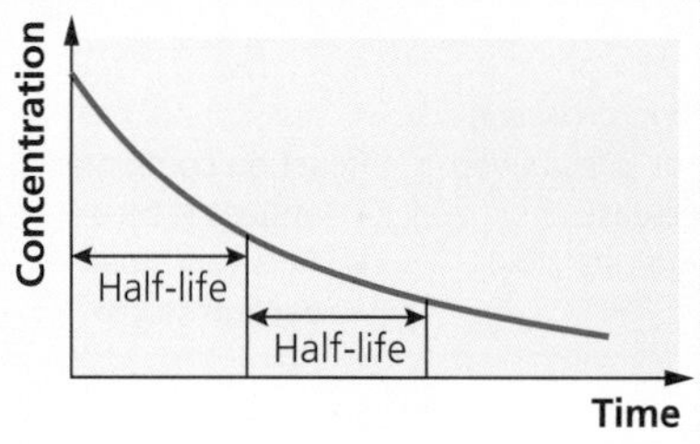 | 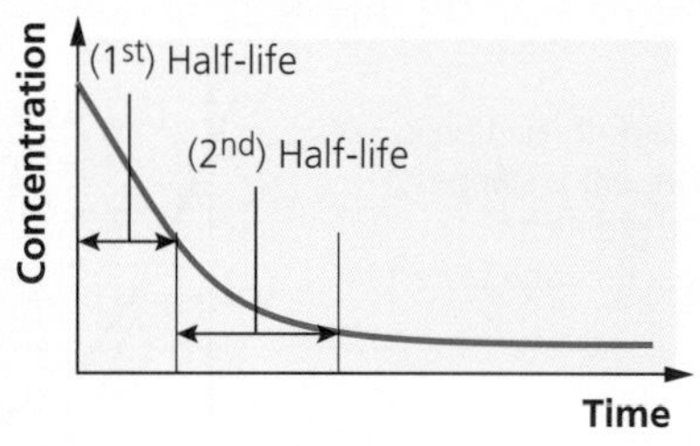 |
| Straight-line graph<br>Concentration falls at a steady rate<br>Half-life decreases with time | Curve<br>Half-life is constant | Curve<br>Half-life increases with time |

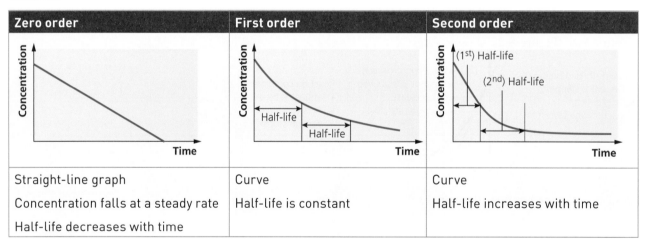

If the reaction is first order, the half-life, $t_{\frac{1}{2}}$, can be determined from the concentration–time graph. Once the half-life is known it can be used to calculate the rate constant, *k*, using the relationship:

$$k = \frac{\ln 2}{t_{\frac{1}{2}}}$$

### Rate–concentration graphs

A concentration–time graph is first plotted and tangents are drawn at several time values on it, giving values of reaction rates. A second graph is now plotted of rate against concentration. See Table 8.2.

**Table 8.2**

| Zero order | First order | Second order |
|---|---|---|
| 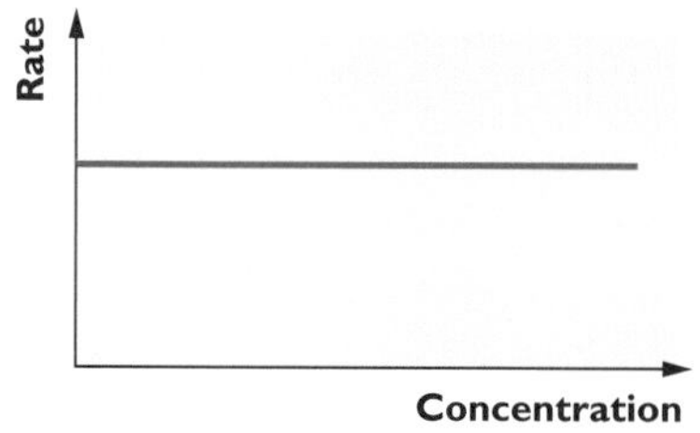  | 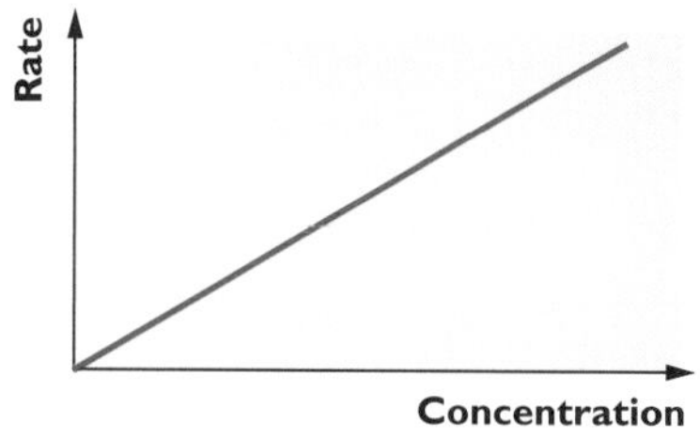  | 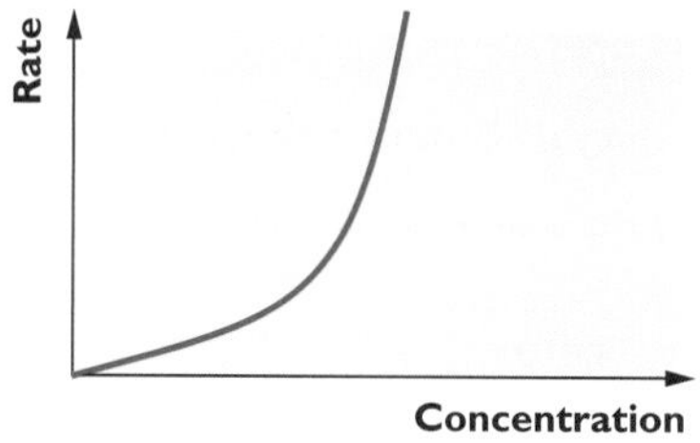  |
| rate ∝ $[X]^0$<br>Rate is constant<br>Rate unaffected by changes in concentration | rate ∝ $[X]^1$<br>Rate doubles as concentration doubles | rate ∝ $[X]^2$<br>Rate quadruples as concentration doubles |

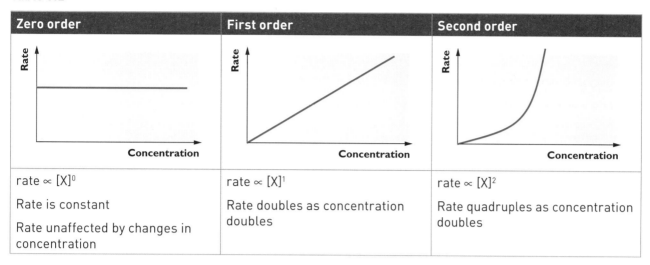

## Measuring rates using the initial rates method

REVISED

For the reaction A + B → C + D experiments are carried out using different initial concentrations of the reactants A and B.

When changing only one variable at a time, three experiments are required:

- In experiments 1 and 2, the concentration of A is changed and the concentration of B is kept constant.
- In experiments 2 and 3, the concentration of B is changed and the concentration of A is kept constant.

A typical set of results is shown in the Table 8.3.

**Table 8.3**

| Experiment | [A(aq)]/mol $dm^{-3}$ | [B(aq)]/mol $dm^{-3}$ | Initial rate/mol $dm^{-3}$ $s^{-1}$ |
|---|---|---|---|
| 1 | $1.0 \times 10^{-2}$ | $1.0 \times 10^{-2}$ | $4.0 \times 10^{-3}$ |
| 2 | $2.0 \times 10^{-2}$ | $1.0 \times 10^{-2}$ | $1.6 \times 10^{-2}$ |
| 3 | $2.0 \times 10^{-2}$ | $2.0 \times 10^{-2}$ | $3.2 \times 10^{-2}$ |

## Order of reaction with respect to each reagent

### Order of reaction with respect to A

Comparing experiments 1 and 2: [B(aq)] is constant and [A(aq)] is doubled. The rate has quadrupled. Therefore, the reaction is second order with respect to A(aq):

rate ∝ $[A(aq)]^2$

### Order of reaction with respect to B

Comparing experiments 2 and 3: [A(aq)] is constant and [B(aq)] is doubled. The rate has doubled. Therefore, the reaction is first order with respect to B(aq):

rate ∝ [B(aq)]

## The rate equation

Combining the two orders with respect to the two reagents gives:

rate $\propto$ [A(aq)]$^2$[B(aq)] or rate = $k$[A]$^2$[B]

The overall order of this reaction is (2 + 1) = third order.

The rate constant, $k$, can be determined by rearranging the rate equation:

$$k = \frac{\text{rate}}{[A]^2[B]}$$

Substituting values from experiment 1 gives:

$$k = \frac{(4.0 \times 10^{-3})}{(1.0 \times 10^{-2})^2 \times (1.0 \times 10^{-2})} = 4.0 \times 10^3\,\text{dm}^6\,\text{mol}^{-2}\,\text{s}^{-1}$$

## Units of rate constants

The units of a rate constant depend upon the rate equation for the reaction. (Table 8.4)

**Table 8.4**

| Order | Rate equation | Units of $k$ |
|---|---|---|
| First | rate = $k$[A] | $s^{-1}$ |
| Second | rate = $k$[A]$^2$ | $mol^{-1}\,dm^3\,s^{-1}$ *or* $dm^3\,mol^{-1}\,s^{-1}$ |
| Third | rate = $k$[A]$^2$[B] or $k$[A]$^3$ | $mol^{-2}\,dm^6\,s^{-1}$ *or* $dm^6\,mol^{-2}\,s^{-1}$ |

There are numerous methods that can be used to determine the rate of a chemical reaction. Wherever possible, the method chosen should not interfere with the reaction taking place, as this could lead to confusing results. There is no need to learn details of individual experiments, but you may be asked to select a method for the continuous monitoring of a reaction.

- If a gas is produced, it is relatively easy to continuously monitor the volume of gas produced.
- If an acid is formed, the pH can be measured using a pH meter.
- If there is any change in colour, it can be followed using a colorimeter.

## Now test yourself

TESTED

1 The rate equation for a reaction is:

**rate = $k$[A][B]$^2$[C]**

(a) What is the overall order of reaction and what are the units of the rate constant, $k$?
(b) For each of the following changes, deduce the effect on the rate of reaction:
  (i) the concentration of A is increased threefold
  (ii) the concentration of B is halved
  (iii) the concentrations of A, B and C are all doubled

2 Suggest a suitable method for measuring the rate of each of the following reactions:
(a) $Br_2(aq) + C_4H_{10}(g) \rightarrow C_4H_9Br(l) + HBr(aq)$
(b) $Mg(s) + 2HCl(aq) \rightarrow MgCl_2(aq) + H_2(g)$
(c) $C_4H_9Br(l) + H_2O(l) \rightarrow C_4H_9OH(l) + H^+(aq) + Br^-(aq)$
(d) $Na_2S_2O_3(aq) + 2HCl(aq) \rightarrow 2NaCl(aq) + SO_2(g) + S(s)$

3 Table 8.5 gives data for the reaction:

**$BrO_3^-(aq) + 5Br^-(aq) + 6H^+(aq) \rightarrow 3Br_2(aq) + 3H_2O(l)$**

Table 8.5

| Experiment | $[BrO_3^-(aq)]$/mol dm$^{-3}$ | $[Br^-(aq)]$/mol dm$^{-3}$ | $[H^+(aq)]$/mol dm$^{-3}$ | Initial rate/mol dm$^{-3}$ s$^{-1}$ |
|---|---|---|---|---|
| 1 | 0.1 | 0.2 | 0.1 | $1.64 \times 10^{-3}$ |
| 2 | 0.2 | 0.1 | 0.1 | $1.64 \times 10^{-3}$ |
| 3 | 0.2 | 0.2 | 0.1 | $3.28 \times 10^{-3}$ |
| 4 | 0.2 | 0.1 | 0.2 | $6.56 \times 10^{-3}$ |
| 5 | 0.25 | 0.25 | 0.25 | X |

(a) Determine the rate equation for this reaction.
(b) Calculate the value of $k$, including its units.
(c) What would be the initial rate of reaction, X, for the initial concentrations shown in the final row of the table?

Answers on p. 216

## Determination of a two-step reaction mechanism

REVISED

The rate-determining step is defined as the slowest step in the reaction.

The rate equation can provide clues about a likely reaction mechanism by identifying the slowest stage of a reaction sequence. For instance, if the rate equation is:

rate = $k[A]^2[B]$

the slow step will involve two molecules of A and one molecule of B. If the rate equation is:

rate = $k[A][B]^2$

the slow step will involve one molecule of A and two molecules of B.

The orders in the rate equation match the number of species involved in the rate-determining step.

Reaction mechanisms often involve many separate steps. You may be asked to use the rate equation and the balanced equation to predict a mechanism for a reaction. In a two-step mechanism, the rate equation indicates the number of molecules of each reactant involved in the *slow* step. The slow step plus the fast step gives the balanced equation.

**Example**

$2H_2(g) + 2NO(g) \rightarrow 2H_2O(l) + N_2(g)$

The rate equation is:

rate = $k[H_2(g)][NO(g)]^2$

Predict a two-step mechanism.

**Answer**

The rate equation tells us that this involves one molecule of $H_2(g)$ and two molecules of NO(g).

A possible two-step mechanism is:

**Slow step**: $1H_2(g) + 2NO(g) \rightarrow H_2O(l) + N_2(g) + O(g)$

**Fast step:** $1H_2(g) + O(g) \rightarrow H_2O(l)$

slow step + fast step = balanced equation

**Balanced equation**: $2H_2(g) + 2NO(g) \rightarrow 2H_2O(l) + N_2(g)$

## Now test yourself

TESTED

4 Iodine monochloride, ICl, reacts with hydrogen:

$2ICl + H_2 \rightarrow 2HCl + I_2$

The rate equation for the reaction is rate = $k[ICl][H_2]$.
Suggest a two-step mechanism for this reaction.

Answer on p. 216

## Effect of temperature on rate constants

REVISED

If the temperature of a reaction is increased, whilst the initial concentrations of the reactants remain constant, the rate of reaction also increases. It follows that the rate constant, $k$, must increase as the temperature increases. The relationship between temperature, $T$, and the rate constant, $k$, can be expressed mathematically as shown in the Arrhenius equation.

### The Arrhenius equation

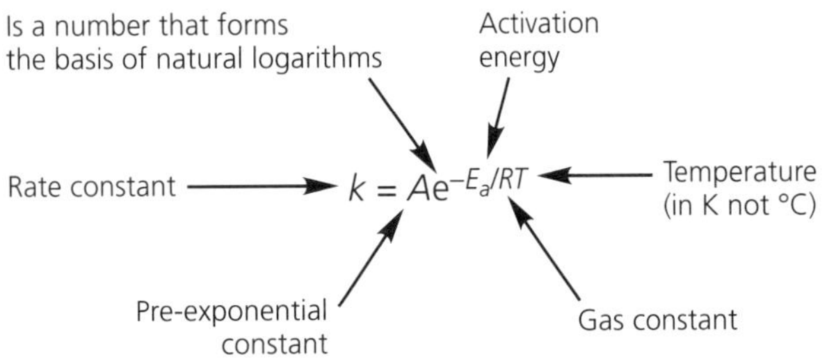


**Figure 8.3 Arrhenius equation**

The constant A has the same units as the rate constant, $k$, which will vary depending on the overall order of the reaction.

If natural logarithms (ln) of the Arrhenius equation are taken, the equation can be written as:

$$\ln k = \ln A - \frac{E_a}{RT}$$

or rearranged to give

$$\ln k = \frac{-E_a}{RT} + \ln A$$

You will recall that a straight-line graph can be described by the equation $y = mx + c$, where $m$ is the gradient and $c$ is the intercept. If $\ln k$ is plotted against $1/T$, the graph will be a straight line with a gradient of $-E_a/R$ and an intercept of $\ln A$ (Figure 8.4).

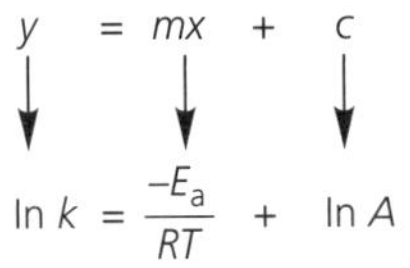


**Figure 8.4**

**Exam tip**

You will not be expected to remember this equation. It will be provided on the *Data Sheet*.

**Exam tip**

Make sure you know how to use your calculator!

**Example 1**

What is the value of the activation energy for a reaction at 367°C which has a pre-exponential factor of $2.45 \times 10^{10}$ and a rate constant of $0.00655\ dm^3 mol^{-1} s^{-1}$?

**Answer**

$$k = Ae^{-E_a/RT}$$

and

$$\ln k = \ln A \frac{-E_a}{RT}$$

The temperature must be in K, so $T = 273 + 367 = 640\,K$.

$R = 8.314\,J\,K^{-1}\,mol^{-1}$ so $RT = 640 \times 8.314 = 5320.96\,J = 5.32\,kJ$. Therefore:

$$\ln(0.00655) = \frac{-E_a}{5.32} + \ln(2.45 \times 10^{10})$$

$$-5.03 = \frac{-E_a}{5.32} + 23.92$$

$$\frac{E_a}{5.32} = 23.92 + 5.03 = 28.95$$

$$E_a = 28.95 \times 5.32 = 154\,kJ\,mol^{-1}$$

**Example 2**

At 500 K the rate constant, $k$, for a reaction is $6.8 \times 10^{-4}\,dm^3\,mol^{-1}\,s^{-1}$.

At 800 K the rate constant, $k$, for the same reaction is $8.2 \times 10^{-2}\,dm^3\,mol^{-1}\,s^{-1}$.

The gas constant $R = 8.314\,J\,K^{-1}\,mol^{-1}$

Determine the activation energy of the reaction.

**Answer**

Use: $\ln k = -E_a/RT + \ln A$ at 500 K and at 800 K.

$R, T$ and $k$ are all known but $E_a$ and $A$ are both unknown.

| 500 K | 800 K |
|---|---|
| $\ln(6.8 \times 10^{-4}) = \frac{-E_a}{(8.314 \times 500)} + \ln A$ | $\ln(8.2 \times 10^{-2}) = \frac{-E_a}{(8.314 \times 500)} + \ln A$ |
| $-7.29 = \frac{-E_a}{(4157)} + \ln A$ | $-2.50 = \frac{-E_a}{(6651)} + \ln A$ |

Isolate $\ln A$ at 500 K such that $\ln A = E_a/(4157) - 7.29$ and substitute into the equation at 800 K:

$$-2.50 = \frac{-E_a}{(6651)} + \frac{-E_a}{(4157)} - 7.29\text{, therefore } 7.29 - 2.50$$

$$= \frac{-E_a}{(6651)} + \frac{-E_a}{(4157)} = 4.79$$

Cross multiply to give:

$$-4157E_a + 6651E_a = 4.79 \times 6651 \times 4157$$

$$2494E_a = 132\,434\,911.5$$

$$E_a = \frac{132\,434\,911.5}{2494} = 53\,101\,J\,mol^{-1}$$

$$E_a = 531.0\,kJ\,mol^{-1}$$

# How far?

The section on chemical equilibrium in Module 3 introduced the idea of a **reversible reaction**, a **dynamic equilibrium** and **le Chatelier's principle and the equilibrium constant $K_c$**.

You should be able to use le Chatelier's principle to deduce what happens to the position of equilibrium when the system is subjected to change (Table 8.6). For example:

$$2NO_2(g) \rightleftharpoons N_2O_4(g) \qquad \Delta H = +100\,kJ\,mol^{-1}$$

Table 8.6

| Increase in temperature | Increase in pressure | Use of a catalyst | Increase in concentration of $NO_2$ |
|---|---|---|---|
| Equilibrium moves to the right because the forward reaction is endothermic | Equilibrium moves to the right because there are fewer molecules of gas on the right-hand side of the equilibrium | Equilibrium position remains unchanged because a catalyst speeds up the forward and reverse reactions equally | Equilibrium moves to the right to reduce the amount of $NO_2$ in the equilibrium |

In a **reversible reaction** the reagents react to form products and the products react to re-form the reagents. The reaction proceeds in both forward and reverse directions, which leads to the formation of a dynamic equilibrium.

## The equilibrium constant, $K_c$

REVISED

The equilibrium law

$K_c$ is the equilibrium constant in terms of equilibrium concentrations. The equilibrium law states that, for an equation:

$$aA + bB \rightleftharpoons cC + dD$$

$$K_c = \frac{[C]^c[D]^d}{[A]^a[B]^b}$$

[A], [B], [C] and [D] are the **equilibrium concentrations** of the reactants and products in the reaction.

Each product and reactant has its equilibrium concentration raised to the **power** of its **balancing number** (*a*, *b*, *c* and *d*) in the equation.

A **dynamic equilibrium** is reached when the rate of the forward reaction equals the rate of the reverse reaction. The concentrations of the reagents and products remain constant; the reagent and the product molecules react continuously.

## Working out $K_c$

REVISED

Consider the equilibrium:

$$H_2(g) + I_2(g) \rightleftharpoons 2HI(g)$$

Applying the equilibrium law:

$$K_c = \frac{[HI(g)]^2}{[H_2(g)][I_2(g)]}$$

At equilibrium: $[H_2(g)] = 0.012\,mol\,dm^{-3}$; $[I_2(g)] = 0.001\,mol\,dm^{-3}$; $[HI(g)] = 0.025\,mol\,dm^{-3}$.

$$K_c = \frac{(0.025)^2}{0.012 \times 0.001} = 52.1$$

### Units of $K_c$

You will have met $K_c$ in Module 3 of the course but, in Module 3, you were not expected to have considered its units. In fact, the units

**Le Chatelier's principle** states that if a closed system at equilibrium is subject to a change, the system will move to *minimise* the effect of that change.

**Equilibrium constant, $K_c$,** for a general reaction:
$aA + bB \rightleftharpoons cC + dD$:

$$K_c = \frac{[C]^c[D]^d}{[A]^a[B]^b}$$

**Effect of change on a system at equilibrium, $K_c$:** $K_c$ is a constant unless the temperature is changed.

of $K_c$ depend upon the equilibrium expression for the reaction. Each concentration value is replaced by its units:

$$K_c = \frac{[HI(g)]^2}{[H_2(g)][I_2(g)]} = \frac{(mol\,dm^{-3})^2}{(mol\,dm^{-3}\,mol\,dm^{-3})}$$

In this equilibrium, the units cancel and $K_c$ has no units.

### Writing expressions for $K_c$

It is essential that you are able to write expressions for $K_c$ and to deduce the units, if any, for each expression. Some examples are given in Table 8.7.

**Table 8.7**

| Equilibrium | $2NO_2(g) \rightleftharpoons N_2O_4(g)$ | $N_2(g) + 3H_2(g) \rightleftharpoons 2NH_3(g)$ | $Br_2(g) + H_2(g) \rightleftharpoons 2HBr(g)$ |
|---|---|---|---|
| $K_c$ | $K_c = \frac{[N_2O_4(g)]}{[NO_2(g)]^2}$ | $K_c = \frac{[NH_3(g)]^2}{[N_2(g)][H_2(g)]^3}$ | $K_c = \frac{[HBr(g)]^2}{[H_2(g)][Br_2(g)]}$ |
| Units | $mol^{-1}\,dm^3$ | $mol^{-2}\,dm^6$ | None |

## Properties of $K_c$

REVISED

$K_c$ indicates how *far* a reaction proceeds but tells us nothing about how *fast* the reaction occurs. The size of $K_c$ indicates the extent of a chemical equilibrium:

- If $K_c$ is big ($K_c = 1000$), the equilibrium lies to the right-hand side and a high percentage of product is formed.
- If $K_c$ is small ($K_c = 1 \times 10^{-3}$), the equilibrium lies to the left-hand side and a low percentage of product is formed.
- If $K_c = 1$, the equilibrium lies halfway between reactants and products.

## Changing $K_c$

REVISED

$K_c$ is a constant, *but* it is temperature dependent — it can be changed by altering the temperature. $K_c$ is unaffected by changes in concentration or pressure.

- In an exothermic reaction, $K_c$ decreases with increasing temperature because raising the temperature reduces the equilibrium yield of products.
- In an endothermic reaction, $K_c$ increases with increasing temperature because raising the temperature increases the equilibrium yield of products.

### Determination of $K_c$ by experiment

A variety of experiments can be carried out to determine equilibrium constants. Whichever method is used, it is essential that the equilibrium must not be disturbed by any measurement taken. For example, the acidity of a component might be measured using a pH meter, which would not affect the position of equilibrium. A titration would not be appropriate because the removal of the hydrogen ions during the titration would cause the equilibrium to rebalance. Other properties that might be used are a change in colour or electrical conductivity.

The equilibrium constant, $K_c$ can be determined from experimental results. The following example illustrates how to answer a typical question.

### Example

0.200 mol $CH_3COOH$ and 0.100 mol $C_2H_5OH$ were mixed together with a trace of acid catalyst in a total volume of 200 $cm^3$. The mixture was allowed to reach equilibrium:

$$CH_3COOH + C_2H_5OH \rightleftharpoons CH_3COOC_2H_5 + H_2O$$

Analysis of the mixture showed that 0.115 mol of $CH_3COOH$ were present at equilibrium. Calculate the equilibrium constant, $K_c$.

#### Answer

**Step 1:** Find the change in moles of each component in the equilibrium.

From the information given, the number of moles of $CH_3COOH$ that reacted = 0.200 − 0.115 = 0.085.

The balanced equation tells us the molar ratio of the reactants and the products.

| **Balanced equation** | $CH_3COOH$ | + | $C_2H_5OH$ | $\rightleftharpoons$ | $CH_3COOC_2H_5$ | + | $H_2O$ |
|---|---|---|---|---|---|---|---|
| **Molar ratio** | 1 mol | | 1 mol | | 1 mol | | 1 mol |
| **Change in moles** | −0.085 | | −0.085 | | +0.085 | | +0.085 |

**Step 2:** Determine the equilibrium concentration of each component.

| **Balanced equation** | $CH_3COOH$ | + | $C_2H_5OH$ | $\rightleftharpoons$ | $CH_3COOC_2H_5$ | + | $H_2O$ |
|---|---|---|---|---|---|---|---|
| **Initial amount/mol** | 0.200 | | 0.100 | | 0 | | 0 |
| **Change in moles** | −0.085 | | −0.085 | | +0.085 | | +0.085 |
| **Equilibrium amount/mol** | 0.115 | | 0.015 | | 0.085 | | 0.085 |
| **Equilibrium concentration/ mol dm$^{-3}$** | 0.115/0.20 | | 0.015/0.20 | | 0.085/0.20 | | 0.085/0.20 |

**Step 3:** Write the expression for $K_c$, substitute values and calculate $K_c$:

$$K_c = \frac{[CH_3COOC_2H_5][H_2O]}{[CH_3COOH][C_2H_5OH]}$$

$$= \frac{0.085/0.20 \times 0.085/0.20}{0.115/0.20 \times 0.015/0.20}$$

$$= \frac{0.425 \times 0.425}{0.575 \times 0.075} = 4.19$$

$K_c$ has no units because the equilibrium concentration units cancel.

**Exam tip**

When calculating a value for $K_c$, first check the units. If the number of species on each side of the equilibrium equation is the same then $K_c$ has no units and it doesn't matter whether you use moles or concentrations of each chemical.

**Typical mistakes**

$K_c$ relates to concentration and its value can only be calculated using concentrations. In answer to a question such as: '5 mol of $NO_2$(g) in a 2 $dm^3$ flask was allowed to reach the equilibrium $2NO_2(g) \rightleftharpoons N_2O_4(g)$. At equilibrium, the mixture contained 3 mols of $NO_2$(g). Calculate $K_c$', many students will simply put the number of moles into the expression for $K_c$. However, it is essential to first convert the moles into concentrations.

## Now test yourself

TESTED

5 Give the expression for the equilibrium constant, $K_c$ for each of the following reactions. In each case, state the units, if any.
   (a) $N_2O_4(g) \rightleftharpoons 2NO_2(g)$
   (b) $2N_2O(g) \rightleftharpoons 2N_2(g) + O_2(g)$
   (c) $2C(s) + O_2(g) \rightleftharpoons 2CO(g)$
   (d) $2CO(g) + O_2(g) \rightleftharpoons 2CO_2(g)$

6 Nitrogen(I) oxide, $N_2O$, decomposes to nitrogen and oxygen according to the equation:

$$2N_2O(g) \rightleftharpoons 2N_2(g) + O_2(g)$$

In an experiment, 1.00 mol of nitrogen(I) oxide is heated in a 1.00 $dm^3$ container until equilibrium is established. The mixture is then analysed and found to contain 0.10 mol of nitrogen(I) oxide.
   (a) Calculate the concentrations of nitrogen and oxygen present in the equilibrium mixture.
   (b) Calculate the equilibrium constant, $K_c$.
   (c) If the experiment were repeated using 1.00 mol of nitrogen(I) oxide in a 2.00 $dm^3$ container, how would the value of $K_c$ change?

Answers on pp. 216–217

## Equilibrium constant from partial pressures, $K_p$

REVISED

Many gaseous reactions also form equilibria and for gases it is more usual to measure pressure rather than concentration. The equilibrium constant for a gaseous reaction is given the symbol $K_p$. At constant temperature the total pressure of a gaseous reaction at equilibrium depends on the number of particles present in a given volume and the contribution of each gas depends on the amount in moles of an individual gas.

In a mixture of gases A, B and C the sum of the three pressures ($P_A$, $P_B$ and $P_C$) equals the total pressure ($P_{total}$) of the mixture:

$$P_{total} = P_A + P_B + P_C$$

In a mixture of gases the gas molecules move around independently, so the **partial pressure** for each gas is the pressure it would exert if it were the only gas in the container.

The **partial pressure** is the pressure that would be exerted by a gas in a mixture of gases if it occupied the same volume on its own at the same temperature.

The ideal gas equation, introduced in Module 3, can be written as $P = nRT/V$ such that the partial pressure of each component gas in the mixture is:

$$P_A = \frac{n_A RT}{V} \qquad P_B = \frac{n_B RT}{V} \qquad P_C = \frac{n_C RT}{V}$$

where $n_A$, $n_B$ and $n_C$ are the amounts in moles of gases A, B and C.

$R$ is a constant and at constant temperature the volume of the mixture is also constant such that:

$$P_A \propto n_A \qquad P_B \propto n_B \qquad P_C \propto n_C$$

The partial pressure of any gas in a mixture can be calculated using:

**partial pressure = mole fraction × total pressure**

Partial pressure of gas B → $P_B$; Total pressure of the mixture → $P_T$; Mole fraction of gas B → $x_B$

$$P_A = x_A \times P_T \qquad P_B = x_B \times P_T \qquad P_C = x_C \times P_T$$

where $x_A$, $x_B$ and $x_C$ are the **mole fractions** of A, B and C. The mole fraction of any component can be calculated by:

$$x_A = \frac{n_A}{(n_A + n_B + n_C)}$$

The **mole fraction** is the amount in moles of a component in a mixture divided by the total amount of all components in moles in the mixture.

The mole fractions of the all the gases must add up to 1: $x_A + x_B + x_C = 1$.

## Expression and units of the equilibrium constant, $K_p$

For a reaction:

$$aW(g) + bX(g) \rightleftharpoons cY(g) + dZ(g)$$

$$K_p = \frac{P_Y^{\,c} \times P_Z^{\,d}}{P_W^{\,a} \times P_X^{\,b}}$$

The units for $K_p$ are worked out in the same way as those for $K_c$ and like $K_c$ are dependent on the amounts in moles on both sides of the equation. Pressures can be measured in several different units but kPa is the correct SI unit.

**Exam tip**

Don't put square brackets round the partial pressures as this implies concentration.

**Example 1**

For the equilibrium $2HI(g) \rightleftharpoons H_2(g) + I_2(g)$:

$K_p = \frac{P_{HI}^2}{P_{H_2} \times P_{I_2}}$ This will have units of $\frac{(kPa)^2}{(kPa)\,(kPa)}$ such that the units cancel and $K_p$ has no units.

**Example 2**

For the equilibrium $N_2(g) + 3H_2(g) \rightleftharpoons 2NH_3(g)$:

$K_p = \frac{(pNH_3(g))^2}{(pN_2(g))(pH_2(g))^3}$ This will have units of $\frac{(kPa)^2}{(kPa)(kPa)^3}$ which is $kPa^{-2}$.

## Calculations involving $K_p$

**Example 1**

$$H_2(g) + I_2(g) \rightleftharpoons 2HI(g)$$

Hydrogen iodide was produced by reacting hydrogen and iodine. At equilibrium the mixture contained 0.1 mol hydrogen, 0.5 mol iodine and 4.5 mol hydrogen iodide. The total pressure of the equilibrium mixture was 250 kPa. Calculate $K_p$.

**Answer**

$$K_p = \frac{P_{HI}^{\;2}}{P_{H_2} \times P_{I_2}}$$

Total amount of moles of gas at equilibrium = 0.1 + 0.5 + 4.5 = 5.1 mol

| | $H_2$(g) | $I_2$(g) | HI(g) |
|---|---|---|---|
| Mole fraction of each gas | 0.1/5.1 | 0.5/5.1 | 4.5/5.1 |
| Partial pressure of each gas | (0.1/5.1) × 250 = 4.9 kPa | (0.5/5.1) × 250 = 24.5 kPa | (4.5/5.1) × 250 = 220.6 kPa |
| Always check that the partial pressures add up to the total pressure | | | 4.9 + 24.5 + 220.6 = 250 kPa |

$$K_p = \frac{220^2}{4.9 \times 24.5} = \frac{48400}{120.05} = 403$$

**Example 2**

6 mol of $SO_2$(g) is mixed with 10 mol of $O_2$(g) and allowed to come to equilibrium at a high temperature. It is found that 5.5 mol of sulfur trioxide has formed and the pressure in the container is 200 kPa:

$$2SO_2(g) + O_2(g) \rightleftharpoons 2SO_3(g)$$

Calculate $K_p$ for this reaction.

**Answer**

$2SO_2(g) + O_2(g) \rightleftharpoons 2SO_3(g)$ can be written as $SO_2(g) + \frac{1}{2}O_2(g) \rightleftharpoons SO_3(g)$.

So 1 mole of $SO_2$ reacts with ½ mol of $O_2$ to form 1 mol of $SO_3$.

| Solidus | $SO_2$ | $O_2$ | $SO_3$ |
|---|---|---|---|
| Initial amount/mol | *A* | *B* | *c* |
| Initial amount/mol | 6 | 10 | 0 |
| Equilibrium amount/mol | (*a* – *x*) | (*b* – ½*x*) | *x* |
| The equilibrium mixture contains 5.5 mol $SO_3$, so *x* = 5.5 | | | |
| Equilibrium amount/mol | 6 – 5.5 = 0.5 | 10 – 5.5 = 4.5 | 5.5 |
| Mole fraction of each gas | 0.5/10.5 = 0.048 | 4.5/10.5 = 0.43 | 5.5/10.5 = 0.52 |
| Partial pressure of each gas | 0.048 × 200 = 9.5 kPa | 0.043 × 200 = 85.7 kPa | 0.52 × 200 = 104.8 |
| Always check that partial pressures add up to total pressure (9.5 + 85.7 + 104.8 = 200) | | | |

$$K_p = \frac{P_{SO_3}{}^2}{P_{SO_3}{}^2 \times P_{O_2}} = \frac{104.82}{9.52 \times 85.7} = \frac{10983.04}{7734.425} = 1.42\,\text{kPa}^{-1}$$

The pressure exerted by each gas is dependent on the number of particles of that gas present and, in a fixed volume, this is related directly to its concentration. Therefore $K_c$ and $K_p$ are therefore also directly related.

## Expressions for $K_c$ and $K_p$ for heterogeneous equilibria

REVISED

In a heterogeneous equilibrium the concentrations of any liquids or solids remain constant and are omitted from the expressions for both $K_c$ and $K_p$.

**Example**

For the equilibria:

$Fe_3O_4(s) + 4H_2(g) \rightleftharpoons 3Fe(s) + 4H_2O(g)$

$$K_c = \frac{[H_2O(g)]^4}{[H_2(g)]^4}$$

$$K_p = \frac{pH_2O(g)^4}{pH_2(g)^4}$$

$CaCO_3(s) \rightleftharpoons CaO(s) + CO_2(g)$

$$K_c = [CO_2(g)]$$

$$K_p = pCO_2(g)$$

## The constancy of equilibrium constants

REVISED

$K_c$ and $K_p$ are temperature dependent and their numerical value will change if temperature is changed. The way in which the value changes depends on the $\Delta H$ value for the forward reaction.

$-\Delta H$ (exothermic) — if the temperature is increased, the numerical values of $K_c$ and $K_p$ decrease because the reverse (endothermic) reaction is favoured and the equilibrium moves to the left.

$+\Delta H$ (endothermic) — if the temperature is increased, the numerical values of $K_c$ and $K_p$ increase because the forward (endothermic) reaction is favoured and the equilibrium moves to the right.

If either concentration, pressure or a catalyst is changed the numerical values of $K_c$ and $K_p$ remain constant as the equilibrium adjusts itself to minimise the effect of the change.

### Now test yourself

TESTED

7 Write an expression for $K_p$ for each of the following equations and give its units.
 (a) $2NO_2(g) \rightleftharpoons N_2O_4(g)$
 (b) $2O_3(g) \rightleftharpoons 3O_2(g)$
 (c) $H_2O(g) + C(s) \rightleftharpoons H_2(g) + CO(g)$

8 $K_p$ for the equilibrium $H_2O(g) + CO(g) \rightleftharpoons CO_2(g) + H_2(g)$ at 700 K is $8.1 \times 10^{-2}$.
 If the partial pressures of the CO(g) and $H_2O(g)$ are both 35 kPa and the partial pressure of $H_2(g)$ is 18 kPa calculate:
 (a) the partial pressure of $CO_2(g)$
 (b) the total pressure of the mixture of gases

9 The following equilibrium can be formed at 470 K:
 $PCl_5(g) \rightleftharpoons PCl_3(g) + Cl_2(g)$
 When 0.30 mol of $PCl_5$ is heated the equilibrium is formed and when it is analysed it is found to contain 0.22 mol of $PCl_3$ and the pressure of the mixture is 222 kPa.
 Calculate $K_p$.

Answers on p. 217

# Acids, bases and buffers

You should be able to define an acid as a proton donor and be able to write equations, including ionic equations, for the reactions of acids.

## Brønsted–Lowry acids and bases

REVISED

The reactions of acids are covered in year 1 and are described fully on pages 32 and 33.

A **Brønsted–Lowry acid** is a proton donor.

A **Brønsted–Lowry base** is a proton acceptor.

### Acid–base pairs

Acids and bases are linked by $H^+$ as **conjugate acid–base pairs**.

By mixing an acid with a base, an equilibrium is set up between two acid–base conjugate pairs (Figure 8.5).

In the forward reaction: →

- $CH_3COOH(aq)$ donates a $H^+$ to the water and, therefore, behaves as an acid
- $H_2O$ accepts a $H^+$ from $CH_3COOH(aq)$ and, therefore, behaves as a base

$$CH_3COOH(aq) + H_2O(l) \rightleftharpoons H_3O^+ + CH_3COO^-(aq)$$

← In the reverse reaction:

- $H_3O^+$ donates a $H^+$ to the $CH_3COO^-(aq)$ and, therefore, behaves as an acid
- $CH_3COO^-(aq)$ accepts a $H^+$ from $H_3O^+$ and, therefore, behaves as a base

**Figure 8.5 Conjugate acid–base pairs**

$CH_3COOH(aq)$ and $CH_3COO^-(aq)$ form an acid–base conjugate pair and $H_3O^+$ and $H_2O(l)$ form a second acid–base conjugate pair.

Consider the equilibrium: $NH_3(g) + H_2O(l) \rightleftharpoons NH_4^+(aq) + OH^-(aq)$

In the forward reaction, the water donates a proton to the ammonia and, therefore, behaves as an acid. The ammonia accepts a proton and, therefore, behaves as a base. In the reverse reaction the ammonium ion is the acid and the hydroxide is the base.

In summary: $NH_3(g) + H_2O(l) \rightleftharpoons NH_4^+(aq) + OH^-(aq)$

| $NH_3(g)$ | $H_2O(l)$ | $NH_4^+(aq)$ | $OH^-(aq)$ |
|---|---|---|---|
| Base 2 | Acid 1 | Acid 2 | Base 1 |

**Exam tip**

All ions have the state symbol (aq). CuO(s) is not written as separate ions as the ions are not free to move in the solid state.

**Exam tip**

When balancing an ionic equation you must balance charge as well as symbols.

In a **conjugate acid–base pair**, the conjugate acid donates $H^+$ and the conjugate base accepts $H^+$.

**Exam tip**

Many questions involve one strong acid and one weak acid, to illustrate acid–base conjugate pairs. Remember: the stronger acid (the acid with the lower pH or $pK_a$ value) will donate a proton to the weaker acid.

### Now test yourself

TESTED

10 For each of the following equilibria, identify the conjugate acid–base pairs.

(a) $HCO_3^- + H_2O \rightleftharpoons H_2CO_3 + OH^-$

(b) $HCO_3^- + OH^- \rightleftharpoons H_2O + CO_3^{2-}$

Answer on p. 217

**Typical mistakes**

Ethanoic acid is mixed with nitric acid forming an equilibrium containing acid–base conjugate pairs. Complete the equation below by filling in the blanks:

$$CH_3CO_2H + HNO_3 \rightleftharpoons \ldots\ldots\ldots + \ldots\ldots\ldots$$

Both $CH_3CO_2H$ and $HNO_3$ are acids and because acids donate protons, the most common *incorrect* answer is $CH_3CO_2^-$ and $NO_3^-$. The correct response is $CH_3CO_2H_2^+ + NO_3^-$.

## Monobasic, dibasic and tribasic acids

REVISED

Monobasic acids contain one acidic hydrogen and include acids such as HCl(aq), $HNO_3$(aq) and $CH_3COOH$(aq). Monobasic acids form only one salt such as NaCl(aq), $NaNO_3$(aq) and $CH_3COONa$(aq), respectively.

Dibasic acids contain two acidic hydrogens; the most common examples are sulfuric acid, $H_2SO_4$(aq) and carbonic acid, $H_2CO_3$(aq). It is possible to form two different salts by reacting a dibasic acid. If one acid proton is replaced by the sodium ion we obtain sodium hydrogensulfate, $NaHSO_4$(aq), but if both are replaced sodium sulfate is produced, $Na_2SO_4$(aq). Sodium hydrogen carbonate, $NaHCO_3$(aq) and sodium carbonate, $Na_2CO_3$(aq) could be formed from carbonic acid.

Phosphoric acid, $H_3PO_4$, is a tri-basic acid as it has three acidic hydrogens and it is possible to form three different salts:

1 sodium dihydrogenphosphate, $NaH_2PO_4$, in which one acidic hydrogen is replaced by the metal ion
2 sodium hydrogenphosphate*, $Na_2HPO_4$, in which two acidic hydrogens are replaced by the metal ions
3 sodium phosphate**, $Na_3PO_4$, in which three acidic hydrogens are replaced by the metal ions

(*Sodium hydrogenphosphate could also be named as di-sodium hydrogenphosphate. **Sodium phosphate could also be named as tri-sodium phosphate.)

## The acid dissociation constant, $K_a$

REVISED

The extent of acid dissociation is shown by an equilibrium constant called the **acid dissociation constant**, $K_a$:

$$HA(aq) \rightleftharpoons H^+(aq) + A^-(aq)$$

$$K_a = \frac{[H^+(aq)][A^-(aq)]}{[HA(aq)]}$$

Units: $K_a$ = mol dm$^{-3}$

A **high $K_a$** value shows that the extent of dissociation is large — the acid is strong.

A **low $K_a$** value shows that the extent of dissociation is small — the acid is weak.

Ethanoic acid ionises as:

$$CH_3COOH(aq) \rightleftharpoons CH_3COO^-(aq) + H^+(aq)$$

$$K_a = \frac{[CH_3COO^-(aq)][H^+(aq)]}{[CH_3COOH(aq)]}$$

The $K_a$ value for ethanoic acid is $1.7 \times 10^{-5}$ mol dm$^{-3}$. This very low value indicates that a solution of ethanoic acid consists largely of ethanoic acid molecules with relatively few ethanoate ions and hydrogen ions.

The $K_a$ value for methanoic acid is $1.6 \times 10^{-4}$ mol dm$^{-3}$, which is almost ten times larger than the value for ethanoic acid. This indicates that methanoic acid, though weak, is stronger than ethanoic acid.

The mineral acids have much higher values for $K_a$. The value for nitric acid is approximately 40 mol dm$^{-3}$; that for sulfuric acid is often just listed as 'very large'.

## $K_a$ and p$K_a$

REVISED

$K_a$ is often expressed as the logarithmic form, **p$K_a$**, which is defined as:

$$pK_a = -\log_{10}K_a.$$

It is a more convenient way of comparing acid strengths.

On this logarithmic scale, each change of one unit on the p$K_a$ scale corresponds to a tenfold change in $K_a$. Like pH, p$K_a$ can be used as a guide to acidity. The lower the p$K_a$ value, the stronger the acid. See, for example, Table 8.8.

**Table 8.8**

| Acid | | $K_a$/mol dm$^{-3}$ | p$K_a$ |
|---|---|---|---|
| Ethanoic acid | $CH_3COOH$ | $1.7 \times 10^{-5}$ | $-\log_{10}(1.7 \times 10^{-5}) = 4.8$ |
| Benzoic acid | $C_6H_5COOH$ | $6.3 \times 10^{-5}$ | $-\log_{10}(6.3 \times 10^{-5}) = 4.2$ |

This indicates that benzoic acid is a stronger acid than ethanoic acid.

## pH and [$H^+$(aq)]

REVISED

### The pH scale

The concentration of $H^+$(aq) ions in acid solutions varies widely between about 10 mol dm$^{-3}$ and about $1 \times 10^{-15}$ mol dm$^{-3}$. The **pH** scale is used to overcome the problem of this wide range of numbers. It is a logarithmic scale — each change of one unit on the pH scale corresponds to a tenfold change in the $H^+$(aq) concentration (Table 8.9).

**pH** is defined by the equation: pH = $-\log_{10}[H^+(aq)]$

**Table 8.9**

| pH | 0 | 1 | 2 | 3 | 4 | 5 | 6 | 7 | 8 | 9 | 10 | 11 | 12 | 13 | 14 |
|---|---|---|---|---|---|---|---|---|---|---|---|---|---|---|---|
| [$H^+$] | 1 | $10^{-1}$ | $10^{-2}$ | $10^{-3}$ | $10^{-4}$ | $10^{-5}$ | $10^{-6}$ | $10^{-7}$ | $10^{-8}$ | $10^{-9}$ | $10^{-10}$ | $10^{-11}$ | $10^{-12}$ | $10^{-13}$ | $10^{-14}$ |

More acidic ← Neutral → More alkaline

You should be able to convert pH to $H^+$(aq) and vice versa using the relationships shown below:

$$pH = -\log_{10}[H^+(aq)]$$

$$[H^+(aq)] = 10^{-pH}$$

### Calculating the pH of strong acids

For a strong acid, we can assume **complete dissociation** and the concentration of $H^+$(aq) can be found from the acid concentration.

**Example 1**

A strong acid, HA, has a concentration of 0.020 mol dm$^{-3}$. What is the pH?

**Answer**

The acid dissociates completely. Therefore:

$$[H^+(aq)] = 0.020\ \text{mol dm}^{-3}$$

$$pH = -\log_{10}[H^+(aq)] = -\log_{10}(0.020) = 1.7$$

**Example 2**

A strong acid, HA, has a pH of 2.4. What is the concentration of $H^+(aq)$?

Answer

The acid dissociates completely. Therefore:

$[H^+(aq)] = 10^{-pH} = 10^{-2.4}\,mol\,dm^{-3}$

$[H^+(aq)] = 3.98 \times 10^{-3}\,mol\,dm^{-3}$

## Calculating the pH of weak acids

Weak acids do not dissociate completely. To calculate the pH of a weak acid, HA, you need to know:

- the concentration of the acid
- the acid dissociation constant, $K_a$.

In the equilibrium of a weak aqueous acid, HA(aq), we assume that only a very small proportion of HA dissociates. Hence the amount of undissociated acid is taken to be the same as the initial concentration of the acid.

We also assume that $[H^+(aq)]$ equals $[A^-(aq)]$.

Using these approximations:

$$K_a = \frac{[H^+(aq)][A^-(aq)]}{[HA(aq)]} = \frac{[H^+(aq)]^2}{[HA(aq)]}$$

**Exam tip**

This approximation should be limited to calculations for 'weaker' weak acids. For 'stronger' weak acids the assumption that the equilibrium amount of undissociated acid is approximately equal to the original concentration of the weak acid may no longer be valid.

**Example**

For a weak acid, $[HA(aq)] = 0.200\,mol\,dm^{-3}$; $K_a = 1.70 \times 10^{-4}\,mol\,dm^{-3}$ at 25°C.

Calculate the pH.

Answer

$$K_a = \frac{[H^+(aq)][A^-(aq)]}{[HA(aq)]} = \frac{[H^+(aq)]^2}{[HA(aq)]}$$

Therefore:

$$1.70 \times 10^{-4} = \frac{[H^+(aq)]^2}{0.200}$$

Rearranging gives:

$(1.70 \times 10^{-4}) \times 0.200 = [H^+(aq)]^2$

$[H^+(aq)] = \sqrt{(1.70 \times 10^{-4}) \times 0.200} = 5.83 \times 10^{-3} = 0.00583$

$pH = -\log_{10}[H^+(aq)] = -\log_{10}(0.00583) = 2.23$

An alternative way of doing this type of calculation is to use the equation:

$pH = -\log_{10}\sqrt{K_a \times [HA(aq)]}$

## Now test yourself

TESTED

11 Calculate the pH of each of the following aqueous solutions:
(a) 0.15 mol dm$^{-3}$ $HNO_3$
(b) 0.15 mol dm$^{-3}$ HCN
(c) 0.15 mol dm$^{-3}$ NaOH
($K_a = 6.2 \times 10^{-10}$ mol dm$^{-3}$)

12 Calculate the pH of a mixture of 20.0 cm$^3$ of 1.00 mol dm$^{-3}$ HCl and 10.0 cm$^3$ of 1.00 mol dm$^{-3}$ NaOH.

Answers on p. 217

## The ionic product of water, $K_w$

REVISED

Water ionises very slightly, acting as both an acid and a base:

| $H_2O(l)$ | + | $H_2O(l)$ | $\rightleftharpoons$ | $H_3O^+(aq)$ | + | $OH^-(aq)$ |
|---|---|---|---|---|---|---|
| Acid 1 | | Base 2 | | Acid 2 | | Base 1 |
| (donates proton) | | (accepts proton) | | (donates proton) | | (accepts proton) |

More simply:

$$H_2O(l) \rightleftharpoons H^+(aq) + OH^-(aq)$$

In water, only a very small proportion of molecules dissociates into $H^+(aq)$ and $OH^-(aq)$ ions and the equilibrium lies well to the left.

Treating water as a weak acid:

$$K_a = \frac{[H^+(aq)][OH^-(aq)]}{[H_2O(l)]}$$

Rearranging gives:

$$K_a \times [H_2O(l)] = [H^+(aq)][OH^-(aq)]$$

- $K_a \times [H_2O(l)]$ is a constant, $K_w$, and is called the **ionic product** of water.
- $K_w = [H^+(aq)][OH^-(aq)] = 1.0 \times 10^{-14}$ mol$^2$ dm$^{-6}$ (at 25°C)
- $K_w$ is temperature dependent and is equal to $1.0 \times 10^{-14}$ mol$^2$ dm$^{-6}$ at 25°C (298 K) only. (At 10°C, (283 K), $K_w = 2.9 \times 10^{-15}$ mol$^2$ dm$^{-6}$; at 40°C (313 K), $K_w = 2.9 \times 10^{-14}$ mol$^2$ dm$^{-6}$).

### $K_w$ can be used to calculate the pH of water

At 25°C: $K_w = [H^+(aq)][OH^-(aq)] = 1.0 \times 10^{-14}$ mol$^2$ dm$^{-6}$

Assuming that $[H^+(aq)] = [OH^-(aq)]$, then $K_w = [H^+(aq)]^2 = 1.0 \times 10^{-14}$ mol$^2$ dm$^{-6}$.

$$[H^+(aq)] = 1.0 \times 10^{-7} \text{ mol}^2 \text{ dm}^{-6}$$

$$pH = -\log_{10}[H^+(aq)] = -\log_{10}(1.0 \times 10^{-7})$$

$$pH = 7.0$$

However, since $K_w$ changes with temperature it follows that the pH of water is equal to 7.0 at 25°C only.

### $K_w$ can be used to calculate the pH of strong alkalis

The pH of a strong alkali, such as NaOH, can be calculated from the concentration of the alkali and the ionic product of water, $K_w$.

**Example**

A strong alkali, KOH, has a concentration of 0.50 mol dm$^{-3}$. What is the pH at 25°C?

**Answer**

KOH dissociates completely:

$$KOH(aq) \rightarrow K^+(aq) + OH^-(aq)$$

Therefore:

$$[OH^-(aq)] = [KOH(aq)] = 0.50\,mol\,dm^{-3}$$

$$K_w = [H^+(aq)][OH^-(aq)] = 1 \times 10^{-14}\,mol^2\,dm^{-6}$$

$$[H^+(aq)] = \frac{K_w}{[OH^-(aq)]} = \frac{1 \times 10^{-14}}{0.50} = 2 \times 10^{-13}\,mol\,dm^{-3}$$

$$pH = -\log_{10}[H^+(aq)]$$

$$= -\log_{10}(2 \times 10^{-13}) = 12.7$$

## Buffer solutions

REVISED

A buffer solution resists changes in pH during the addition of an acid or an alkali. It maintains a near constant pH by removing most of any acid or alkali that is added to the solution.

A buffer solution can be a mixture of a weak acid, HA, and its conjugate base, $A^-$:

$$HA(aq) \rightleftharpoons H^+(aq) + A^-(aq)$$

**Weak acid Conjugate base**

Buffer mixtures can be formed in one of two ways:

- By mixing a weak acid and a salt of the weak acid — $CH_3COOH$ (the weak acid) and $CH_3COO^-Na^+$ (the conjugate base).
- By mixing an **excess** of a weak acid and a strong base — excess $CH_3COOH$ (the weak acid) and NaOH (the strong base). The acid and base react to form the salt of the weak acid but because there is excess acid a mixture of the weak acid and its salt are formed.

The pH at which the buffer operates depends on the $K_a$ of the weak acid and the relative concentrations of the weak acid and the conjugate base.

In a mixture of $CH_3COOH$ and $CH_3COO^-Na^+$, the $CH_3COOH$ partially dissociates, giving low concentrations of $CH_3COO^-(aq)$ and $H^+(aq)$:

$$CH_3COOH(aq) \rightleftharpoons CH_3COO^-(aq) + H^+(aq)$$

$CH_3COO^-Na^+$ dissociates completely, giving high concentrations of $CH_3COO^-(aq)$:

$$CH_3COO^-Na^+(aq) \rightarrow CH_3COO^-(aq) + Na^+(aq)$$

The high $CH_3COO^-(aq)$ concentration forces the equilibrium to the left-hand side and results in the buffer solution containing a low concentration of $H^+(aq)]$ and high concentrations of $CH_3COOH(aq)$ and $CH_3COO^-(aq)$.

A buffer solution contains *two* important components:

- a high concentration of the weak acid, $[CH_3COOH(aq)]$
- a high concentration of the conjugate base, $[CH_3COO^-(aq)]$

On addition of an acid, $H^+(aq)$, the high concentration of the conjugate base $CH_3COO^-(aq)$ removes most of the added $H^+(aq)$ by forming $CH_3COOH(aq)$:

$$CH_3COO^-(aq) + H^+(aq) \rightarrow CH_3COOH(aq)$$

On addition of an alkali, $OH^-(aq)$, the high concentration of $CH_3COOH(aq)$ removes most of the added $OH^-(aq)$ by forming $CH_3COO^-(aq)$:

$$CH_3COOH(aq) + OH^-(aq) \rightarrow H_2O(l) + CH_3COO^-(aq)$$

A buffer cannot cancel out the effect of any acid or alkali that is added. The buffer removes most of the added acid or alkali and *minimises* any changes in pH.

## Calculations involving buffer solutions

The pH of a buffer solution depends upon the acid dissociation constant, $K_a$, of the acid and the molar ratio of the weak acid and its conjugate base.

For a buffer containing the weak acid, HA, and its conjugate base, $A^-$:

$$K_a = \frac{[H^+(aq)][A^-(aq)]}{[HA(aq)]}$$

Therefore:

$$[H^+(aq)] = \frac{K_a[HA(aq)]}{[A^-(aq)]}$$

so: $pH = -\log[H^+(aq)]$

$$pH = \frac{-\log [A^-]}{[HA]}$$

It follows that the pH of a buffer can be altered by adjusting the weak acid, HA, to conjugate base, $A^-$, ratio.

**Example**

(a) Calculate the pH of a buffer with concentrations of 0.10 mol dm$^{-3}$ $CH_3COOH(aq)$ and 0.10 mol dm$^{-3}$ $CH_3COO^-(aq)$. For $CH_3COOH$, $K_a = 1.7 \times 10^{-5}$ mol dm$^{-3}$.

(b) What happens to the pH if the concentration of $CH_3COOH(aq)$ is changed to 0.30 mol dm$^{-3}$?

**Answer**

(a) First, calculate $[H^+(aq)]$:

$$[H^+(aq)] = \frac{K_a[HA(aq)]}{[A^-(aq)]}$$

$$= \frac{1.7 \times 10^{-5} \times 0.10}{0.10} = 1.7 \times 10^{-5}\ \text{mol dm}^{-3}$$

**Exam tip**

Buffers can be prepared from a weak acid and a strong base, providing that the weak acid is in excess. If 100 cm$^3$ of 0.2 mol dm$^{-3}$ $CH_3COOH(aq)$ is mixed with 100 cm$^3$ of 0.1 mol dm$^{-3}$ $NaOH(aq)$, the resultant solution contains undissociated $CH_3COOH(aq)$ and $CH_3COO^-(aq)$. This solution is a buffer.

Then use [H⁺(aq)] to calculate pH:

$$pH = -\log_{10} [H^+(aq)]$$

$$= -\log_{10} (1.7 \times 10^{-5}) = 4.77$$

The pH of the buffer solution is 4.77.

(b) First, calculate [H⁺(aq)]:

$$[H^+(aq)] = \frac{K_a [HA(aq)]}{[A^-(aq)]}$$

$$= \frac{1.7 \times 10^{-5} \times 0.30}{0.10} = 5.1 \times 10^{-5} \text{mol dm}^{-3}$$

Then use [H⁺(aq)] to calculate pH:

$$pH = -\log_{10}[H^+(aq)]$$

$$= -\log_{10}(5.1 \times 10^{-5}) = 4.29$$

The pH of the buffer solution is 4.29.

## Control of pH in blood

REVISED

In the human body the blood plasma has a normal pH of 7.35–7.45. If the pH falls below 7.0 or rises above 7.8 the results could be fatal. The buffer systems in the blood are extremely effective and protect the fluid from large changes in pH. Blood contains a number of buffering systems, the major one being the carbonic acid–hydogencarbonate system:

$$H_2O(l) + CO_2(g) \rightleftharpoons H_2CO_3 \rightleftharpoons HCO_3^- + H^+$$

$H_2CO_3$ is carbonic acid; $HCO_3^-$ is hydrogencarbonate.

Adding an acid to the system increases the concentration of $H^+(aq)$, driving the equilibrium to the left. This increases the concentration of carbonic acid, $H_2CO_3$, which in turn is decreased by an increased breathing rate. More carbon dioxide is exhaled resulting in more $H_2CO_3$ breaking down to replace the exhaled $CO_2$. The two equilibria together resist the increase in acidity.

## pH changes and indicators

REVISED

**Indicators** are substances that change colour with a change in pH. Many indicators are weak acids and can be represented by HIn. The weak acid, HIn, and its conjugate base, $In^-$, have different colours, for example for methyl orange:

| | | | |
|---|---|---|---|
| RED | | | YELLOW |
| HIn(aq) | ⇌ | H⁺(aq) + | In⁻(aq) |
| Weak acid | | | Conjugate base |

At the end point of a titration HIn (red) and $In^-$ (yellow) are present in equal concentrations. Therefore, the colour at the end point is orange. The pH at the end point is equal to the $pK_{in}$ of the indicator.

### pH ranges for common indicators

An indicator changes colour over a range of about two pH units within which is the $pK_{in}$ value of the indicator (Figure 8.6).

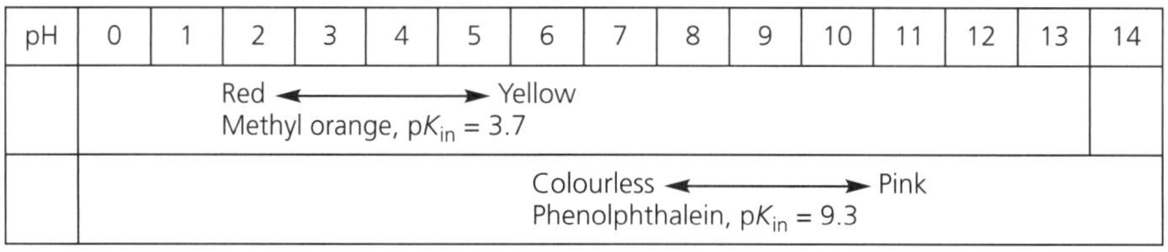


**Figure 8.6** Common indicators

## Choosing an indicator

When the acid and the base have completely reacted, this is known as the **equivalence point**. At the equivalence point of the titration there is a sharp change in pH for a very small addition of acid or base.

The choice of a suitable indicator is best shown using titration curves, which show the changes in pH during a titration (Figure 8.7).

### Key features of titration curves

- The pH changes rapidly at the near vertical portion of the titration curve. This is the end point of the titration.
- The sharp change in pH is brought about by a very small addition of alkali, typically the addition of one drop.
- The indicator is only suitable if its p$K_{in}$ value is within the pH range of the near vertical portion of the titration curve.

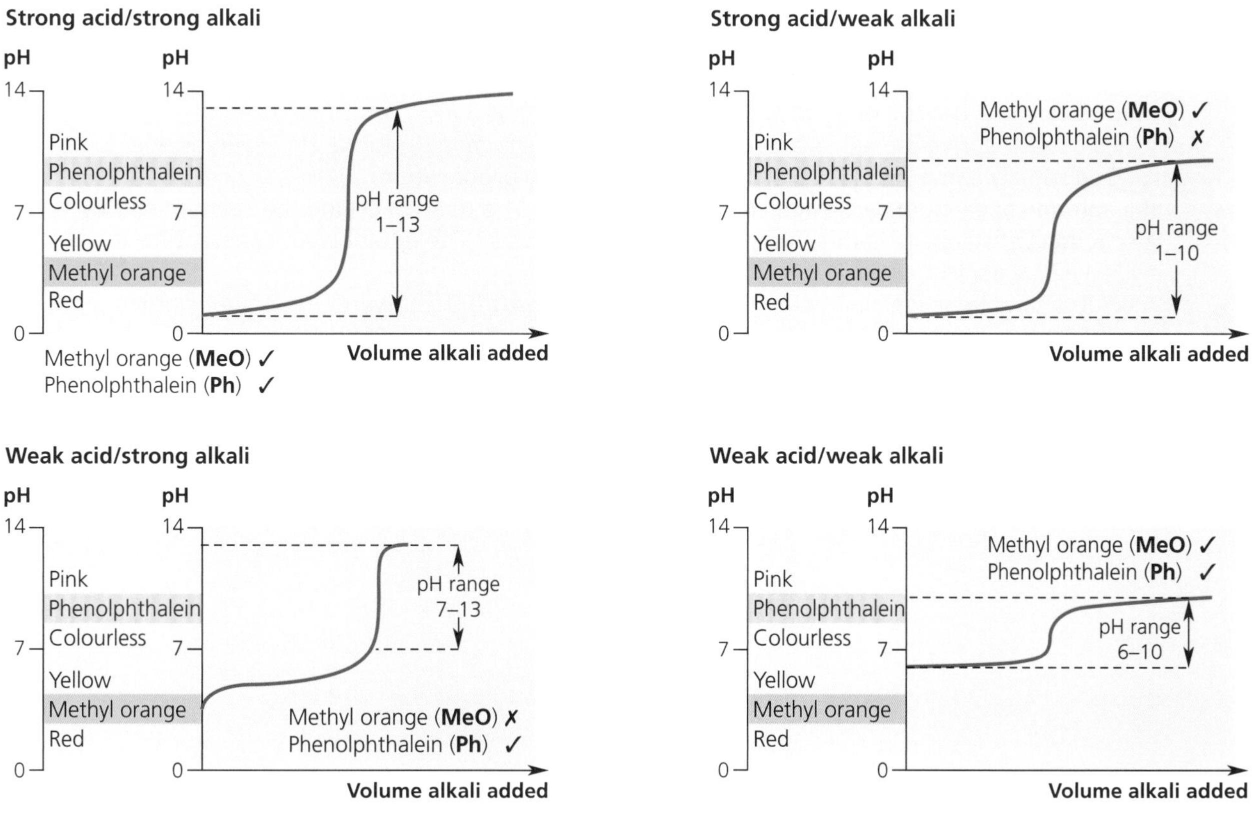


**Figure 8.7** Titration curves

## Now test yourself

TESTED

13 (a) The pH of a solution of ethanoic acid is 2.70. $K_a$ for the acid is $1.7 \times 10^{-5}$ mol dm$^{-3}$. Calculate the concentration of the ethanoic acid solution.

(b) Calculate the mass of sodium ethanoate that must be added to the acid to create a buffer solution of pH 4.0. (Assume that the sodium ethanoate does not cause an increase in volume as it dissolves.)

14 The $K_{in}$ value of chlorophenol red is $6.31 \times 10^{-7}$. It is yellow in acid solutions and red in alkaline solutions.

(a) Calculate the pH that is the mid-point for the colour change.

(b) Using chlorophenol red as your example, describe how an indicator works

(c) Give the colour of chlorophenol red when it is added to the following solutions. Explain your answers.

(i) 0.0001 mol dm$^{-3}$ hydrochloric acid

(ii) pure water

15 Aspirin is an effective pain killer although its use has, to some extent, been discouraged because in some instances it can cause the stomach to bleed. This appears to be triggered by the molecular form of aspirin dissolving in the covalent lipids in the stomach lining.

Aspirin contains a carboxylic acid and an ester. It is quite readily hydrolysed:

$$C_6H_4(OCOCH_3)CO_2H + H_2O \rightleftharpoons C_6H_4(OH)CO_2H + CH_3COOH$$

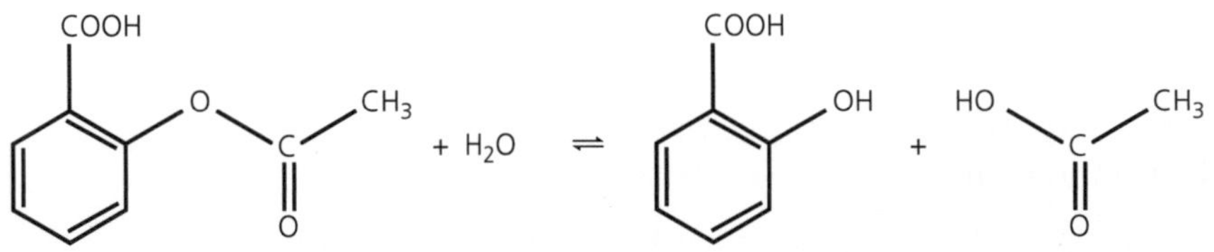


Because of the ease of hydrolysis, aspirin has a limited shelf life.

(a) Assuming that the pH of stomach acid is approximately 1, explain why stomach bleeding might be a problem.

(b) The blood is buffered at a pH of 7.4. Calculate whether aspirin in the blood exists largely in its unionised molecular form or as an anion. ($K_a$ for aspirin is $3 \times 10^{-4}$ mol dm$^{-3}$.)

Aspirin is usually administered as a calcium salt since this is more soluble. However, as aspirin is hydrolysed rapidly above pH 8.5, care has to be taken in its preparation.

(c) If a solution of calcium hydroxide containing 0.741 g dm$^{-3}$ is used to create the calcium salt by a reaction with aspirin, is this likely to result in hydrolysis? The equilibrium constant for the hydrolysis of aspirin is 0.35.

(d) A 0.900 g sample of aspirin becomes damp and absorbs 0.100 g of water. An equilibrium is established and analysis shows that 0.117 g of ethanoic acid is present in the equilibrium mixture. Calculate the percentage of aspirin that has been hydrolysed.

Answers on pp. 217–218

## Exam practice

1 The reaction between hydrogen and nitrogen monoxide is a redox reaction and results in the formation of nitrogen and water.

(a) (i) Write a balanced equation for the reaction. [1]

(ii) Identify the oxidising agent in the reaction. Justify your answer. [2]

(b) The rate equation for the reaction is:

rate = $k[H_2(g)][NO(g)]^2$

Using $1.2 \times 10^{-2}$ mol dm$^{-3}$ $H_2(g)$ and $6.0 \times 10^{-3}$ mol dm$^{-3}$ NO(g), the initial rate of this reaction was $3.6 \times 10^{-2}$ mol dm$^{-3}$ s$^{-1}$. Calculate the rate constant, *k*, for this reaction. Quote your answer to two significant figures. State the units of the rate constant, *k*. [4]

(c) Calculate the initial rate of reaction when each of the following changes is made. Show your working.

(i) The concentration of hydrogen is tripled. [1]

(ii) The concentration of the nitrogen monoxide is halved. [1]

(iii) The concentration of both is doubled. [1]

(d) Dinitrogen pentoxide decomposes according to the equation:

$2N_2O_5(g) \rightarrow 4NO_2(g) + O_2(g)$

The decomposition is first order with respect to $N_2O_5(g)$.

The decomposition proceeds by a two-step mechanism with the rate-determining step taking place first.

(i) Write a rate equation for this reaction. [1]

(ii) Explain the term *rate-determining step*. [1]

(iii) Suggest the two steps for this reaction and write their equations. Show clearly that the two steps equate to the balanced equation given above. [3]

2 Hydrogen and iodine react according to the equation:

$H_2(g) + I_2(g) \rightleftharpoons 2HI(g)$ $\Delta H = +53.0$ kJ mol$^{-1}$

(a) State le Chatelier's principle. [1]

(b) Use le Chatelier's principle to predict what happens to the position of the equilibrium when:

(i) the temperature is increased

(ii) the pressure is increased

(iii) a catalyst is used

Justify each of your predictions. [6]

(c) Write an expression for $K_c$ for the equilibrium. State the units, if any. [2]

(d) (i) When 0.18 mol of $I_2$ and 0.5 mol $H_2$ were placed in a 500 cm$^3$ sealed container and allowed to reach equilibrium, the equilibrium mixture was found to contain 0.010§mol of $I_2$. Calculate $K_c$. [5]

(ii) Explain what would happen to the value of $K_c$ if the experiment were repeated with the 500 cm$^3$ container replaced by one with a volume of 1 dm$^3$. [2]

3 (a) (i) A weak organic acid, HA, has the percentage composition by mass: C, 40%; H, 6.7%; O, 53.3%. Calculate the empirical formula of HA. [2]

(ii) The relative molecular mass of HA is 60.0. What is its molecular formula? [1]

(b) 1.20 g of HA were dissolved in 250.0 cm$^3$ of water. Calculate the pH of the resulting solution. Show all your working.

($K_a$ of HA = $1.7 \times 10^{-5}$ mol dm$^{-3}$) [5]

(c) A 0.04 mol dm$^{-3}$ solution of HA was titrated with a 0.05 mol dm$^{-3}$ solution of sodium hydroxide.

(i) Calculate the pH of the NaOH(aq). ($K_w = 1.0 \times 10^{-14}$ mol$^2$ dm$^{-6}$) [2]

(ii) Calculate the volume of NaOH(aq) required to neutralise 25.0 cm$^3$ of solution HA. [3]

(iii) Sketch a graph to show the change in pH during the titration. [3]

(d) Indicators can be used to determine the end point of a titration. Which of the following would be most suitable for this titration? Justify your answer and suggest what you would see at the end point. [3]

| Indicator | Acid colour | pH range | Alkaline colour |
|---|---|---|---|
| Thymol blue (acid) | Red | 1.2–2.8 | Yellow |
| Bromocresol purple | Yellow | 5.2–6.8 | Purple |
| Thymol blue (base) | Yellow | 8.0–9.6 | Blue |

4 A patient suffering from a duodenal ulcer displays increased acidity in their gastric juices. The exact acidity of the patient's gastric juice is monitored by measuring the pH.

(a) (i) Define pH. [1]

(ii) The patient's gastric juice was found to have a hydrochloric acid concentration of $8.0 \times 10^{-2}$ mol dm$^{-3}$. Calculate the pH of the gastric juice. [1]

(b) One of the most common medications designed for the relief of excess stomach acidity is aluminium hydroxide, $Al(OH)_3$.

(i) Write an equation for the reaction between HCl and $Al(OH)_3$. [1]

(ii) On another day, the patient's gastric juice was found to have a pH of 1.3. The patient produces 2 dm$^3$ of gastric juice in a day. This volume of gastric juice is to be treated with tablets containing $Al(OH)_3$ in order to raise the pH to 2.0. Calculate the mass of aluminium hydroxide required to raise the pH of 2 dm$^3$ of gastric juice from 1.3 to 2.0. [5]

(c) The control of the blood pH is important. This is achieved by the presence of $HCO_3^-$ ions in blood plasma. Using appropriate equations, explain how $HCO_3^-$ acts as a buffer solution. [3]

## Answers and quick quiz 8 online

ONLINE

## Summary

You should now have an understanding of:

- orders, rate equations and rate constants
- rate-determining step
- Arrhenius equation
- equilibrium, $K_c$
- equilibrium, $K_p$
- Brønsted–Lowry acids and bases
- p$K_a$ and pH
- buffers
- neutralisation

# 9 Energy

## Lattice enthalpy

### Review of basic ideas on energetics

REVISED

Chemical reactions are usually accompanied by a change in enthalpy (energy), $\Delta H$, normally in the form of heat energy. Reactions tend to be either **exothermic** or **endothermic**:

- An exothermic reaction loses energy to the surroundings and $\Delta H$ is negative.
- An endothermic reaction gains energy from the surroundings and $\Delta H$ is positive.

#### Standard enthalpy changes

All standard enthalpy changes are measured under **standard conditions** of temperature and pressure:

- temperature — 298 K (25°C)
- pressure — 101 kPa

Standard conditions are referred to as s.t.p.

The standard enthalpy change of formation and of combustion were both covered in year 1 of the course and are illustrated in Table 5.1 on page 59.

**Average bond enthalpy** is the enthalpy change on breaking 1 mol of a covalent bond in a gaseous molecule under standard conditions of 298 K and 101 kPa.

#### Activation energy

**Activation energy** is the minimum energy required for colliding particles to react. In any chemical reaction bonds are broken and new bonds are formed. Breaking bonds is an endothermic process that requires energy. The energy requirement contributes to the activation energy of a reaction.

#### Hess's law

**Hess's law** states that the enthalpy change for a reaction is the same irrespective of the route taken, provided that the initial and final conditions are the same.

### Lattice enthalpy and Born–Haber cycles

REVISED

**Lattice enthalpy** indicates the strength of the ionic bonds in an ionic lattice. For example:

$$Na^+(g) + Cl^-(g) \rightarrow Na^+Cl^-(s)$$

It is almost impossible to measure lattice enthalpy experimentally such that lattice enthalpy is calculated using a **Born–Haber** cycle. A Born–Haber cycle is similar to a Hess's cycle, enabling calculation of changes that cannot be measured directly.

> The **lattice enthalpy** ($\Delta_{LE}H^{\ominus}$) of an ionic compound is the enthalpy change that accompanies the formation of 1 mol of an ionic compound from its constituent gaseous ions. $\Delta_{LE}H^{\ominus}$ is exothermic.

The lattice enthalpy of sodium chloride can be calculated by considering the standard enthalpy of formation of NaCl(s). In order to form an ionic solid, both sodium and chlorine have to undergo a number of changes. These are outlined in Figure 9.1.

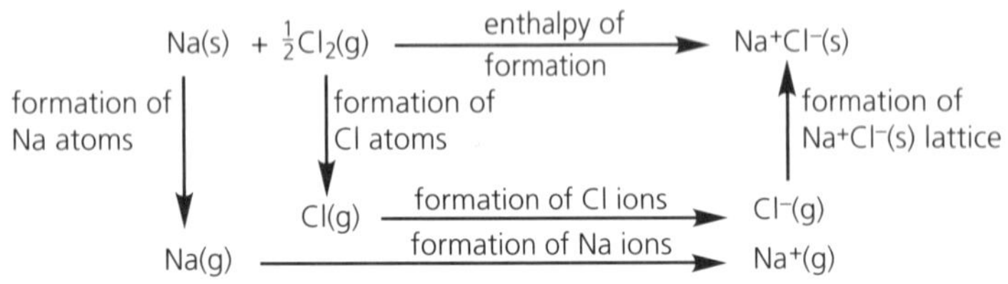


**Figure 9.1 Sodium chloride cycle**

All of the changes in the cycle can be measured experimentally except for the formation of the $Na^+Cl^-$(s) lattice from its gaseous ions — the lattice enthalpy. However, because enthalpies for the other steps can be measured, the lattice enthalpy can be calculated. The cycle above has to be converted into a Born–Haber cycle, which is a combination of an enthalpy profile diagram and a Hess's cycle. The full Born–Haber cycle for sodium chloride is shown in Figure 9.2

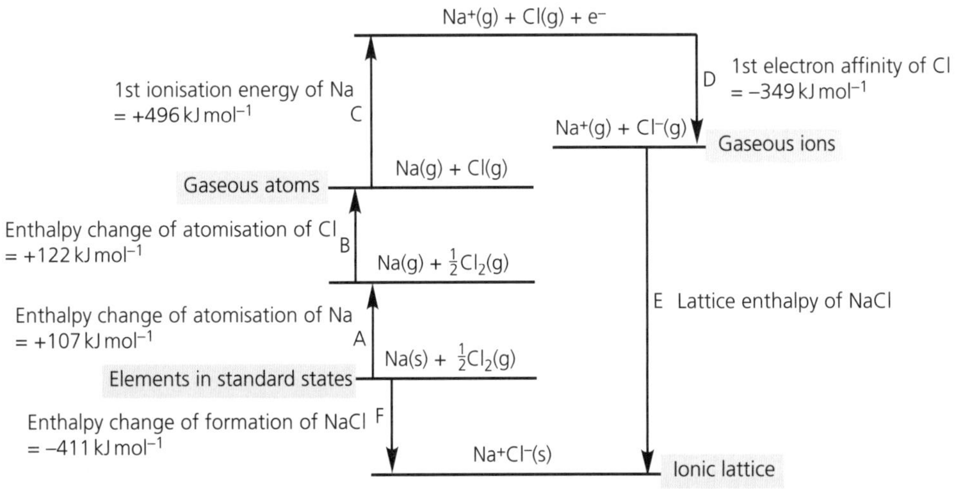


**Figure 9.2 Born–Haber cycle for the formation of sodium chloride**

Using Hess's law: A + B + C + D + E = F

$$\Delta_{at}H^{\ominus}\,Na(g) + \Delta_{at}H^{\ominus}\,Cl(g) + \Delta_{IE}H^{\ominus}Na(g) + \Delta_{EA}H^{\ominus}Cl(g) + E = \Delta_f H^{\ominus}Na^+Cl^-(s)$$

$$+107 \quad + \quad 122 \quad + \quad 496 \quad + \quad (-349) \quad + \quad E = -411$$

Hence, the lattice energy of $Na^+Cl^-$(s), $E = -787\,kJ\,mol^{-1}$

**Exam tip**

When constructing a Born–Haber cycle it is essential to show the change from *elements* to *gaseous atoms* to *gaseous ions* to *ionic lattice*.

## Definitions of enthalpy changes

REVISED

### Formation of an ionic compound

This is represented by step F in Figure 9.4.

**The standard enthalpy change of formation ($\Delta_f H^{\ominus}$)** is the enthalpy change when 1 mol of a substance is formed from its elements, in their natural states, under standard conditions. The standard enthalpy change of formation is usually exothermic for an ionic compound.

$$Na(s) + \tfrac{1}{2}Cl_2(g) \rightarrow Na^+Cl^-(s) \qquad \Delta_f H^{\ominus} = -411\,kJ\,mol^{-1}$$

## Formation of gaseous atoms

This is represented by steps A and B in Figure 9.4.

**The standard enthalpy change of atomisation, ($\Delta_{at}H^{\ominus}$)** of an element is the enthalpy change accompanying the formation of 1 mol of gaseous atoms from the element in its standard state. The standard enthalpy change of atomisation is always endothermic.

$Na(s) \rightarrow Na(g)$ $\Delta_{at}H^{\ominus} = +107\,kJ\,mol^{-1}$

$\frac{1}{2}Cl_2(g) \rightarrow Cl(g)$ $\Delta_{at}H^{\ominus} = +122\,kJ\,mol^{-1}$

## Formation of positive ions

This is represented by step C in Figure 9.4.

The **first ionisation energy ($\Delta_{IE}H^{\ominus}$)** of an element is the enthalpy change that accompanies the removal of one electron from each atom in 1 mol of gaseous atoms to form 1 mol of gaseous 1+ ions. The first ionisation energy is always endothermic.

$Na(g) \rightarrow Na^+(g) + e^-$ $\Delta_{IE}H^{\ominus} = +496\,kJ\,mol^{-1}$

## Formation of negative ions

This is represented by step D in Figure 9.4.

The **first electron affinity ($\Delta_{EA}H^{\ominus}$)** of an element is the enthalpy change that accompanies the addition of one electron to each atom in 1 mol of gaseous atoms to form 1 mol of gaseous 1− ions. The first electron affinity is always exothermic.

$Cl(g) + e^- \rightarrow Cl^-(g)$ $\Delta_{EA}H^{\ominus} = -349\,kJ\,mol^{-1}$

## Formation of ionic compound

This is represented by step E in Figure 9.4.

The **lattice enthalpy ($\Delta_{LE}H^{\ominus}$)** of an ionic compound is the enthalpy change accompanying the formation of 1 mol of an ionic compound from its constituent gaseous ions. The lattice enthalpy is always exothermic.

$Na^+(g) + Cl^-(g) \rightarrow Na^+Cl^-(s)$ $\Delta_{LE}H^{\ominus} = -787\,kJ\,mol^{-1}$

# Calculation of lattice enthalpy

REVISED

The lattice enthalpy for magnesium chloride and for magnesium oxide can be calculated using the data shown in Table 9.3

**Table 9.1 Data required for calculating the lattice enthalpies of magnesium chloride**

| | Standard enthalpy change | Equation | $\Delta H/kJ\,mol^{-1}$ |
|---|---|---|---|
| A | Formation of $MgCl_2(s)$ | $Mg(s) + Cl_2(g) \rightarrow MgCl_2(s)$ | −641 |
| B | Atomisation of magnesium | $Mg(s) \rightarrow Mg(g)$ | +148 |
| C | Atomisation of chlorine | $\frac{1}{2}Cl_2(g) \rightarrow Cl(g)$ | +122 |
| D | First ionisation energy of Mg | $Mg(g) \rightarrow Mg^+(g) + 1e^-$ | +738 |
| E | Second ionisation energy of Mg | $Mg^+(g) \rightarrow Mg^{2+}(g) + 1e^-$ | +1451 |
| F | First electron affinity of Cl | $Cl(g) + 1e^- \rightarrow Cl^-(g)$ | −349 |

The Born–Haber cycle for magnesium chloride is shown in Figure 9.3.

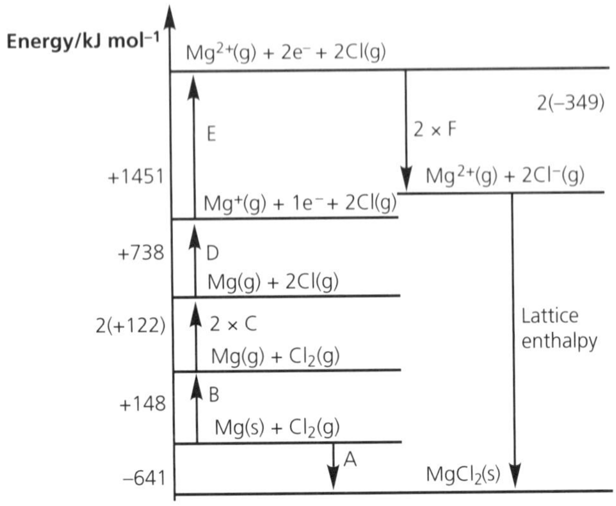


**Figure 9.3** **Born–Haber cycle for magnesium chloride**

Applying Hess's law to the Born–Haber cycle in Figure 9.5 gives:

A = B + 2C + D + E + 2F + lattice enthalphy

lattice enthalpy = A − B − 2C − D − E − 2F

The lattice enthalpy of magnesium chloride is:

= −641 −148 −244 − 738 −1451 − (−698)

= $-2524\,kJ\,mol^{-1}$

## Factors affecting the size of lattice enthalpies

REVISED

The strength of an ionic lattice and the value of its lattice enthalpy depend upon ionic radius and ionic charge.

### Effect of ionic size

As the **ionic radius increases** the charge density decreases and the attraction between the ions decreases such that the lattice energy becomes *less* negative.

### Effect of ionic charge

The strongest ionic lattices contain **small, highly charged ions**.

As the **ionic charge increases** the charge density increases and the attraction between the ions increases such that the lattice energy becomes *more* negative.

**Exam tip**

Note that lattice energy has a negative value. When describing lattice enthalpies you should use the term 'becomes less/more negative', *not* 'becomes bigger/smaller'.

## Now test yourself

TESTED

1 Use the data provided to:
  (a) construct a Born–Haber cycle for potassium oxide
  (b) calculate the lattice enthalpy of potassium oxide
  Enthalpy of atomisation of potassium = $+89.5\,kJ\,mol^{-1}$
  First ionisation enthalpy of potassium = $+420.0\,kJ\,mol^{-1}$
  Enthalpy of atomisation of oxygen = $+249.4\,kJ\,mol^{-1}$
  First electron affinity of oxygen = $-141.4\,kJ\,mol^{-11}$
  Second electron affinity of oxygen = $+790.8\,kJ\,mol^{-1}$
  Enthalpy of formation of potassium oxide = $-361.5\,kJ\,mol^{-1}$

Answer on p. 218

## Enthalpy change of hydration

REVISED

The concept of a Born–Haber cycle can be extended to provide a partial explanation of the solubility of substances in water. To do this, the **enthalpy of hydration** of an ion has to be used.

It is, therefore, the enthalpy change for the process:

$$X^{n+}(g) \rightarrow X^{n+}(aq)$$

In the case of hydration of NaCl the attraction is between the cation, $Na^+$, and the oxygen atom of a water molecule, and between the anion, $Cl^-$, and the hydrogen atom of the water molecule (Figure 9.4). This occurs because of the dipoles present in water, which you should be familiar with from year 1 of the course.

The **enthalpy of hydration**, $\Delta_{hyd}H^{\ominus}$ of an ion is the enthalpy change that occurs when 1 mol of gaseous ions is completely hydrated by water at 25°C and 101 kPa.

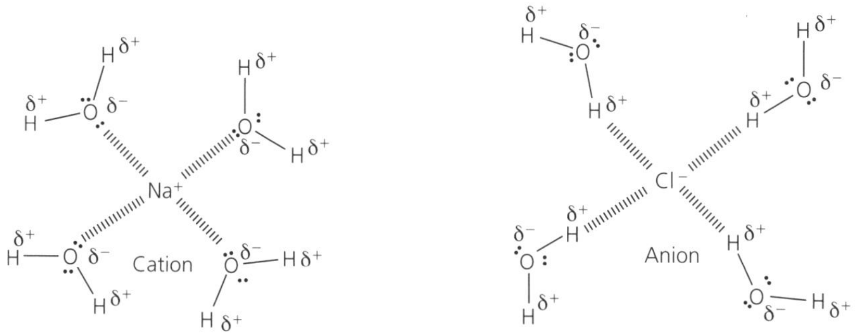


**Figure 9.4 Hydration of sodium chloride**

Like lattice enthalpy, the enthalpy change of hydration depends on the ionic radius and the size of the charge of the ion. As with lattice enthalpy, the greater the charge density, the greater the attraction.

Values of lattice enthalpies and enthalpies of hydration relate to the **enthalpy of solution**. A typical enthalpy cycle for sodium chloride is shown in Figure 9.5.

**The enthalpy of solution,** $\Delta_{sol}H^{\ominus}$ of a compound is the enthalpy change when 1 mol of that compound dissolves completely in excess water.

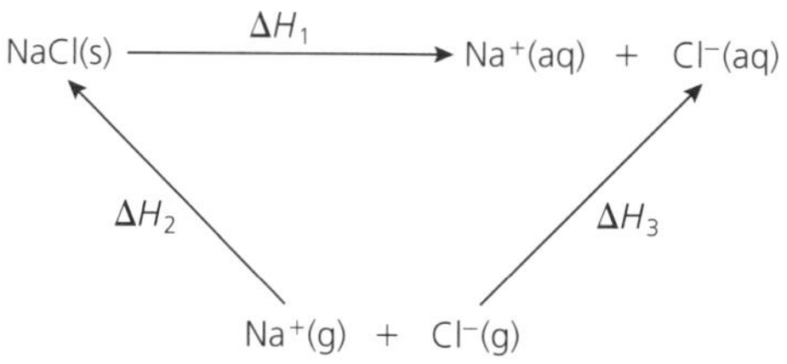


**Figure 9.5**

Applying Hess's law:

- $\Delta H_1$ is the enthalpy of solution.
- $\Delta H_2$ is the lattice enthalpy of sodium chloride ($-781\,kJ\,mol^{-1}$).
- $\Delta H_3$ is the enthalpy of hydration of the sodium ion ($-418\,kJ\,mol^{-1}$) + the enthalpy of hydration of the chloride ion ($-338\,kJ\,mol^{-1}$) = $-756\,kJ\,mol^{-1}$

$$\Delta H_2 + \Delta H_1 = \Delta H_3$$

$$\Delta H_1 = \Delta H_3 - \Delta H_2 = -756 + 781 = +25\,kJ\,mol^{-1}$$

The dissolving of sodium chloride is endothermic, yet sodium chloride dissolves readily in water at 25°C. This suggests that there is some other factor that is encouraging the dissolving to take place. This is an energy-related quantity called **entropy**, which is discussed in the next section.

**Exam tip**

This topic could be examined by providing you with a Born–Haber diagram and asking you to deduce the value of any one step. For sodium chloride, it would look like the diagram shown below:

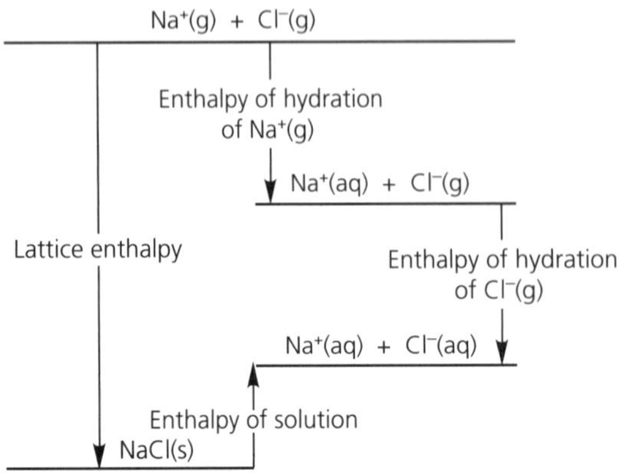


## Now test yourself

TESTED

2 Use the following enthalpies to calculate:
(a) the enthalpy of solution of silver chloride
(b) the enthalpy of hydration of iodide ions, $I^-(aq)$
Enthalpy of hydration of $Ag^+ = -464.4\,kJ\,mol^{-1}$
Enthalpy of hydration of $Cl^- = -384.1\,kJ\,mol^{-1}$
Enthalpy of solution of AgI = $+96.9\,kJ\,mol^{-1}$
Lattice enthalpy of AgCl = $-890\,kJ\,mol^{-1}$
Lattice enthalpy of AgI = $-867\,kJ\,mol^{-1}$
(c) Compare your answer to part (b) with the enthalpy of hydration of $Cl^-(aq)$ ($-384.1\,kJ\,mol^{-1}$). Explain your answer.
(d) Compare the relative solubilities of AgCl and AgI.

Answer on pp. 218–219

# Enthalpy and entropy

## Entropy

REVISED

When a reaction occurs energy is either absorbed (endothermic) or released (exothermic) in the form of heat. In addition, some energy is either absorbed or released as a result of the redistribution of the particles when the products are formed. This quantity of energy depends largely on the physical state of the substances and on the temperature.

Entropy is the term used to measure this quantity of energy. It is given the symbol, *S*.

Solids are more ordered than liquids, and liquids are more ordered than gases. It follows that most energy (entropy) is required to hold a solid in its ordered state. The particles of a gas are less constrained than in a liquid and energy (entropy) is not used because their freedom of movement is not restricted.

The enthalpy change for the melting of ice to water at 0°C is:

$$H_2O(s) \rightarrow H_2O(l) \qquad \Delta H = +6.02\,kJ\,mol^{-1}$$

The conversion therefore looks not to be possible — yet ice does melt at 0°C. This is because, as melting occurs, the change in entropy releases sufficient energy to counteract the positive enthalpy. The energy required to hold the rigid structure of the ice in place is released as the less constrained molecules of water are produced.

Two important differences between enthalpy and entropy are shown in Table 9.2.

**Table 9.2 Differences between enthalpy and entropy**

| Enthalpy | Entropy |
|---|---|
| If enthalpy is released when a reaction occurs, $\Delta H$ is negative | If entropy increases when a reaction occurs, $\Delta S$ is positive |
| The energy unit is usually kilojoules, kJ | The energy unit is usually joules, J |

Entropy always increases ($\Delta S$ is positive) when there is a greater opportunity for energy to be spread out as a result of a change. The system becomes more disordered. It follows that entropy increases when:

- a solid becomes a liquid
- a liquid becomes a gas
- a solid dissolves in a liquid to form a solution
- a reaction produces products with a greater degree of freedom of movement — for example, this could be because a gas is produced when a solid reacts, as in the decomposition of calcium carbonate:

$$CaCO_3(s) \rightarrow CaO(s) + CO_2(g)$$

- a reaction produces more particles in the same state, as in the combustion of propane:

$$C_3H_8(g) + 5O_2(g) \rightarrow 3CO_2(g) + 4H_2O(g)$$

**Exam tip**

You will not be asked to explain what 'entropy' is because this is a very difficult concept about which even experts disagree. You may be asked to predict whether entropy increases in a reaction — just use the state symbols as a guide. Compare the number of moles of gas, liquid or solid on each side of the equation.

## Now test yourself

TESTED

3 For each of the following reactions, predict whether the entropy change will be positive or negative:

(a) $H_2O(g) \rightarrow H_2O(s)$
(b) $NaOH(s) \rightarrow NaOH(aq)$
(c) $2Mg(s) + O_2(g) \rightarrow 2MgO(s)$
(d) $2SO_2(g) + O_2(g) \rightarrow 2SO_3(g)$

Answer on p. 219

## Calculating entropy changes

REVISED

Calculations to determine $\Delta S$ are similar to calculations for $\Delta H$, although it must be remembered that if $\Delta S$ is positive, it means that entropy is increased.

The change in entropy, $\Delta S$, can be calculated using the formula:

$$\Delta S = \Sigma(\text{entropy of products}) - \Sigma(\text{entropy of reactants})$$

**Example**

Calculate the entropy change for the following reaction under standard conditions:

$3O_2(g) \rightarrow 2O_3(g)$

| | $S^{\ominus}$/J mol$^{-1}$ K$^{-1}$ |
|---|---|
| $O_3$ | 238.8 |
| $O_2$ | 205 |

Answer

$\Delta S = \Sigma$(entropy of products) – $\Sigma$(entropy of reactants)

$\Delta S = 2 \times (238.8) - 3 \times (205)$

$= -137.4\ \text{J mol}^{-1}\ \text{K}^{-1}$

You should be able to anticipate the sign of $\Delta S$ by the fact that 3 mol of $O_2$ gas have been converted to 2 mol of $O_3$ gas. When a reaction produces fewer particles in the same state, $\Delta S$ is negative.

## Now test yourself

TESTED

4 Substances A, B and C are iodine, ammonia and methanol, but not necessarily in that order. Given the following entropies, identify which substance corresponds to which letter. Explain your answer.
A: 192.5 J mol$^{-1}$ K$^{-1}$ B: 58.4 J mol$^{-1}$ K$^{-1}$ C: 127.2 J mol$^{-1}$ K$^{-1}$
5 Calculate the entropy change when sodium reacts with oxygen.
$S^{\ominus}$(sodium) = 51.0 J mol$^{-1}$ K$^{-1}$; $S^{\ominus}$(oxygen) = 102.5 J mol$^{-1}$ K$^{-1}$; $S^{\ominus}$(sodium oxide) = 72.8 J mol$^{-1}$ K$^{-1}$

Answer on p. 219

## Free energy

REVISED

The change in the entropy of a reaction can be combined with the change in enthalpy to provide an answer to the question of whether a chemical reaction is feasible.

A new term must be introduced. This is **free energy** (or Gibbs free energy), which is given the symbol $G$.

The free energy change of a reaction relates to the enthalpy and entropy changes by the equation:

$$\Delta G = \Delta H - T\Delta S$$

$\Delta G$ provides a definite answer as to whether a given reaction is feasible. If $\Delta G$ is negative, the reaction is feasible; if $\Delta G$ is positive, the reaction is not feasible.

**Exam tip**

If $\Delta H$ and $\Delta S$ are both positive the reaction is always feasible. If they are both negative, the reaction is not feasible.

| | |
|---|---|
| $\Delta H$ is negative; $\Delta S$ is negative | $\Delta H$ favours the reaction but $T\Delta S$ resists the change. The reaction will be feasible when $\Delta H > T\Delta S$ and is therefore more likely to be feasible at low temperatures. |
| $\Delta H$ is positive; $\Delta S$ is positive | $\Delta H$ resists the reaction but $T\Delta S$ favours the change. The reaction will be feasible when $\Delta H < T\Delta S$ and is therefore more likely to be feasible at high temperatures. |

**Typical mistake**

When using the expression $\Delta G = \Delta H - T\Delta S$, you must remember that, whereas the units of $\Delta G$ and $\Delta H$ are kJ mol$^{-1}$, $\Delta S$ is measured in J mol$^{-1}$ K$^{-1}$. Therefore $\Delta S$ has to be converted into kJ mol$^{-1}$ K$^{-1}$ by dividing by 1000.

## Feasibility of a reaction

REVISED

A reaction is feasible if $\Delta G$ is negative. When $\Delta G = 0$, the system is at equilibrium and the reaction is about to be feasible.

Using $\Delta G = \Delta H - T\Delta S$ when $\Delta G = 0$ it follows that $\Delta H = T\Delta S$. The temperature at which the reaction becomes feasible can be calculated by using: $T = \Delta H/\Delta S$.

### Calculating free energy changes

If tables of information are provided, then calculating $\Delta G$ is similar to the process of calculating $\Delta H$.

**Example**

Use the data in the table to calculate the temperature at which the reaction $2NO(g) + O_2(g) \rightarrow 2NO_2(g)$ reaches equilibrium.

| | $\Delta_f H^\ominus$/kJ mol$^{-1}$ | $S^\ominus$/J mol$^{-1}$ K$^{-1}$ |
|---|---|---|
| NO(g) | 90.4 | 210.5 |
| $O_2(g)$ | 0 | 204.9 |
| $NO_2(g)$ | 33.2 | 240.0 |

**Answer**

$\Delta H = \Sigma$(enthalpy of products) – $\Sigma$(enthalpy of reactants)

$\Delta S = \Sigma$(entropy of products) – $\Sigma$(entropy of reactants)

At equilibrium, $\Delta G = 0$ so $T = \dfrac{\Delta H}{\Delta S}$

$\Delta H$ for the reaction is $(2 \times 33.2) - (2 \times 90.4) = -114.4\,\text{kJ mol}^{-1}$

$\Delta S = (2 \times 240.0) - ((2 \times 210.5) + 204.9) = -145.9\,\text{J mol}^{-1}\,\text{K}^{-1}$

Therefore (remembering to convert the energy unit of $\Delta S$ from J into kJ):

$T = \dfrac{-114.4}{-0.1459} = 784\,\text{K}$ or 511°C

# Redox and electrode potentials

## Ionic equations

REVISED

To write ionic equations correctly, it is essential to balance *both* symbol and charge. State symbols should always be included.

**Typical mistakes**

Students are aware that symbols have to be balanced, but they often ignore charge, which must also be balanced. For example, when asked to balance the equation:

$...IO_3^-(aq) + ...I^-(aq) + ...H^+(aq) \rightarrow ...I_2(s) + ...H_2O(l)$, the most common response is:

$...IO_3^-(aq) + ...I^-(aq) + 6H^+(aq) \rightarrow ...I_2(s) + 3H_2O(l)$

which balances the symbols but not the charges. The correct response is:

$IO_3^-(aq) + 5I^-(aq) + 6H^+(aq) \rightarrow 3I_2(s) + 3H_2O(l)$, which balances both.

**Exam tip**

When you have balanced an equation *always* double-check to make sure that the charges balance as well as the symbols. In the equation illustrated in 'Typical mistakes', each side of the equation has a net charge of zero, hence it is balanced.

The reaction between an acid and a base to produce a salt and water can be represented by an ionic equation. For example, when an aqueous hydroxide reacts with an acid, the ionic equation is:

$H^+(aq) + OH^-(aq) \rightarrow H_2O(l)$

Both sides of the equation have a net charge of zero.

When the base magnesium oxide reacts with an acid the ionic equation is:

$MgO(s) + 2H^+(aq) \rightarrow Mg^{2+}(aq) + H_2O(l)$

In an ionic solid such as MgO, the ions are not free to move, so they are not written as separate ions.

Both sides of the equation have a net charge of 2+.

The reaction between an acid and a carbonate to produce a salt, carbon dioxide and water can be represented by an ionic equation:

$CO_3^{2-}(aq) + 2H^+(aq) \rightarrow CO_2(g) + H_2O(l)$

Both sides of the equation have a net charge of zero.

## Now test yourself

TESTED

6 Write ionic equations for each of the following reactions:
(a) aqueous potassium carbonate and nitric acid
(b) solid calcium carbonate and hydrochloric acid
(c) precipitation of calcium carbonate from aqueous calcium chloride and aqueous sodium carbonate
(d) neutralisation of aqueous calcium hydroxide and hydrochloric acid
(e) precipitation of copper(II) hydroxide from aqueous copper nitrate and aqueous potassium hydroxide
(f) zinc oxide solid and nitric acid.

Answer on p. 219

## Redox reactions and oxidation numbers

REVISED

The displacement reaction between chlorine and bromide is an example of a redox reaction that you met in Module 3 in year 1 of the course (Figure 9.6).

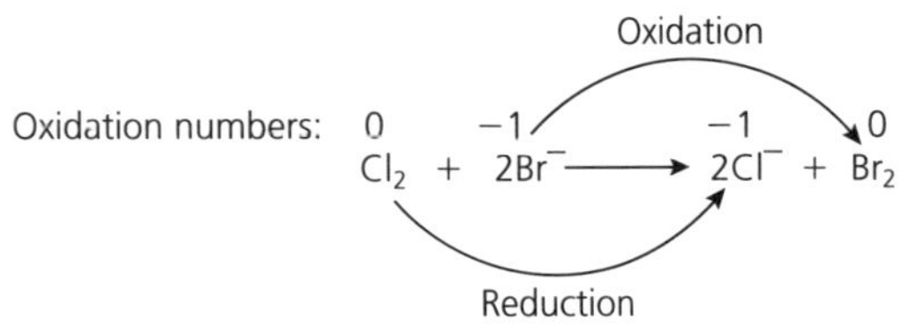


**Figure 9.6 Oxidation–reduction reaction**

Oxidation number is a convenient way of identifying quickly whether a substance has undergone either oxidation or reduction. In order to work out the oxidation number, you must first learn a few simple rules.

The rules for working out oxidation number were covered in year 1 and are shown on page 35.

If you make sure you apply these rules rigidly in the sequence indicated it should be relatively simple to deduce any oxidation number.

If during a reaction the oxidation number of a substance:

- **increases** the substance has been **oxidised** and the substance behaves as a **reducing agent**
- **decreases** the substance has been **reduced** and the substance behaves as an **oxidising agent**

An **oxidising agent** accepts electrons from another reagent and during the course of the reaction is itself reduced.

A **reducing agent** gives electrons to another reagent and during the course of the reaction is itself oxidised.

Consider the reaction of zinc and aqueous copper sulfate:

$Zn(s) + CuSO_4(aq) \rightarrow ZnSO_4(aq) + Cu(s)$

It may be helpful to write the oxidation numbers above each element in the equation:

Oxidation numbers: 0 +2 +6 −2 +2 +6 −2 0

$Zn(s) + CuSO_4(aq) \rightarrow ZnSO_4(aq) + Cu(s)$

In any redox reaction the oxidation number of one element increases and the oxidation number of a second element decreases. The oxidation number of zinc increases from 0 to +2. The oxidation number of copper decreases from +2 to 0. The ionic equation is:

$Zn(s) + Cu^{2+}(aq) \rightarrow Zn^{2+}(aq) + Cu(s)$

The zinc is oxidised. Each zinc atom loses two electrons and becomes a $Zn^{2+}$ ion. The electrons are taken up by a $Cu^{2+}$ ion, which is reduced to a copper atom, Cu.

The ionic half-equations are:

$Zn(s) \rightarrow Zn^{2+}(aq) + 2e^-$ oxidation (loss of electrons)

$Cu^{2+}(aq) + 2e^- \rightarrow Cu(s)$ reduction (gain of electrons)

In this reaction the Zn(s) is the reducing agent and the $Cu^{2+}$(aq) is the oxidising agent.

It is also be possible to use ionic half-equations to construct a full ionic equation. When Cu(s) is added to aqueous $AgNO_3$(aq), $Cu^{2+}$(aq) and Ag(s) are formed. The ionic half-equations are:

$Cu(s) \rightarrow Cu^{2+}(aq) + 2e^-$ oxidation (loss of electrons)

$Ag^+(aq) + e^- \rightarrow Ag(s)$ reduction (gain of electrons)

In any pair of ionic half-equations, the number of electrons released (by oxidation) is the same as the number required for the reduction. Cu(s) supplies two electrons as it is oxidised to $Cu^{2+}$(aq). Each $Ag^+$(aq) requires only one electron to be reduced to Ag(s). Therefore, it is necessary to use two $Ag^+$(aq) for each Cu(s):

$Cu(s) \rightarrow Cu^{2+}(aq) + 2e^-$

$2Ag^+(aq) + 2e^- \rightarrow 2Ag(s)$

The overall equation is obtained by adding the two half-equations together, excluding the electrons:

$2Ag^+(aq) + Cu(s) \rightarrow 2Ag(s) + Cu^{2+}(aq)$

In this reaction the Cu(s) is the reducing agent and the $Ag^+$(aq) is the oxidising agent.

The overall equation can now be written:

$2AgNO_3\ (aq) + Cu(s) \rightarrow 2Ag(s) + Cu(NO_3)_2(aq)$

Acidic solution of complex ions such as a $Cr_2O_7^{2-}$(aq) and $MnO_4^{2-}$(aq) are good oxidising agents. The chromium in $Cr_2O_7^{2-}$(aq) changes to $Cr^{3+}$(aq) and the manganese in $MnO_4^{2-}$(aq) changes to $Mn^{2+}$(aq). Using this knowledge it should be possible to construct half ionic equations:

$$Cr_2O_7^{2-}(aq) \longrightarrow Cr^{3+}(aq)$$

There are 2 Cr on the left-hand side so we need 2 Cr on the right-hand side

$$Cr_2O_7^{2-}(aq) \longrightarrow 2Cr^{3+}(aq)$$

The oxygens are always balanced by producing water as a product
There are 7 oxygens on the left-hand side so we need 7 waters on the right-hand side

$$Cr_2O_7^{2-}(aq) \longrightarrow 2Cr^{3+}(aq) + 7H_2O(l)$$

There are now 14 hydrogens on the right-hand side so we need to counterbalance and put 14 hydrogen ions on the left-hand side

$$14H^+ + Cr_2O_7^{2-}(aq) \longrightarrow 2Cr^{3+}(aq) + 7H_2O(l)$$

The symbols are now balanced but we need to balance charge by adding electrons to the left-hand side

$$14H^+ + Cr_2O_7^{2-}(aq) \longrightarrow 2Cr^{3+}(aq) + 7H_2O(l)$$

Charge on left-hand side = (14+) + (2-) = 12+

Charge on right-hand side = 2(3+) = 6+

We need to balance charge by adding 6 electrons to the left-hand side

$$14H^+ + Cr_2O_7^{2-}(aq) + 6e^- \longrightarrow 2Cr^{3+}(aq) + 7H_2O(l)$$

Symbols and charge are now balanced

## Now test yourself

TESTED

7 Use each of the following pairs of half-equations to construct an overall equation for the reaction. You must balance each half-equation before constructing the overall equation.

(a) $MnO_4^-(aq) + H^+(aq) \rightarrow Mn^{2+}(aq) + H_2O(l)$
$V^{2+}(aq) \rightarrow V^{3+}(aq)$

(b) $MnO_4^-(aq) + H^+(aq) \rightarrow Mn^{2+}(aq) + H_2O(l)$
$V^{2+}(aq) + H_2O \rightarrow VO_3^-(aq) + H^+(aq)$

(c) $Cr_2O_7^{2-}(aq) + H^+(aq) \rightarrow Cr^{3+}(aq) + H_2O(l)$
$SO_2(aq) + H_2O(l) \rightarrow SO_4^{2-}(aq) + H^+(aq)$

(d) $NO_3^-(aq) + H^+(aq) \rightarrow NO(g) + H_2O(l)$
$Cu(s) \rightarrow Cu^{2+}(aq)$

Answer on p. 219

## Redox titrations

REVISED

Titration calculations based on experimental results for the redox titrations are covered fully in the transition elements section.

## Electrode potentials

REVISED

The **standard electrode potential** is the potential difference (the difference in voltage) between one half-cell (e.g. a metal in contact with its metal ions) and the standard hydrogen electrode, when measured under standard conditions.

The **standard cell potential** is the voltage formed when two half-cells are connected. It is measured using a voltmeter of high resistance under standard conditions.

A diagram representing the standard hydrogen electrode is shown in Figure 9.7.

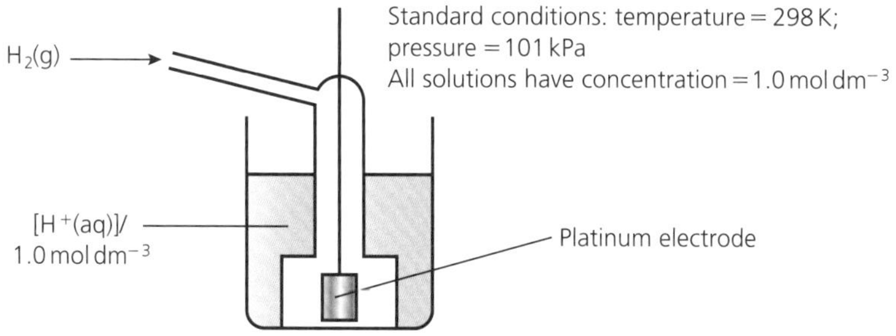


**Figure 9.7** A standard hydrogen electrode

This cell is connected via an external circuit and through a salt bridge to the other cell. The voltage measured gives the electrode potential of this cell compared with the half-reaction:

$$2H^+(aq) + 2e^- \rightarrow H_2(g)$$

which is given the arbitrary value of zero.

## Measuring the standard electrode potentials

**(1)** Metals (Figue 9.8)

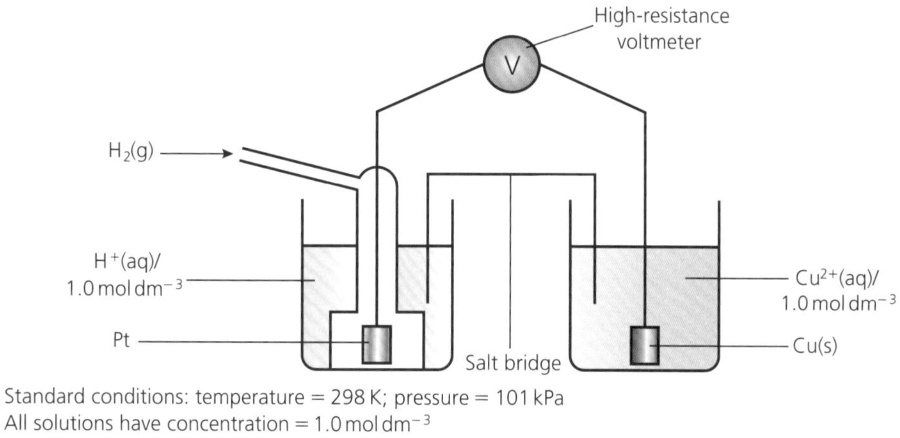


**Figure 9.8** Measuring standard electrode potentials for metals

**(2)** Non-metals/ions of the same element in different oxidation states (Figure 9.9)

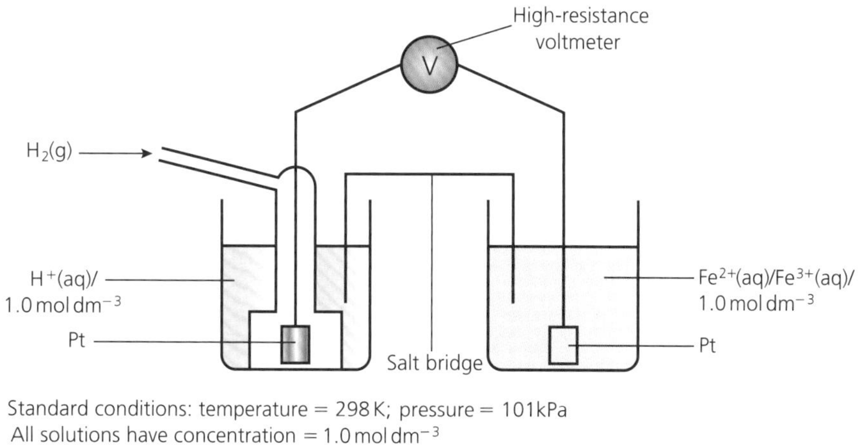


**Figure 9.9** Measuring standard electrode potentials for non-metals

The salt bridge is made of a porous material soaked in a saturated solution of $KNO_3$. The salt bridge completes the circuit without mixing the solutions by allowing the passage of ions.

**Typical mistakes**

If asked to draw a sketch to show how to measure the electrode potential for $Fe^{2+}/Fe^{3+}$ many students incorrectly draw:

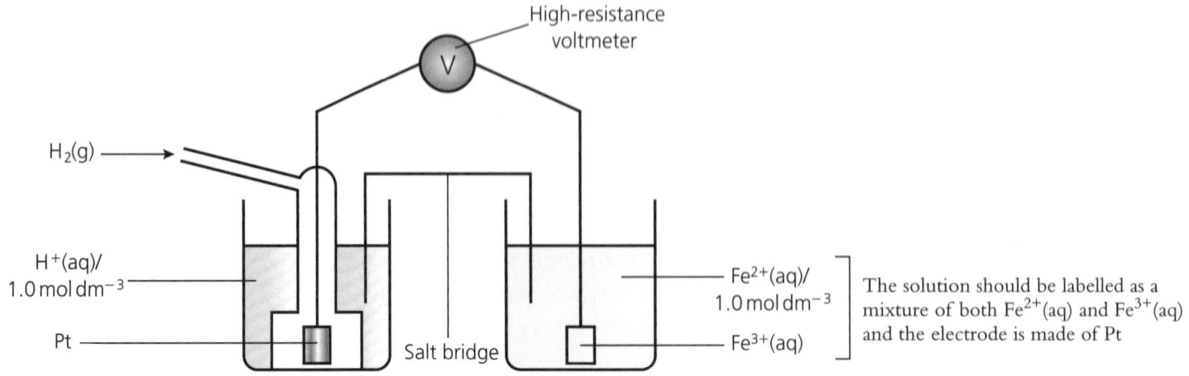


Standard conditions: temperature = 298 K; pressure = 101 kPa
All solutions have concentration = 1.0 mol dm$^{-3}$

Some common cell potentials are listed in the Table 9.3.

**Table 9.3 Common cell potentials**

| | Half-cell | $E^\ominus$/volts |
|---|---|---|
| A | $F_2(g) + 2e^- \rightleftharpoons 2F^-(aq)$ | +2.87 |
| B | $MnO_4^-(aq) + 8H^+(aq) + 5e^- \rightleftharpoons Mn^{2+}(aq) + 4H_2O(l)$ | +1.52 |
| C | $Cl_2(g) + 2e^- \rightleftharpoons 2Cl^-(aq)$ | +1.36 |
| D | $Cr_2O_7^{2-}(aq) + 14H^+(aq) + 6e^- \rightleftharpoons 2Cr^{3+}(aq) + 7H_2O(l)$ | +1.33 |
| E | $Ag^+(aq) + e^- \rightleftharpoons Ag(s)$ | +0.80 |
| F | $Fe^{3+}(aq) + e^- \rightleftharpoons Fe^{2+}(aq)$ | +0.77 |
| G | $Cu^{2+}(aq) + 2e^- \rightleftharpoons Cu(s)$ | +0.34 |
| **H** | $\mathbf{2H^+(aq) + 2e^- \rightleftharpoons H_2(g)}$ | **0.00** |
| I | $Zn^{2+}(aq) + 2e^- \rightleftharpoons Zn(s)$ | −0.76 |
| J | $K^+(aq) + e^- \rightleftharpoons K(s)$ | −2.92 |

For half-cells with positive $E^\ominus$ (A–G) the forward reaction is favoured, gaining electrons; for half-cells with a negative $E^\ominus$ (I and J) the reverse reaction is favoured, losing electrons.

- $F_2$(g) has the highest positive $E^\ominus$ and gains electrons readily to form $F^-$(aq) ions. Therefore, fluorine is a powerful oxidising agent.
- K(s) loses an electron readily to form $K^+$(aq). Therefore, potassium is a powerful reducing agent.

For a reaction to proceed, the overall cell potential must be positive. It can be calculated by using the appropriate two half-cells. The $E^\ominus$ values for the zinc and copper systems are:

$Zn^{2+}(aq) + 2e^- \rightleftharpoons Zn(s)$ **−0.76 V**

$Cu^{2+}(aq) + 2e^- \rightleftharpoons Cu(s)$ **+0.34 V**

One of these equations has to be reversed to give a positive value of the cell potential. Reversing the zinc half-cell gives:

$Zn(s) \rightarrow Zn^{2+}(aq) + 2e^-$ **+0.76 V**

To calculate the overall cell potential, this is combined with the copper half-cell, thus:

$Zn(s) \rightarrow Zn^{2+}(aq) + 2e^-$ +0.76 V

$Cu^{2+}(aq) + 2e^- \rightarrow Cu(s)$ +0.34 V

Cell potential = +1.10 V

**Example**

Acidified $MnO_4^-(aq)$ is a strong oxidising agent. It is used in the preparation of $Cl_2(g)$ by the oxidation of $Cl^-(aq)$ ions. Calculate the cell potential and deduce the balanced equation.

$MnO_4^-(aq) + 8H^+(aq) + 5e^- \rightleftharpoons Mn^{2+} + 4H_2O(l)$ $E^\ominus = +1.52\,V$

$Cl_2(g) + 2e^- \rightleftharpoons 2Cl^-(aq)$ $E^\ominus = +1.36\,V$

**Answer**

Both electrode potentials are positive, but $H^+(aq)/MnO_4^-(aq)$ is more positive and is, therefore, more likely to be preferred. Here, the chlorine half-equation has to be reversed:

$MnO_4^-(aq) + 8H^+(aq) + 5e^- \rightleftharpoons Mn^{2+} + 4H_2O(l)$ $E^\ominus = +1.52\,V$

$2Cl^- \rightarrow Cl_2(g) + 2e^-$ $E^\ominus = -1.36\,V$

Cell potential = +0.16 V

Both half-equations must have the same number of electrons. The $MnO_4^-$ half-equation is multiplied by 2 to give $10e^-$; the $Cl^-$ half-equation is multiplied by 5.

$2MnO_4^-(aq) + 16H^+(aq) + 10e^- \rightarrow 2Mn^{2+}(aq) + 8H_2O(l)$

$10Cl^-(aq) \rightarrow 5Cl_2(g) + 10e^-$

The overall equation is:

$2MnO_4^-(aq) + 16H^+(aq) + 10Cl^- \rightarrow 2Mn^{2+}(aq) + 8H_2O(l) + 5Cl_2(g)$

**Exam tip**

When balancing an equation always check that it is balanced for both symbol and charge. The reaction between $MnO_4^-$ and $Cl^-$ shown above has a net charge of +4 on each side of the equation. Hence, it is balanced.

## Now test yourself

TESTED

8 $Mg^{2+}(aq) + 2e^- \rightleftharpoons Mg(s)$ $E^\ominus = -2.37\,V$

$Zn^{2+}(aq) + 2e^- \rightleftharpoons Zn(s)$ $E^\ominus = -0.76\,V$

$Sn^{4+}(aq) + e^- \rightleftharpoons Sn^{2+}(aq)$ $E^\ominus = +0.15\,V$

$I_2(aq) + 2e^- \rightleftharpoons 2I^-(aq)$ $E^\ominus = +0.54\,V$

$Fe^{3+}(aq) + e^- \rightleftharpoons Fe^{2+}(aq)$ $E^\ominus = +0.77\,V$

$Br_2(aq) + 2e^- \rightleftharpoons 2Br^-(aq)$ $E^\ominus = +1.09\,V$

Use the standard electrode potentials, $E^\ominus$, listed above to calculate the cell potential for each of the following pairs of half-cells:

(a) $Mg(s)/Mg^{2+}(aq)$ and $Zn(s)/Zn^{2+}(aq)$
(b) $Sn^{4+}(aq)/Sn^{2+}(aq)$ and $Fe^{3+}(aq)/Fe^{2+}(aq)$
(c) $I_2(aq)/2I^-(aq)$ and $Br_2(aq)/2Br^-(aq)$
(d) $Zn(s)/Zn^{2+}(aq)$ and $I_2(aq)/2I^-(aq)$
(e) $Sn^{4+}(aq)/Sn^{2+}(aq)$ and $Br_2(aq)/2Br^-(aq)$

Answer on p. 219

## The effect of concentration on the feasibility of reactions

REVISED

A positive cell potential indicates that a reaction is feasible. However, it gives no indication of how fast a reaction will occur. The cell potential of the reaction between $H^+(aq)/MnO_4^-(aq)$ and $Cl^-$ is only +0.16 V, but the reaction takes place quickly despite the low overall potential.

The cell potentials are calculated assuming standard conditions. According to le Chatelier's principle, if the concentration of one component in a half-cell is changed, the equilibrium will move to minimise the effect of the change.

Consider the equilibrium:

$$Fe^{3+}(aq) + e^- \rightleftharpoons Fe^{2+}(aq) \qquad E^\ominus = +0.77\,V$$

If the concentration of $Fe^{2+}(aq)$ is reduced, the equilibrium position will move to the right, causing the value of the electrode potential to increase. If the concentration of $Fe^{3+}(aq)$ is reduced, the equilibrium will move to the left and the value of $E^\ominus$ will decrease. In each case, an extremely large change would be required to make any noticeable difference. As a general rule of thumb, a tenfold change in concentration changes the electrode potential of a half-reaction by 0.06 V or less.

### Now test yourself

TESTED

9 Dental amalgam contains about 40% mercury (Hg) combined with an alloy that is made largely of silver and tin. (Small amounts of copper and zinc are also present.) A number of redox reactions are possible with the amalgam as an electrode and saliva in the mouth as the electrolyte.
Two examples are:

$$Hg^+ + e^- \rightleftharpoons Ag/Hg\ (amalgam) \qquad E = +0.85\,V$$

$$Sn^{2+} + 2e^- \rightleftharpoons Sn/Hg\ (amalgam) \qquad E = -0.13\,V$$

If a piece of aluminium foil is bitten by teeth containing an amalgam, an unpleasant sharp pain is experienced. This results from a temporary cell being set up between the amalgam and the aluminium. Describe what happens in the cell and why it results in pain being felt.

Answers on pp. 219–220

## Storage and fuel cells

REVISED

### Storage cells

Storage cells are commonly referred to as batteries. Electrode potential can be used to predict the possible voltage of a battery.

**Example**

An 'alkaline battery' has a cathode made from graphite and manganese(IV) oxide and an anode made of either zinc or nickel-plated steel. The electrolyte is potassium hydroxide.

The reactions that take place are:

At the anode: $Zn + 2OH^- \rightarrow ZnO + H_2O + 2e^-$
At the cathode: $2MnO_2 + H_2O + 2e^- \rightarrow Mn_2O_3 + 2OH^-$

By adding the two equations together an overall equation for the cell can be constructed:

$$Zn + 2OH^- + 2MnO_2 + H_2O + 2e^- \rightarrow ZnO + H_2O + 2e^- + Mn_2O_3 + 2OH^-$$

The electrons, $H_2O$ and $OH^-$ cancel to give the net reaction:

$$Zn + 2MnO_2 \rightarrow ZnO + Mn_2O_3$$

**Exam tip**

There is no need to remember the details or construction of any particular cell, but you may be asked in an exam to interpret provided data.

Many other storage cells are made and the intense research into the development of batteries for use in vehicles has led to a number of different constructions. A disadvantage of all storage cells is that the reactants are used up and the overall voltage is not constant. Li-based cells present a risk from fire and from toxicity.

## Fuel cells

A fuel cell produces electrical power from the chemical reaction of a fuel (for example, hydrogen, hydrocarbons or alcohols) with oxygen. The fuel cell operates like a conventional storage cell, except that the fuels are supplied externally as gases. The cell will therefore operate more or less indefinitely so long as the fuel supply is maintained.

In all fuel cells the overall reaction is equivalent to the combustion of that fuel.

The hydrogen/oxygen fuel cell (Figure 9.10) is used widely and illustrates the principles behind fuel cells in general.

In an acidic solution, hydrogen is converted to hydrogen ions at the cathode while, at the anode, oxygen reacts with hydrogen ions to make water:

$$H_2(g) \rightleftharpoons 2H^+(aq) + 2e^- \qquad E^\ominus = 0.00\,V$$

$$\tfrac{1}{2}O_2(g) + 2H^+(aq) + 2e^- \rightleftharpoons H_2O(l) \qquad E^\ominus = +1.23\,V$$

The overall reaction is:

$$H_2(g) + \tfrac{1}{2}O_2(g) \rightarrow H_2O(l)$$

which is equivalent to the combustion of the fuel. The voltage produced is 1.23 V.

In alkaline solution, hydrogen reacts with hydroxide ions to form water and oxygen reacts with water to form hydroxide ions:

$$H_2(g) + 2OH^-(aq) \rightleftharpoons 2H_2O(l) + 2e^- \qquad E^\ominus = +0.83\,V$$

$$\tfrac{1}{2}O_2(g) + H_2O(l) + 2e^- \rightleftharpoons 2OH^-(aq) \qquad E^\ominus = +0.40\,V$$

The overall reaction is:

$$H_2(g) + \tfrac{1}{2}O_2(g) \rightarrow H_2O(l)$$

which is equivalent to the combustion of the fuel, and the voltage produced is again 1.23 V.

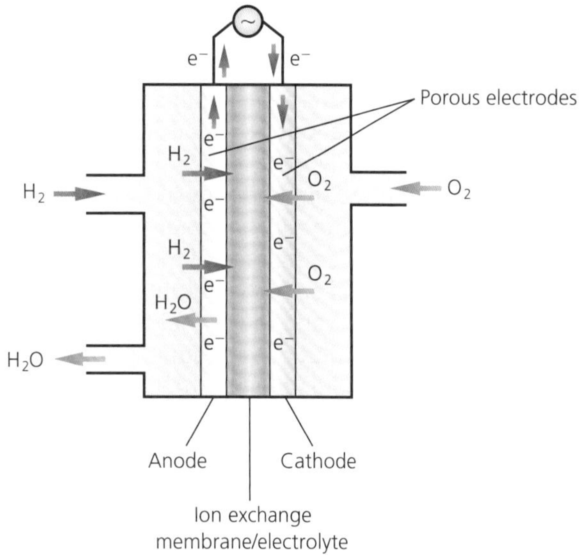


**Figure 9.10** A hydrogen/oxygen fuel cell

Other fuel cells can be constructed using different 'fuels'. For example, an ethanol fuel cell uses ethanol instead of hydrogen. The overall reaction that is occurring within the cell is again equivalent to burning the fuel, this time ethanol. In an acidic medium the reactions at each electrode are:

- at the positive electrode: $3O_2 + 12H^+ + 12e^- \rightarrow 6H_2O$
- at the negative electrode: $C_2H_5OH + 3H_2O \rightarrow 2CO_2 + 12H^+ + 12e^-$

And combining these two equations so that the supply of electrons is balanced gives:

$$3O_2 + 12H^+ + C_2H_5OH + 3H_2O + 12e^- \rightarrow 6H_2O + CO_2 + 12H^+ + 12e^-$$

Cancelling the $12H^+$, the $+ 12e^-$ and removing $3H_2O$ from both sides of the equation then gives the equation for the combustion of ethanol:

$$C_2H_5OH + 3O_2 \rightarrow 2CO_2 + 3H_2O$$

which is equivalent to the combustion of the fuel.

## Exam practice

1 (a) (i) Explain what is meant by the term lattice enthalpy. [2]

(ii) Write an equation to show what is meant by the lattice enthalpy of magnesium chloride. [2]

(b) Use the Born–Haber cycle in Figure 9.11 to answer the questions that follow.

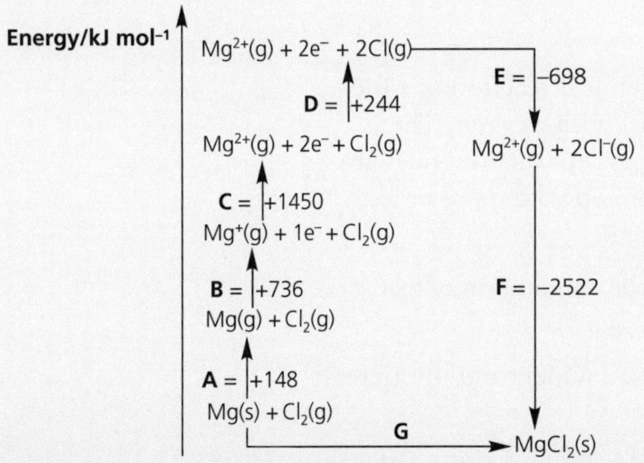


**Figure 9.11**

(i) Identify which step represents the second ionisation energy of magnesium. [1]

(ii) Write an equation that illustrates the second ionisation energy of magnesium. [1]

(iii) Explain why the enthalpy value for the second ionisation energy of magnesium is about twice the value of the first ionisation energy. [2]

(iv) Write an equation that illustrates the first electron affinity of chlorine. [2]

(v) State the energy, in $kJ\,mol^{-1}$, for the first electron affinity of chlorine. [1]

(vi) Calculate the enthalpy of formation of magnesium chloride. [2]

(c) The lattice enthalpy for magnesium bromide is $-2440\,kJ\,mol^{-1}$. Explain the difference in the values of the lattice enthalpies of magnesium bromide and magnesium chloride. [1]

(d) Magnesium bromide is soluble in water. The enthalpy of hydration of magnesium ions is $-1921\,kJ\,mol^{-1}$ and the enthalpy of hydration of the bromide ion is $-336\,kJ\,mol^{-1}$. Calculate the enthalpy of solution of magnesium bromide. [2]

(e) Using enthalpies of solution is not always a reliable way of predicting whether a substance will be soluble in water.

(i) What other energy change should be considered in making a prediction of solubility? [1]

(ii) Explain whether this other energy change is likely to suggest that a substance will be more or less soluble in water. [2]

(f) Describe how you could distinguish between aqueous solutions of magnesium bromide and magnesium chloride. State the observations you would make. [3]

2 (a) Use the data below to calculate the standard enthalpy change for the reaction:

$C(s) + CO_2(g) \rightarrow 2CO(g)$

$\Delta_f H^{\ominus}(CO_2) = -393.7\,kJ\,mol^{-1}$

$\Delta_f H^{\ominus}(CO) = -110.5\,kJ\,mol^{-1}$ [2]

(b) Use the data below to calculate the standard entropy change for the reaction:

$C(s) + CO_2(g) \rightarrow 2CO(g)$

$S^{\ominus}(CO_2) = 213.8\,J\,mol^{-1}\,K^{-1}$

$S^{\ominus}(C) = 5.7\,J\,mol^{-1}\,K^{-1}$

$S^{\ominus}(CO) = 197.9\,J\,mol^{-1}\,K^{-1}$ [2]

(c) (i) State the relationship between $\Delta G$, $\Delta H$ and $\Delta S$. [1]

(ii) Use your answers to (a) and (b) to determine the value of $\Delta G^{\ominus}$ for the reaction of carbon dioxide and carbon under standard conditions of 298 K and 101 kPa. [2]

(d) Calculate the minimum temperature in °C required for the reaction between carbon dioxide and carbon to become feasible. [3]

3 (a) Draw a diagram to show how to measure the standard electrode potential of the half-cell:

$Fe^{3+}(aq) + e^- \rightleftharpoons Fe^{2+}(aq)$

State the conditions necessary. [6]

(b) Use the following electrode potentials to predict whether, under standard conditions, $Fe^{3+}(aq)$ will be able to react with:

(i) $I^-(aq)$

(ii) $Br^-(aq)$

$I_2(aq) + 2e^- \rightleftharpoons 2I^-(aq)$ $E^{\ominus} = +0.54\,V$

$Fe^{3+}(aq) + e^- \rightleftharpoons Fe^{2+}(aq)$ $E^{\ominus} = +0.77\,V$

$Br_2(aq) + 2e^- \rightleftharpoons 2Br^-(aq)$ $E^{\ominus} = +1.09\,V$

If a reaction is possible, state what you would observe as the reaction takes place. [5]

(c) $I^-(aq)$ reacts with acidified $KMnO_4$ to form $Mn^{2+}(aq)$ ions and $I_2(aq)$. Write half-equations for each of these reagents and use them to construct a balanced ionic equation for the reaction. [3]

## Answers and quick quiz 9 online

ONLINE

## Summary

You should now have an understanding of:

- lattice enthalpy
- Born–Haber and related enthalpy cycles
- entropy, enthalpy and free energy
- redox
- electrode potentials
- storage and fuel cells

# 10 Transition elements

## Transition elements

The **transition elements** occur in period 4 of the periodic table (Table 10.1).

The 4*s* sub-shell is at a lower energy level than the 3*d* sub-shell and therefore the 4*s* sub-shell fills before the 3*d* sub-shell. The orbitals in the 3*d* sub-shell are first occupied singly to prevent any repulsion caused by pairing.

The majority of transition elements form ions in more than one oxidation state. When transition elements form ions they do so by losing electrons from the 4*s* orbitals before the 3*d* orbitals. Sc and Zn each form ions in one oxidation state only: $Sc^{3+}$ and $Zn^{2+}$. The electron configurations of these ions are $[Ar]3d^0$ and $[Ar]3d^{10}$, respectively. Neither fits the definition of a transition element.

**Typical mistakes**

Students usually get the full electron configuration of a transition metal correct. However, when asked for the electron configuration of a transition metal *ion* many incorrectly remove the 3*d* electrons before the 4*s*. The electron configuration of ${}_{26}Fe^{2+}$ is $1s^22s^22p^63s^23p^63d^6$, *not* $1s^22s^22p^63s^23p^63d^44s^2$.

Table 10.1 Electron configuration of the elements in period 4

| Element | Electron configuration |
|---|---|
| Sc | $[Ar]3d^14s^2$ |
| Ti | $[Ar]3d^24s^2$ |
| V | $[Ar]3d^34s^2$ |
| *Cr | $[Ar]3d^54s^1$ |
| Mn | $[Ar]3d^54s^2$ |
| Fe | $[Ar]3d^64s^2$ |
| Co | $[Ar]3d^74s^2$ |
| Ni | $[Ar]3d^84s^2$ |
| **Cu | $[Ar]3d^{10}4s^1$ |
| Zn | $[Ar]3d^{10}4s^2$ |

*Chromium has one electron in each orbital of the 4*s* and 3*d* sub-shells, giving the configuration as $[Ar]3d^54s^1$, which is more stable than $[Ar]3d^44s^2$.

**Copper has a full 3*d* sub-shell, giving the configuration as $[Ar]3d^{10}4s^1$, which is more stable than $[Ar]3d^94s^2$.

A **transition element** is defined as a *d*-block element that forms one or more stable ion that has partly filled *d*-orbitals.

## Properties

REVISED

- The transition elements are all metals and therefore they are good conductors of heat and electricity.
- They are denser than other metals. They have smaller atoms than the metals in groups 1 and 2, so the atoms pack together more closely, hence increasing the density.
- They have higher melting and boiling points than other metals. This can be explained by considering the size of their atoms. Within the metallic lattice, ions are smaller than those of the *s*-block metals, which results in greater 'delocalised electron density' and hence a stronger metallic bond.
- They have compounds with two or more oxidation states. This is because successive ionisation energies of transition metals increase only gradually. All the transition metals can form an ion of oxidation state +2, representing the loss of the two 4*s* electrons. The maximum oxidation state possible cannot exceed the total number of 4*s* and 3*d* electrons in the electron configuration.

Table 10.2 lists the common oxidation states of the transition elements

**Table 10.2**

| Ti | V | Cr | Mn | Fe | Co | Ni | Cu |
|---|---|---|---|---|---|---|---|
| +4, +3, +2 | +5, +4, +3, +2 | +6, +3, +2 | +7, +6, +4 +3, +2 | +3, +2 | +3, +2 | +2, +3 | +2, +1 |

- They have at least one oxidation state in which compounds and ions are coloured. The colours are often distinctive and can be used as a means of identification — for example, $Cu^{2+}$(aq) ions are blue, $Cr^{3+}$(aq) ions are green, $Cr_2O_7^{2-}$(aq) ions are orange and $MnO_4^-$(aq) ions are purple.
- Many transition metals and their compounds are used as heterogeneous catalysts. Examples include:
  - iron in the Haber process
  - $MnO_2$(s) for the decomposition of $H_2O_2$(l)
  - $Cu^{2+}$(aq) for the reaction of Zn with acids

  There are many benefits of using catalysts, not least the reduction of energy costs, however, there are significant risks from the toxicity of many transition elements.

## Ligands and complex ions

Transition metal ions are small and have a high charge density. They strongly attract electron-rich species called **ligands**, forming **complex ions**.

Common ligands include: $H_2O$:, :$Cl^-$, :$NH_3$ and :$CN^-$, all of which have at least one lone pair of electrons. The shape of the complex ion is determined by the number of coordinate bonds around the central metal ion.

A **ligand** is a molecule or ion that bonds to a metal ion, forming a coordinate (dative covalent) bond by donating a lone pair of electrons into a vacant *d*-orbital.

A **complex ion** is defined as a central metal ion surrounded by ligands.

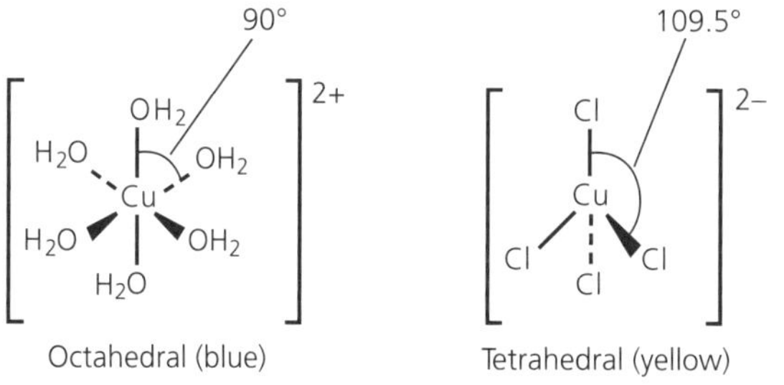


**Figure 10.1**

## Coordination number

The **coordination number** of a transition metal indicates how many ligands there are around the metal ion.

Complex ions with ligands such as $H_2O$ and $NH_3$ are usually 6-coordinate and octahedral in shape.

Complex ions with $Cl^-$ ligands are usually 4-coordinate and tetrahedral in shape.

Ligands form a dative coordinate bond with a central transition metal ion. Some ligands are able to form two dative coordinate bonds with the central transition metal ion; these are known as **bidentate ligands**.

The **coordination number** is defined as the total number of coordinate bonds from the ligands to the central transition metal ion in a complex ion.

1,2-diaminoethane is a common bidentate ligand. Each nitrogen atom has a lone pair of electrons and each can form a dative bond (Figure 10.2).

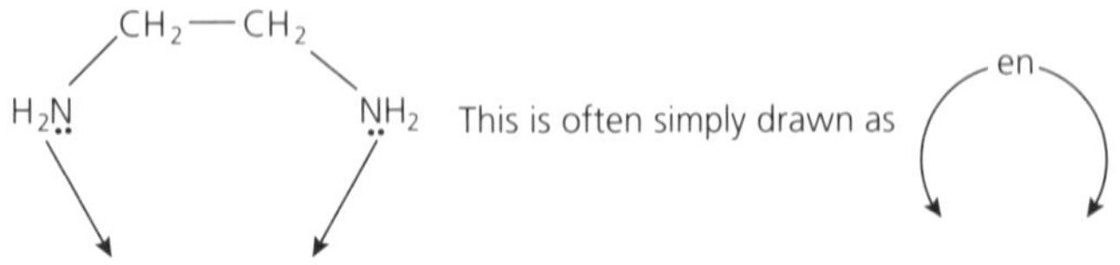


**Figure 10.2**

## Stereoisomerism in complex ions

Isomerism is commonplace in organic compounds. It also occurs in some inorganic substances.

The square planar structure of $Ni(NH_3)_2Cl_2$ has two isomeric forms (Figure 10.3) with the ammonia molecules and chloride ions being either on opposite sides of the complex ion (the *trans* form) or alongside each other (the *cis* form).

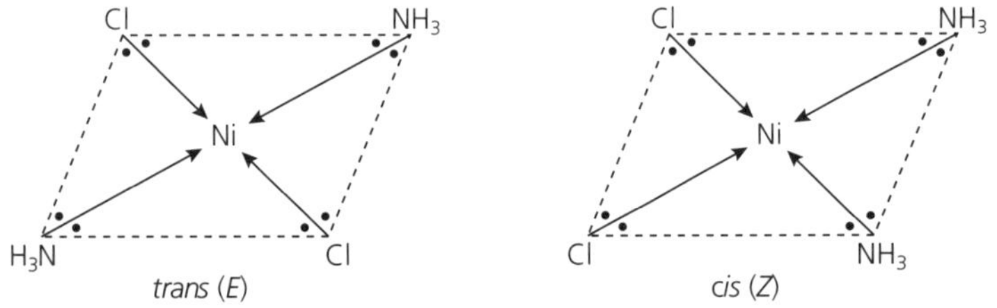


**Figure 10.3**

Complex ions have various uses. A particularly interesting example is the *cis* (*Z*) form of the molecule $PtCl_2(NH_3)_2$. (The platinum is present as platinum(II), so the complex therefore has no overall charge). The structure of $PtCl_2(NH_3)_2$ is shown in Figure 10.4.

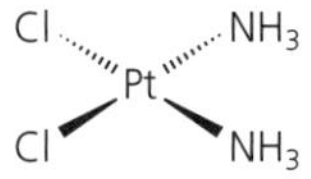


**Figure 10.4**

This compound is known as *cis*-platin. It is used during chemotherapy as an anti-cancer drug. It is a colourless liquid that is usually administered as a drip into a vein. It works by binding onto the DNA of cancerous cells and preventing their division. The importance of the exact shape and structure of the molecule is emphasised by the fact that the *trans* molecule is ineffective.

Optical isomerism is also possible in complexes coordinated with polydentate ligands. The nickel(II) 1,2-diaminoethane complex ion is an example (Figure 10.5).

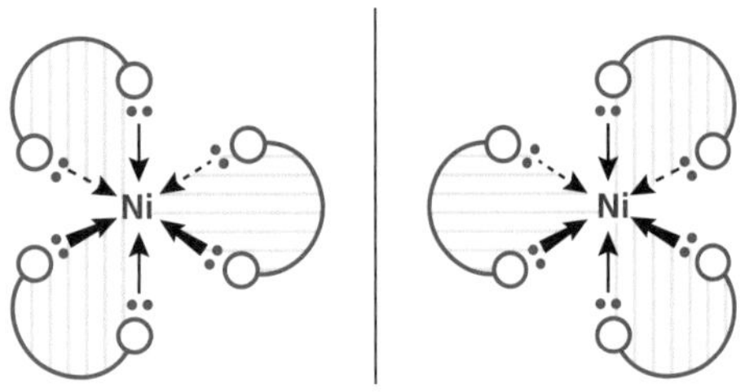


**Figure 10.5** **Optical isomers of nickel (II) 1, 2-diaminoethane**

**Exam tip**

Any ion or molecule that has two nitrogens can act as a bidentate ligand and form complexes like this $Ni(en)_3^{2+}$ complex.

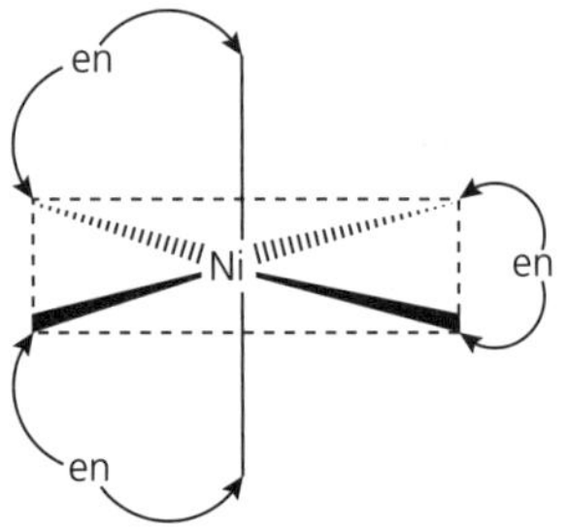


To draw the complex all you have to do is replace 'en' with whatever you are given in the question. Diols and dicarboxylic acids can also behave as bidentate ligands because the oxygen atoms have lone pairs of electrons.

As is the case with organic molecules, it is the asymmetry of the structure that leads to this property. The two molecules shown cannot be superimposed on each other.

## Ligand substitution of complex ions

A ligand substitution reaction takes place when a ligand in a complex ion exchanges with another ligand.

### Exchange between $H_2O$ and $NH_3$ ligands

Water and ammonia ligands have similar sizes, so the coordination number does not change during ligand exchange. An example is the formation of $[Cr(NH_3)_6]^{3+}$ from $[Cr(H_2O)_6]^{3+}$ (Figure 10.6).

**Typical mistakes**

It is easy to lose marks by drawing the complex ion carelessly, showing the coordinate (dative) bond going from the wrong atom. In $H_2O$, the bond always goes from the oxygen, *not* the hydrogen; in $NH_3$ it always goes from the nitrogen.

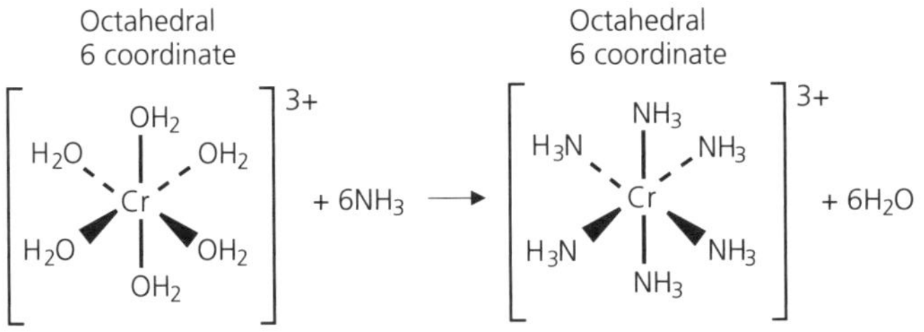


$$[Cr(H_2O)_6]^{3+} + 6NH_3 \rightleftharpoons [Cr(NH_3)_6]^{3+} + 6H_2O$$

**Figure 10.6 Ligand exchange to form $[Cr(H_2O)_6]^{3+}$**

### Exchange between $H_2O$ and $Cl^-$ ligands

Water molecules and chloride ions have **different sizes**, so the coordination number changes during ligand exchange. An example is the formation of $[CoCl_4]^{2-}$ from $[Co(H_2O)_6]^{2+}$ (Figure 10.7).

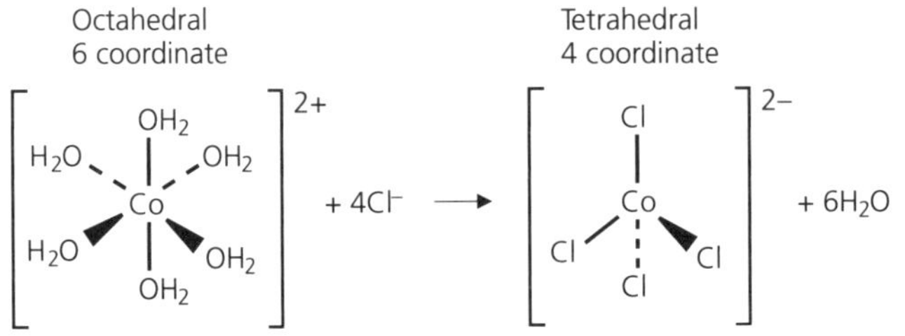


Pink solution $[Co(H_2O)_6]^{2+}$ + $4Cl^-$ → Blue solution $[CoCl_4]^{2-}$ + $6H_2O$

**Figure 10.7 Ligand exchange to form $[Cocl_4]^{2-}$**

## Precipitation reactions

REVISED

A precipitation reaction takes place between aqueous alkali and an aqueous solution of a metal(II) or metal(III) cation. This results in formation of a precipitate of the metal hydroxide, often with a characteristic colour. A suitable aqueous alkali is NaOH(aq) or $NH_3$(aq). The colour of the precipitate can be used as a means of identification. Some precipitation reactions can be represented simply, as in table 10.3.

**Table 10.3**

| Ion | Reaction | Colour of precipitate | Comments |
|---|---|---|---|
| $Cu^{2+}(aq)$ | $Cu^{2+}(aq) + 2OH^-(aq) \rightarrow Cu(OH)_2(s)$ | Light blue | See note 2 below |
| $Fe^{2+}(aq)$ | $Fe^{2+}(aq) + 2OH^-(aq) \rightarrow Fe(OH)_2(s)$ | Green | Slowly oxidises to $Fe(OH)_3$, which is brown |
| $Fe^{3+}(aq)$ | $Fe^{3+}(aq) + 3OH^-(aq) \rightarrow Fe(OH)_3(s)$ | Rust | |
| $Mn^{2+}(aq)$ | $Mn^{2+}(aq) + 2OH^-(aq) \rightarrow Mn(OH)_2(s)$ | Pale pink, almost white | Readily oxidises to $Mn_2O_3$, which is brown |
| $Cr^{3+}(aq)$ | $Cr^{3+}(aq) + 3OH^-(aq) \rightarrow Cr(OH)_3(s)$ | Dark green | See note 3 below |

**Note 1** This table shows the equations in their simplest format. They could each be written in full to show all of the ligands: e.g. $Cu(H_2O)_6^{2+}(aq) + 2OH^-(aq) \rightarrow Cu(H_2O)_4(OH)_2(s) + 2H_2O(l)$.

**Note 2** If aqueous ammonia is used in excess, the blue precipitate of $Cu(OH)_2(s)$ dissolves to form a much darker blue solution due to the formation of $[Cu(NH_3)_4(H_2O)_2]^{2+}$.

**Note 3** The precipitate of $Cr(OH)_3$ will dissolve if:
- aqueous ammonia is added in excess. The solution obtained contains the ion $Cr(NH_3)_6^{3+}$.
- aqueous sodium hydroxide is added in excess. The green solution obtained contains the ion $[Cr(OH)_6]^{3-}$.

## Now test yourself

TESTED ☐

1 Explain the following:
   (a) When 1,2-diaminoethane is added to a light blue, aqueous copper sulfate solution the colour of solution intensifies to dark blue.
   (b) When hydrochloric acid is added to the dark blue solution from part (a), the colour returns to the lighter blue.

2 Suggest explanations for each of the following:
   (a) When concentrated hydrochloric acid is added to aqueous cobalt(II) chloride solution, the colour of the solution changes from pink to blue.
   (b) When water is added to some of the blue solution from part (a), the colour changes back to pink.
   (c) When aqueous silver nitrate is added to some of the blue solution from part (a) the solution changes to pink again and a precipitate is formed.

3 Salts that contain a 'complexed' cation with an 'uncomplexed' anion can be crystallised. For example, cobalt forms a salt, **A**, of formula $[Co(NH_3)_6]Cl_3$ that is orange in colour.
   Isomers of this cobalt complex can be made that retain the same number of chlorines but with a chloride ion taking the place of one of the ammonia molecules in the ligand. An example is salt, **B**, which has the formula $[Co(NH_3)_5(Cl)]Cl_2$.
   (a) If equal volumes of solutions of the two salts **A** and **B** of the same concentration are reacted separately with excess aqueous silver nitrate, salt **A** produces a precipitate that has a mass which is 1.5 greater than that produced by salt **B**. Explain why.
   (b) Two different salts, **C** and **D**, can be made that contain $Co^{3+}$ coordinated with four ammonia ligands. Each salt also contains three chlorines. When the experiment in (a) is repeated separately with **C** and **D**, each produces a mass of precipitate that is half the mass obtained from compound **B**. Suggest structures for **C** and **D** and explain your answer.

Answers on p. 220

## Redox reactions

REVISED ☐

### Oxidation number

Oxidation number is a convenient way of identifying quickly whether a substance has undergone either oxidation or reduction.

## The iron(II)–manganate(VII) reaction

The most common redox reaction involving transition elements that you will meet is the reaction between $Fe^{2+}(aq)$ and $MnO_4^-(aq)$.

**Step 1:** Write an ionic half-equation for each transition metal.

In this reaction, $Fe^{2+}(aq)$ is oxidised to $Fe^{3+}(aq)$. This can be written as a half-equation:

$Fe^{2+} \rightarrow Fe^{3+} + 1e^-$ (equation 1)

Like any balanced equation, both the symbols and the charges have to balance.

If $Fe^{2+}$ is oxidised, it follows that $MnO_4^-$ must be reduced. It is reduced to $Mn^{2+}$. The first step in constructing a half-equation for this reduction is to recognise the change in oxidation state of the Mn.

As the oxidation number of oxygen is usually −2, it follows that in $MnO_4^-$ the oxidation number of Mn is +7. The oxidation number of the Mn in $Mn^{2+}$ is +2. Hence, the oxidation number of Mn changes from +7 to +2, so $5e^-$ must be gained:

$MnO_4^- + 5e^- \rightarrow Mn^{2+}$

This half-equation is *not* balanced. The reaction will not take place unless the $MnO_4^-$ is acidified. Each oxygen in the $MnO_4^-$ forms a water molecule. Since there are four oxygens in $MnO_4^-$, four water molecules will be formed, requiring $8H^+$:

$MnO_4^- + 8H^+ + 5e^- \rightarrow Mn^{2+} + 4H_2O$ (equation 2)

Like any balanced equation, both the symbols and the charges have to balance — each side has a net charge of 2+.

Each half-equation is now balanced:

$Fe^{2+} \rightarrow Fe^{3+} + 1e^-$ (equation 1)

$MnO_4^- + 8H^+ + 5e^- \rightarrow Mn^{2+} + 4H_2O$ (equation 2)

**Step 2:** Rewrite the half-equations so that the number of electrons in both is the same.

In this case, we need to multiply equation 1 by 5, giving:

$5Fe^{2+} \rightarrow 5Fe^{3+} + 5e^-$

Equation 2 remains the same:

$MnO_4^- + 8H^+ + 5e^- \rightarrow Mn^{2+} + 4H_2O$

**Step 3:** Add the last two half-equations together to cancel out the electrons.

So the overall reaction equation is:

$5Fe^{2+} + MnO_4^- + 8H^+ \rightarrow 5Fe^{3+} + Mn^{2+} + 4H_2O$

Net charge on the left-hand side = (10+) + (1−) + (8+) = 17+

Net charge on the right-hand side = (15+) + (2+) = 17+

Like any balanced equation, the symbols and the charges have to balance.

## Now test yourself

TESTED

4 Deduce the oxidation number of the transition element in each of the following:

(a) $[Zn(NH_3)_4(H_2O)_2]^{2+}$ (b) $[Fe(CN)_6]^{4-}$ (c) $[Co(NH_3)_5Cl]^{2+}$

(d) $[Co(C_2O_4)_3]^{4-}$ (e) $[Cr(CH_3COO)_2(H_2O)_4]^{+}$

Answers on p. 220

## Redox reactions

**Table 10.4**

| **Interconversions between $Fe^{2+}$ and $Fe^{3+}$** | | $E^\ominus$ |
|---|---|---|
| $Fe^{2+}$ to $Fe^{3+}$ | $Fe^{3+}(aq) + e^- \rightleftharpoons Fe^{2+}(aq)$ | $E^\ominus = +0.77\,V$ |
| | $MnO_4^-(aq) + 8H^+(aq) + 5e \rightleftharpoons Mn^{2+}(aq) + 4H_2O(l)$ | $E^\ominus = +1.51\,V$ |
| | $MnO_4^-(aq) + 8H^+(aq) + 5Fe^{2+}(aq) \rightarrow 5Fe^{3+}(aq) + Mn^{2+}(aq) + 4H_2O(l)$ | $E^\ominus = +0.74\,V$ |
| $Fe^{3+}$ to $Fe^{2+}$ | $Fe^{3+}(aq) + e^- \rightleftharpoons Fe^{2+}(aq)$ | $E^\ominus = +0.77\,V$ |
| | $I_2(aq) + 2e^- \rightleftharpoons 2I^-(aq)$ | $E^\ominus = +0.54\,V$ |
| | $2Fe^{3+}(aq) + 2I^-(aq) \rightleftharpoons 2Fe^{2+}(aq) + I_2(aq)$ | $E^\ominus = +0.23\,V$ |
| **Interconversions between $Cr^{3+}$ and $Cr_2O_7^{2-}$** | | $E^\ominus$ |
| $Cr_2O_7^{2-}$ to $Cr^{3+}$ | $Cr_2O_7^{2-}(aq) + 14H^+ + 6e^- \rightleftharpoons 2Cr^{3+}(aq) + 7H_2O$ | $E^\ominus = +1.33\,V$ |
| | $Zn^{2+}(aq) + 2e^- \rightleftharpoons Zn(s)$ | $E^\ominus = -0.76\,V$ |
| | $3Zn(s) + Cr_2O_7^{2-}(aq) + 14H^+ \rightleftharpoons 3Zn^{2+}(aq) + 2Cr^{3+}(aq) + 7H_2O$ | $E^\ominus = +2.09\,V$ |
| $Cr^{3+}$ to $Cr_2O_7^{2-}$ | Oxidation of $Cr^{3+}(aq)$ is quite difficult because the oxidising agent must have an electrode potential that exceeds 1.33 V. See note 1 below. | |
| **Interconversions between $Cu^{2+}$ and $Cu^+$** | | $E^\ominus$ |
| $Cu^{2+}$ to $Cu^+$ | $Cu^{2+}(aq) + e^- \rightleftharpoons Cu^+(aq)$ | $E^\ominus = +0.15\,V$ |
| | $I_2(aq) + 2e^- \rightleftharpoons 2I^-(aq)$ | $E^\ominus = +0.54\,V$ |
| | The overall cell potential is therefore −0.39 V and this suggests the reaction will not be feasible. However, in this case the exceptionally low solubility of copper(I) iodide causes the reaction to take place. As the reagents are mixed a very tiny amount of $Cu^+$ is formed but it is sufficient to begin the precipitation of copper(I) iodide ($Cu_2I_2$), which then drags the equilibria to produce more $I^-$ and the process continues until the reaction is complete. A grey/white precipitate of copper(I) iodide is produced but it will be coloured brown by the iodine produced. The net reaction is: $2Cu^{2+}(aq) + 2I^-(aq) \rightleftharpoons Cu_2I_2(s) + I_2(aq)$ | |
| $Cu^+$ to $Cu^{2+}$ | $Cu^{2+}(aq) + e^- \rightleftharpoons Cu^+(aq)$ | $E^\ominus = +0.15\,V$ |
| | $Cu^+(aq) + e^- \rightleftharpoons Cu(s)$ | $E^\ominus = +0.34\,V$ |
| | $2Cu^+(aq) \rightleftharpoons Cu^{2+}(aq) + Cu(s)$ | $E^\ominus = +0.19\,V$ |

**Note 1** Hydrogen peroxide reacts with $Cr^{3+}(aq)$ in alkaline solution to form the yellow chromate(VI) ion $CrO_4^{2-}(aq)$. The relevant half-equations must be constructed using $OH^-(aq)$ rather than $H^+(aq)$:

$Cr^{3+}(aq) + 8OH^-(aq) \rightleftharpoons CrO_4^{2-}(aq) + 4H_2O(l) + 3e^-$

$H_2O_2(aq) \rightleftharpoons 2OH^-(aq) + 2e^-$

and these combine to give an overall equation:

$2Cr^{3+}(aq) + 3H_2O_2(aq) + 10OH^-(aq) \rightleftharpoons 2CrO_4^{2-}(aq) + 8H_2O(l)$

The chromate, $CrO_4^{2-}(aq)$, can be converted into the dichromate, $Cr_2O_7^{2-}(aq)$, simply by adding excess hydrogen ions:

$2CrO_4^{2-}(aq) + 2H^+(l) \rightleftharpoons Cr_2O_7^{2-}(aq) + H_2O(l)$

## Redox titrations

Transition metal ions are often coloured and the colour changes that occur when they react can be used to show when a titration has reached its end point. The reaction of $Fe^{2+}$ with $MnO_4^-$ is a good example. $MnO_4^-$ is purple while $Mn^{2+}$ is a very pale pink or almost colourless. When purple $MnO_4^-$ is added from a burette into acidified $Fe^{2+}$ it immediately turns pale pink or colourless as the $MnO_4^-$ reacts with the acidified $Fe^{2+}$. When all of the $Fe^{2+}$ has reacted, the purple colour of further $MnO_4^-$ added remains. The end point of this titration is when a faint, permanent, pink colour is seen.

The reaction between $Fe^{2+}$ and $MnO_4^-$ is often tested in the context of a titration calculation.

**Example**

Five iron tablets with a combined mass of 0.900 g were dissolved in acid and made up to 100 cm$^3$ of solution. In a titration, 10.0 cm$^3$ of this solution reacted exactly with 10.4 cm$^3$ of 0.0100 mol dm$^{-3}$ potassium manganate(VII). What is the percentage by mass of iron in the tablets?

**Answer**

**Step 1:** Write the balanced equation:

$$5Fe^{2+}(aq) + MnO_4^-(aq) + 8H^+(aq) \rightarrow 5Fe^{3+}(aq) + Mn^{2+}(aq) + 4H_2O(l)$$

Use the balanced equation to obtain the mole ratio of $Fe^{2+}$ to $MnO_4^-$, which is 5:1.

Calculate the number of moles of $MnO_4^-$ by using the concentration, $c$, and the reacting volume, $v$, of $KMnO_4$.

From the titration results, the amount of $KMnO_4$ can be calculated:

$$\text{amount of } KMnO_4 = \frac{c \times v}{1000} = \frac{0.0100 \times 10.4}{1000} = 1.04 \times 10^{-4}\text{ mol}$$

From the mole ratio, the amount of $Fe^{2+}$ can be determined.

The $Fe^{2+}$ to $MnO_4^-$ ratio is 5:1. The amount of $KMnO_4$ is $1.04 \times 10^{-4}$ mol.

Therefore, $5 \times 1.04 \times 10^{-4}$ mol $Fe^{2+}$ reacts with $1.04 \times 10^{-4}$ mol $MnO_4^-$.

**amount of $Fe^{2+}$ reacted = $5.20 \times 10^{-4}$ mol**

**Step 2:** Find the amount of $Fe^{2+}$ in the solution prepared from the tablets

10.0 cm$^3$ of $Fe^{2+}(aq)$ contains $5.20 \times 10^{-4}$ mol $Fe^{2+}(aq)$.

100 cm$^3$ solution of iron tablets contains $10 \times (5.20 \times 10^{-4}) = 5.20 \times 10^{-3}$ mol $Fe^{2+}$.

**Step 3:** Find the percentage of $Fe^{2+}$ in the tablets ($A_r$: Fe, 55.8)

$5.20 \times 10^{-3}$ mol $Fe^{2+}$ has a mass of $5.20 \times 10^{-3} \times 55.8 = 0.290$ g.

$$\% \text{ of } Fe^{2+} \text{ in tablets} = \frac{\text{mass of } Fe^{2+}}{\text{mass of tablets}} \times 100 = \frac{0.290}{0.900} \times 100 = 32.2\%$$

You also need to know the redox titration between iodine and thiosulfate ions:

$$2S_2O_3^{2-}(aq) + I_2(s) \rightarrow S_4O_6^{2-}(aq) + 2I^-(aq) \qquad \text{(equation 1)}$$

This titration is not usually used directly to determine the concentration of an iodine solution. Rather, it allows the determination of the concentration of a reagent that generates iodine as a result of a reaction.

An example is the determination of the concentration of a copper(II) sulfate solution. A known volume of copper (II) sulfate is reacted with excess potassium iodide:

$$2Cu^{2+}(aq) + 4I^{-}(aq) \rightarrow Cu_2I_2(s) + I_2(s) \qquad \text{(equation 2)}$$

$Cu_2I_2$ is copper(I) iodide, which forms as a grey-white precipitate. The reaction is, therefore, a redox process in which $Cu^{2+}$ is reduced and $I^-$ is oxidised.

The iodine produced is then titrated against a solution of sodium thiosulfate of known concentration.

At the start of the titration, the solution appears brown–purple because of the presence of the iodine. As the titration proceeds, this colour fades to yellow and the end point is reached when the solution is colourless. In practice, this colour change is quite difficult to see, mainly because of the presence of the copper(I) iodide precipitate. To help, some starch solution is added as the end point is approached. This gives rise to a dark-blue coloration that disappears sharply at the end point.

It can be seen that from:

- equation 2 that 2 mol of $Cu^{2+}$ react to produce 1 mol of $I_2$
- equation 1 that 1 mol of $I_2$ reacts with 2 mol of $S_2O_3^{2-}$

It follows therefore that for every 1 mole of $Cu^{2+}$, 1 mole of $S_2O_3^{2-}$ is required. So the amount (in moles) of thiosulfate used is equivalent to the amount (in moles) of copper(II) ions present originally.

## Now test yourself

TESTED

5 A solution is made that contains the $VO^{2+}(aq)$ ion. When 25.0 cm$^3$ of the solution is titrated against 0.0150 mol dm$^{-3}$ $MnO_4^-(aq)$ ions in the presence of excess sulfuric acid, it is found that 23.3 cm$^3$ are required to reach the end point. The equation for the oxidation of $VO^{2+}(aq)$ ions is:

$$VO^{2+}(aq) + 2H_2O(l) \rightarrow VO_3^-(aq) + 4H^+(aq) + e^-$$

Calculate the concentration in mol dm$^{-3}$ of the solution containing $VO^{2+}(aq)$.

6 A general purpose solder contains antimony, lead and tin. When reacted with an acid, the solder dissolves to form a solution containing $Sb^{3+}(aq)$, $Pb^{2+}(aq)$ and $Sn^{2+}(aq)$. Neither $Sb^{3+}(aq)$ nor $Pb^{2+}(aq)$ reacts with dichromate ($Cr_2O_7^{2-}$) ions. $Sn^{2+}(aq)$ is oxidised to $Sn^{4+}(aq)$ by an acidified solution of potassium dichromate(VI).

In an experiment, 10.00 g of solder is dissolved in acid to make 1.00 dm$^3$ of solution. When 25.0 cm$^3$ of this solution is titrated against an acidified potassium dichromate solution of concentration 0.0175 mol dm$^{-3}$, 20.0 cm$^3$ of the dichromate are required to reach an end point. The equation for the reduction of $Cr_2O_7^{2-}(aq)$ is:

$$Cr_2O_7^{2-}(aq) + 14H^+(aq) + 6e^- \rightarrow 2Cr^{3+}(aq) + 7H_2O(l)$$

(a) Write an overall equation for the reaction of $Sn^{2+}(aq)$ with $Cr_2O_7^{2-}(aq)$.
(b) Calculate the concentration of $Sn^{2+}(aq)$ in the solution in mol dm$^{-3}$.
(c) Calculate the percentage by mass of tin in the solder.

Answers on pp. 220–221

# Qualitative analysis

During year 1 of the course, you have met several reactions that can be used to identify the presence of particular ions. These are shown in Table 4.4 on page 56. In year 2 of the course, you are also expected to be able to detect transition metal ions. These are shown in Table 10.1 on page 159.

# Exam practice

1 (a) (i) What is meant by the term *transition element*? [2]

(ii) Copy and complete the electron configuration of the iron atom: $1s^2 2s^2 2p^6$... [1]

(iii) Write the electron configuration of an $Fe^{2+}$ ion and an $Fe^{3+}$ ion. [2]

(b) (i) Aqueous $Fe^{2+}$ ions react with aqueous hydroxide ions. Write an ionic equation for this reaction and state what you would see. [2]

(ii) The product formed in the reaction between aqueous $Fe^{2+}$ ions and aqueous hydroxide ions slowly darkens and eventually turns 'rusty'. What has happened to cause this colour change? [1]

(c) The dichromate ion, $Cr_2O_7^{2-}$, is an oxidising agent that is used in laboratory analysis. It reacts with acidified $Fe^{2+}$ ions to form $Cr^{3+}$ and $Fe^{3+}$ ions:

$$Cr_2O_7^{2-}(aq) + 14H^+(aq) + 6e^- \rightarrow 2Cr^{3+}(aq) + 7H_2O(l)$$

$$Fe^{2+}(aq) \rightarrow Fe^{3+}(aq) + e^-$$

(i) Construct the full ionic equation for this reaction. [1]

(ii) Calculate the volume of 0.0100 mol dm$^{-3}$ potassium dichromate required to react with 20.0 cm$^3$ of 0.0500 mol dm$^{-3}$ acidified iron(II) sulfate. [3]

2 (a) Explain the meaning of the terms *ligand* and *coordinate bond.* [2]

(b) Stereoisomerism is sometimes shown by transition metal complex ions. Using a suitable named example in each case, show how transition metal complex ions can form:

(i) *cis–trans* isomers

(ii) optical isomers [8]

(c) Ligand exchange may occur when transition metal complex ions react. This will take place if a new complex ion that has a greater stability can be formed. An example of a ligand exchange reaction is the formation of $[CoCl_4]^{2-}$ from $[Co(H_2O)_6]^{2+}$.

(i) The stability of a complex ion is expressed by its stability constant. Define the stability constant of $[CoCl_4]^{2-}$. [2]

(ii) Describe how you would convert $[Co(H_2O)_6]^{2+}$ into $[CoCl_4]^{2-}$. What would you see as the reaction takes place? [3]

3 Synoptic question

*Most questions on this paper are based on the specification content, but you are likely to be given data and asked to use those data to answer the question. This might involve extended writing or a more lengthy calculation. The question that follows is along these lines.*

Copper reacts with nitric acid. $HNO_3$, but the products of the reaction depend on the concentration of the acid.

If the nitric acid is dilute, the following reaction takes place:

$$Cu(s) \rightarrow Cu^{2+}(aq) + 2e^-$$

$$4H^+(aq) + NO_3^-(aq) + 3e^- \rightarrow NO(g) + 2H_2O(l)$$

If the nitric acid is concentrated, the reaction is:

$$Cu(s) \rightarrow Cu^{2+}(aq) + 2e^-$$

$$2H^+(aq) + NO_3^-(aq) + e^- \rightarrow NO_2(g) + H_2O(l)$$

(a) Write balanced equations for each of the above reactions. [5]

(b) In an experiment, some nitric acid is reacted with 1.27 g of copper. It is found that 320 cm$^3$ of gas is produced. Deduce whether the acid used in this experiment was dilute or concentrated. Show *all* your working. [4]

## Answers and quick quiz 10 online

ONLINE

# Summary

You should now have an understanding of:

- general properties of transition elements
- ligands and complex ions
- ligand substitution reactions
- precipitation reactions
- redox reactions and titrations
- qualitative analysis

# 11 Aromatic compounds, carbonyls and acids

## Arenes

### Structure of benzene

REVISED

The French chemist August Kekulé suggested that benzene was a cyclic molecule with alternating C=C double bonds and C–C single bonds (Figure 11.1).

However, three pieces of evidence casts doubt against this type of structure:

- Compounds that contain C=C double bonds readily decolorise bromine *but* benzene only reacts with bromine when hot and exposed to ultraviolet light or in the presence of a halogen carrier.
- On average, the length of a C–C single bond is 154 pm while the average length of a C=C double bond is 134 pm. All the bonds in benzene are 139 pm. This suggests an intermediate bond somewhere between a double bond and a single bond.
- Experimentally determined enthalpy changes for the hydrogenation of cyclohexene and benzene give a value for benzene that is about 150 kJ mol$^{-1}$ lower than that expected from the alternating double bond–single bond model (Figure 11.2).

**Figure 11.1 Kekulé structure of benzene**

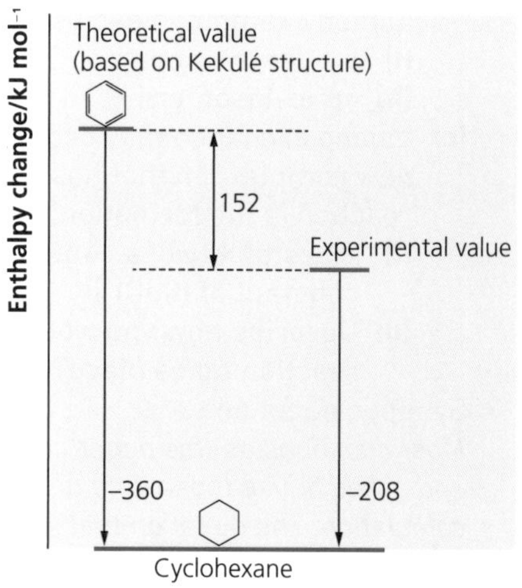


**Figure 11.2**

The current model of benzene is that each carbon atom contributes one electron to a π-delocalised ring of electrons above and below the plane of atoms. Each carbon has one *p*-orbital at right angles to the plane of atoms and adjacent *p*-orbitals overlap so that delocalisation is extended over all six carbon atoms. The π-delocalised ring accounts for the increased stability of benzene as well as explaining the reluctance to react with bromine. In addition, it explains why all six carbon–carbon bond lengths are identical. Benzene is usually represented by the skeletal formula shown in Figure 11.3.

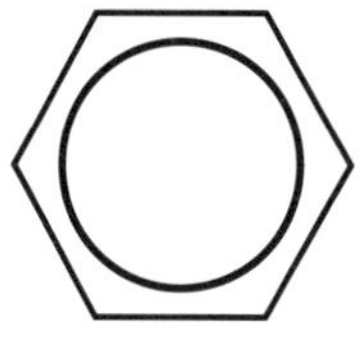

**Figure 11.3 Skeletal formula of benzene**

**Exam tip**

The structure of benzene demonstrates the 'tentative nature of scientific knowledge'. The exact structure of benzene is still open to debate and is acceptable to use either structure to represent benzene.

### Electrophilic substitution

REVISED

The π-delocalised rings make benzene very stable and the electron density in benzene is relatively low. However, benzene does react with **electrophiles** that have a *full* positive charge — an induced dipole in a molecule is not normally sufficient.

An **electrophile** is an electron-pair acceptor that forms a dative covalent bond in a reaction.

Catalysts are used to generate electrophiles such as $NO_2^+$, $Cl^+$, $Br^+$, $CH_3^+$ and $CH_3CO^+$. The general equation is:

$$C_6H_6 + X^+ \rightarrow C_6H_5X + H^+$$

where $X^+$ is the electrophile.

The electrophilic substitution reactions of aromatic compounds can be summarised as: nitration, halogenation, alkylation and acylation. The mechanism can be broken down into three stages:
● generation of the electrophile
● electrophilic substitution (of H by the electrophile) at the ring
● regeneration of the catalyst

## Nitration of benzene

**Reagents:** $HNO_3$ and $H_2SO_4$ (catalyst)

**Conditions:** approximately 60°C

**Balanced equation:** $C_6H_6 + HNO_3 \rightarrow C_6H_5NO_2 + H_2O$

**Mechanism:**
● Generation of the electrophile:

$$H_2SO_4 + HNO_3 \rightleftharpoons HSO_4^- + H_2NO_3^+$$

Sulfuric acid donates
a proton to nitric acid

Protonated nitric acid is
very unstable and can
break down to form

$$H_2O \qquad {}^+NO_2$$

Nitronium ion

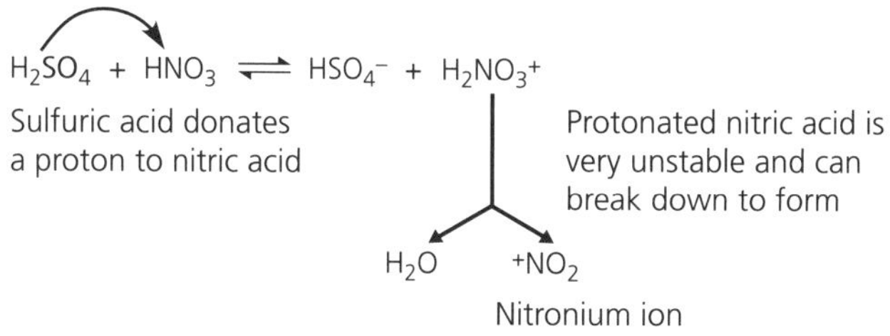

● Electrophilic attack at the benzene ring:

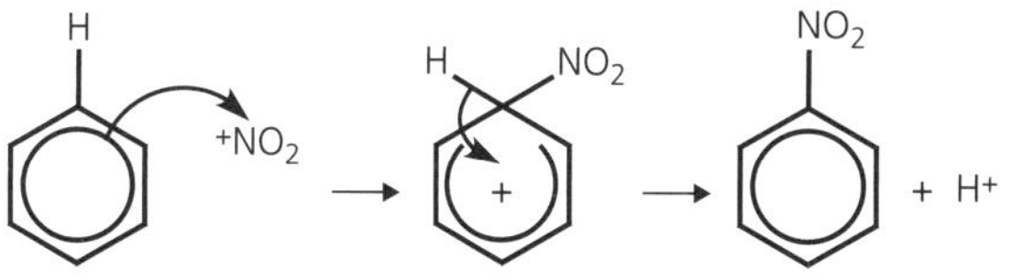

● Regeneration of the catalyst:

$$H^+ + HSO_4^- \rightarrow H_2SO_4$$

> **Typical mistakes**
>
> Students often take a great deal of care when drawing out the mechanism. They ensure the curly arrows are correctly placed but often lose a mark by forgetting to include the $H^+$, which is substituted from the ring.

## Halogenation, alkylation and acylation of benzene

REVISED

The mechanism is essentially the same for all three reactions; only the reagents vary.

## Halogenation of benzene

**Reagents:** $Cl_2$ and $AlCl_3$ (catalyst)

**Conditions:** anhydrous ($AlCl_3$ reacts with water)

**Balanced equation:** $C_6H_6 + Cl_2 \rightarrow C_6H_5Cl + HCl$

**Mechanism:**

$$Cl{-}Cl + AlCl_3 \longrightarrow Cl^+ + AlCl_4^-$$

**Step 1**
Formation of the electrophile

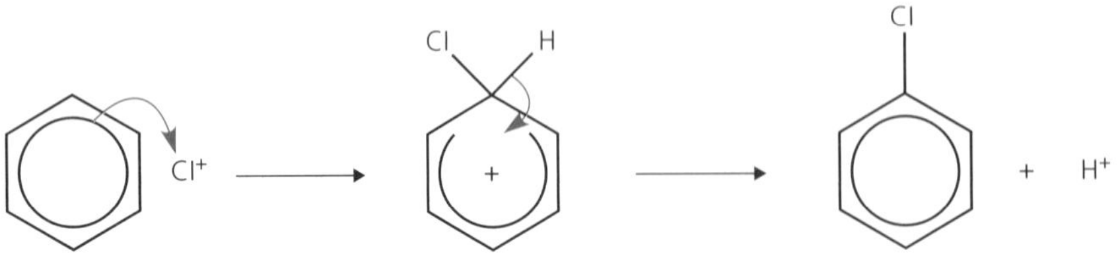


**Step 2**
Substitution of H by the electrophile

$$AlCl_4^- + H^+ \longrightarrow AlCl_3 + HCl$$

**Step 3**
Regeneration of the catalyst (halogen carrier)

The chlorination of benzene is a Friedel–Crafts reaction in which $AlCl_3$ behaves as a halogen carrier. Halogen carriers are able to accept a halide ion and to 'carry it' through the reaction. At the end of the reaction, the halide ion is released and the hydrogen halide is formed. All aluminium halides, iron(III) halides and iron can behave as halogen carriers.

## Alkylation of benzene

**Reagents:** $CH_3Cl$ and $AlCl_3$ (catalyst)

**Conditions:** anhydrous ($AlCl_3$ reacts with water)

**Balanced equation:** $C_6H_6 + CH_3Cl \rightarrow C_6H_5CH_3 + HCl$

**Mechanism:**

$$H_3C{-}Cl + AlCl_3 \longrightarrow CH_3^+ + AlCl_4^-$$

**Step 1**
Formation of the electrophile

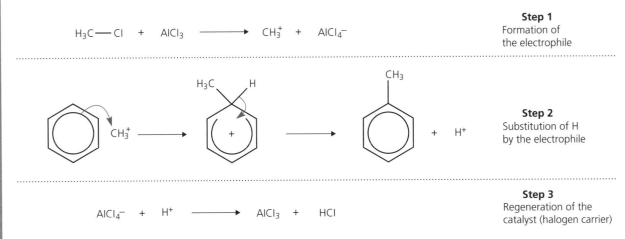

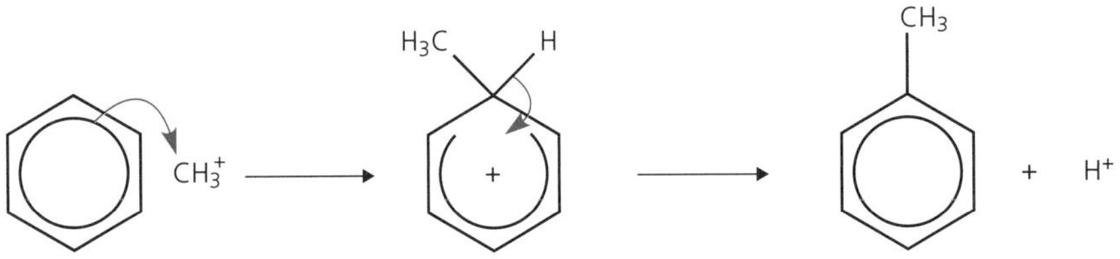


**Step 2**
Substitution of H by the electrophile

$$AlCl_4^- + H^+ \longrightarrow AlCl_3 + HCl$$

**Step 3**
Regeneration of the catalyst (halogen carrier)

## Acylation of benzene

**Reagents:** $CH_3COCl$ and $AlCl_3$ (catalyst)

**Conditions:** anhydrous ($AlCl_3$ reacts with water)

**Balanced equation:** $C_6H_6 + CH_3COCl \rightarrow C_6H_5COCH_3 + HCl$

**Mechanism:**

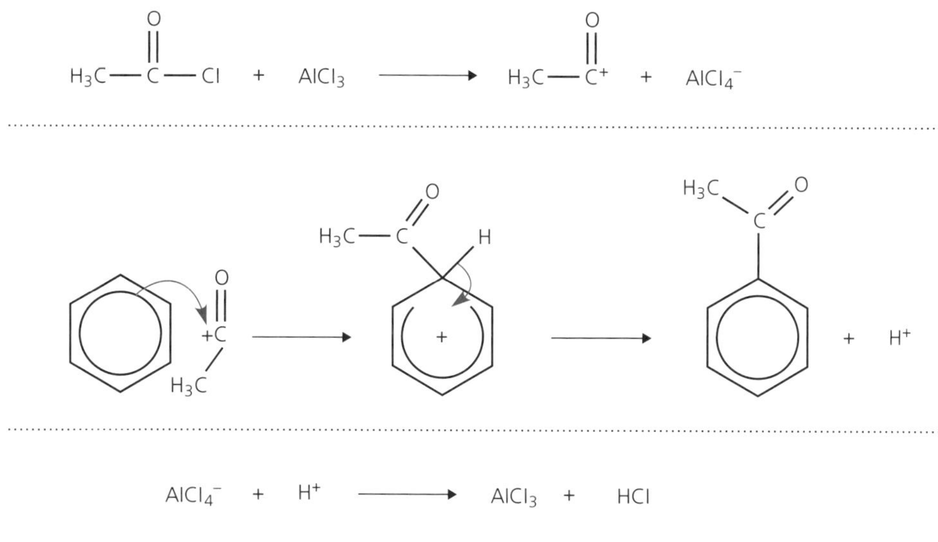

Step 1
Formation of
the electrophile

Step 2
Substitution of H
by the electrophile

$$AlCl_4^- + H^+ \longrightarrow AlCl_3 + HCl$$

Step 3
Regeneration of the
catalyst (halogen carrier)

## Bromination of alkenes and arenes

You will recall from Module 4 that alkenes, such as cyclohexene, react readily with bromine in the absence of sunlight, undergoing **electrophilic addition** reactions:

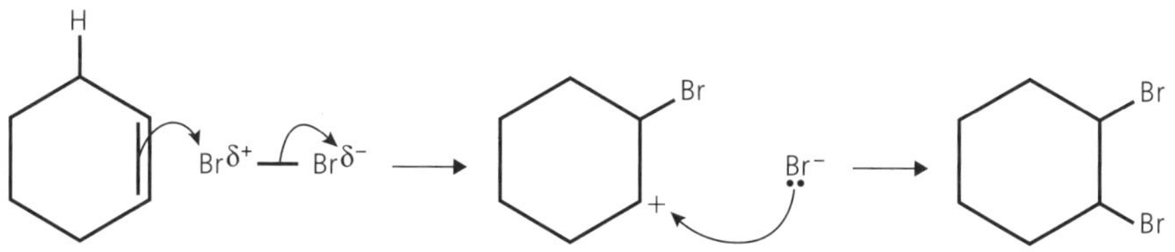

The reaction is rapid and is initiated by the induced dipole in bromine.

Benzene also reacts with bromine but is more resistant, reacting much less readily than an alkene, such as cyclohexene. Benzene requires an electrophile with a full positive charge, $Br^+$, which is generated in the presence of a halogen carrier. The resultant reaction is electrophilic substitution, *not* electrophilic addition. This is explained by the stability of the π-delocalised ring of electrons that is retained in most reactions of all arenes.

The relative ease of reaction of cyclohexene can be explained by the electron density:
● Cyclohexene has a C=C double bond that has high electron density.
● The π-electrons are localised between the two carbon atoms in the C=C double bond.
● The electron density is sufficient to induce a dipole in the Br–Br bond and an electrophile is generated.
● The electrophile is attracted to cyclohexene because of its high electron density.

## Now test yourself

TESTED

1 Methylbenzene, $C_6H_5CH_3$, can be nitrated to form $CH_3C_6H_4NO_2$. Draw and name the isomers.
2 Methylbenzene, $C_6H_5CH_3$, can be further nitrated to form 2,4,6-trinitromethylbenzene. Write a balanced equation for this reaction.

Answers on p. 221

## Phenols

REVISED

In phenols, the –OH group is attached directly to the benzene ring. Phenol behaves as a weak **acid**. It also undergoes electrophilic substitution reactions much more readily than benzene.

An **acid** is a proton donor.

### Now test yourself

TESTED

3 What is the molecular formula of 4-methylphenol?

Answer on p. 221

**Exam tip**

If you remember the definition of a salt it is easy to work out the formula of an organic salt. Simply replace the acidic $H^+$ in the phenol (or carboxylic acid) with the metal ion (usually $Na^+$).

Phenol forms **salts** by the reaction with both sodium and sodium hydroxide, but phenol is not sufficiently acidic to react with carbonates:

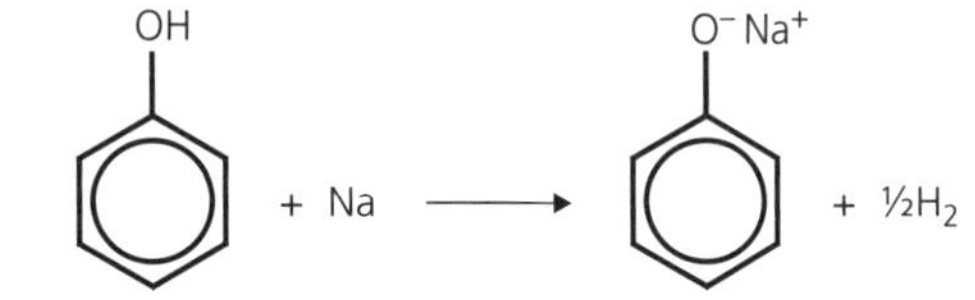


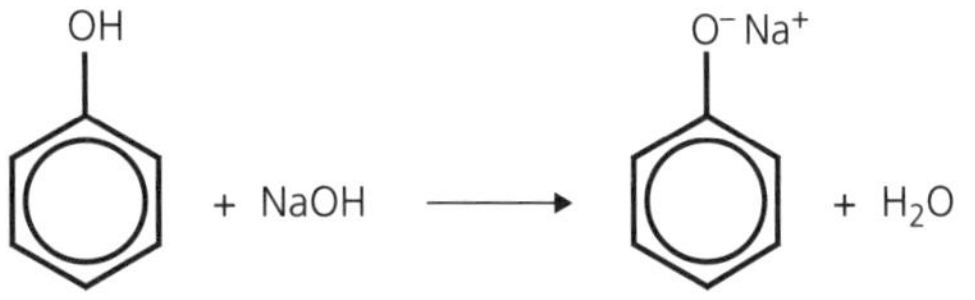


A **salt** is formed when an acid has one or more of its hydrogen ions replaced by a metal ion or an ammonium ion, $NH_4^+$.

Unlike benzene, phenol readily undergoes electrophilic substitution without the aid of a catalyst. Phenol can be nitrated with dilute nitric acid to form 2-nitrophenol.

Phenol also reacts readily with bromine and does not require a halogen carrier. The bromine is decolorised and white crystals of 2,4,6-tribromophenol are formed:

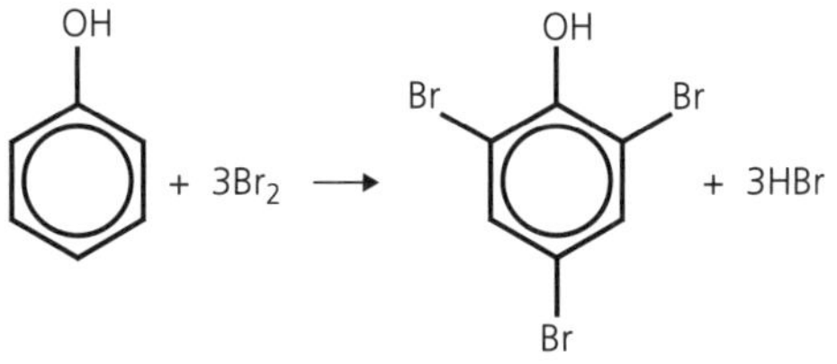


This is explained by the activation of the ring in phenol due to delocalisation of one of the lone pairs of electrons on the oxygen atom into the ring. This increases the electron density, which in turn polarises the halogen and increases the attraction for the halogen. The result is increased reactivity of phenol.

### Now test yourself

TESTED

4 Benzene, phenol and cyclohexene all react with bromine.
  (a) For each reaction:
    - name the type of reaction
    - state the reagents and conditions (if any)
    - identify the organic product and state any observations
  (b) Explain the different rates of reaction of bromine with each of the following pairs of compounds:
    (i) benzene and phenol
    (ii) benzene and cyclohexene

Answers on p. 221

## Reactions of substituted aromatic compounds

Substituted aromatic compounds also react by the same mechanism as benzene, but the substituent affects the rate of reaction, as in phenol, and also affects the position of substitution on the ring (Figure 11.4).

Alkyl groups such as $CH_3$, along with OH and $NH_2$ groups, direct the electrophile to the 2 and 4 (and 6) positions on the ring.

Electron-withdrawing groups like $NO_2$ direct further substitution to the 3 position on the ring and also inhibit any further reaction at the ring.

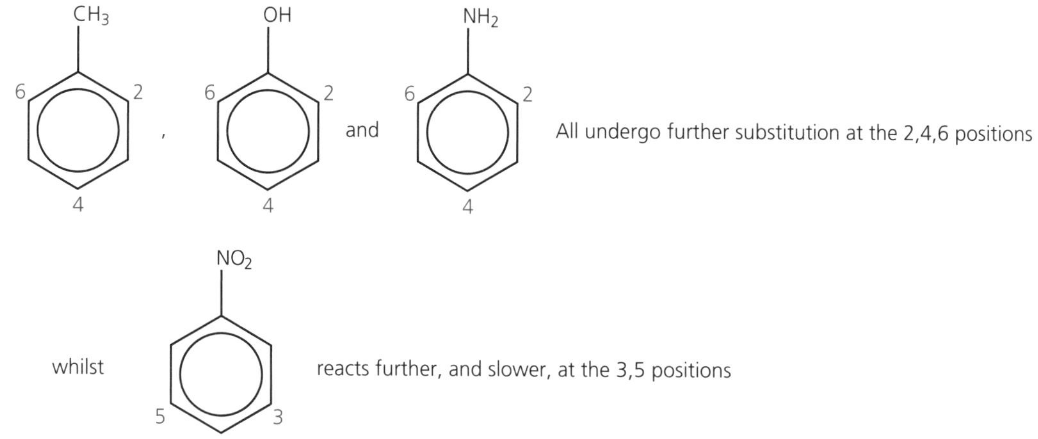


**Figure 11.4 Effect of substituents on position of substitution**

### Now test yourself

TESTED

5 Starting with benzene, suggest a two-stage synthesis of 3-nitromethylbenzene.

Answer on p. 221

# Carbonyl compounds

The presence of the carbonyl group, C=O, in a molecule means that it is unsaturated. The position of the C=O group on the carbon chain determines whether or not the molecule is classified as an aldehyde or a ketone. Aldehydes *always* have the C=O at the end of the carbon chain (Figure 11.5).

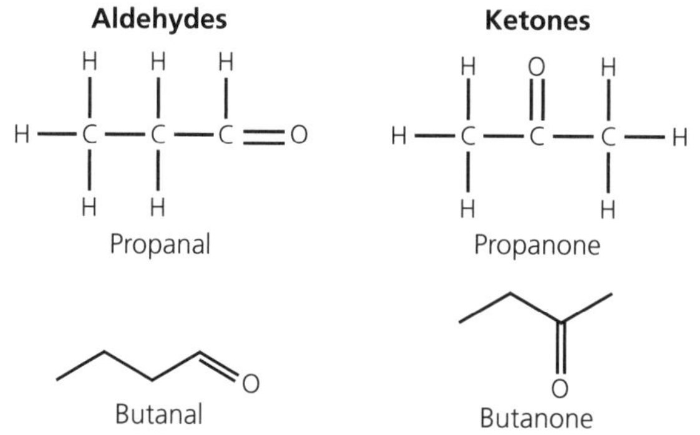


**Figure 11.5 Examples of aldehydes and ketones**

You met the carbonyl group in Module 4 when you studied the chemistry of alcohols. Aldehydes and ketones are formed by the oxidation of alcohols using $Cr_2O_7^{2-}/H^+$ (e.g. $K_2Cr_2O_7/H_2SO_4$). This is bright orange and changes to green during the redox process. When oxidising a primary alcohol the choice of apparatus is important. Refluxing produces a carboxylic acid; distillation produces an aldehyde.

Oxidation of a primary alcohol to an **aldehyde** by distillation, for example:

$CH_3CH_2OH + [O] \rightarrow CH_3CHO + H_2O$

Ethanol → Ethanal

Oxidation of a primary alcohol to a **carboxylic acid** by refluxing, for example:

$CH_3CH_2OH + 2[O] \rightarrow CH_3CO_2H + H_2O$

Ethanol → Ethanoic acid

Oxidation of a secondary alcohol to a **ketone**, for example:

$CH_3CHOHCH_3 + [O] \rightarrow CH_3COCH_3 + H_2O$

Propan-2-ol → Propan-2-one

## Reactions of carbonyl compounds

REVISED

### Reduction

Aldehydes and ketones can be reduced to their respective alcohols. Sodium tetrahydridoborate(III), $NaBH_4$, is a suitable reducing agent. [H] is used to represent the reducing agent in equations representing organic reduction reactions.

Aldehydes are reduced to primary alcohols, for example:

$CH_3CH_2CHO + 2[H] \rightarrow CH_3CH_2CH_2OH$

Ketones are reduced to secondary alcohols, for example:

$CH_3COCH_3 + 2[H] \rightarrow CH_3CH(OH)CH_3$

$NaBH_4$ is the source of the hydride ion, $H:^-$, which is a **nucleophile**. The intermediate formed reacts with the solvent, $H_2O$, to form the alcohol.

A **nucleophile** is an electron-pair donor that forms a dative covalent bond in a reaction.

The mechanism of the reduction of ethanal with aqueous $NaBH_4$ is as follows:

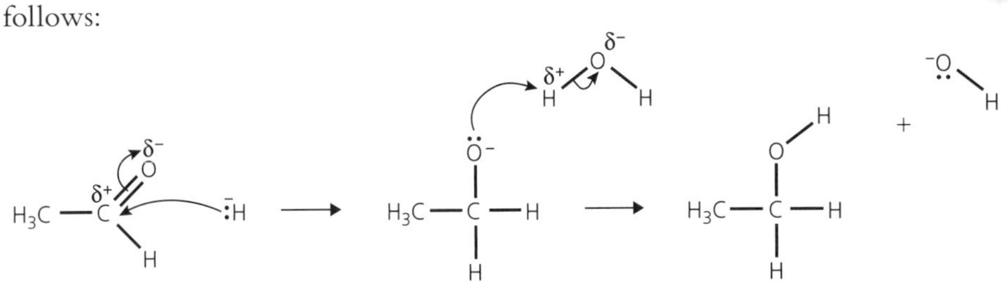

**Ethanal** **Ethanol**

Ketones behave similarly. The mechanism of the reduction of propanone with aqueous $NaBH_4$ is as follows:

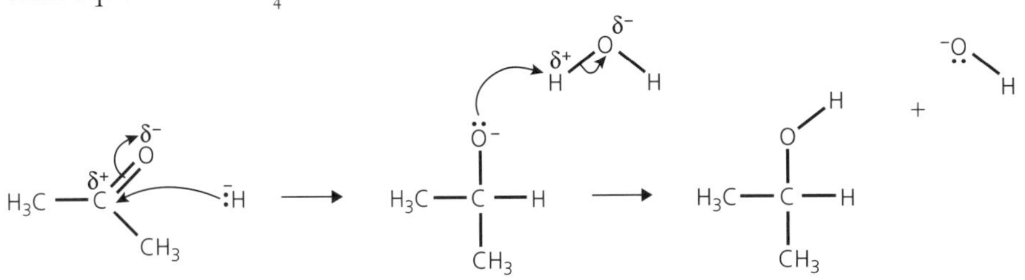

**Propanone** **Propan-2-ol**

**Exam tip**

The nucleophilic addition mechanism is simplified if an acid, $H^+(aq)$, is added. The mechanism becomes:

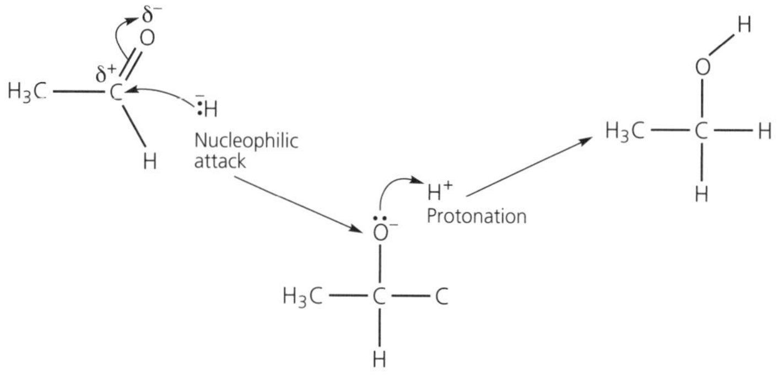


## Now test yourself

TESTED

6 Butan-2-ol can be prepared by the reduction of a carbonyl compound. Identify the carbonyl compound, and state the reagents and conditions. Write a balanced equation and, with the aid of curly arrows, describe the mechanism.

Answer on p. 221

## Nucleophilic addition with the cyanide ion, $^-$:CN

Hydrogen cyanide can be used as the source of the cyanide nucleophile, $^-$:CN, but the rate of reaction is very slow. It is more common to use potassium cyanide, KCN, and an acid.

The mechanism can again be broken down into two steps:

- nucleophilic attack to produce an intermediate anion
- reaction with a proton, $H^+$, from either water or from an acid to produce the product

The product contains two functional groups: an alcohol (–OH) and the cyanide group, which is known as a nitrile (–C≡N). The organic product is always a 2-hydroxynitrile (Figure 11.6).

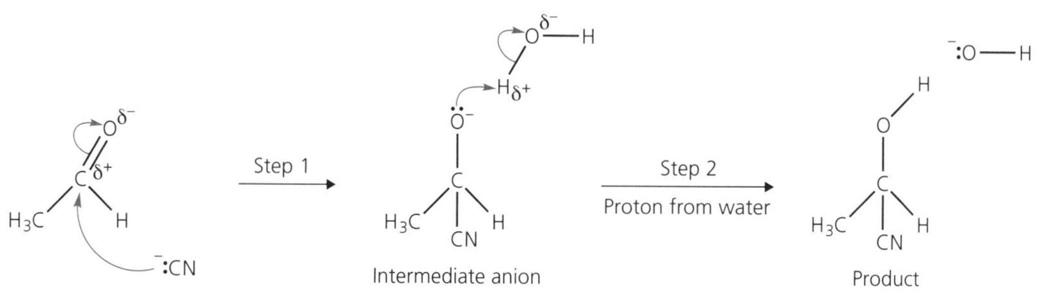


**Figure 11.6 Reaction of cyanide with ethanal**

In this reaction **ethanal** is converted into 2-hydroxy**propane**nitrile. You will note that the product contains one more carbon atom than the reagent. This reaction can be used to extend the length of the carbon chain in organic synthesis.

Ketones behave similarly — they react with KCN in the presence of an acid to form a 2-hydroxynitrile (Figure 11.7).

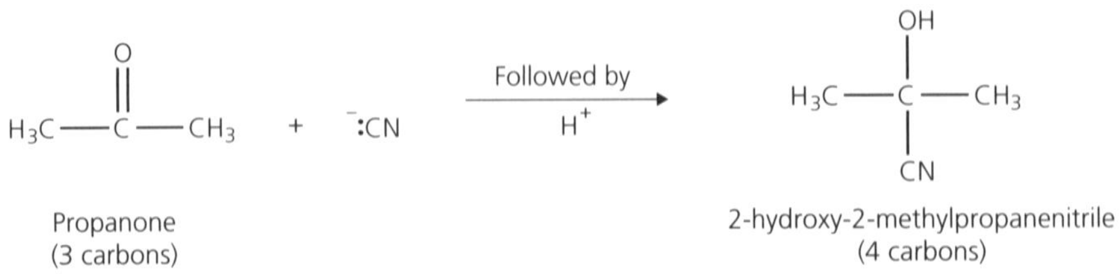


**Figure 11.7 Reaction of cyanide with propanone**

In this reaction propanone is converted into 2-hydroxy-2,methylpropanenitrile. You will note that the product again contains one more carbon atom than the reagent.

> **Exam tip**
>
> When naming a nitrile, the nitrile group always takes position 1 on the chain and always appears at the end of the name. Alcohols usually end with ...ol but 'hydroxy' at the start of the name can also be used.

## Now test yourself

TESTED

7 Name the following nitrile compounds.
(a) $CH_3CH_2CN$
(b) $CH_3(CH_2)_2CH(OH)(CN)$
(c)

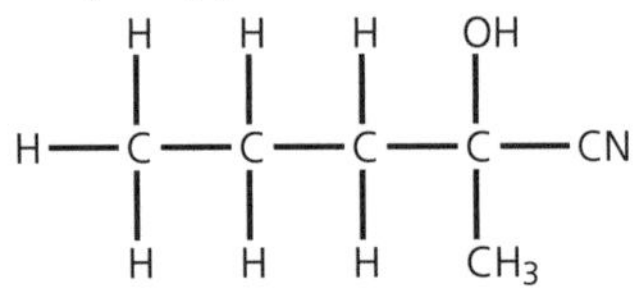


8 Write an equation and describe the mechanism for the reduction of phenylethanone, $C_6H_5COCH_3$.

Answers on p. 222

## Characteristic tests for carbonyl compounds

REVISED

### Use of 2,4-dinitrophenylhydrazine

Students are not expected to be able to recall the formula of 2,4-dinitrophenylhydrazine (the abbreviation 2,4-DNPH is acceptable). The reactions with 2,4-DNPH are important for two reasons:

- 2,4-DNPH reacts with a carbonyl compound to produce a distinctively coloured precipitate, which is usually bright red, orange or yellow. Therefore, this reaction can be used to identify the presence of a carbonyl group.
- The brightly coloured organic product (the 2,4-DNPH derivative) is relatively easy to purify by recrystallisation. Therefore, the melting point of the brightly coloured precipitate can be measured. Each derivative has a different melting point, the value of which can be used to identify the specific carbonyl compound.

## Use of Tollens' reagent

REVISED

Aldehydes and ketones can be distinguished by a series of redox reactions. Aldehydes are readily oxidised to carboxylic acids whereas ketones are not easily oxidised.

Aldehydes react with Tollens' reagent, which is an aqueous solution of $Ag^+$ ions in an excess of ammonia, $Ag(NH_3)_2^+$. When Tollens' reagent is reacted with an aldehyde and warmed gently in a water bath at about 60°C, silver metal is precipitated, which forms a distinctive silver mirror.

This is a redox reaction in which $Ag^+$ ions are reduced to silver metal and the aldehyde is oxidised to a carboxylic acid. The $Ag^+$ ion gains an electron and is, therefore, reduced to silver:

$$Ag^+ + e^- \xrightarrow{\text{Reduction}} Ag \text{ (silver mirror)}$$

The aldehyde is oxidised to a carboxylic acid:

Tollens' reagent does not react with ketones because they are not readily oxidised.

Oxidation of an aldehyde to a carboxylic acid can also be achieved by refluxing with acidified dichromate ($H^+/Cr_2O_7^{2-}$). There is a colour change from orange to green.

Oxidation of an aldehyde to a carboxylic acid can be followed using infrared spectroscopy. The relevant absorptions are shown in Table 11.1.

**Table 11.1 IR absorptions of C=O and O–H groups**

| Group | Compounds | IR absorption |
|---|---|---|
| C=O | Aldehydes, ketones, carboxylic acids | 1630–1820 $cm^{-1}$ |
| O–H | Carboxylic acids | 2500–3300 $cm^{-1}$ (very broad) |

The IR spectrum of ethanal is shown in Figure 11.8. The absorption due to the carbonyl group can be seen.

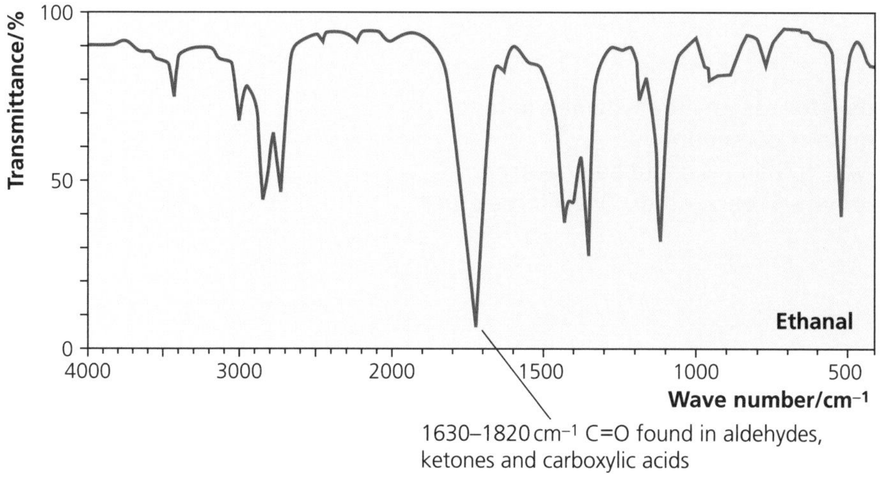


**Figure 11.8 Infrared spectrum of ethanal**

The IR spectrum of ethanoic acid is shown in Figure 11.9. This spectrum shows the absorptions for both the C=O and O–H groups.

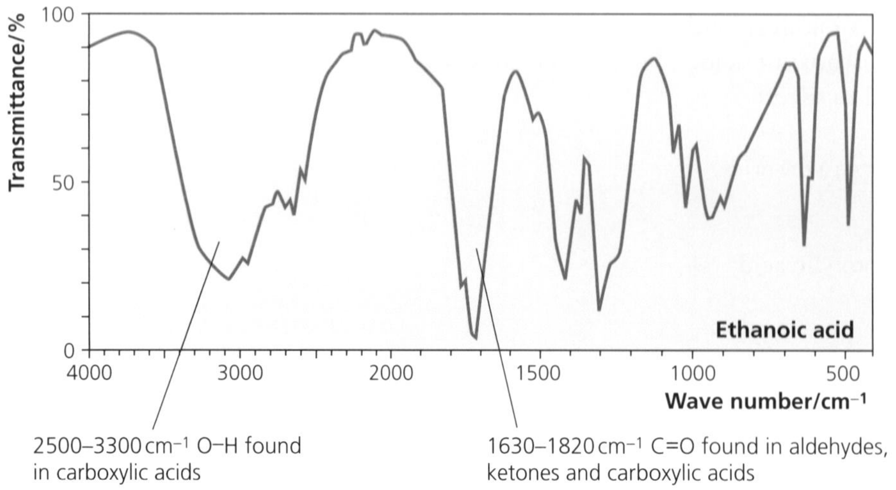


**Figure 11.9 Infrared spectrum of ethanoic acid**

## Now test yourself

TESTED

9 (a) Name each of the following compounds:

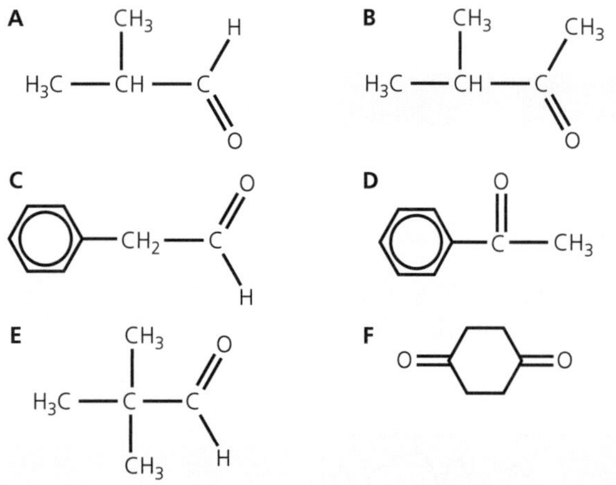

(b) Classify each of compounds A to F as an aldehyde or a ketone.
(c) What is the molecular formula of compound F?
(d) Identify the alcohols from which C and D could be prepared.
(e) Compounds B and E are isomers of each other. Draw *three* other isomers of B and E.

Answer on p. 222

# Carboxylic acids and esters

## Carboxylic acids

REVISED

All carboxylic acids contain the functional group:

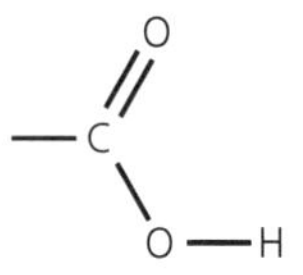

The carboxylic acid group can be attached to either a chain (aliphatic) or to a ring (aromatic), for example:

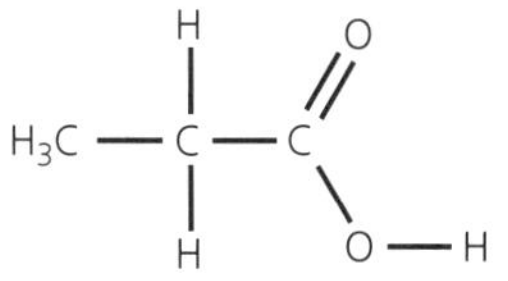

Propanoic acid

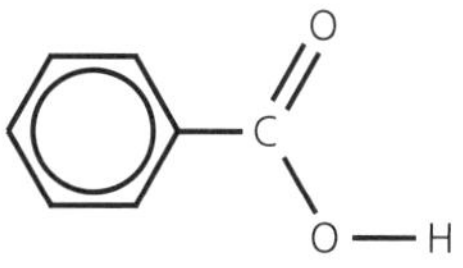

Benzoic acid

Carboxylic acids such as methanoic acid and ethanoic acid are soluble in water. The solubility is explained by the ability of carboxylic acids to form hydrogen bonds with water:

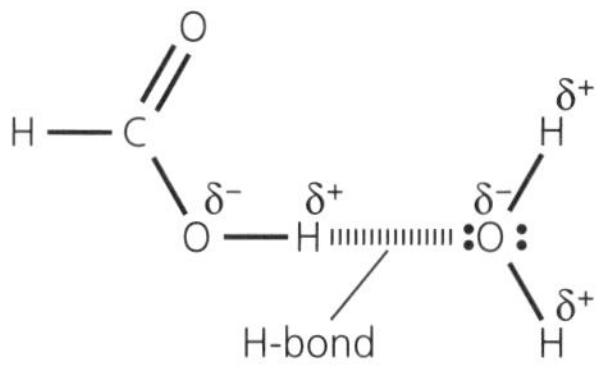


Methanoic acid is soluble in water because it can form H-bonds with water molecules

The solubility of carboxylic acids decreases with increased molar mass.

Carboxylic acids are acidic. Therefore they donate protons. However, they are weak acids, so dissociate only partially into their ions:

$$CH_3CO_2H(aq) \rightleftharpoons CH_3CO_2^-(aq) + H^+(aq)$$

They show typical reactions of acids and can form salts (carboxylates). In each of the examples that follows, the acid is ethanoic acid and the salt formed is sodium ethanoate:

- acid + base → salt + water

$$CH_3CO_2H(aq) + NaOH(aq) \rightarrow CH_3CO_2^-Na^+(aq) + H_2O(l)$$

- acid + (reactive) metal → salt + water

$$CH_3CO_2H(aq) + Na(s) \rightarrow CH_3CO_2^-Na^+ + \tfrac{1}{2}H_2$$

- acid + carbonate → salt + water + carbon dioxide

$$CH_3CO_2H(aq) + Na_2CO_3(aq) \rightarrow CH_3CO_2^-Na^+(aq) + H_2O(l) + CO_2(g)$$

The reaction with a carbonate is used as a test for a carboxylic acid. When an acid is added to a solution of a carbonate, bubbles (effervescence/fizzing) of carbon dioxide are seen.

## Now test yourself

TESTED

10 12.0 g of ethanoic acid were reacted with methanol in the presence of concentrated sulfuric acid. 3.70 g of the ester, methylethanoate, were isolated.
  (a) Write a balanced equation for the reaction and explain the role of the concentrated sulfuric acid.
  (b) Calculate the percentage yield.
  (c) Calculate the atom economy.
  (d) Suggest why the percentage yield is so low.

11 Write a balanced equation, including state symbols, for the reaction of $HCO_2H$ with:
  (a) Na(s)
  (b) $NaHCO_3(aq)$

Answers on p. 222

### Exam tip

The reaction of a carboxylic acid with sodium produces bubbles (in this case, of hydrogen), but it cannot be used as a test for a carboxylic acid because phenols also react with sodium to produce a salt and bubbles. However, phenols are not acidic enough to react with carbonates.

## Esters

REVISED

Carboxylic acids react with alcohols to form esters. This type of reaction is known as **esterification**. It is reversible and is usually carried out in the presence of an acid catalyst, such as concentrated sulfuric acid. The general reaction can be summarised as follows:

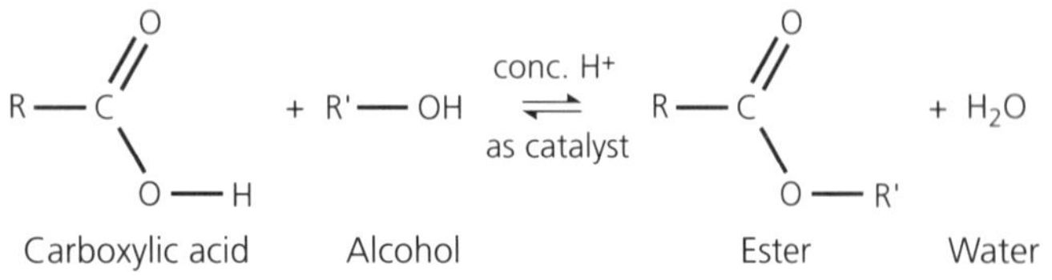


Esters are named from the alcohol and the carboxylic acid from which they are derived. The first part of the name relates to the alcohol and the second part of the name relates to the acid, for example:

methyl ethanoate
- methyl: Comes from methanol, $CH_3OH$
- ethanoate: Comes from ethanoic acid, $CH_3CO_2H$

ethyl methanoate
- ethyl: Comes from ethanol, $CH_3CH_2OH$
- methanoate: Comes from methanoic acid, $HCO_2H$

When organic compounds react, the reaction usually occurs between the two functional groups, in this case the alcohol and the carboxylic acid. It is helpful to draw the two reacting molecules with the functional groups facing each other:

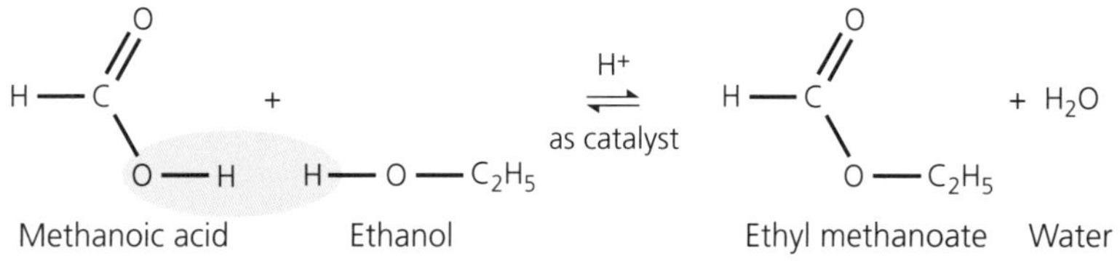


The formation of an ester by the reaction between a carboxylic acid and an ester is a reversible reaction and it follows that the yield is often low. An ester can also be prepared by the reaction of an acid anhydride with an alcohol.

Acid anhydrides contain the 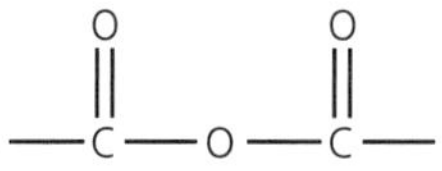 functional group.

Acid anhydrides react with alcohols to produce an ester and a carboxylic acid:

acid anhydride + alcohol → ester + carboxylic acid

Ethanoic anhydride is the most common anhydride. The formation of ethyl ethanoate (and ethanoic acid) from ethanoic anhydride is shown in Figure 11.10.

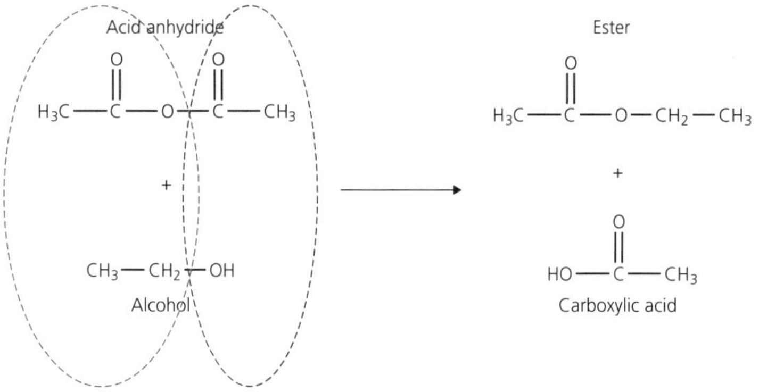


**Figure 11.10** Formation of ethyl ethanoate from ethanoic anhydride

**Typical mistakes**

Students often quote $H_2SO_4(aq)$ as the catalyst and lose the mark because (aq) indicates that water is present. Water is a product in the esterification reaction. The presence of additional water would drive the equilibrium to the left and inhibit the formation of the ester.

The advantages of preparing an ester from an acid anhydride are that the reaction is not reversible and it occurs readily.

Esters are used in flavourings and perfumes. They often contribute to the flavour associated with fruits.

Esters react with water. The **hydrolysis** reaction is slow and is carried out under reflux in the presence of either an acid, $H^+(aq)$, or a **base**, $OH^-(aq)$. Acid–catalysed hydrolysis leads to the formation of the carboxylic acid and the alcohol:

> A **base** is a proton acceptor.

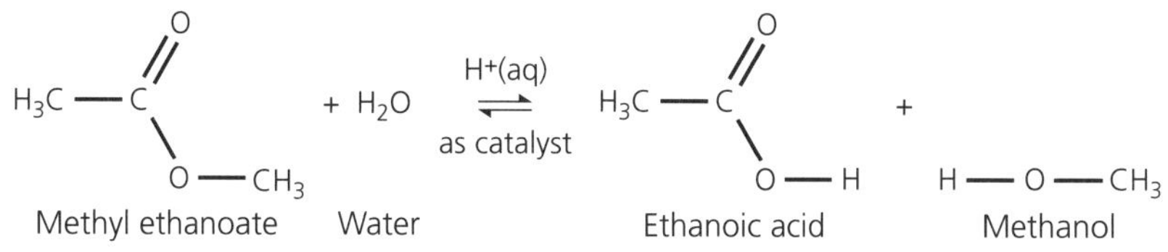

Hydrolysis in the presence of a base leads to the formation of the salt of the carboxylic acid (the carboxylate) and the alcohol. The base speeds up the hydrolysis but the base is used up as it reacts with the carboxylic acid produced:

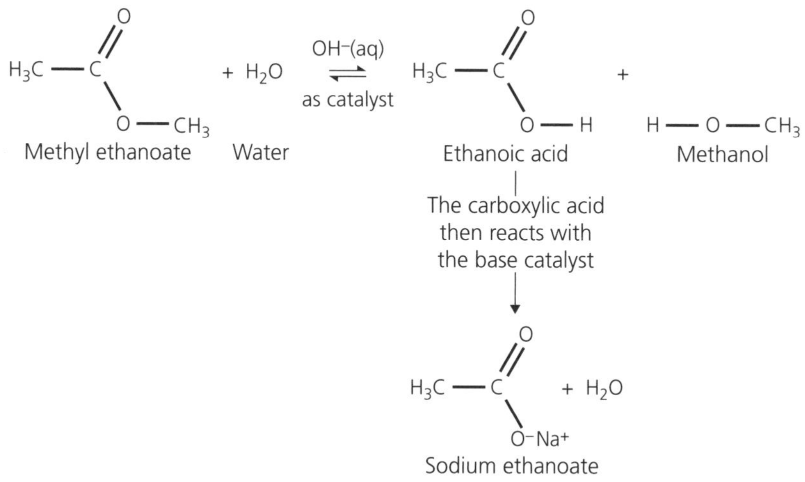

## Now test yourself

TESTED ☐

12 Propylethanoate can be hydrolysed by refluxing with NaOH(aq).
   (a) Explain what is meant by *refluxing*.
   (b) Write a balanced equation for the reaction. Name the products.

Answer on p. 222

# Acyl chlorides

REVISED ☐

## Preparation of acyl chlorides

Carboxylic acids, like alcohols, can be chlorinated by reaction with sulfur dichloride oxide (thionyl chloride), $SOCl_2$.

$$CH_3COOH + SOCl_2 \rightarrow CH_3COCl + SO_2 + HCl$$

## Reactions of acyl chlorides

Acyl halides are very reactive and they are hard to control but they can be used to make a variety of other chemicals.

The overall reaction of acid chlorides can be summarised as:

| RCO–Cl | + | H–Y | → | RCO–Y | + | H–Cl |
|---|---|---|---|---|---|---|
| acyl chloride | | reagent | | organic product | | |

The reagent, H–Y, can be as shown in Table 11.2.

**Table 11.2 Reagents and products in reactions of acyl chlorides**

| Reagent | Example | Organic product |
|---|---|---|
| H–OH | $H_2O$ (water) | RCOOH<br>carboxylic acid |
| H–OR | $CH_3OH$ (alcohol)* | RCOOR<br>ester |
| H–$NH_2$ | $NH_3$ (ammonia) | $RCONH_2$<br>primary amide |
| H–NH–R | $CH_3NH_2$ (amine) | RCONHR<br>secondary amide |
| *Phenols, $C_6H_5OH$, also react with acid halides. | | |

The reactions of acid halides are summarised in Figure 11.11.

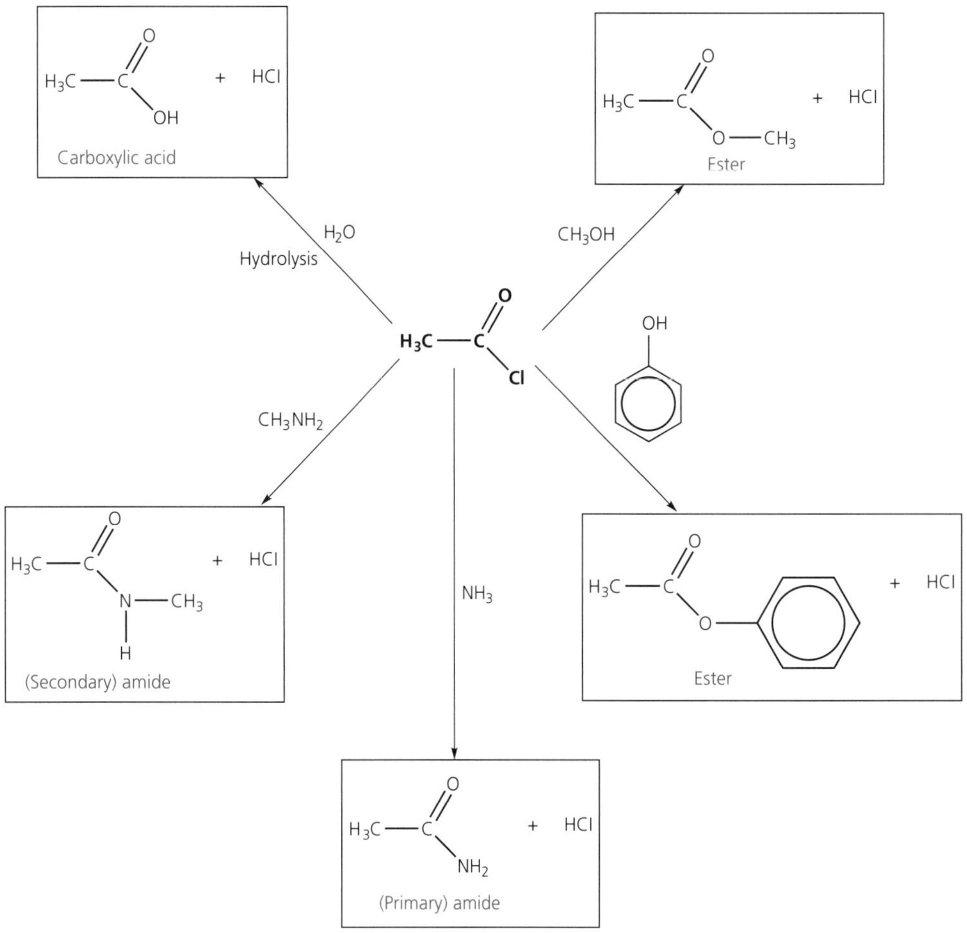


**Figure 11.11 Reactions of acid halides**

Acid halides are very versatile and can be used to produce a wide range of other functional groups. You will recall that esters can be made by reacting alcohols with carboxylic acids, but the reaction is reversible and the yield of the ester is therefore low. Alcohols react readily with acid chlorides to produce esters. The yield is much higher as the reaction is not reversible.

## Exam practice

1 Methylbenzene is an important industrial chemical. It is used in the production of polyurethane plastic foams and fibres such as Lycra®. The production of such foams and fibres involves the nitration of methylbenzene.

(a) Methylbenzene undergoes electrophilic substitution with the nitronium ion, $NO_2^+$, to form 4-nitromethylbenzene, $CH_3C_6H_4NO_2$.

(i) With the aid of curly arrows, show the mechanism for the formation of 4-nitromethylbenzene. [3]

(ii) In an experiment, 9.20 g of methylbenzene were used and 5.48 g of pure 4-nitromethylbenzene were isolated. Calculate the percentage yield and the atom economy of the reaction. [5]

(b)

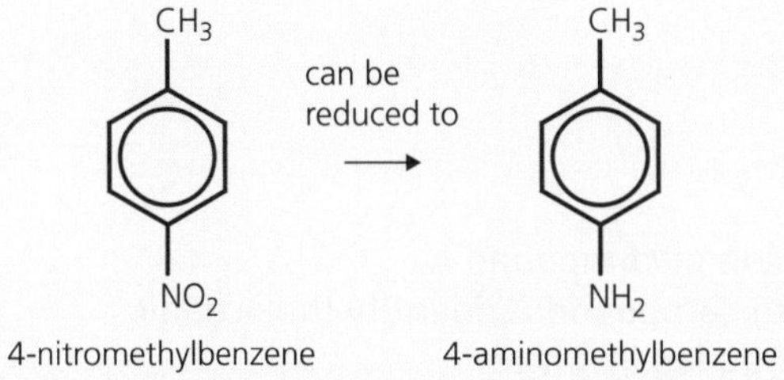


**Figure 11.12 Reduction of 4-nitromethylbenzene**

(i) Suggest a suitable reducing agent or a suitable reducing mixture for the reaction in Figure 11.12. [1]

(ii) Construct a balanced equation for this reduction. Use [H] to represent the reducing agent. [2]

(c) There are six structural isomers of dinitromethylbenzene, $CH_3C_6H_3(NO_2)_2$. Four are drawn for in Figure 11.13. Draw the structure of the other *two* isomers. [2]

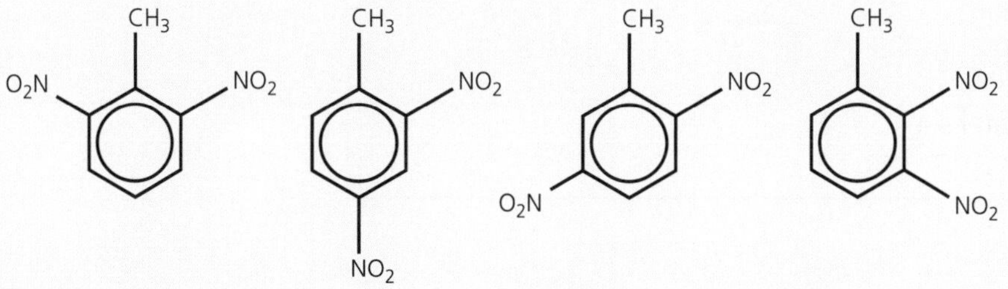


**Figure 11.13**

(d) The manufacture of Lycra® involves one of these six isomers. A small section of Lycra® is shown in Figure 11.14.

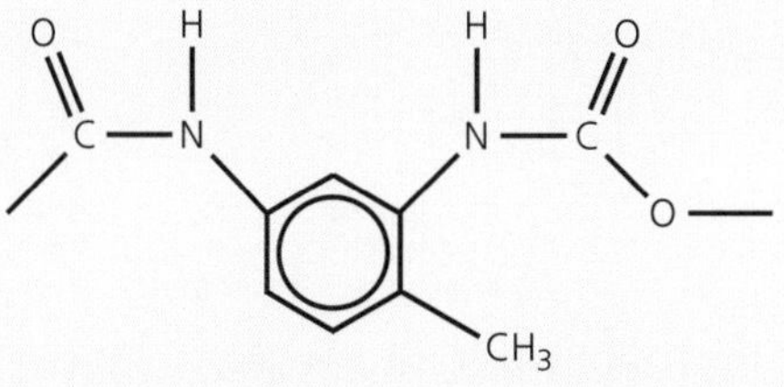


**Figure 11.14**

Draw the structure of the isomer of dinitromethylbenzene used in the manufacture of Lycra®. [1]

2 Propan-1-ol can be oxidised to both propanal and to propanoic acid.

(a) (i) State a suitable oxidising mixture. [2]

(ii) State what you would see during the oxidations. [1]

Using [O] to represent the oxidising mixture, write balanced equations to show the oxidation of:

(iii) propan-1-ol to propanal [1]

(iv) propan-1-ol to propanoic acid [1]

(v) Describe a simple *chemical* test to distinguish between propanal and propanoic acid. State what you would see. [2]

(b) Compound X contains carbon, hydrogen and oxygen only. The relative molecular mass of compound X is 102.0. When 5.1 g of compound X is burned in excess oxygen, 6.0 $dm^3$ $CO_2$ is produced. Compound X can be hydrolysed to form propan-1-ol and one other organic compound. Use *all* of the information in the question to deduce the molecular formula of compound X. Draw the structure of compound X. Show all your working. [5]

3 Compound A has the structure shown in Figure 11.15.

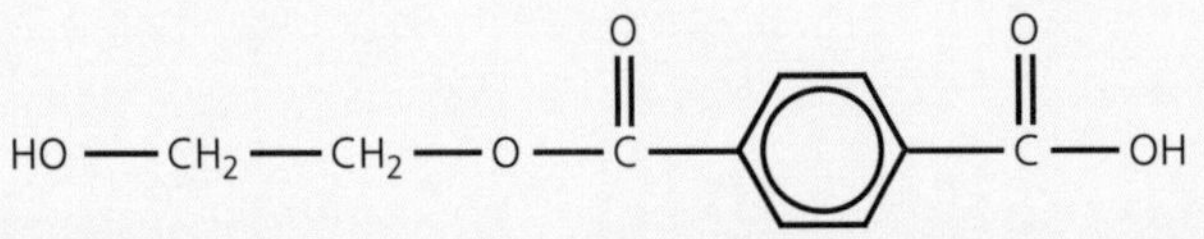


**Figure 11.15**

(a) Deduce the empirical formula and molecular formula of compound A. [2]

(b) Suggest *three* different reagents that will react with compound A. Identify the organic product(s) of each reaction and name the type of reaction involved. [9]

## Answers and quick quiz 11 online

ONLINE

## Summary

You should now have an understanding of:

- benzene and aromatic compounds
- electrophilic substitution
- phenols
- carbonyl compounds
- carboxylic acids and esters
- acyl chlorides

# 12 Nitrogen compounds, polymers and synthesis

## Amines

### Basicity and preparation of amines

Amines are weak bases since the lone pair of electrons on the nitrogen can accept a proton from water to form a dative covalent bond:

$$C_2H_5-\overset{\overset{\displaystyle H}{|}}{\underset{\underset{\displaystyle H}{|}}{N}}: + H_2O \longrightarrow \left(C_2H_5-\overset{\overset{\displaystyle H}{|}}{\underset{\underset{\displaystyle H}{|}}{N}}: \longrightarrow H\right)^+ + OH^-$$

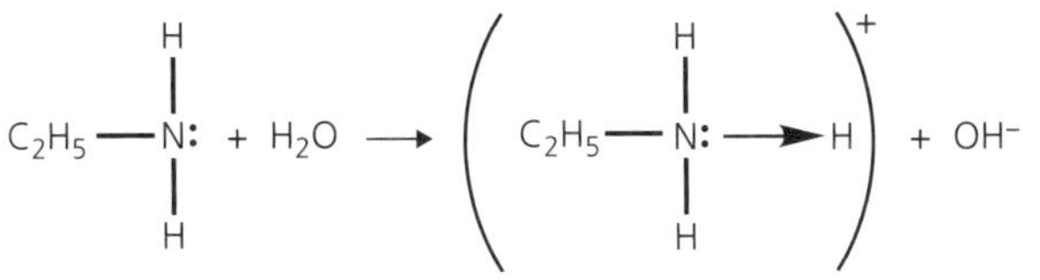

Consequently, amines react with acids to form salts. Two examples are:

$$C_2H_5NH_2 + HCl \rightarrow C_2H_5NH_3{}^+Cl^-$$
**Ethylamine**

$$C_6H_5NH_2 + H_2SO_4 \rightarrow C_6H_5NH_3{}^+HSO_4{}^-$$
**Phenylamine**

In the second reaction, $(C_6H_5NH_3{}^+)_2SO_4{}^{2-}$ could also be formed.

### Preparation of amines

Primary aliphatic amines such as ethylamine, $CH_3CH_2NH_2$, can be prepared by the nucleophilic substitution reaction between a haloalkane and excess ethanolic ammonia:

$$CH_3CH_2Cl + :NH_3 \text{ (alc)} \rightarrow CH_3CH_2\overset{..}{N}H_2 + HCl$$
$$\text{nucleophile}$$

The reaction mixture has to be heated under pressure.

Secondary aliphatic amines such as diethylamine, $CH_3CH_2NHCH_2CH_3$, can be prepared by the nucleophilic substitution reaction between a haloalkane and a primary amine:

$$CH_3CH_2Cl + CH_3CH_2\overset{..}{N}H_3 \rightarrow CH_3CH_2\overset{..}{N}HCH_2CH_3 + HCl$$
$$\text{nucleophile}$$

Aromatic amines such as phenylamine, $C_6H_5NH_2$, can be prepared by heating nitrobenzene, under reflux, with tin and concentrated hydrochloric acid. This is a reduction reaction in which the reducing agent is formed from the reaction between tin and concentrated hydrochloric acid. Using [H] to represent the reducing agent, the equation for this reaction is:

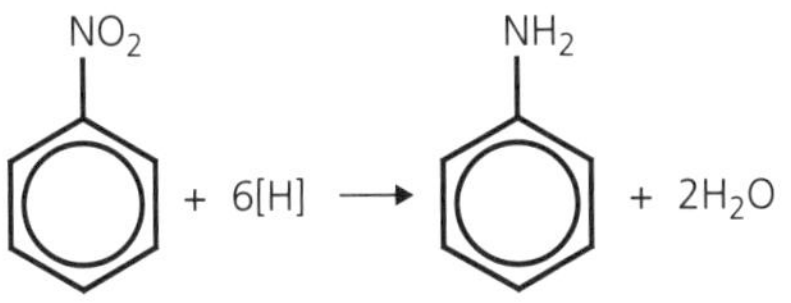

> **Exam tip**
>
> An amine has a lone pair of electrons on the nitrogen and can also behave as a base so will therefore react with an acid. For example, $CH_3CH_2NH_2$ reacts with the HCl also produced to form the salt $CH_3CH_2NH_3{}^+Cl^-$.

NO_2 ⬡ + 6[H] → NH_2 ⬡ + 2H_2O

## Now test yourself

TESTED

1 Chloromethane, $CH_3Cl$, and ammonia react to form a mixture of amines including $CH_3NH_2$, $(CH_3)_2NH$ and $(CH_3)_3N$.
(a) Write equations for the formation of each amine
(b) Explain the conditions you would use to ensure maximum possible yield of $CH_3NH_2$.

Answer on p. 222

# Amino acids, amides and chirality

## Amino acids

REVISED

The general formula of an α-**amino acid** is $RCH(NH_2)COOH$, where R represents the side-chain (Figure 12.1)

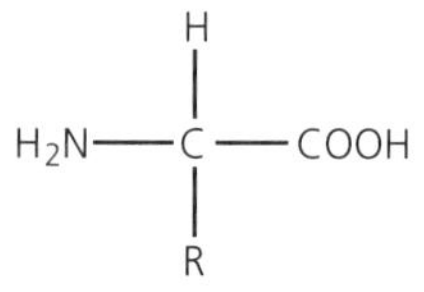


**Figure 12.1 General structural formula of an amino acid**

The general formula of an α-**amino acid** is $RCH(NH_2)COOH$. The amine group ($NH_2$) and the carboxylic acid group (COOH) are bonded to the same carbon atom.

The simplest α-amino acid is aminoethanoic acid, or glycine, where the R group is hydrogen. In 2-aminopropanoic acid or alanine, the R group is $CH_3$. (Figure 12.2)

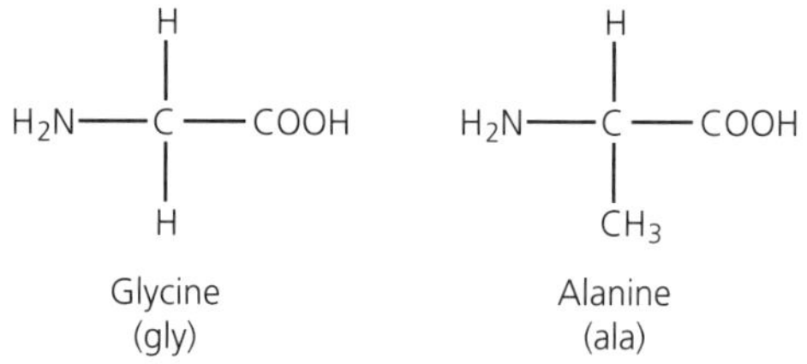


**Figure 12.2 Amino acids glycine and alanine**

Alanine has two optical isomers; glycine is not optically active. This is because alanine has an asymmetric (chiral) carbon atom whereas glycine does not.

Amino acids are bi-functional because they contain two functional groups — carboxylic acid and amine.

### Reaction of the carboxylic acid group

An amino acid can react with a base to produce a salt, for example:

$$CH_2NH_2CO_2H(aq) + NaOH(aq) \rightarrow CH_2NH_2CO_2^-Na^+(aq) + H_2O(l)$$

**Glycine**

As well as reacting with alkalis, amino acids also react with metals, carbonates and metal oxides:

$$2H_2NCH(R)COOH + 2K \rightarrow 2H_2NCH(R)COO^-K^+ + H_2$$

$$2H_2NCH(R)COOH + Na_2CO_3 \rightarrow 2H_2NCH(R)COO^-Na^+ + H_2O + CO_2$$

$$2H_2NCH(R)COOH + CaO \rightarrow (H_2NCH(R)COO^-)_2Ca^{2+} + H_2O$$

An amino acid can react with an alcohol to produce an ester, for example:

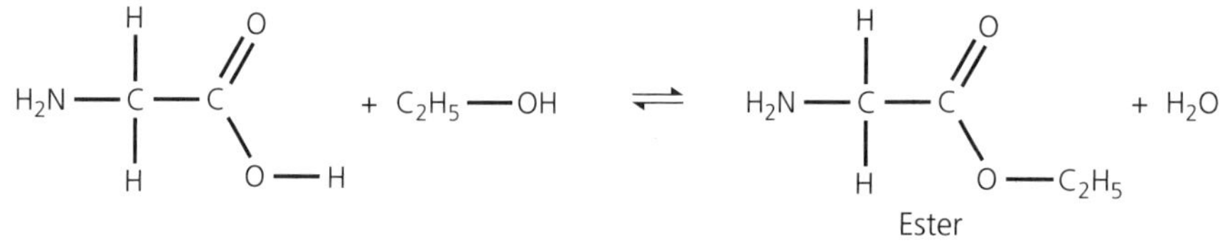

### Reaction of the amine group

Amino acids can also behave as a primary amine and will react with an acid to produce a salt:

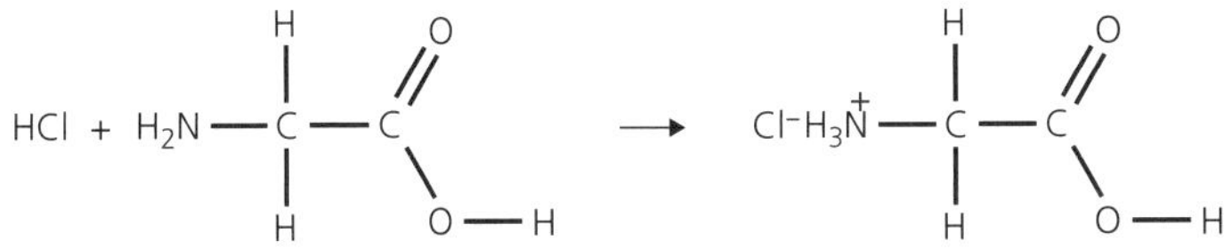

Amino acids also display properties that depend on both functional groups. These reactions can result in the formation of peptides, polypeptides and proteins; they are not included in the specification and will not be tested.

## Amides

REVISED

Primary amides have the general formula R-$CONH_2$ and include compounds such as those in Figure 12.3.

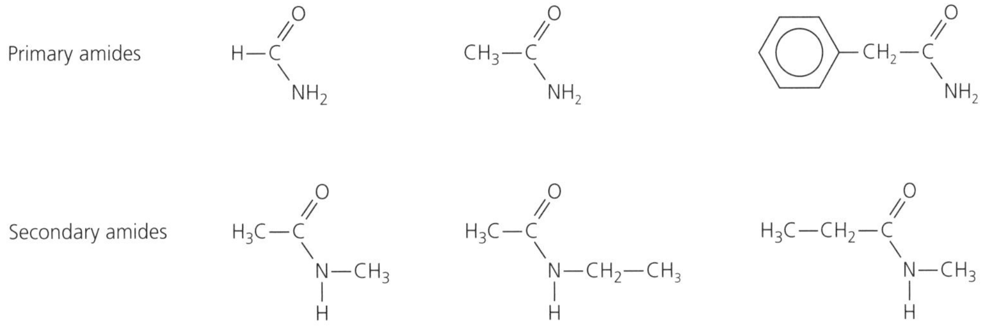


**Figure 12.3 Primary and secondary amides**

The amide group is polar:

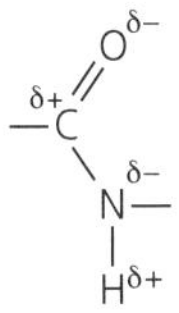

and like the ester group can be hydrolysed:

- Hydrolysis by heating with a mineral acid, usually HCl(aq):

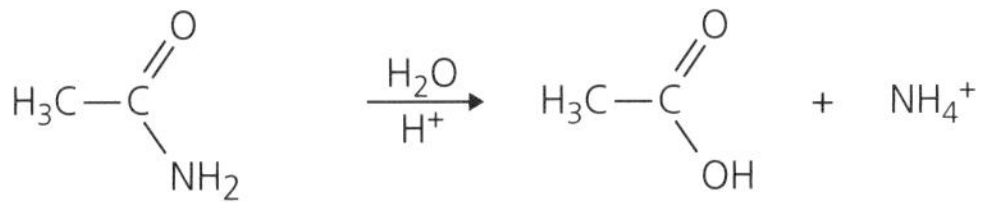

$NH_3$ is initially formed but it reacts with the $H^+$ to form the ammonium salt

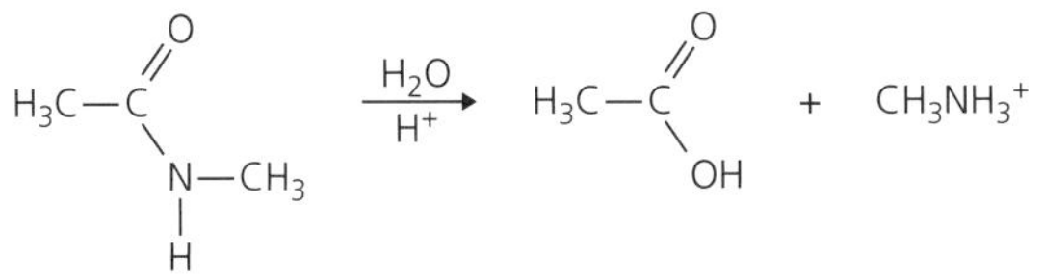

$CH_3NH_2$ is initially formed but it reacts with the $H^+$ to form the ethylamine salt

- Hydrolysis by heating with an alakali such as NaOH(aq):

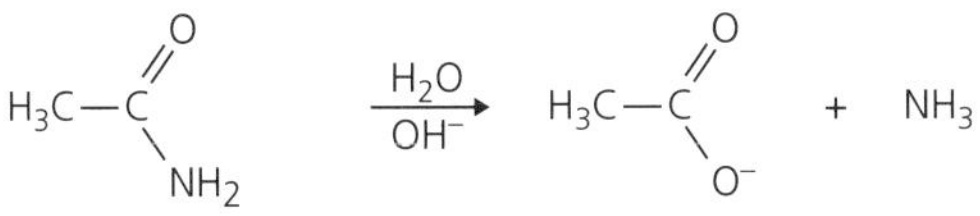

$CH_3COOH$ is initially formed but it reacts with the $OH^-$ to form the ethanoate salt and water

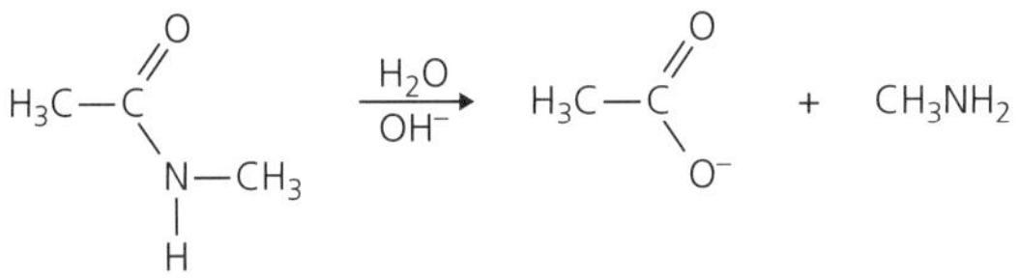

$CH_3COOH$ is initially formed but it reacts with the $OH^-$ to form the ethanoate salt and water

## Chirality

REVISED

A **chiral** (asymmetric) carbon atom is a carbon atom that is bonded to four different atoms or groups. Amino acids, $RC^{\star}H(NH_2)COOH$, with the exception of glycine, $CH_2(NH_2)COOH$, are optically active because the carbon atom C* is bonded to four different atoms or groups. The optical isomers of alanine are shown below in Figure 12.4.

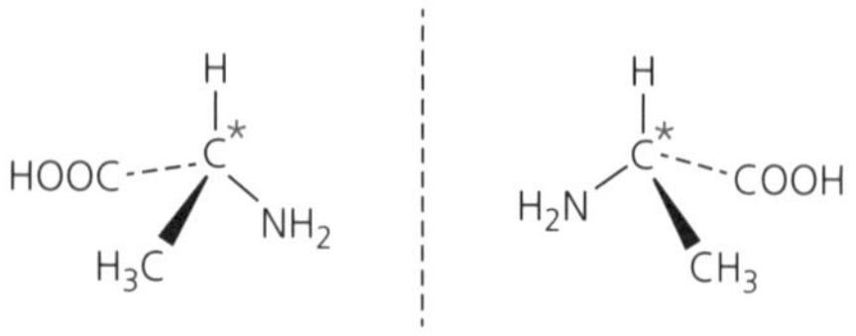


**Figure 12.4 Optical isomers of alanine**

> **Typical mistakes**
>
> Students lose marks for careless drawings of isomers. The diagrams below all lose marks. Compare them with the correct diagrams above.
>
> 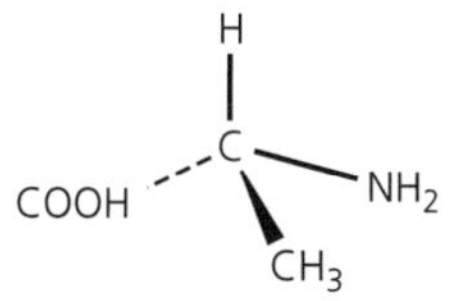
> 
>
> The COOH must be linked to the central carbon by the C not the H
>
> 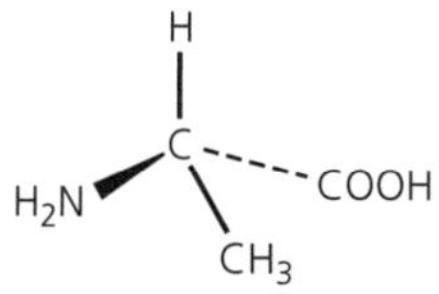
> 
>
> The two ⟋ bonds have to be next to each other

## Now test yourself

TESTED

2 (a) Draw the optical isomers of phenylalanine:

$C_6H_5CH_2CH(NH_2)COOH$

(b) Write an equation for the reaction of phenylalanine with:

(i) HCl

(ii) $CH_3OH$

(iii) $SOCl_2$

3 During the late 1950s and early 1960s thalidomide (Figur 12.5) was given to pregnant women to combat morning sickness.

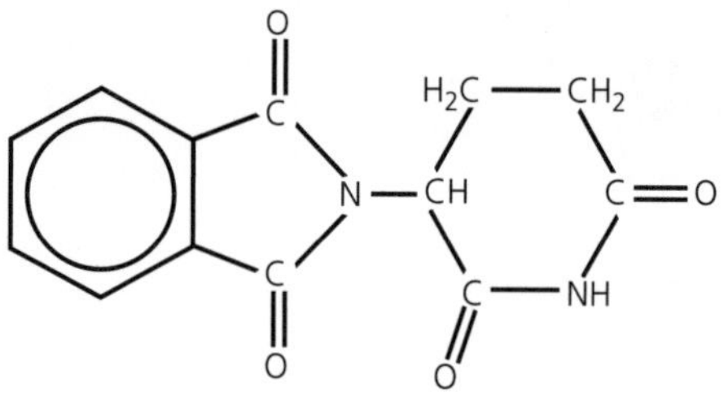


Figure 12.5

(a) What is the molecular formula of thalidomide?

(b) Copy the structure of thalidomide and identify the chiral carbon by drawing an asterisk next to it.

Answers on p. 222

# Polyesters and polyamides

There are two categories of polymer: addition polymers and condensation polymers. Addition polymers were covered in Module 4.

## Condensation polymers

REVISED

Condensation polymers are formed when monomers react together and 'condense' out a small molecule such as $H_2O$ or HCl. There are two main types: polyesters and polyamides.

### Polyesters

Terylene® is a common polyester made by reacting the monomers ethene-1,2-diol and benzene-1,4-dicarboxylic acid (Figure 12.6).

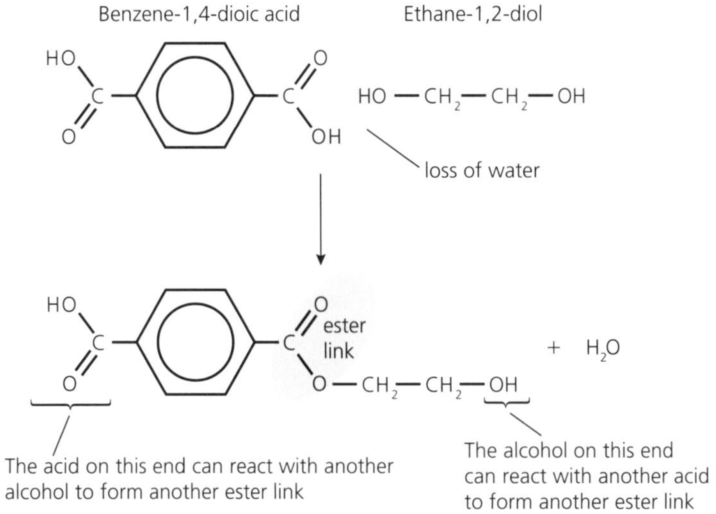


**Figure 12.6 Formatiom of Terylene®**

The resulting polymer is almost linear. This means that the polymer chains can be packed closely together. The close packing produces strong intermolecular forces that enable the polymer to be spun into thread.

### Polyamides

Polyamides are prepared from two monomers, one with an amine group at each end and the other with a carboxylic acid group at each end. Nylon-6,6 is made from the two monomers 1,6-diaminohexane and hexane-1,6-dicarboxylic acid Figure 12.7. It is called nylon-6,6 because each monomer contains six carbon atoms.

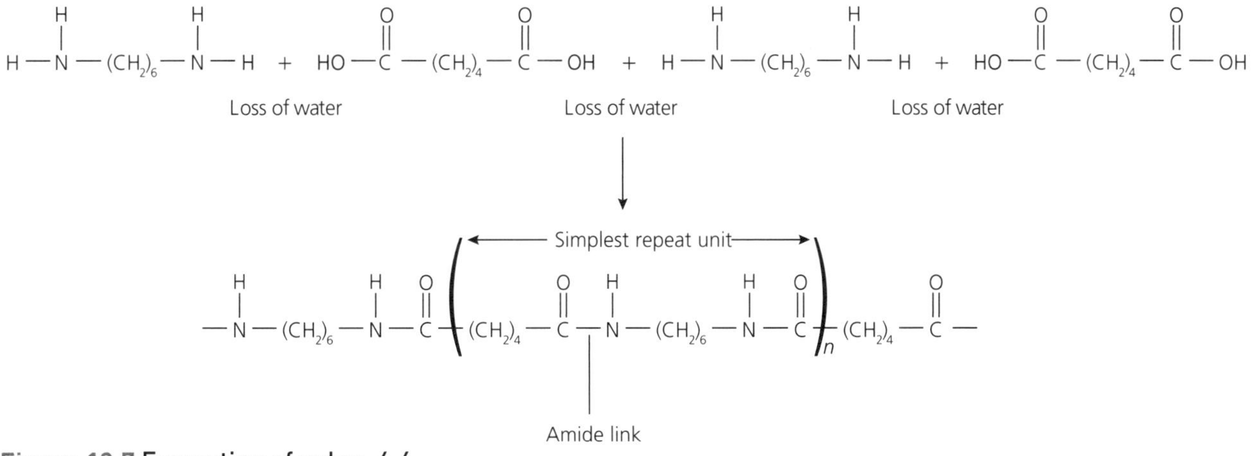


**Figure 12.7 Formation of nylon-6,6**

Nylon forms a strong, flexible fibre when it is melt-spun.

Kevlar® is another polyamide. It is stronger than steel and fire resistant. It is used for making bulletproof vests, crash helmets and for protective clothing used by fire fighters. It is made from two monomers: benzene-1,4-diamine and benzene-1,4 dicarboxylic acid (Figure 12.8).

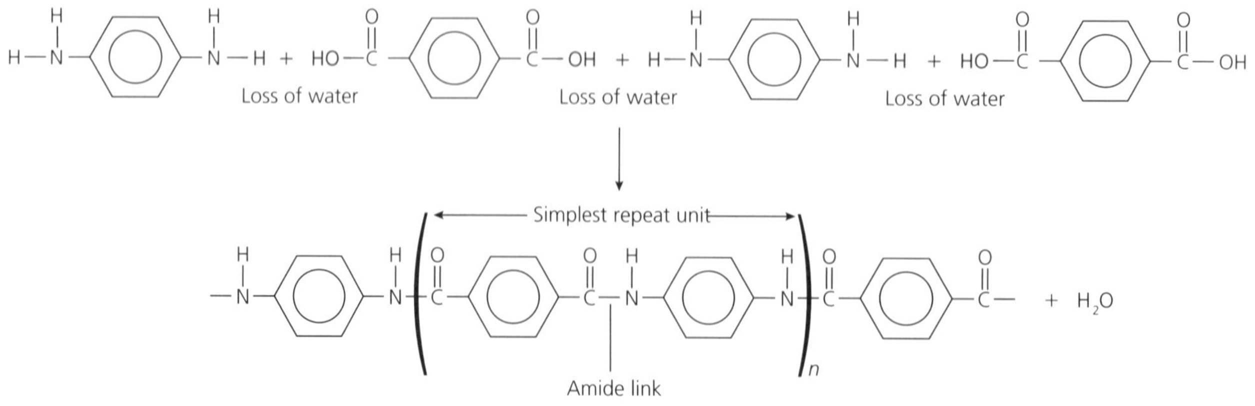


**Figure 12.8 Formation of Kevlar®**

## Now test yourself

TESTED

4 Draw *two* repeat units of the polymer that could be formed from:

(a)

$$HOH_2C — CH_2 — CH_2 — CH_2OH \ + \ HO — \overset{O}{\overset{\|}{C}} — (CH_2)_3 — \overset{O}{\overset{\|}{C}} — OH$$

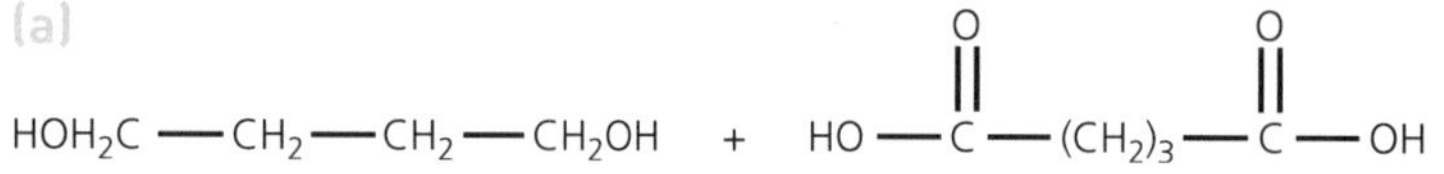


(b)

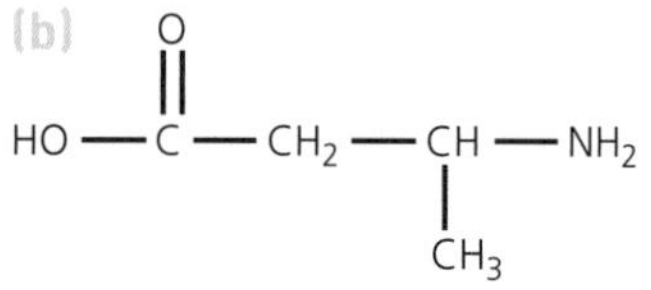


5 (a) Nylon is not a single material but a group of chemicals made from diamines and dioic acids (or dioyl chlorides).
  (i) Identify the monomers used to make:
  - nylon-4,6
  - nylon-6,4
  - nylon-6,10

  (ii) Different nylons have different melting points. Suggest why nylon-4,6 has a lower melting point than nylon-6,10.

(b) Nylon-6 can be made from the cyclic amide caprolactam, molecular formula $C_5H_{11}NO$.
  (i) Draw the structure of caprolactam.
  (ii) Draw *two* repeat units of nylon-6 formed from caprolactam.

Answers on pp. 223

## Acid and base hydrolysis

REVISED

The ester link in a polyester and the amide link in a polyamide are both polar links and are subject to acid-catalysed and base-catalysed hydrolysis (Figure 12.9).

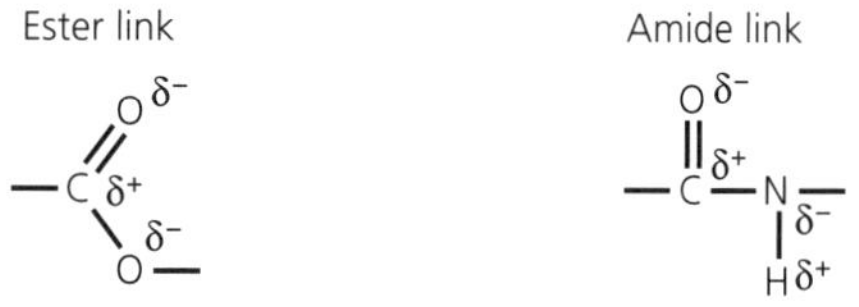

**Figure 12.9**

Acid hydrolysis of a polyester results in the formation of a diol and a dioic acid:

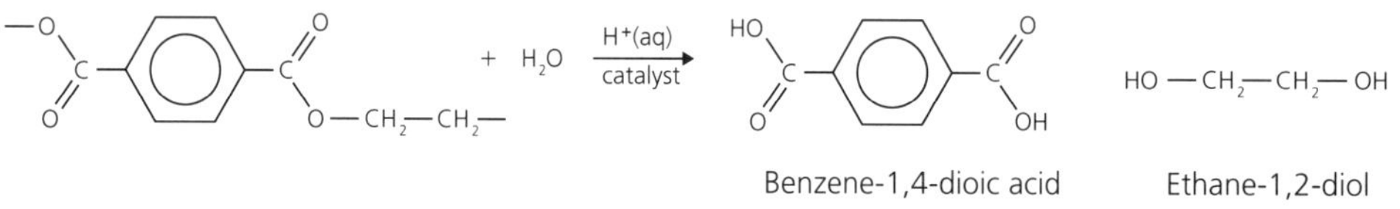

Base hydrolysis of a polyester also forms a diol, but the dioic acid formed then reacts with the base catalyst to form the dioate salt. The products of refluxing Terylene® with an aqueous solution of sodium hydroxide are:

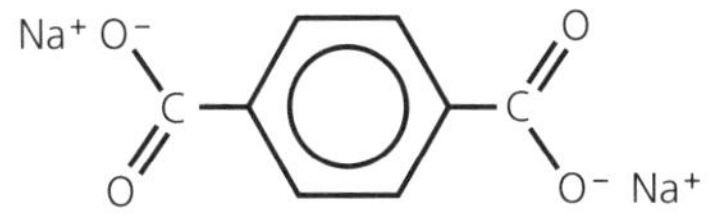


and $HO-CH_2-CH_2-OH$

Polyamides can also be hydrolysed:

- Acid-catalysed hydrolysis results in the formation of the dioic acid and the di-salt of the diamine.
- Base-catalysed hydrolysis results in the formation of the diamine and the dioate salt of the dioic acid.

Hydrolysis of polyamides is summarised in the reaction scheme in Figure 12.10.

> **Typical mistakes**
>
> The products of the hydrolysis of polyesters and polyamides are often deduced incorrectly because many students assume that hydrolysis breaks the polymer back to the monomers. Hydrolysis occurs at a significant rate only in the presence of either an acid or base catalyst.
> The presence of the catalyst results in the formation of the corresponding salts of the monomers.

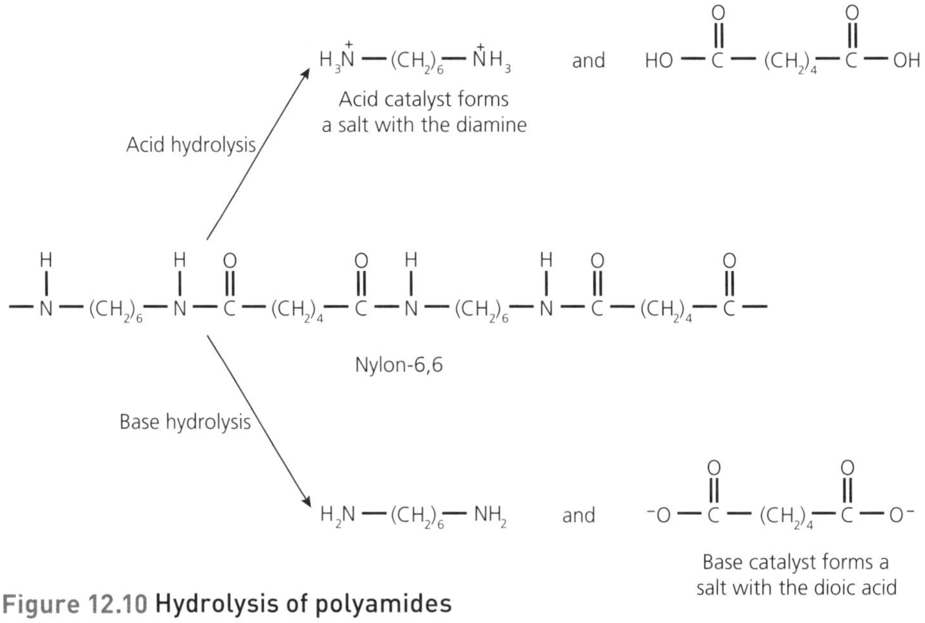


**Figure 12.10 Hydrolysis of polyamides**

## Now test yourself

TESTED

6 Identify the products formed by both acid and base hydrolysis of the polymer shown in Figure 12.11.

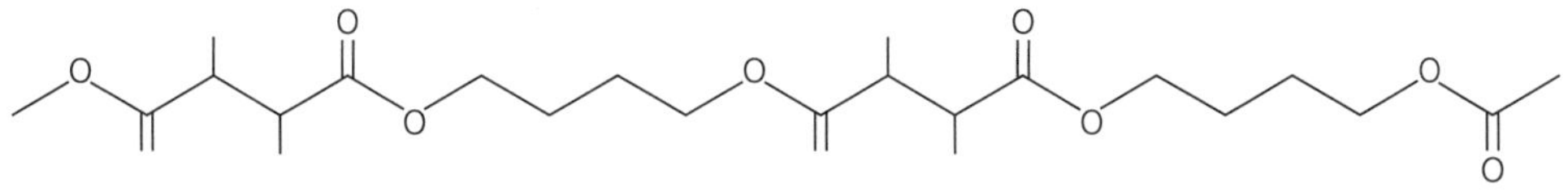

Figure 12.11

Answer on p. 223

Chemists are aware of the impact on the environment of using compounds derived from fossils fuels and also of the problems associated with the disposal of plastic waste. Condensation polymers can be disposed of by hydrolysis. Photodegradable polymers are being developed. An example is poly(lactic acid), PLA, which is prepared from 2-hydoxypropanoic (lactic) acid, $CH_3CH(OH)COOH$. A molecule of lactic acid contains an alcohol group (–OH) and a carboxylic acid group (–COOH). These can react together to produce an ester linkage.

The introduction of polymers such as PLA reflects the role of chemists in minimising the impact on the environment through the use of renewable sources and by the development of degradable polymers. PLA is particularly attractive as a sustainable alternative to products derived from petrochemicals, since the monomer can be produced by the bacterial fermentation of agricultural by-products, such as cornstarch or sugar cane, which are **renewable** feedstocks. Polylactic acid is fully compostable and degrades to carbon dioxide and water in a relatively short period of time.

**Renewable** relates to an essential chemical that can be replaced. An example is cornstarch, which is used in the production of PLA — more cornstarch can be produced by growing more corn.

PLA is more expensive than many petroleum-derived commodity plastics, but its price has been falling as more production comes online. The degree to which the price will fall and the degree to which PLA will be able to compete with non-sustainable, petroleum-derived polymers is uncertain.

**Exam tip**

Examiners are always looking for new ways to test routine chemistry and often set questions containing structures of complex molecules. Remember that, no matter how complex the molecule, only the functional groups react. A good starting point is to identify the functional groups within any complex molecule, as in the following example:

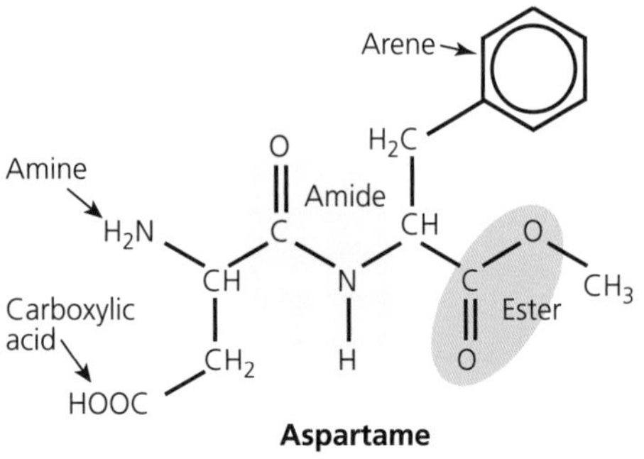
Arene
Amine
Amide
Carboxylic acid
Ester
Aspartame

# Carbon–carbon bond formation

Chemists are continuously looking to develop new chemicals. In order to build new molecules it is essential to increase the length of the carbon chain. You should be aware of three different ways in this can be achieved.

## Method 1

REVISED

Haloalkanes react with ethanolic cyanide(nitrile) ions, $^{-}C{\equiv}N$, to form a nitrile:

$$CH_3CH_2Cl + {}^{-}C{\equiv}N \rightarrow CH_3CH_2C{\equiv}N + Cl^-$$

**Chloroethane (2 carbons)** → **Propanenitrile (3 carbons)**

The mechanism involves nucleophilic substitution:

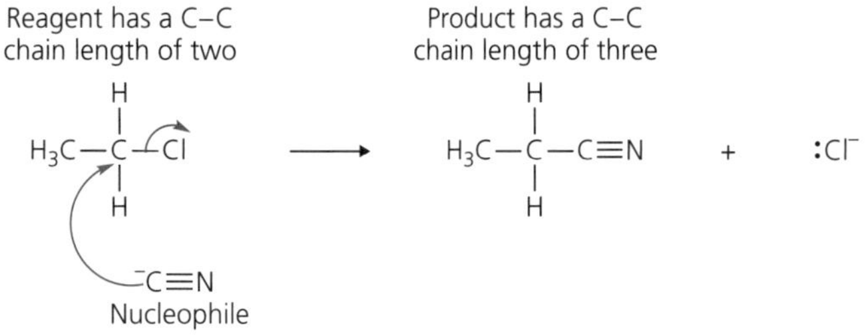
Reagent has a C–C chain length of two
Product has a C–C chain length of three
Nucleophile

## Method 2

Aldehydes and ketones react with HC≡N to form a hydroxy-nitrile:

$$CH_3CH_2CHO + HC≡N → CH_3CH_2CH(OH)C≡N$$

Propanal               2-Hydroxybutanenitrile

(3 carbons)             (4 carbons)

The mechanism involves nucleophilic addition (see page 175).

## Method 3

The formation of an aromatic C–C by alkylation (using a haloalkane) or by acylation (using an acyl chloride) in the presence of a halogen carrier. See pages 170–171.

The mechanism involves electrophilic substitution (see page 171).

The nitrile group formed by methods 1 and 2 can be converted to amines or carboxylic acids (Figure 12.12).

**Reduction**    $H_3C—C≡N \quad + \quad 4[H]$    $\xrightarrow[\text{or } H_2 \text{ and Ni}]{\substack{\text{Reduction using either} \\ \text{LiAlH}_4 \text{ or Na in ethanol}}}$    $H_3C—CH_2—NH_2$

**Hydrolysis**

$H_3C—C≡N \quad \xrightarrow[\substack{\text{Hydrolysis occurs and water} \\ \text{adds to form an acid amide}}]{H_2O/H^+(aq)} \quad H_3C—\overset{\displaystyle O}{\overset{\|}{C}}—NH_2$

The amide is then hydrolysed to form the carboxylic acid and an ammonium salt

$H_3C—\overset{\displaystyle O}{\overset{\|}{C}}—NH_2 \quad \xrightarrow[\substack{\text{Hydrolysis occurs again and water} \\ \text{adds to form a carboxylic acid}}]{H_2O/H^+(aq)} \quad H_3C—\overset{\displaystyle O}{\overset{\|}{C}}—OH \ + \ NH_4^+$

The net reaction for acid hydolysis is:

$$CH_3CN \ + \ 2H_2O \ + \ H^+ \longrightarrow CH_2COOH \ + \ NH_4^+$$

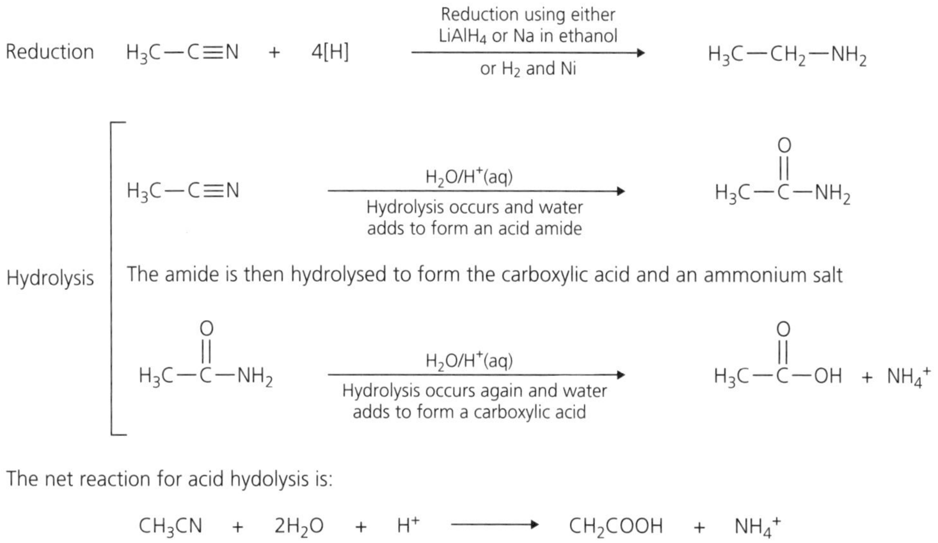

**Figure 12.12 Reactions of nitriles to form amines and carboxylic acids**

# Organic synthesis

Compounds such as aldosterone, $C_{21}H_{28}O_5$, are complex molecules (Figure 12.13).

But the chemistry of complex molecules depends on the functional groups within the molecule.

Your knowledge of functional groups should now cover: alkanes, alkenes, alcohols, haloalkanes, aldehydes, ketones, carboxylic acids, esters, acid chlorides, amines and amides. Table 12.1 summarises the reactions of these groups.

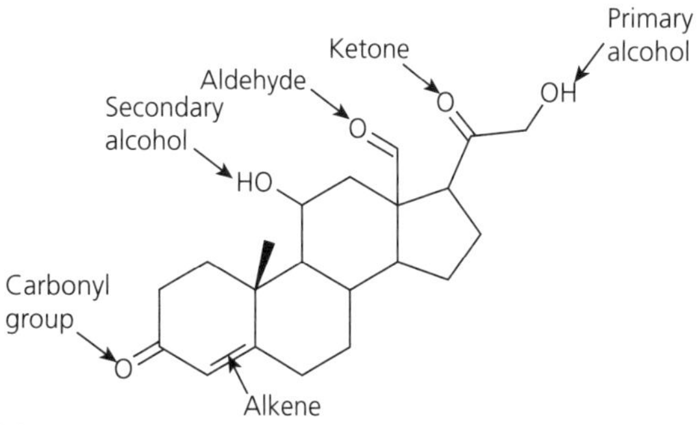

**Figure 12.13**

Table 12.1 Summary of reactions of functional groups

| Functional group | | Type of reaction | Reagents that react |
|---|---|---|---|
| **Name** | **Group** | | |
| Alkene | 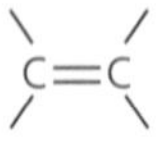 | Electrophilic addition | $H_2$, HBr, $Br_2$ $H_2O(g)$ |
| Alcohol | R–OH | Oxidation<br>Esterification<br>Elimination | $H^+/Cr_2O_7^{2-}$<br>RCOOH (carboxylic acids)<br>$H_2SO_4$ |
| Haloalkane | R–Cl | Nucleophilic substitution | Common nucleophiles include: $:OH^-$, $:NH_3$, $:CN^-$ |
| Aldehyde | 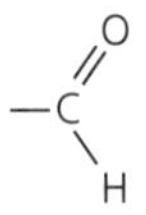 | Nucleophilic addition<br>Oxidation | $:H^-/NaBH_4$, HCN<br>$H^+/Cr_2O_7^{2-}$ |
| Ketone | 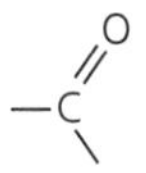 | Nucleophilic addition | $:H^-/NaBH_4$, HCN |
| Carboxylic acid | 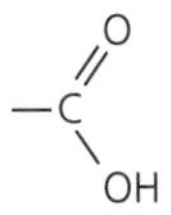 | Acidic reactions<br>Esterification | Na, NaOH, $Na_2CO_3$<br>Alcohols, ROH |
| Ester | 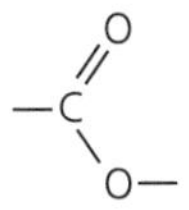 | Hydrolysis | $H^+(aq)$, $OH^-(aq)$ |
| Acyl chloride | 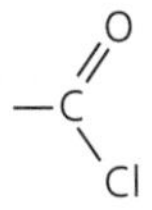 | Condensation | $H_2O$, ROH, $NH_3$, $RNH_2$ |
| Amine | $R–NH_2$ or 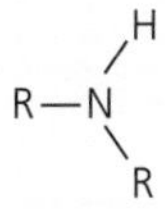 | Basic reactions<br>Nucleophilic reactions | HCl<br>Haloalkanes, R–Cl |
| Amide | 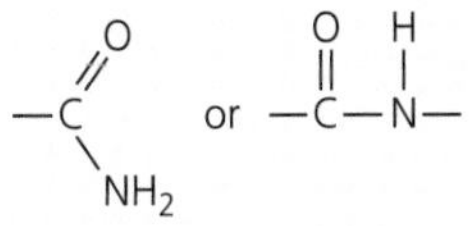 | Hydrolysis | $H^+(aq)$, $OH^-(aq)$ |
| Nitrile | —C≡N | Hydrolysis<br>Reduction | $H^+(aq)$, $OH^-(aq)$<br>Na in ethanol (or $LiAlH_4$) |

## Now test yourself

TESTED

7 Predict four different reactions of aldosterone. In each reaction, state which functional group will react and name the functional group that will be formed.

Answer on p. 223

It may not be possible to convert one chemical into another using a single reaction — intermediate compounds have to be formed.

## Example 1

Use a two-stage synthesis to convert bromoethane into ethyl ethanoate.

**Step 1** – start with the target molecule and identify the compounds that could readily be converted directly into the target — concentrate on the functional group.

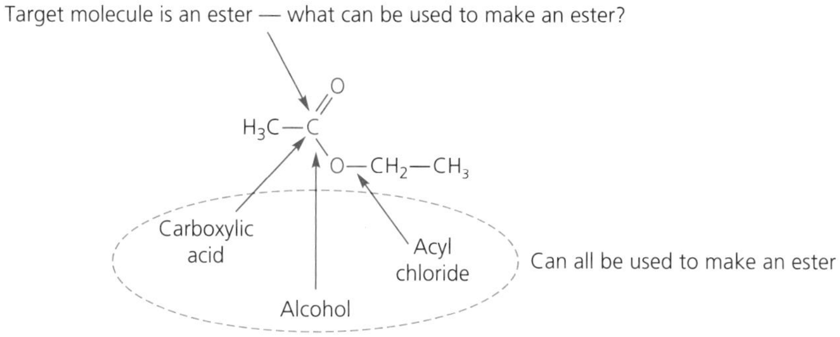

Target molecule is an ester — what can be used to make an ester?

Carboxylic acid
Acyl chloride
Alcohol

Can all be used to make an ester

**Step 2** – look at the starting molecule, bromoethane — what reactions of haloalkanes do you know?

Amine     Alcohol     Nitrile

$CH_3 - CH_2 - Br$
Starting molecule

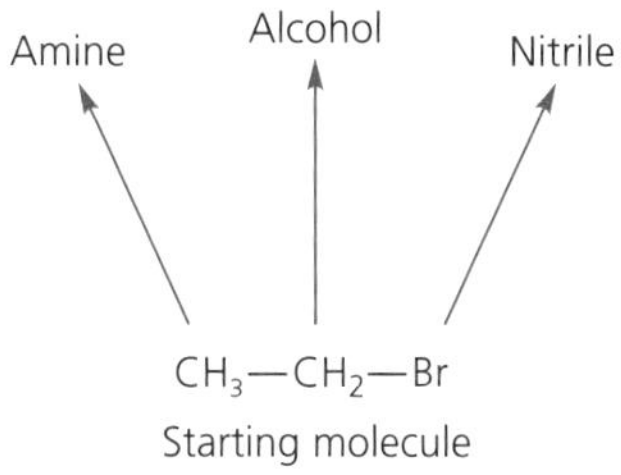

You should now see a possible two-stage synthetic route from your starting molecule to the target molecule. In this case, the route can go via the alcohol:

Starting $\quad\quad\quad$ Intermediate $\quad\quad\quad\quad\quad\quad$ Target

$$CH_3 - CH_2 - Br \xrightarrow{NaOH/H_2O} CH_3 - CH_2 - OH \xrightarrow[H^+ \text{ catalyst}]{CH_3COOH} CH_3 - C(=O) - O - CH_2 - CH_3$$

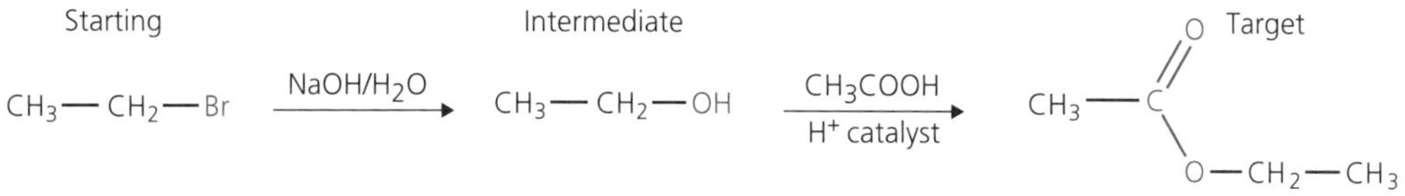

## Example 2

Use a two-stage synthesis to convert ethanal into 2-hydroxypropanoic acid.

**Step 1** – start with the target molecule and identify the compounds that could readily be converted directly into the target — concentrate on the functional groups.

Target molecule is a hydroxyl carboxylic acid. This contains two functional groups:

Target molecule is a hydroxy carboxylic acid; this contains two functional groups

Secondary alcohol     Carboxylic acid

Ketone
Alkene
Haloalkane

Acyl chloride
Primary alcohol
Aldehyde

Hydroxynitrile

**Step 2** – look at the starting molecule, ethanal — what reactions of aldehydes do you know?

Hydroxynitrile

Primary alcohol

Carboxylic acid

$H_3C - C(=O) - H$

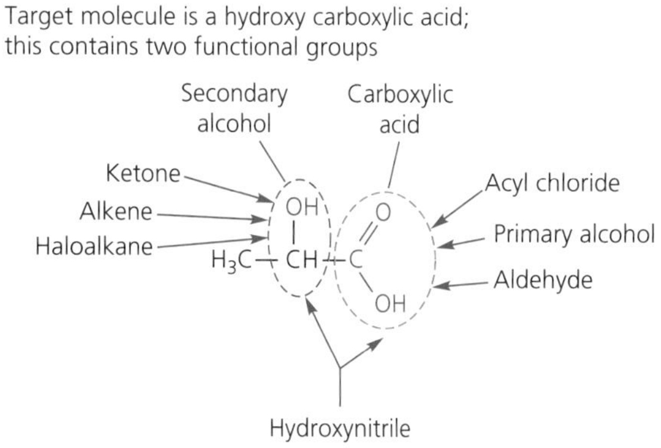

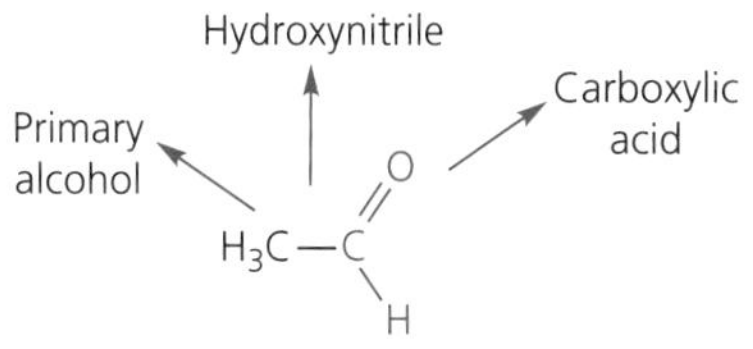

You should now see a possible two-stage synthetic route from your starting molecule to the target molecule. In this case, the route can go via the hydroxynitrile:

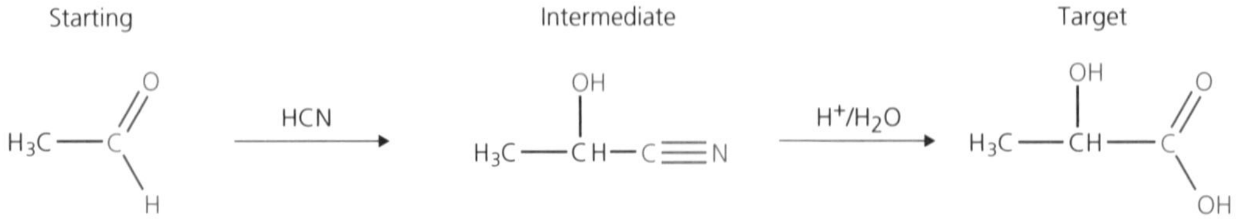

Chemists normally seek a synthetic route that has the least number of stages and which, therefore, produces a higher yield of the product. It is rare for any one reaction to be 100% efficient; normally the percentage yield is significantly below the theoretical yield.

## Now test yourself

TESTED ☐

8 Each of the following conversions involves multistage synthesis.
   (a) propene → propanone
   (b) 3-chloropropan-1-ol → 3-hydoxypropene
   (c) phenylethanone → poly(phenylethene)
   For each conversion:
   • Explain how it could be achieved.
   • Write an equation and state the special conditions, if any, for each stage in the synthesis.

Answer on p. 224

## Exam practice

1 Propene is an important industrial chemical essential in the production of a wide range of polymers, plastics and fibres. By far the greatest use of propene is as the monomer for polymerisation to poly(propene).
   (a) (i) Draw the monomer propene. [1]
       (ii) Draw a section of poly(propene) to show *two* repeat units. [2]
   (b) There are difficulties caused by waste polymers such as poly(propene). Not only are they non-biodegradable but when burned they produce a wide range of toxic fumes such as acrolein, $CH_2=CHCHO$, which has a choking odour and is the major cause of death of those suffocated in house fires. Identify the *two* functional groups present in acrolein and describe how you could test to show the presence of each group. Describe what you would see with each test. [6]

2 Consider the reaction scheme shown in Figure 12.14.

$$CH_2CHCOOH \longrightarrow H_3C-\overset{\overset{\displaystyle OH}{|}}{CH}-COOH \xrightarrow{H^+/Cr_2O_7^{2-}} \text{Compound C}$$

Compound A        Compound B

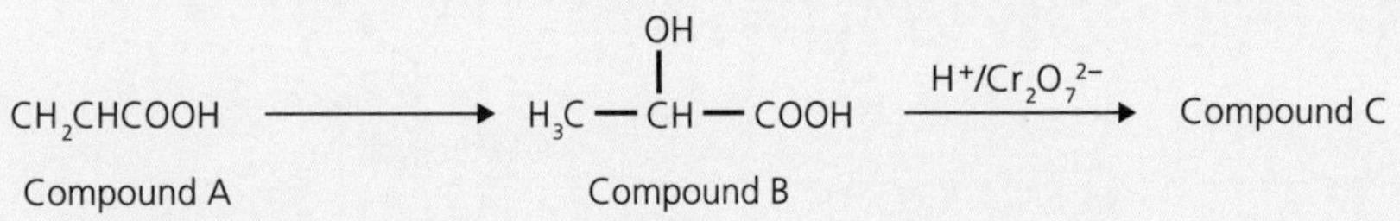

**Figure 12.14**

   (a) (i) Name compound A. [1]
       (ii) Write a balanced equation for the conversion of compound A into compound B. [1]
   (b) Compound B, lactic acid, is found in cheese and exists as one of two stereoisomers.
       (i) Draw the two stereoisomers of compound B. [2]
       (ii) Explain whether or not compound B, prepared by the reaction scheme, would contain both stereoisomers. [1]
   (c) (i) Draw the structure of compound C. [1]
       (ii) Compound C can be reduced to propane-1,2-diol. Using [H] to represent the reducing agent, construct a balanced equation for this reduction. [3]

**3 (a)** Aspartame (Figure 12.15) is used as an artificial sweetener.

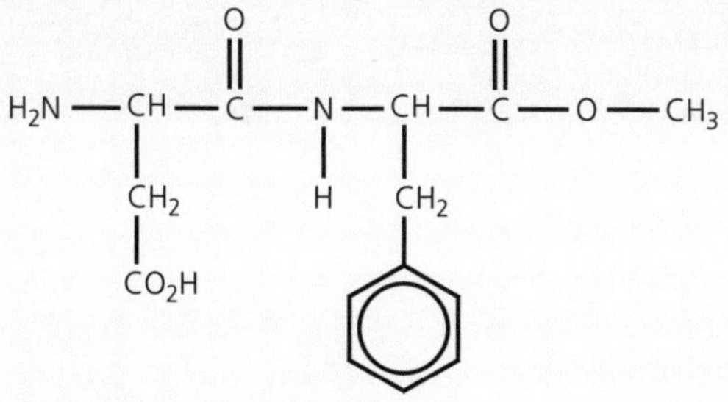

**Figure 12.15** **Aspartame**

(i) Aspartame contains five functional groups including the benzene ring. Name the other *four* functional groups. [4]

(ii) *Two* of the four functional groups can be hydrolysed. Circle these groups on the diagram above. [2]

(iii) Show the structures of the organic products formed by the acid hydrolysis of aspartame. [3]

**(b)** (i) Aspartame has two chiral carbon atoms. Identify each with an asterisk (*). [2]

(ii) Explain what is meant by the term *chiral* and deduce the number of possible stereoisomers. [2]

**(c)** Aspartame can be made from aspartic acid (Figure 12.16):

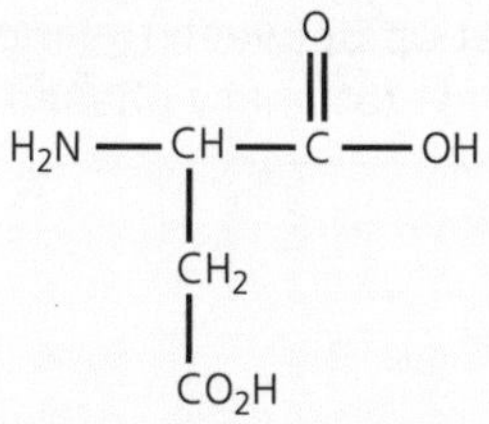

**Figure 12.16** **Aspartic acid**

Suggest the structure of a compound that could react with aspartic acid to make aspartame. [1]

## Answers and quick quiz 12 online

ONLINE

## Summary

You should now have an understanding of:

- amines
- amino acids, amides and chirality
- condensation polymers
- carbon–carbon bond formation
- organic synthesis

# 13 Analysis

## Chromatography

Chromatography is an analytical technique that involves the small-scale separation of components within a mixture. All types of chromatography contain a **stationary phase** and a **mobile phase**.

Different types of chromatography, for example thin-layer chromatography (TLC) and gas chromatography (EC), separate the components in a mixture by either **adsorption** or by **relative solubility (partition)**, TLC and EC are summarised in Table 13.1.

**Adsorption** If the stationary phase is a solid, separation depends on the adsorption of each component onto the surface of the stationary phase.

Separation by **relative solubility (partition)** is achieved when solutes are not equally soluble in the mobile and stationary phases. An equilibrium is set up between the mobile and stationary phases.

**Table 13.1**

| | TLC | GC |
|---|---|---|
| Stationary phase | The thin layer | The packing in the column |
| Mobile phase | The solvent | The gas |
| Separation by | Adsorption | Either adsorption or relative solubility* |
| Measurements | Qualitative | Qualitative and quantitative |
| Interpretation | Use $R_f$ values | Use retention times |
| *depends on whether or not the stationary phase in the column is a liquid or solid | | |

### Thin-layer chromatography (TLC)

REVISED

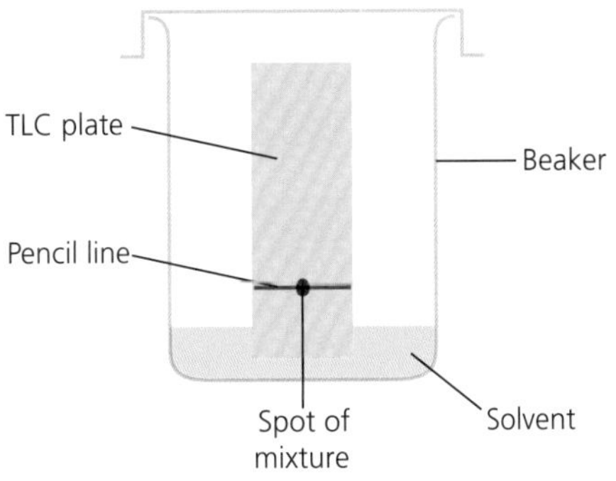


**Figure 13.1 Apparatus for thin-layer chromatography**

The components in a mixture can be identified by using **$R_f$ values**. $R_f$ stands for 'retardation factor' and is measured by using the equation:

The **$R_f$ value** is the distance moved by a component divided by the distance moved by the solvent (Figure 13.2).

$$R_f = \frac{\text{distance moved by spot/solute}}{\text{distance moved by solvent}}$$

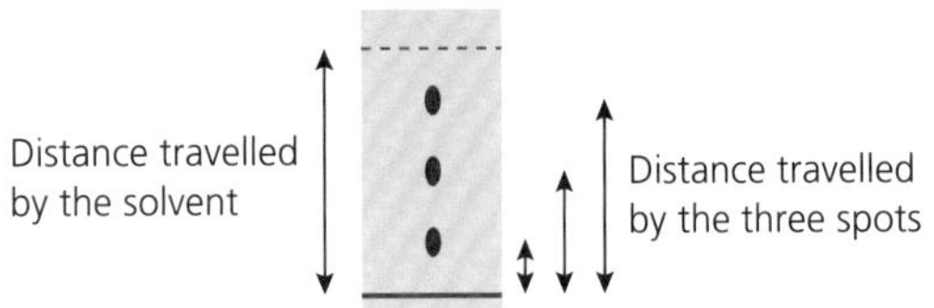


**Figure 13.2 Example of a TLC plate showing the distances moved by the solvent and components of a mixture**

# Gas chromatography (GC)

REVISED

The time between the injection of the sample and the emergence of a component from the column is called the **retention time**. Retention time depends on volatility of the solute and the relative solubility of the solutes in the mobile and stationary phases.

**Retention time** is the time taken from the injection of the sample for a component to leave the column.

The area underneath each peak gives an indication of the relative amounts of each component. The relative amounts of the components can be estimated by assuming that the peak is a triangle and by using the equation:

**area = base × ½ height**

If the peak is very narrow it is sufficient to estimate the amount by measuring the height of the peak.

Peak areas are now measured automatically and relative peak areas can be calculated.

The area under each peak is measured and can be expressed as either a percentage peak area or as a relative peak area. The calculations for the six peaks in the chromatogram in Figure 13.3 are shown in Table 13.2.

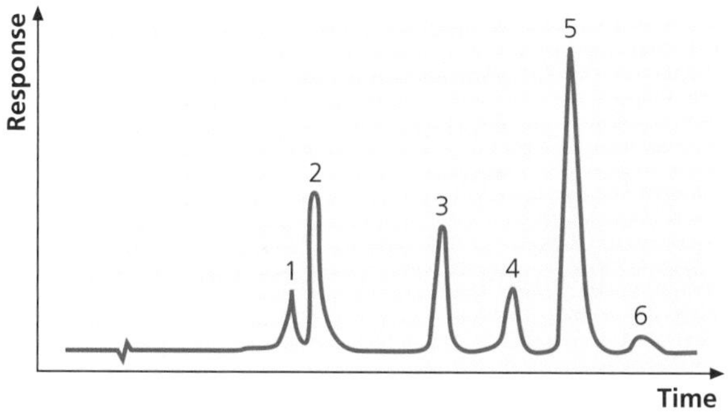


**Figure 13.3 Example of a gas chromatogram**

**Table 13.2**

| Peak | Area of peak | % area of peak | Relative peak areas |
|---|---|---|---|
| 1 | 2200 | 7.36 | 2.13 |
| 2 | 6500 | 21.75 | 6.30 |
| 3 | 5140 | 17.20 | 4.98 |
| 4 | 2769 | 9.27 | 2.69 |
| 5 | 12240 | 40.96 | 11.87 |
| 6 | 1032 | 3.45 | 1.00 |
| Total area of all peaks | 29881 | | |

Analysis by chromatography has its limitations, in that similar compounds often have similar $R_f$ values or similar retention times. It is likely that in a mixture of gases such as methane, ethane, propane and butane some of the peaks would overlap. These limitations have been largely overcome by coupling GC with mass spectrometry.

# GC–MS

REVISED

The combination of gas chromatography and mass spectrometry provides a powerful analytical tool that is used widely in areas such as forensics, environmental analysis, airport security, food and drink analysis and in medical applications.

The components in a mixture are separated by gas chromatography and then each component is analysed separately by mass spectrometry. The component is vaporised and then ionised. The process of fragmentation was outlined in Module 4.

Even in simple molecules there are a large number of lines in the mass spectrum. The combination of the lines and their size is specific to the individual compound — the fragmentation peaks are said to be a **fingerprint** of the molecule. This fingerprint can be cross-matched against a computer database to identify the compound.

**Exam tip**

Remember that it is a positive gaseous ion that is detected in a mass spectrometer. If, for example, you are asked to identify the ion responsible for the peak at $m/z$ = 15, the answer is $CH_3^+(g)$, *not* $CH_3^+$ or $CH_3(g)$ or $CH_3$.

## Tests for organic functional groups

REVISED

Functional groups can be identified by simple qualitative tests. These 'wet tests' are summarised in Table 13.3.

**Table 13.3 Tests for organic functional groups**

| Test | Observation | Conclusions |
| --- | --- | --- |
| pH of solution (add litmus) | Red | Carboxylic acid or phenol |
| $Br_2$ | Decolorises and/or white ppt | Alkene, phenol or phenylamine |
| Na | Gas ($H_2$) given off, bubbles, fizzes | Carboxylic acid or phenol or alcohol |
| $Na_2CO_3$ | Gas ($CO_2$) given off, bubbles, fizzes | Carboxylic acid |
| $AgNO_3$(aq)/ethanol in water bath at about 60 °C | White ppt<br>Cream ppt<br>Yellow ppt | Chloroalkane<br>Bromoalkane<br>Iodoalkane |
| 2,4DNPH | Orange ppt | Aldehyde or ketone |
| Tollens reagent $Ag^+(NH_3)_2$ | Silver mirror | Aldehyde |
| Heat with $H^+/Cr_2O_7^{2-}$ | Orange to green | Primary alcohol, secondary alcohol or aldehyde |
| Water | White fumes of HCl | Acid chloride |
| Warm with NaOH | Smell of $NH_3$ gas (which turns litmus blue) | Amide |
| There is no simple test for an ester. Esters are detected by first eliminating all other functional groups. Smell is not accepted as a chemical test. | | |

# Spectroscopy

## NMR spectroscopy

REVISED

NMR spectroscopy involves the interaction of nuclei with radio waves, which are at the low-energy end of the electromagnetic spectrum.

If the nucleus of an atom contains an odd number of protons and/or neutrons, the nucleus has a net nuclear spin that can be detected by using radio frequency — for example, $^{1}H$ and $^{13}C$ can both be detected.

The nucleus behaves like a tiny bar magnet and as it spins it generates a magnetic moment. Adjacent nuclei also have magnetic moments. Therefore, each nucleus is affected by neighbouring nuclei. The frequency at which each nucleus absorbs radio waves depends on its environment.

If the nucleus of an atom contains an even number of protons and an even number of neutrons the nucleus does *not* have a net nuclear spin and *cannot* be detected by using radio frequency — for example, $^{12}C$ and $^{16}O$ cannot be detected.

$^{1}H$ and $^{13}C$ both absorb energy in the radio-wave part of the spectrum. However, the frequency of the radio waves absorbed depends on the surrounding atoms, i.e. the exact frequency absorbed depends on the chemical environment. This variation in the frequency absorbed is the key to the determination of structure. It is known as the chemical shift, $\delta$. All absorptions are measured relative to TMS, tetramethylsilane, $(CH_3)_4Si$. The chemical shift, $\delta$, of TMS is set at zero.

TMS is used as a standard because:
- it is chemically inert and does not react with the sample
- it is volatile and easy to remove at the end of the procedure
- it absorbs at a higher frequency than other organic compounds

Therefore, its mass spectrum does not overlap with that of the sample.

**Exam tip**

You do not have to learn the chemical shift values of any of these peaks. All relevant absorptions for $^1$H-NMR and $^{13}$C-NMR are listed in the *Data Booklet*, which you will be given in the examination. However, it is essential that you are able to recognise different chemical environments.

## Proton ($^1$H) NMR spectroscopy

Ethanol, $C_2H_5OH$, contains six hydrogen atoms, but they are not all identical.
- The three hydrogens in the $CH_3$ group are all in the same environment and are labelled $H_a$.
- The two hydrogens in the middle $CH_2$ group (labelled $H_b$) are in the same environment and are labelled $H_b$.
- The hydrogen in the OH group is different from all of the rest and is labelled $H_c$(Figure 13.4).

So the six hydrogens in ethanol are in three different environments. Therefore, the $^1$H-NMR spectrum of ethanol contains three different peaks ($H_a$, $H_b$ and $H_c$) with different chemical shifts (Figure 13.5).

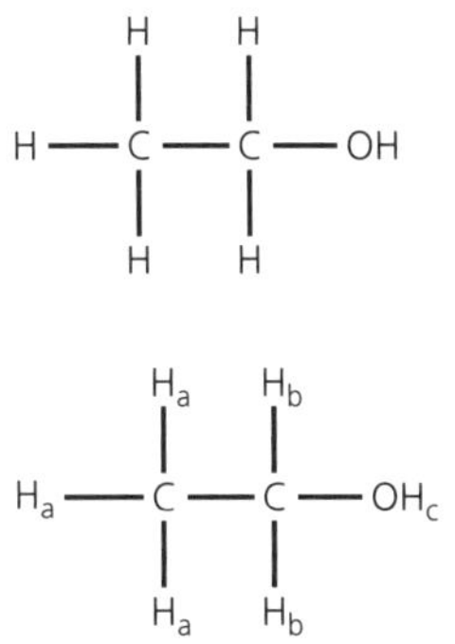

**Figure 13.4 Ethanol contains hydrogens in three different environments**

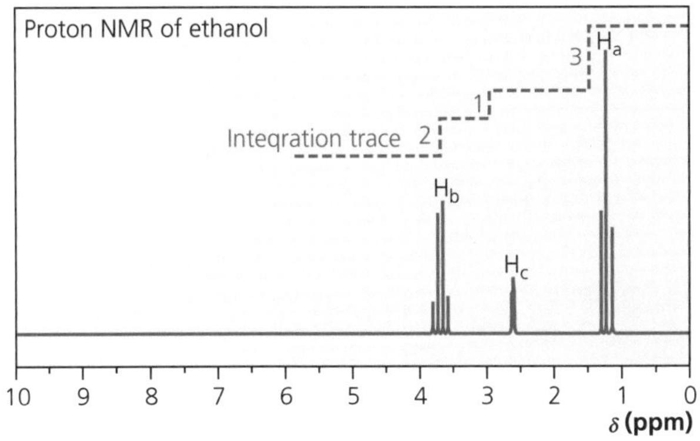


**Figure 13.5 $^1$H-NMR spectrum of ethanol**

The three peaks are of different sizes and may be split. The relative size of each peak reflects the number of hydrogens in each environment:
- $H_a$ — there are three hydrogens in this environment.
- $H_b$ — there are two hydrogens in this environment.
- $H_c$ — there is one hydrogen in this environment.

It follows that the relative intensity of the peaks $H_a$, $H_b$ and $H_c$ is 3:2:1.

The hydrogens attached to one carbon atom influence the hydrogens on adjacent carbon atoms. This is called the **spin–spin splitting pattern**. The easiest way to predict the splitting pattern is to count the number of hydrogens on the adjacent carbon atoms and then use the **'*n* + 1'** rule, where *n* is the number of hydrogens on the adjacent carbon atoms.

In the NMR spectrum of ethanol, each of the peaks will be split differently:

- $H_a$ is next to two hydrogens in $CH_2$ and hence the peak is split into (2 + 1) — a **triplet**.
- $H_b$ is next to three hydrogens in $CH_3$ and hence the peak is split into (3 + 1) — a **quartet**.
- $H_c$ is not attached to a carbon atom and hence does not undergo spin–spin coupling. It is, therefore, a **singlet**.

We would, therefore, expect the high-resolution NMR spectrum of ethanol to have three peaks of relative intensity 3:2:1, split into a triplet, a quartet and a singlet, respectively.

The exact position (the chemical shift) of each peak can be obtained from the *Data Sheet*, which will be supplied in any examination.

In the $^1$H-NMR spectrum of ethanol, the $-CH_3$ ($H_a$) has a chemical shift between 0.7 ppm and 1.6 ppm, the $-CH_2-$ ($H_b$) has a chemical shift between 2.0 ppm and 4.3 ppm and the $-OH$ ($H_c$) has a chemical shift between 1.0 ppm and 5.5 ppm (Figure 13.5).

## Use of $D_2O$

The O–**H** and the N–**H** peaks have chemical shifts that differ between compounds and sometimes lie outside the range 0.5–12.0 ppm. Therefore, they are difficult to assign. When alcohols, carboxylic acids or amines are dissolved in water there is a rapid exchange between the protons in the functional groups (**labile protons**) and the protons in the water. For example:

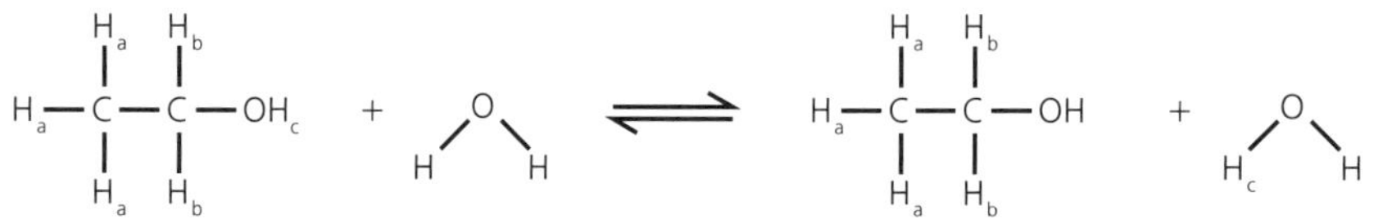

If water is replaced by deuterated water, $^2H_2O$, the peak at $H_c$ disappears. The $H_c$ proton is replaced by deuterium, $^2H$, which does not absorb in this region of the spectrum.

Deuterated water, $^2H_2O$ can be written as $D_2O$. Ethanol dissolved in deuterated water can be represented as:

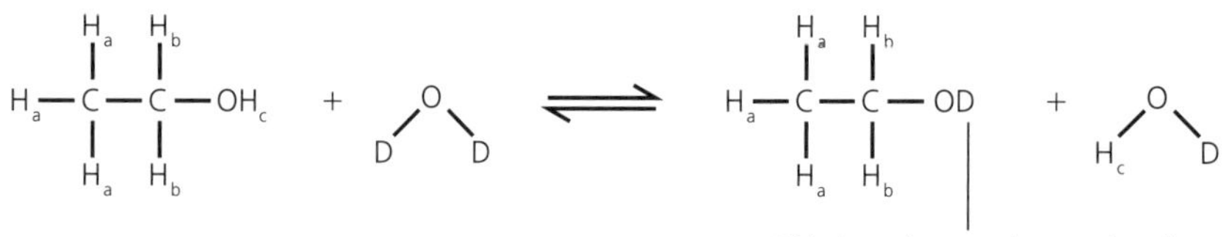

This is no longer detected and
the peak for Hc disappears


The use of $^2H_2O$ to identify labile protons is a valuable technique in proton ($^1$H) NMR.

When samples are prepared for NMR it may be necessary to dissolve them in a suitable solvent. Solvents containing protons are unsuitable because the protons would be detected and interfere with the spectrum. This is overcome by using a deuterated solvent, such as $CDCl_3$.

## Now test yourself

TESTED

1 (a) Identify the number of different hydrogen environments in each of the following:

(i)

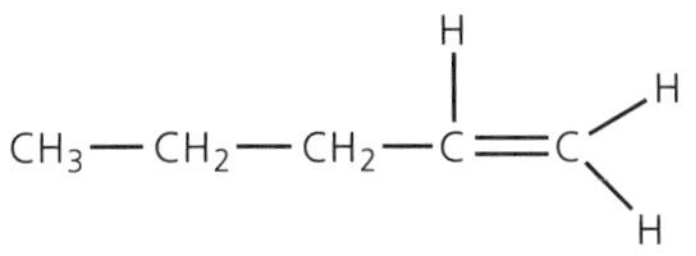

(ii)

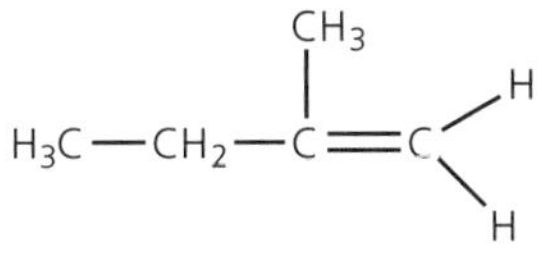

(iii)

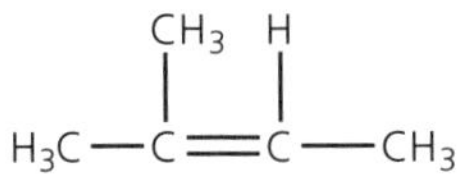

(iv)

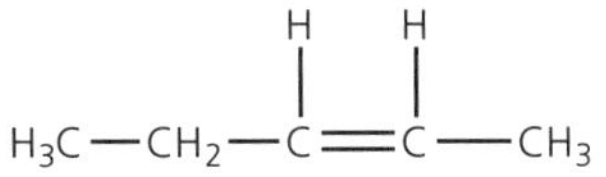

(b) State the splitting of the peaks in (a)(iii) above.

(c) Identify the number of different hydrogen environments in each of the following:

(i)

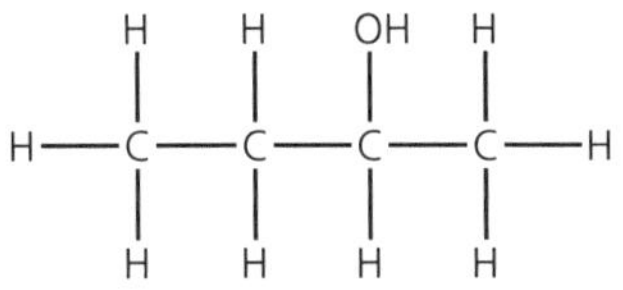

(ii)

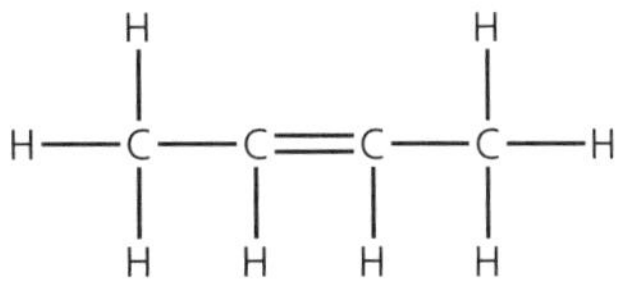

(iii)

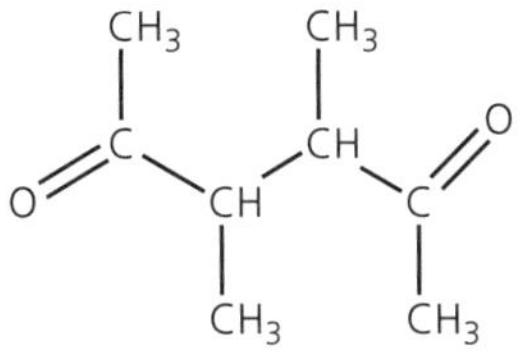

(iv)

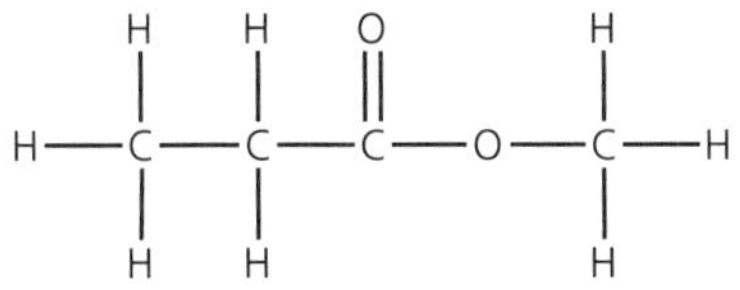

(v)

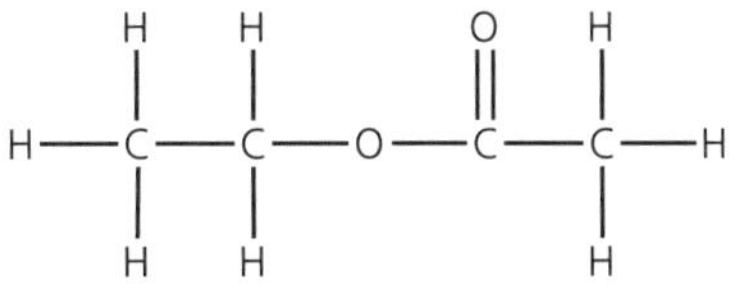

(vi)

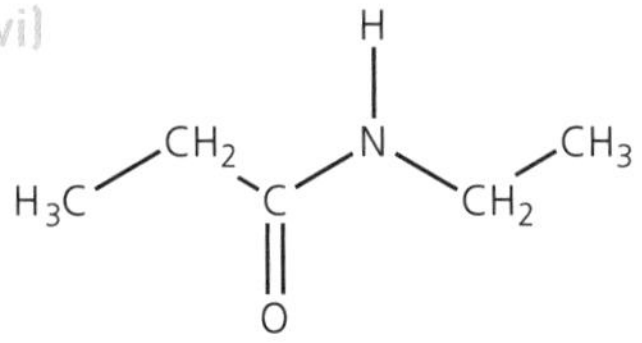

(d) State the splitting of the peaks in (c)(iv) above.

2 In the $^1H$ NMR of each of the following:

(i)

(i)

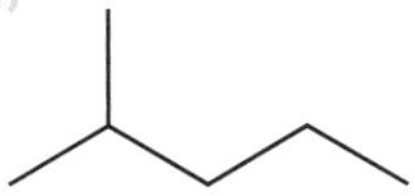

(iii)

(iv)

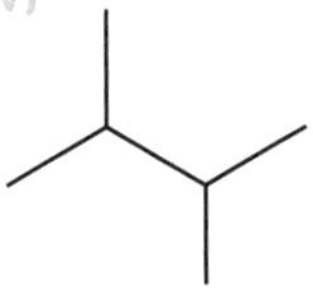

(v)

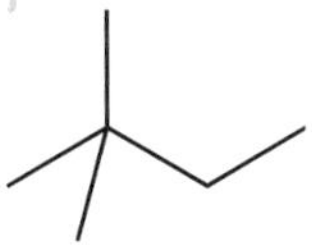

(a) State the number of peaks.

(b) Use the *Data Sheet* to identify the chemical shift range of each peak.

(c) State the number of peaks if $D_2O$ is added prior to running the NMR.

Answers on pp. 224–225

## $^{13}$C-NMR spectroscopy

Carbon-12, $^{12}C$, is the most abundant isotope of carbon. It does not have spin because it has an even number of protons and an even number of neutrons. The second isotope of carbon, carbon-13, $^{13}C$, can be detected using low-energy radio waves and it is possible to generate carbon-13

NMR spectra. The $^{13}C$ atom is about 6000 times more difficult to detect than $^{1}H$ atoms because of its low abundance (only about 1.1% of naturally occurring carbon is $^{13}C$) and its low magnetic moment. Interaction between adjacent $^{13}C$ atoms is unlikely because of their low abundance. $^{13}C$ atoms do interact with adjacent protons but these interactions are removed by decoupling and all absorptions appear as singlets. Each peak represents a different carbon environment.

Ethanol has two carbons atoms, $C_1$ and $C_2$:

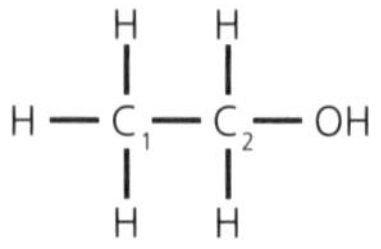

Therefore, there are two separate peaks, one for each carbon environment (Figure 13.6).

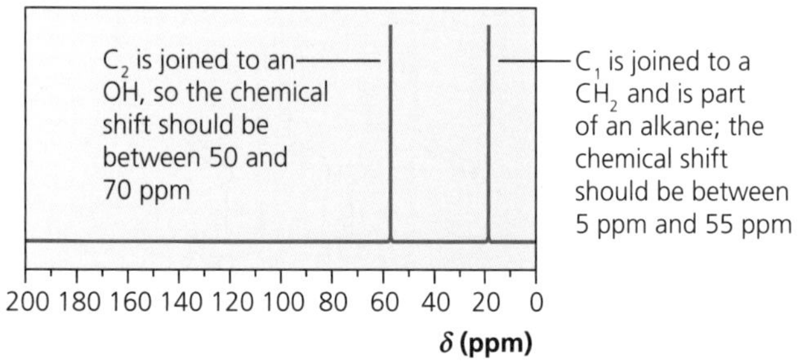

C2 is joined to an OH, so the chemical shift should be between 50 and 70 ppm
C1 is joined to a CH2 and is part of an alkane; the chemical shift should be between 5 ppm and 55 ppm
200 180 160 140 120 100 80 60 40 20 0
δ (ppm)

**Figure 13.6** $^{13}$**C-NMR spectrum of ethanol**

The key to interpreting carbon-13 NMR spectra is to identify the number of different carbon environments and then to match them with the groups in the *Data Sheet*.

**Example**

Determine the number of carbon environments in propan-2-ol. For each environment predict the chemical shift, $\delta$.

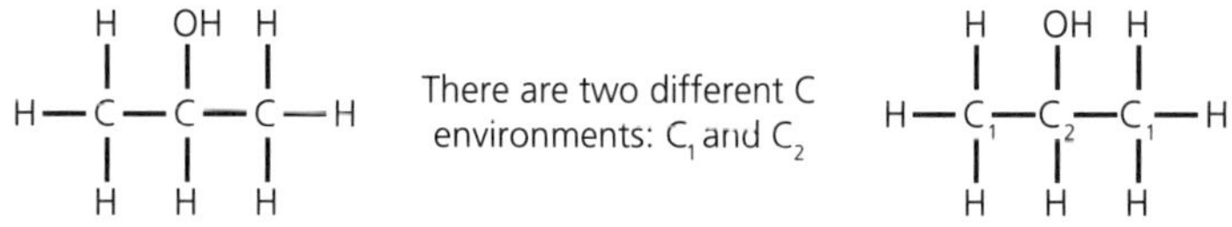

There are two different C environments: C1 and C2

**Answer**

The $^{13}C$-NMR spectrum should therefore contain two peaks:

- $C_2$ is next to an OH group and should therefore have a $\delta$ value between 50 ppm and 90 ppm.
- $C_1$ is part of an alkyl group and should therefore have a $\delta$ value between 10 ppm and 50 ppm. However, because the adjacent carbon is bonded to an OH, it will be towards the high end of the range.

The $^{13}C$ spectrum of propan-2-ol is shown in Figure 13.7.

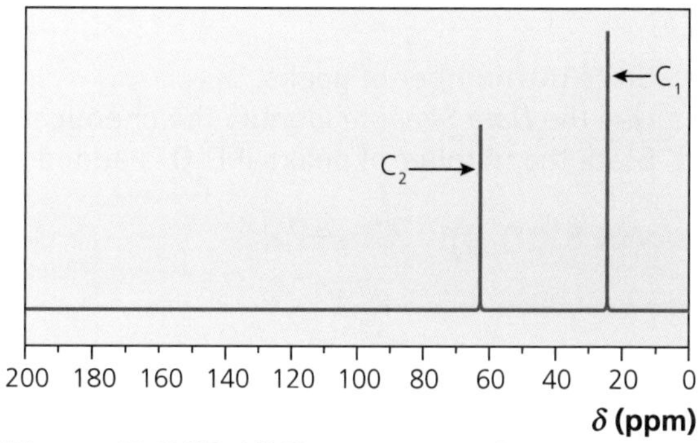

C1
C2
200 180 160 140 120 100 80 60 40 20 0
δ (ppm)

**Figure 13.7** $^{13}$**C-NMR spectrum of propan-2-ol**

## Now test yourself

TESTED

3 Identify the number of different carbon environments in each of the following.

(a)

(i)

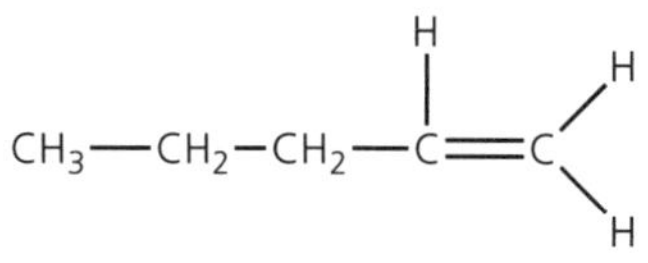

(ii)

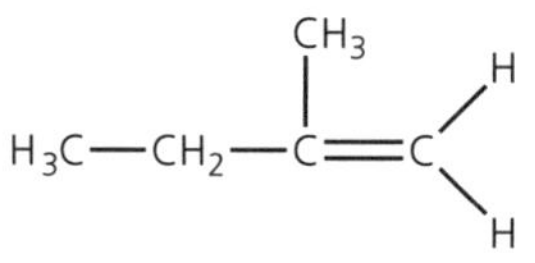

(iii)

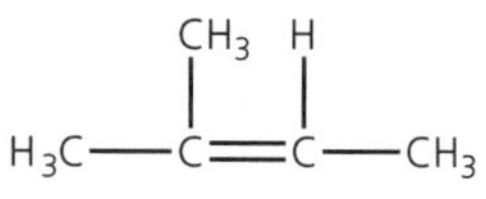

(iv)

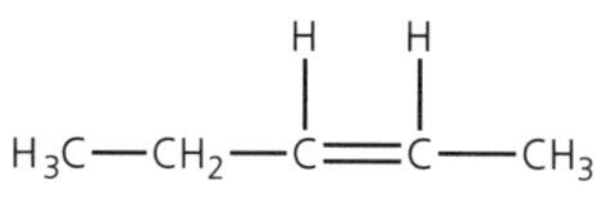

(b)

(i)

(ii)

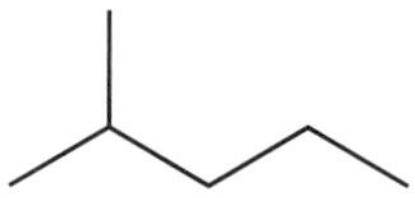

(iii)

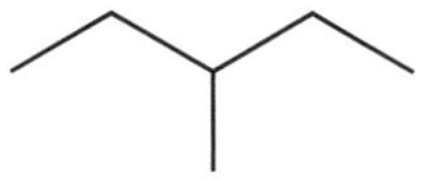

(iv)

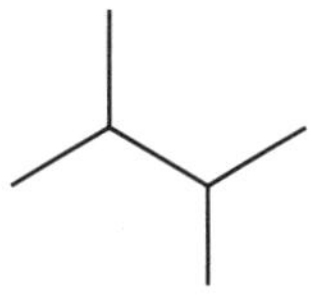

(v)

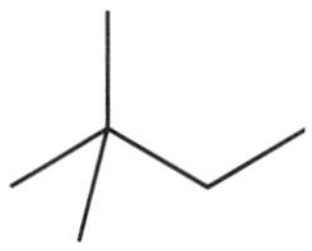

4 In the $^{13}$C-NMR spectrum for each of the following state the number of peaks and use the *Data Sheet* to identify the chemical shift range of each peak.

(i)

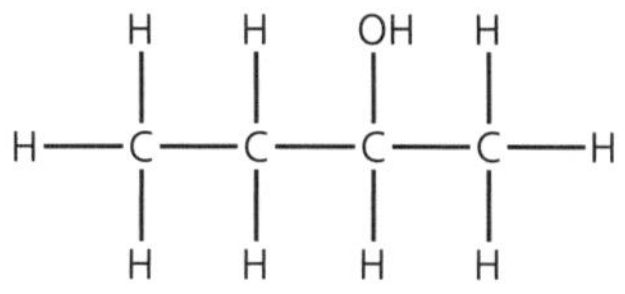

(ii)

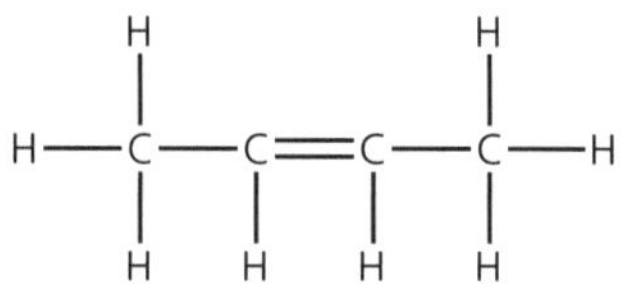

(iii)

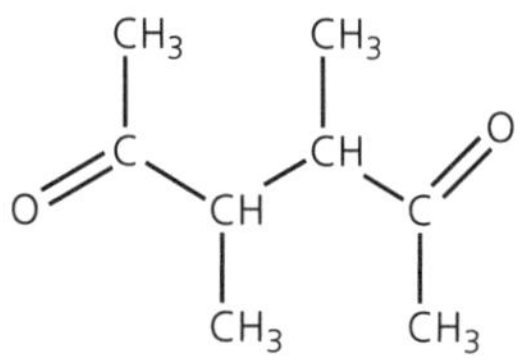

(iv)

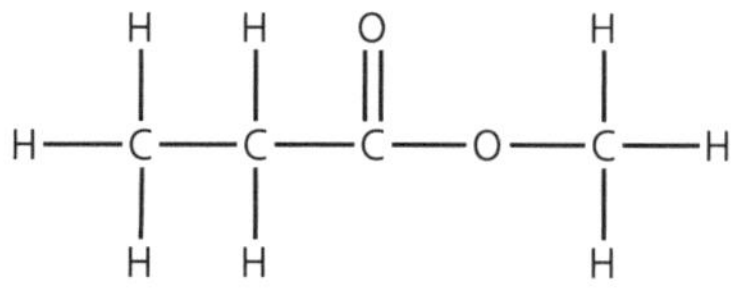

(v)

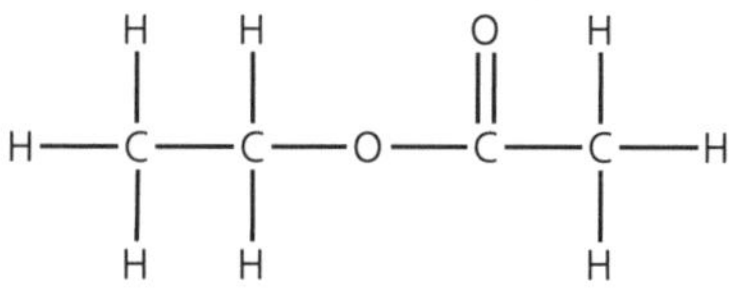

(vi)

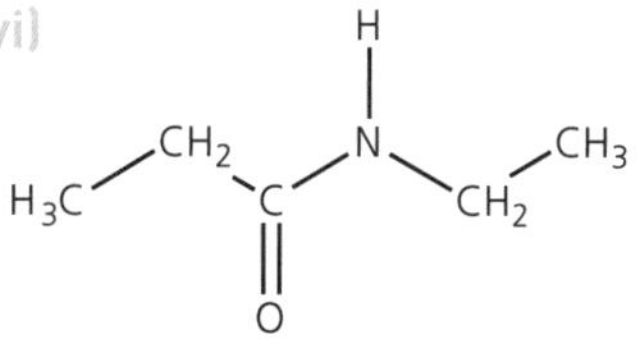

Answers on p. 226

## Combined techniques

REVISED

Analytical chemistry is rather like detective work — pieces of evidence are gathered from different places. Usually no single piece of evidence is conclusive but when the pieces of evidence are slotted together, the combination is definitive. Gathering together the evidence is a bit like doing a jigsaw.

**Exam tip**

You may be faced with three or four different spectra that you have to use to identify a molecule. A good simple approach is as follows:

1. Use the mass spectrum to identify the molecular ion and hence the molar mass.
2. Start with the infrared spectrum and check for absorptions due to C=O and/or O–H.
3. If you know the molar mass and the functional group it should be possible to deduce the molecular formula.
4. The number of peaks in the $^{13}$C-NMR spectrum indicates the number of different carbon environments.
5. The number of peaks in the $^{1}$H-NMR spectrum indicates the number of different hydrogen environments.
6. Use the splitting patterns in the $^{1}$H-NMR spectrum to determine the adjacent hydrogen environments.
7. Match the chemical shifts with each peak.

## Now test yourself

TESTED

5 Cyclopentanone, $C_5H_8O$, is shown in Figure 13.8.

Figure 13.8 **Cyclopentanone**

(a) Explain why the $^{1}$H-NMR spectrum of cyclopentanone has two peaks and the $^{13}$C-NMR spectrum has three peaks.
(b) Using the *Data Sheet*, predict the value of the chemical shift, $\delta$, for each peak in the $^{13}$C-NMR spectrum.
(c) Using the *Data Sheet*, suggest the chemical shift value, $\delta$, the splitting pattern and the relative peak areas for each peak in the $^{1}$H-NMR spectrum.

6 Identify compound X from the spectra in Figure 13.9.

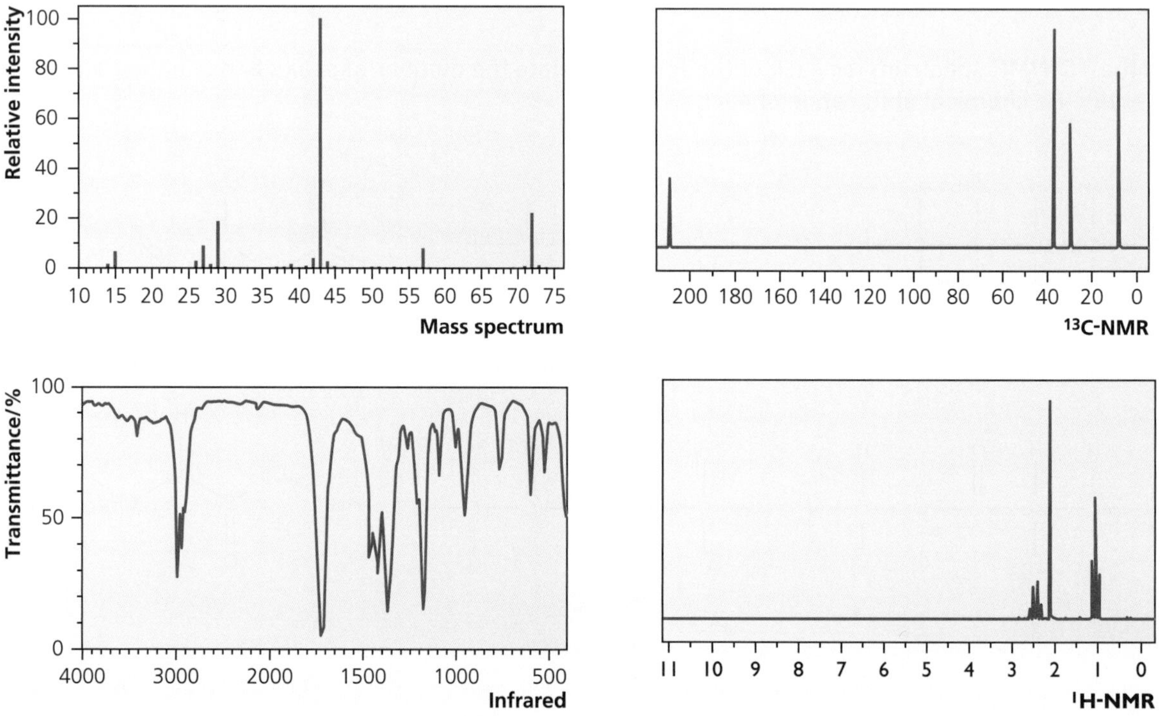


Figure 13.9 **Spectra for unknown compound**

7 Predict the number of peaks in the $^{13}$C-NMR spectrum of each of the following compounds, A–F:

A
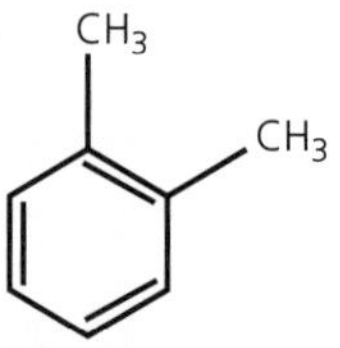


B
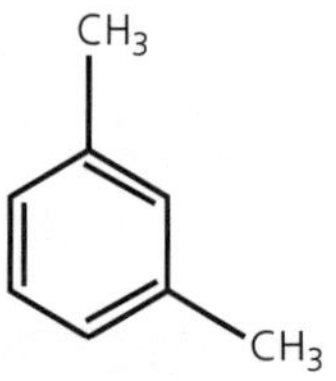


C

D
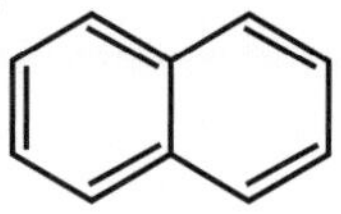

E
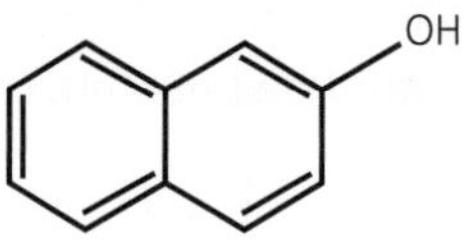


F
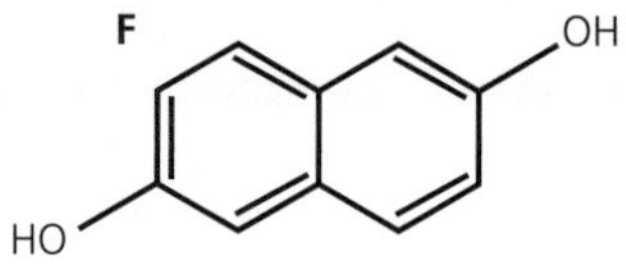


Answers on p. 226

# Exam practice

1 Compounds A and B are structural isomers.

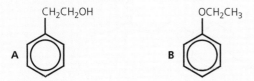

**(a)** The mass spectrum of one of the compounds is shown in Figure 13.10. Explain how the fragmentation pattern allows you to deduce that it is *not* compound B. [2]

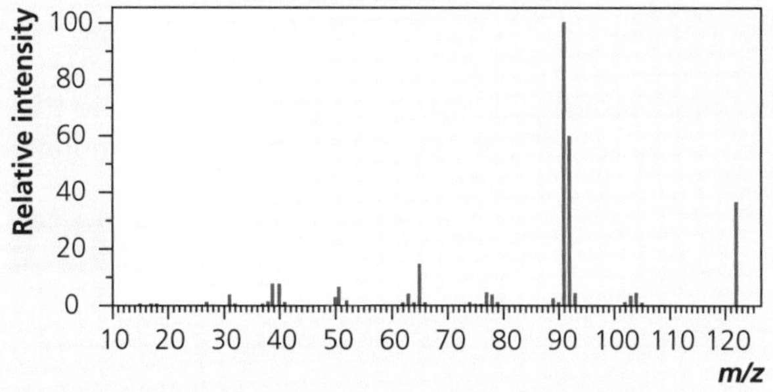


**Figure 13.10** **Mass spectrum of compound A**

**(b)** One of the compounds A or B gives the infrared spectrum shown in Figure 13.11.

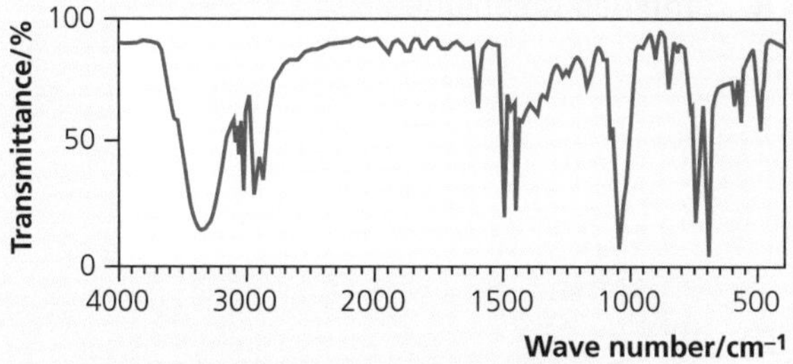


**Figure 13.11** **IR spectrum of compound A or B**

Using the *Data Sheet*, identify which of the two compounds A or B has this spectrum. Explain your reasoning carefully. [2]

**(c)** One of the compounds A and B gives the $^1$H-NMR spectrum in Figure 13.12.

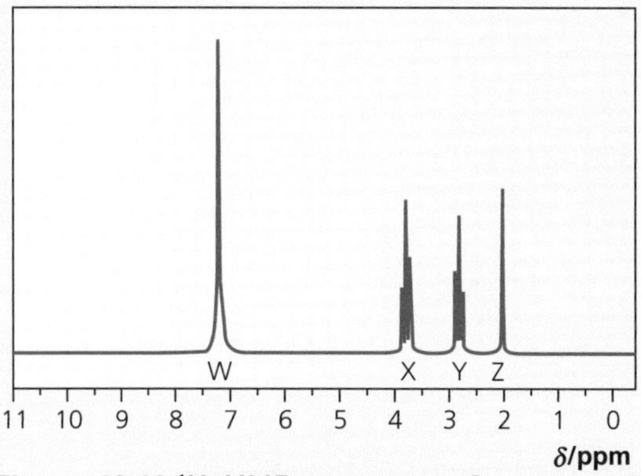


**Figure 13.12** **$^1$H-NMR spectrum of compound A or B**

$D_2O$ was added and a second spectrum was run. The peak Z at $\delta$ 2.0 disappeared. Using the *Data Sheet*, suggest the identity of the protons responsible for the groups of peaks W, X, Y and Z. For each group of peaks, explain your reasoning carefully. Use *all* of the information given. [8]

2 (a) A sample of torn clothing was found at the scene of a crime. The clothing had a yellow stain, which was thought to be either compound A or compound B (Figure 13.13)

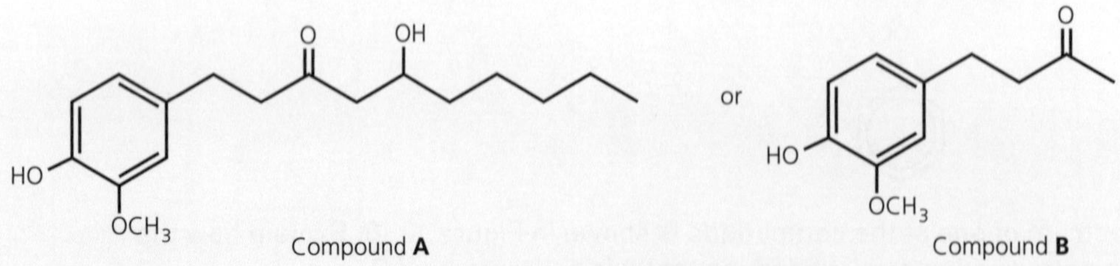


**Figure 13.13**

Explain how a forensic scientist could determine which, if either, of compound A or compound B was responsible for the yellow stain. [5]

(b) Suggest a chemical test that could be used to distinguish between compounds A and B. State the reagent(s) and conditions and explain what you would expect to see. Identify the organic product. [3]

## Answers and quick quiz 13 online

ONLINE

## Summary

You should now have an understanding of:

- chromatography
- tests for functional groups
- NMR spectroscopy
- $^{13}$C-NMR spectroscopy
- $^{1}$H-NMR spectroscopy
- combined techniques

# Synoptic assessment

## Synoptic assessment

Synoptic assessment tests the ability to link together different areas of chemistry. Students will be expected to draw together knowledge, understanding and skills from different aspects of the subject.

It is anticipated that all examinations/components will contain synoptic assessment.

In Modules 3, 4, 5 and 6 the subject content links strongly with the content met in Module 2 and includes:

- atoms, moles and equations
- acid and redox reactions
- bonding and structure

In the second year of the course Module 5 is strongly linked to Modules 2 and 3, whilst Module 6 follows on from Module 4.

The questions that follow indicate what synoptic questions may look like.

### Synoptic questions

TESTED

1 Rhubarb leaves contain poisonous ethanedioic acid, $(COOH)_2$. A dose of about 24 g of ethanedioic acid would probably be fatal if consumed by an adult. On heating, the ethanedioate ions react with potassium manganate(VII) solution and so this forms the basis for a titration. The ethanedioate ions are oxidised to carbon dioxide.
Four large rhubarb leaves are heated with water to extract the ethanedioic acid. The solution is filtered and the solution obtained is diluted to 250 $cm^3$ in a volumetric flask.
25.0 $cm^3$ samples of the solution are acidified with dilute sulfuric acid. 23.90 $cm^3$ of 0.0200 mol $dm^{-3}$ potassium manganate(VII) are required to reach the end point in a titration.
Calculate how many large rhubarb leaves would be needed to kill an adult.

2 A compound of formula $NaXO_3$ is produced from element X. An aqueous solution of $NaXO_3$ is made with a concentration of 0.0500 mol $dm^{-3}$. When excess potassium iodide solution is added to 25.0 $cm^3$ of this solution, iodine is produced. When this is titrated against a solution of sodium thiosulfate containing 13.63 g $dm^{-3}$, 29.00 $cm^3$ of the solution is required to react completely with the iodine.
Deduce the change in oxidation state of element X in the reaction.

3 Benzene reacts with alkenes in the presence of an acid catalyst in the following way:

$$C_6H_6 + C_nH_{2n} \xrightarrow{H^+ \text{ catalyst}} C_6H_5C_nH_{2n+1}$$

The initial step in the reaction is the $H^+$ catalyst reacting with the alkene to form a carbocation, $C_nH_{2n+1}^{\ +}$.
In the presence of an acid catalyst, benzene reacts with propene to form an aromatic hydrocarbon with molecular formula $C_9H_{12}$.

(a) Outline, with the aid of curly arrows, the reaction between benzene and propene in the presence of $H^+$.

(b) Explain why it is possible to form two isomers of $C_9H_{12}$.

(c) Alkyl groups such as $CH_3$ are electron releasing. They can push electrons along a σ-bond. This is called an inductive effect and can stabilise a carbonium ion. Use this and your understanding of the mechanism to explain why the major product of the reaction between benzene and propene is $C_6H_5CH(CH_3)_2$ and not $C_6H_5CH_2CH_2CH_3$.

4 A carbonyl compound that contains at least one hydrogen atom on the carbon atom adjacent to the carbonyl group (i.e. CHC=O) can, in the presence of a base such as NaOH, undergo a condensation reaction. For example, propanone forms 4-hydroxy-4-methylpentan-2-one:

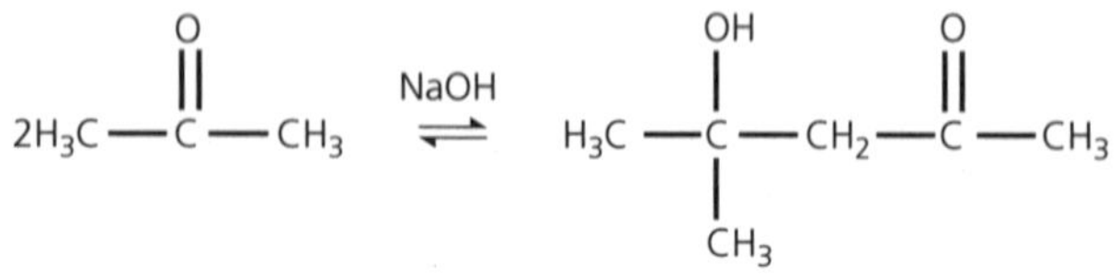

Use this information and your knowledge of the reactions in the specification to suggest how but-2-enal, $CH_3CHCHCHO$, could be made from ethanal.

5 Compound X, an ester, was prepared by reacting ethanol with compound Y, a carboxylic acid. The atom economy for the preparation of the ester (compound X) is 86.567%.
The $^{13}C$ NMR and the proton NMR of the carboxylic acid (compound Y) are shown below.
Identify compounds X and Y. Show all of your working.

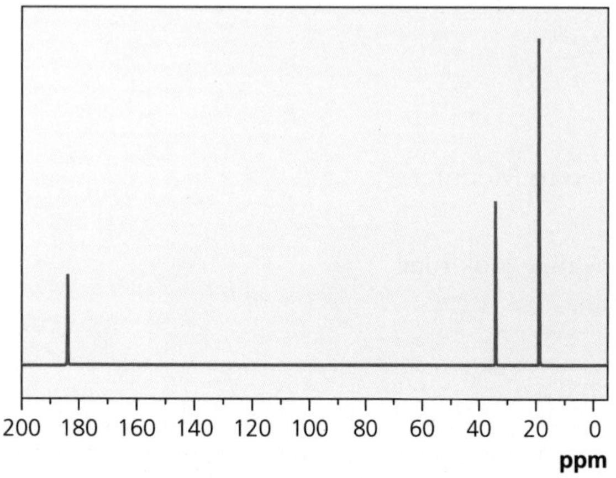


6 Devise a *three*-step conversion of propene into 2-methylpropanoic acid.
For each step write an equation, stating any essential conditions.
Assume the percentage yield for each stage is 40%. What volume of propene, at r.t.p., would you start with in order to produce 7.04 g 2-methylpropanoic acid?

## Answers on p. 227–229

ONLINE

# Now test yourself answers

## Chapter 1

1 (a) extremely flammable
(b) dangerous for the environment
(c) explosive
(d) corrosive
(e) toxic
(f) oxidising
(g) irritant
(h) radioactive

2 1 with F, 2 with H, 3 with D, 4 with A, 5 with C, 6 with I, 7 with B, 8 with E, 9 with G

3 (a) (i) 2%
(ii) 1%
(iii) 0.2%
(iv) 0.48%
(v) 0.1%
(b) (i) 16.7%
(ii) 3.3%
(To measure a temperature rise the initial and final temperatures have to be measured — so the error is doubled.)

4 (a) (i) 735
(ii) 698
(iii) 0.000346
(b) (i) $7.3 \times 10^2$
(ii) $7.0 \times 10^2$
(iii) $3.5 \times 10^{-4}$

5 The student should ignore the rough reading and the 24.50 $cm^3$. The average titre is (23.50 + 23.60)/2 = 23.55 $cm^3$, but this is usually quoted to 1 decimal place, so the average titre is 23.6 $cm^3$.

## Chapter 2

1 $^{16}O$ has 8p, 8n and 8e
$^{23}Na^+$ has 11p, 12n and 10e
$^{19}F^-$ has 9p, 10n, 10e

2 $\frac{(85 \times 72.2) + (87 \times 27.8)}{100} = \frac{6137 + 2418.6}{100} = \frac{8555.6}{100}$
= 85.556 = 85.6 (3 s.f.)

3 $\frac{10x + 11(100 - x)}{100} = 10.8$
Rearrange to find $x = 1100 - 1080 = 20$
Hence 20% $^{10}B$ and 80% $^{11}B$

4 (a) $Mg(OH)_2 = 24.3 + 16.0 + 16.0 + 1.0 + 1.0 = 58.3$
(b) $Na_2SO_4.10H_2O = 142.1 + 180.0 = 322.1$
($Na_2SO_4 = 23.0 + 23.0 + 32.1 + 64.0 = 142.1$ and $10H_2O = 10 \times 18.0 = 180.0$)

5 (a) Isotopes are atoms of the same element that have different numbers of neutrons.
(b) $^6Li$ has 3p, 3e and 3n; $^7Li$ also has 3p and 3e, but has 4n.
(c) $\frac{(12 \times 6) + (88 \times 7)}{100} = \frac{688}{100} = 6.88$

6 (a) $MgCl_2$
(b) $Al_2(SO_4)_3$

7 $Rb_2SO_4$

8 $MnBr_2$

9 (a) $ZnO(s) + 2HCl(aq) \rightarrow ZnCl_2(aq) + H_2O(l)$
(b) $CH_4(g) + 2O_2(g) \rightarrow CO_2(g) + 2H_2O(l)$

10 (a) $Ag_2SO_4$
(b) $Al(NO_3)_3$
(c) $Fe(NO_3)_3$

11 (a) $\frac{8.0}{32.1} = 0.25$
(b) $\frac{1.68}{56.1} = 0.0299$

12 (a) Use $m = n \times M$, molar mass of $AlCl_3$ = 133.5, $m = 0.04 \times 133.5 = 5.34$ g
(b) Use $m = n \times M$, molar mass of $Al(OH)_3$ = 78, $m = 0.45 \times 78 = 35.1$ g

13 $M = \frac{m}{n} = \frac{2.60}{0.05} = 52$; hence the element is Cr

14 $M = \frac{m}{n} = \frac{2.432}{0.02} = 121.6 = M(OH)_2$
$2 \times OH = 2 \times 17 = 34$; hence mass of X is $121.6 - 34 = 87.6$ = Sr

15 50 $cm^3$ nitrogen and 25 $cm^3$ oxygen

16 (a) 7.33 g
(b) 0.625 g

17 $PV = nRT$, $n = \frac{PV}{RT} = \frac{101 \times 0.610}{8.314 \times 310} = 0.0239$ mol
molar mass = $\frac{3.81}{0.0238}$ = 159.4 g $mol^{-1}$
Bromine, $Br_2$, has molar mass = $2 \times 79.9$ = 159.8 g $mol^{-1}$

18 (a) 0.1 mol
(b) $2.5 \times 10^{-3}$ or 0.0025 mol

19 moles of NaOH = 0.05; mass of NaOH = 2.0 g

20 (a) Diluted by factor of 10, hence concentration = 0.2 mol dm$^{-3}$

(b) Diluted by factor of 5, hence concentration = 0.4 mol dm$^{-3}$

21 (a) $K_2CO_3(s) + 2HCl(aq) \rightarrow 2KCl(aq) + CO_2(g) + H_2O(l)$

(b) $1.00 \times 10^{-3}$ mol

(c) $2.00 \times 10^{-3}$ mol

(d) 0.07 mol dm$^{-3}$

22 moles of ethanol = $\frac{4.60}{46.0} = 0.10$

moles of ethyl methanoate = $\frac{5.92}{74.0} = 0.08$

% yield = $\frac{0.08}{0.10} \times 100 = 80.0\%$

23 molar mass of desired product = 32.0 g mol$^{-1}$

molar mass of all products = 32.0 + 119 = 151 g mol$^{-1}$

atom economy = $\frac{32.0}{119} \times 100 = 21.2\%$

24 (a) $Ca(NO_3)_2$

(b) $Al_2(SO_4)_3$

(c) $(CH_3COO^-)_2Mg^{2+}$

25 (a) full equation $CH_3COOH(aq) + NaOH(aq) \rightarrow CH_3COO^-Na^+(aq) + H_2O(l)$

ionic equation $H^+(aq) + OH^-(aq) \rightarrow H_2O(l)$

(b) full equation $CaCO_3(s) + 2HNO_3(aq) \rightarrow Ca(NO_3)_2(aq) + H_2O(l) + CO_2(g)$

ionic equation $CO_3^{2-}(aq) + 2H^+(aq) \rightarrow H_2O(l) + CO_2(g)$

26 (a)

| $H_2O$ | $NaOH$ | $KNO_3$ | $NH_3$ | $N_2O$ |
|---|---|---|---|---|
| +1 −2 | +1 −2 +1 | +1 +5 −2 | −3 +1 | +1 −2 |

(b)

| $SO_4^{2-}$ | $CO_3^{2-}$ | $NH_4^+$ | $MnO_4^-$ | $Cr_2O_7^{2-}$ |
|---|---|---|---|---|
| +6 −2 | +4 −2 | −3 +1 | +7 −2 | +6 −2 |

27

| Zn + | $CuSO_4 \rightarrow$ | Cu + | $ZnSO_4$ |
|---|---|---|---|
| 0 | +2 +6 −2 | 0 | +2 +6 −2 |

Zn has been oxidised as its oxidation number changes from 0 to +2.

## Chapter 3

1 (a) Element X is in group 15 as there is a large increase in ionisation energy between the fifth and sixth ionisations. Element X is in group 15 and in the third period so it must be phosphorus.

(b) The third ionisation energy is represented by $X^{2+}(g) \rightarrow X^{3+}(g) + e^-$

2 Factor 1 atomic radius — K is bigger than Na

Factor 2 shielding — K has more electrons than Na

Factor 3 nuclear charge — K has a greater nuclear charge than Na

Factors 1 and 2 outweigh factor 3.

3 N $1s^22s^22p^3$

$Al^{3+}$ $1s^22s^22p^6$

$P^{3-}$ $1s^22s^22p^63s^23p^6$

$Fe^{3+}$ $1s^22s^22p^63s^23p^63d^5$

4 (a) angular

(b) pyramidal

(c) angular

(d) tetrahedral

(e) trigonal planar

(f) trigonal planar

## Chapter 4

1 (a) Magnesium: atomic radius decreases across a period, shielding is the same and magnesium has the greater nuclear charge.

(b) Magnesium: atomic radius increases down a group and magnesium has less shielding. These two factors outweigh the greater nuclear charge of calcium.

(c) Neon: sodium has the larger radius and has more shielding, which outweigh the increased nuclear charge of sodium. However, neon has a full outer shell, which is extremely stable.

2 Group 4, as there is a large jump in ionisation energy between the fourth and fifth ionisations.

3 $Ca(s) + \frac{1}{2}O_2(g) \rightarrow CaO(s)$

Ca has been oxidised. Its oxidation number changes from 0 to +2.

$Ca(s) + 2H_2O(l) \rightarrow Ca(OH)_2(aq) + H_2(g)$

Ca has been oxidised. Its oxidation number changes from 0 to +2.

4 (a) $Ba(NO_3)_2$

(b) $(CH_3COO^-)_2Sr^{2+}$

(c) $Ca_3(PO_4)_2$

5 $SrCO_3(s) + 2HNO_3(aq) \rightarrow Sr(NO_3)_2(aq) + H_2O(l) + CO_2(g)$

6 $2Cl_2 + 4NaOH \rightarrow 3NaCl + NaClO_2 + 2H_2O$

7 (a) $Cl_2(g) + C_2H_2(g) \rightarrow 2C(s) + 2HCl(g)$

(b) The oxidation number of Cl in $Cl_2$ is 0; in HCl it is −1. This shows that the Cl has been reduced, which means that $Cl_2$ is the oxidising agent.

(c) The reaction should be more explosive as fluorine is a better oxidising agent than chlorine. This is because fluorine gains electrons more easily as it is smaller and there is less shielding.

8 Add each solid separately to a beaker containing HCl(aq) — the one that fizzes is $BaCO_3$.

Add the other two solids to a beaker of water — the one that is insoluble is $BaSO_4$.

Add $AgNO_3(aq)$ to the dissolved $BaCl_2(aq)$ and a white precipitate will be formed.

# Chapter 5

1 Standard enthalpy change of formation, $\Delta_f H^\ominus$, is the enthalpy change when 1 mol of a substance is formed from its elements, in their natural state, under standard conditions of 298 K and 101 kPa.

$3C(s) + 3H_2(g) + \frac{1}{2}O_2(g) \rightarrow CH_3CH_2CHO(l)$

2 Standard enthalpy change of combustion, $\Delta_c H^\ominus$, is the enthalpy change when 1 mol of a substance is burnt completely, in an excess of oxygen, under standard conditions of 298 K and 101 kPa.

$CH_3COCH_3(l) + 4O_2(g) \rightarrow 3CO_2(g) + 3H_2O(l)$

3 $\Delta H = \frac{q}{n} = \frac{mc\Delta t}{n}$

$q = 75.0 \times 4.20 \times 4.6 = 1449\ J = 1.449\ kJ$

Using $n = cV$, moles of $HNO_3 = \frac{1.00 \times 25.0}{1000} = 0.0250$

$\Delta H = \frac{q}{n} = \frac{1.449}{0.025} = 57.96 = 58\ kJ\ mol^{-1}$

4 **Step 1** Write an equation for $\Delta_f H$ of propane:
$3C(s) + 4H_2(g) \rightarrow C_3H_8(g)$

**Step 2** Construct the enthalpy triangle by writing the combustion products at the bottom:

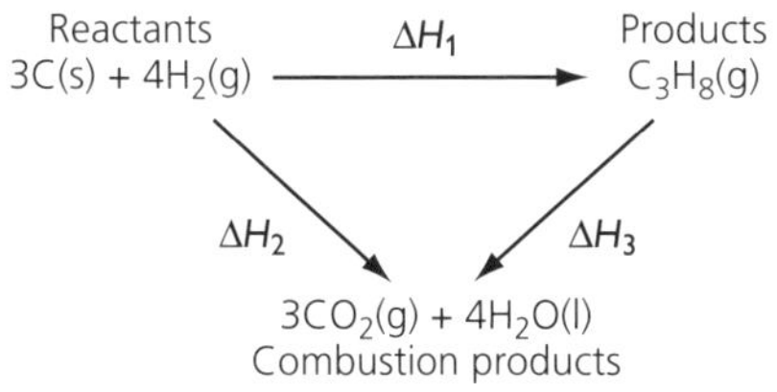


**Step 3** Apply Hess's law using the clockwise = anticlockwise rule

$\Delta H_1 + \Delta H_3 = \Delta H_2$, hence $\Delta H_1 = \Delta H_2 - \Delta H_3$

$\Delta H_2 = 3 \times (\Delta_c H(C(s)) + 4 \times (\Delta_c H(H_2(g))$

$= (3 \times -394) + (4 \times -286) = -2326\ kJ\ mol^{-1}$

$\Delta H_3 = -2219\ kJ\ mol^{-1}$

$\Delta H_1 = \Delta H_2 - \Delta H_3 = (-2326) - (-2219) = -107\ kJ\ mol^{-1}$

5 Activation energy is the minimum energy needed for colliding particles to react.

6 Increasing the pressure on a gaseous reaction has the same effect as increasing the concentration of the reactants because it results in a decrease in volume, so the concentration increases. Increased concentration results in an increased likelihood of a collision, so the rate of reaction increases.

7 Enthalpy profile diagram:

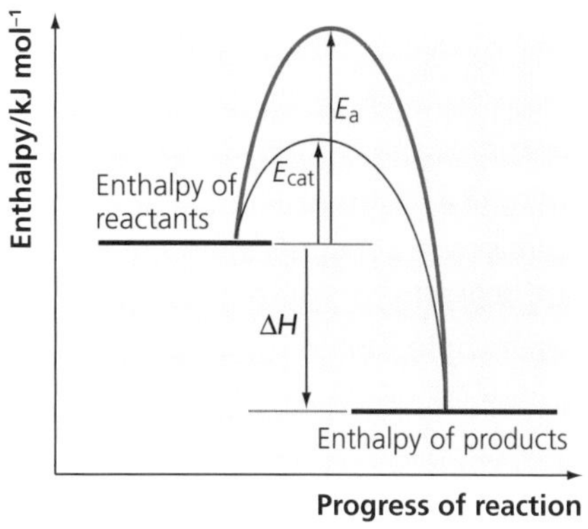


Boltzmann distribution:

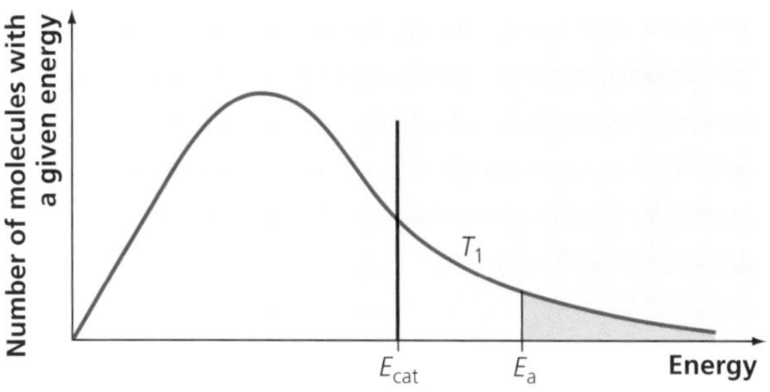


$E_a$ is the activation energy of the uncatalysed reaction and $E_{cat}$ is the activation energy of the catalysed reaction. A catalyst lowers the activation energy, but does not alter the $\Delta H$ value for the reaction and does not change the Boltzmann distribution. It changes the number of particles with energy greater than or equal to the new activation energy, $E_{cat}$. This is illustrated in the Boltzmann distribution where the areas under the curve indicate the proportion of particles with energy greater than the activation energies.

8 A heterogeneous catalyst is one that is in a different phase from the reactants.

Example: $N_2(g) + 3H_2(g) \rightleftharpoons 2NH_3(g)$ with Fe(s) as the catalyst

A homogeneous catalyst is one that is in the same phase as the reactants.

Example: esterification of ethanol and ethanoic acid (both in solution) with concentrated sulfuric acid (also in solution) as the catalyst:

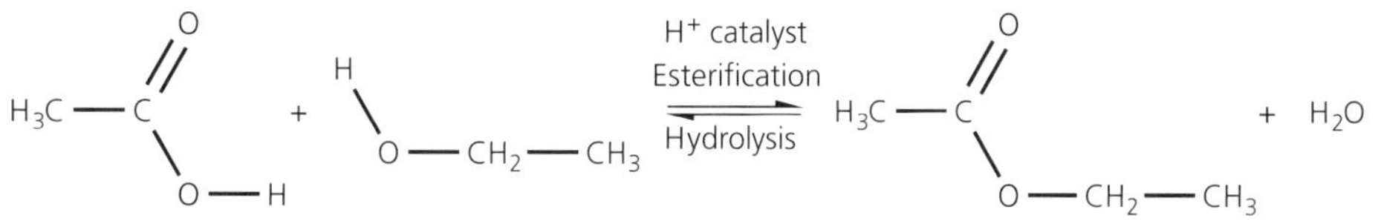


Ethanoic acid · Ethanol · Ethyl ethanoate · Water

9 A reversible reaction is one that proceeds in both the forward and reverse directions. Equilibrium is achieved when the rate of the forward reaction equals the rate of the reverse reaction. Equilibrium can only be achieved in a closed system. The equilibrium is described as dynamic because the reactants and products react continuously; the concentrations of the reactants and the products remain constant.

10 Le Chatelier's principle states that if a closed system under equilibrium is subject to a change, the system moves to minimise the effect of that change.

11 (a) The temperature is increased — the $\Delta H$ value is negative, so the forward reaction is exothermic. If the temperature is increased the system will try to minimise this effect by favouring the reverse endothermic process, so the equilibrium position will move to the left.

(b) The pressure is decreased — the system will try to minimise this effect by increasing the pressure. Therefore the equilibrium position moves towards the side with the most moles of gas, i.e. to the left-hand side.

(c) $N_2O_4$(g) is removed — the system will try to minimise this effect by increasing the amount of $N_2O_4$(g), so the equilibrium position will move to the right.

12 $K_c = \frac{[N_2O_4(g)]}{[NO_2(g)]^2}$

(a) At this temperature the equilibrium lies to the left and favours the reagents.

(b) $0.0025 = \frac{[N_2O_4(g)]}{[1.0]^2}$; hence $[N_2O_4(g)] =$ 0.0025 mol dm$^{-3}$

13 $K_c = \frac{[NO(g)]^2[Cl_2(g)]}{[NOCl(g)]^2} = \frac{[(0.32)^2(0.16)]}{(3.42)^2}$

$= 1.4 \times 10^{-3}$ mol dm$^{-3}$

## Chapter 6

1 (a)

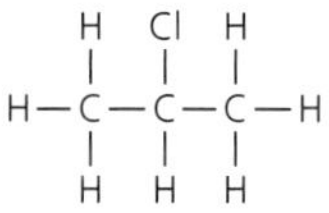

(b)

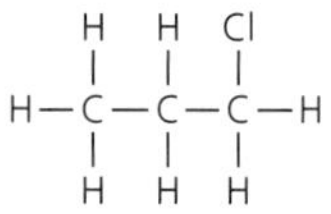

(c)

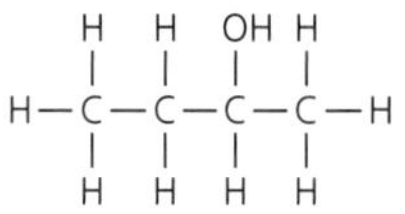

(d)

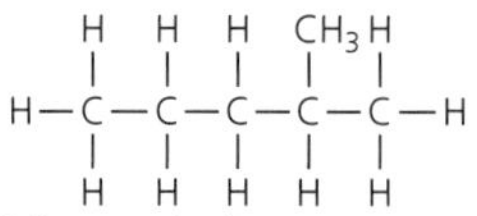

(e)

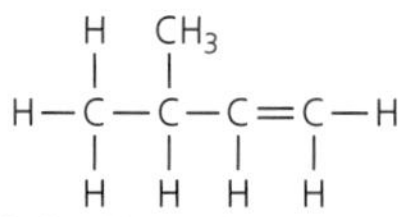

2 (a) 3-methylpentane (b) 2,2-dimethylpropane

(c) but-1-ene (d) propane-1,3-diol

3 (a) 2-bromopropane (b) but-2-ene

(c) 2,2-dimethylpropane (d) 3-methylpentane

4 (a) ratio of volume of alkane A:$CO_2$:$H_2O$ = 100:300:400 (1:3:4)

Hence the alkane contains 3C and 8H, so the formula is $C_3H_8$.

(b) 10.8 g $H_2O$ is $\frac{10.8}{18} = 0.6$ mol

Hence 0.1 mol of alkane B produces 0.6 mol $H_2O$, hence the alkane must contain 12H and therefore the formula of the alkane is $C_5H_{12}$.

5 Cyclobutane is $C_4H_8$

Equation: $C_4H_8 + Cl_2 \rightarrow C_4H_7Cl + HCl$

Mechanism:

Initiation $Cl_2 \rightarrow 2Cl\bullet$ generates radicals

Propagation $Cl\bullet + C_4H_8 \rightarrow HCl + \bullet C_4H_7$ maintains radicals

$\bullet C_4H_7 + Cl_2 \rightarrow C_4H_7Cl + Cl\bullet$

Termination $Cl\bullet + \bullet C_4H_7 \rightarrow C_4H_7Cl$ loss of radicals

Homolytic fission — breaking a covalent bond so that each atom in the covalent bond receives one of the shared pair of electrons.

Radicals are neutral atoms or groups of atoms that contain a single unpaired electron.

Substitution reactions usually occur in saturated molecules and one atom (or group of atoms) is replaced by another atom (or group of atoms).

6 Isomers of $C_6H_{14}$ are:

A

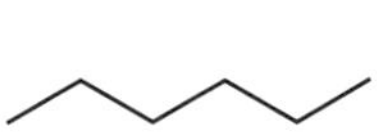

Hexane

B

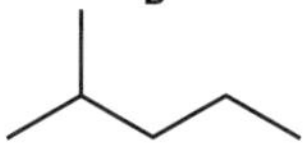

2-methylpentane

C

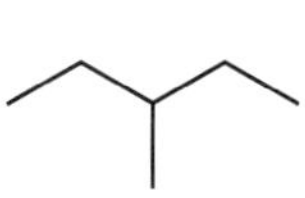

3-methylpentane

D

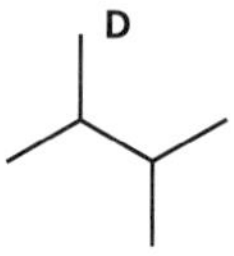

2,3-dimethylbutane

E

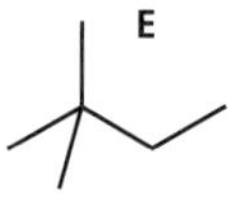

2,2-dimethylbutane

D and E have the lowest boiling points.

7

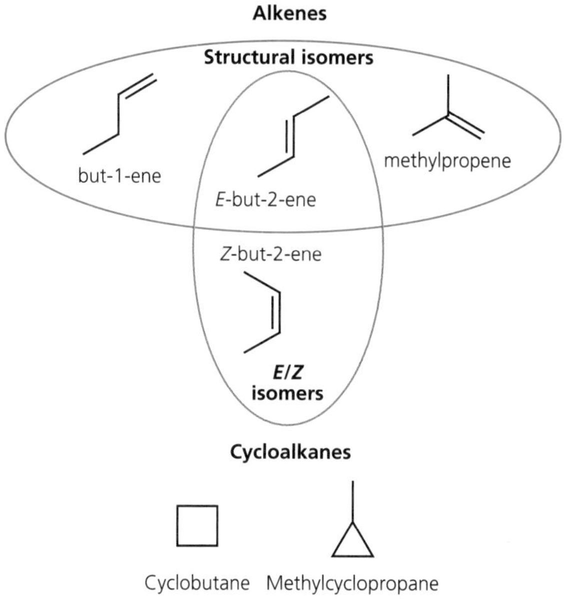

8 (a) (i) $C_3H_6 + 4\frac{1}{2}O_2 \rightarrow 3CO_2 + 3H_2O$

(ii) $CH_2CHCH_2CH_3 + H_2 \rightarrow CH_3CH_2CH_2CH_3$

(iii) $CH_3CHCHCH_3 + H_2O \rightarrow CH_3CH_2CH(OH)CH_3$

(b) $CH_2CHCHCH_2 + 2Br_2 \rightarrow BrCH_2CHBrCHBrCH_2Br$. The bromine would be decolorised. The product is 1,2,3,4-tetrabromobutane.

(c) But-2-ene is symmetrical. Whichever way $H_2O$ adds across the double bond, butan-2-ol can be the only product. But-1-ene is not symmetrical, so it is possible to produce both butan-1-ol and butan-2-ol.

9 (a) An electrophile is an electron-pair acceptor.

(b) $C_6H_{10} + Br_2 \rightarrow C_6H_{10}Br_2$

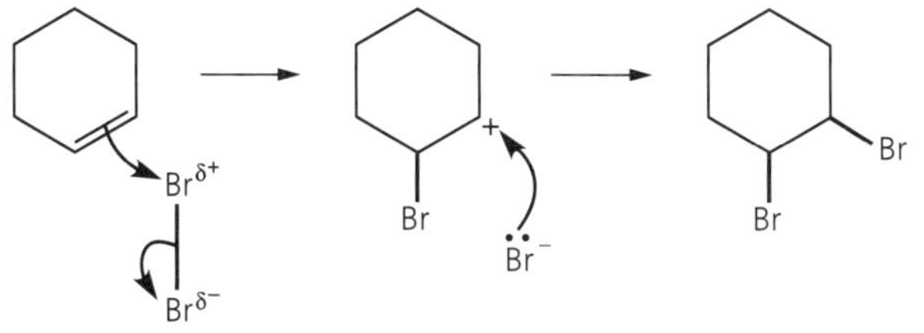


(c) When $Br_2$ reacts with an alkane the Br–Br bond is broken homolytically and one electron goes to each Br, producing two Br radicals.

When bromine reacts with an alkene the Br–Br bond is broken heterolytically and the two electrons go to one of the Br (forming a nucleophile and an electrophile).

10

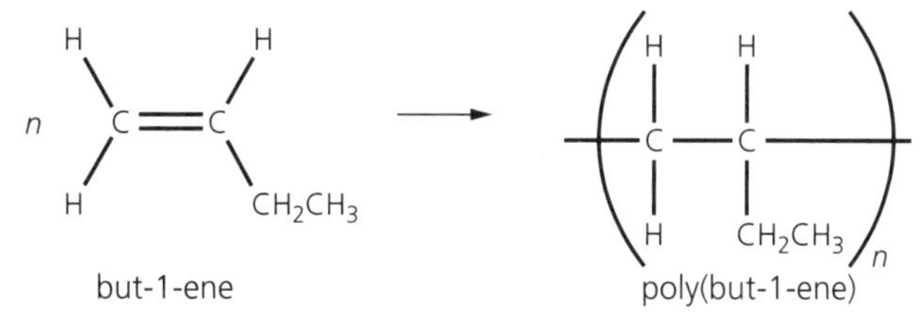


Two repeat units

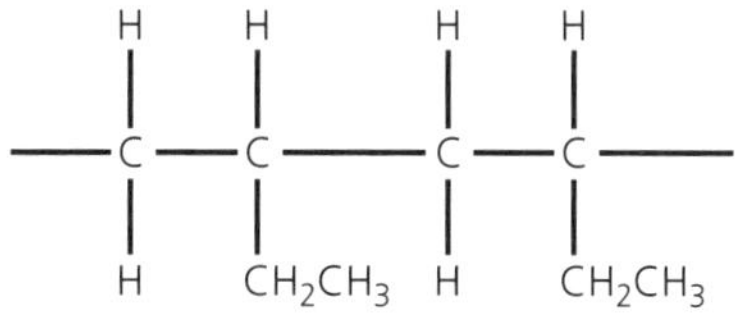

## Chapter 7

1 A = 2-methylbutan-2-ol, B = 3-methylbutan-2-ol, C= 2-methylbutan-1-ol, D = cyclohexanol, E = cyclobutanol, F = but-2-en-1-ol or 1-hydroxybut-2-ene

2 (a) $C_3H_7OH + 4\frac{1}{2}O_2 \rightarrow 3CO_2 + 4H_2O$

It is common to see this written incorrectly as $C_3H_7OH + 5O_2 \rightarrow 3CO_2 + 4H_2O$ because many students forget to count the oxygen in the alcohol.

(b) $C_5H_{11}OH \rightarrow C_5H_{10} + H_2O$

It is better to write the equation as:

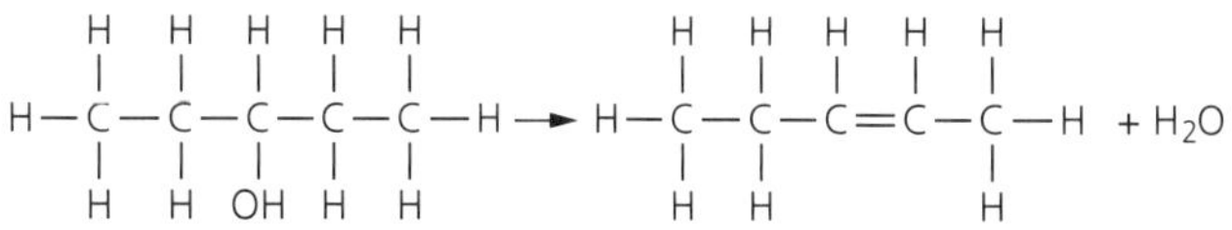

(c) $C_4H_9OH + [O] \rightarrow CH_3CH_2COCH_3 + H_2O$

or

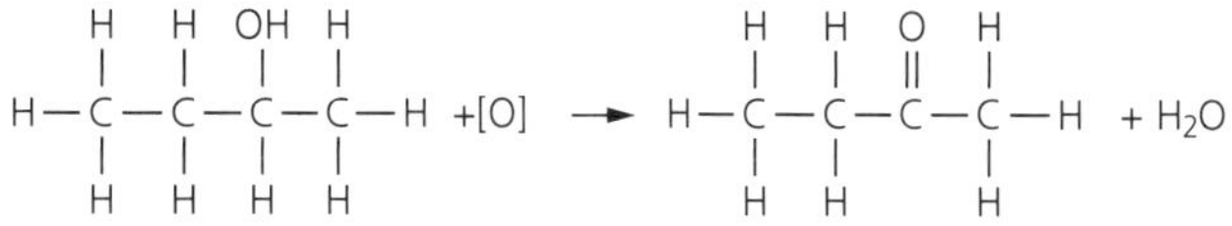

3 Reflux is a process of continuous evaporation and condensation that prevents volatile components from escaping. It does not lead to separation of products.

Distillation is a process of evaporation followed by condensation, which allows the most volatile component to be separated.

4 The dehydration of pentan-3-ol gives only one alkene, pent-2-ene, because pentan-3-ol is symmetrical. However, pent-2-ene exists as *E*/*Z* isomers.

Pentan-2-ol is not symmetrical and produces both pent-1-ene and pent-2-ene. Pent-2-ene exists as *E*/*Z* isomers.

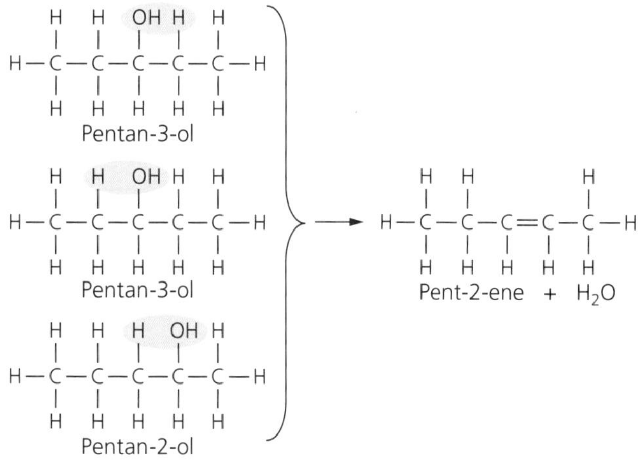


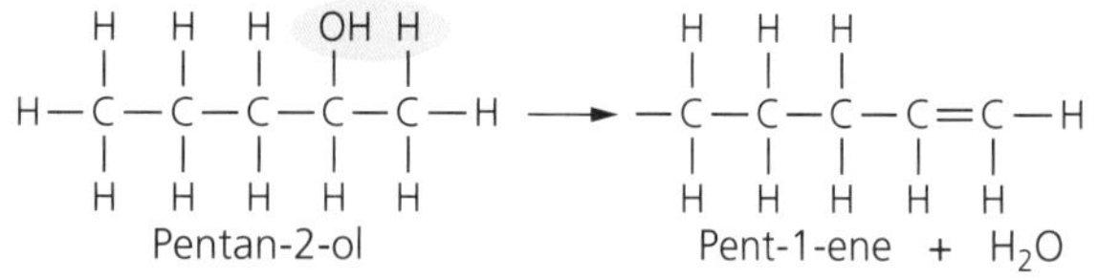


However, pent-2-ene can exist as *E*/*Z* isomers

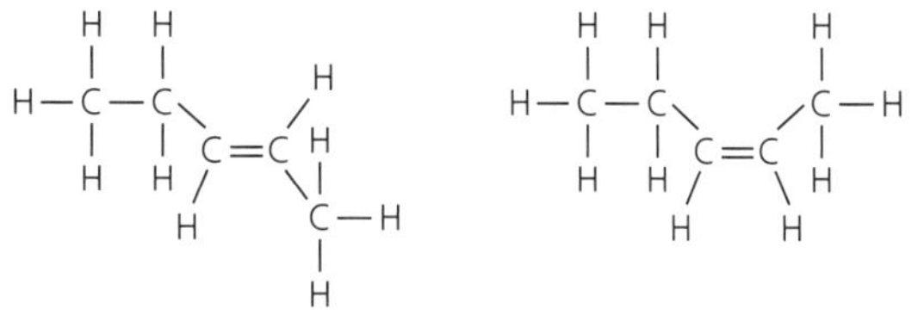

5 (a) A = 2-chloro-2-methylbutane, B = 2-chloro-3-methylbutane, C = 1-chloro-2-methylbutane, D = bromocyclohexane, E = 1,1,1-trichloro-2,2-difluoroethane, F = 2,3-dibromopropene

**(b)** A is tertiary, B is secondary and C is primary.

**(c)** $C_6H_{11}Br + OH^- \rightarrow C_6H_{11}OH + Br^-$

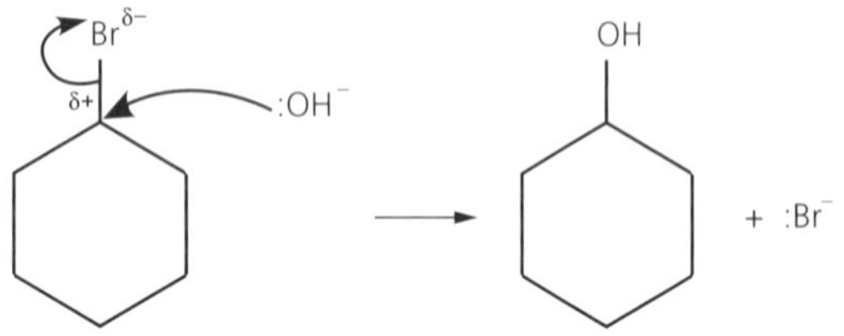


The marks would be for:

- correct dipoles
- curly arrow from C–Br bond to $Br^{\delta-}$
- curly arrow from $:OH^-$ to $C^{\delta+}$
- correct products

**(d)** A radical is a particle with an unpaired electron. In the symbol for a radical the unpaired electron is usually shown as a dot, e.g. Cl•.

The radical most likely to be formed is Cl• because the C–Cl bond is weaker than the C–F bond.

**6** Compound A: decolorises $Br_2$, therefore is an alkene; is oxidised by acidified dichromate, therefore is an alcohol. Compound A is $CH_3CHCHCH_2OH$. (It is difficult to spot the C=C double bond: $CH_3CH{=}CHCH_2OH$.)

**7** **(a)** methane → chloromethane (reagents: $Cl_2(g)$, conditions: UV light)

chloromethane → methanol (reagents: NaOH(aq), conditions: heat)

**(b)** propene → propan-2-ol (reagents: steam, conditions: high temperature/pressure)

propan-2-ol → propanone (reagents: acidified dichromate, conditions: heat under reflux)

**8** The bonds vibrate.

**9** The ability of the gas to absorb infrared radiation.

The atmospheric concentration of the gas.

The length of time the gas stays in the atmosphere — the residence time.

**10** **(a)** **(i)** No broad peak at about 3000 $cm^{-1}$, therefore O–H is not present.

**(ii)** Peak at about 1700 $cm^{-1}$, therefore C=O (carbonyl) is present.

**(b)** molar mass = 58.0

**(c)** Compound A contains C=O, which has mass 28.0 (12.0 + 16.0).

The molar mass = 58.0, so the rest of the molecule must have a mass of 30.0.

Hence, there must be two carbon atoms (24.0) and six hydrogen atoms.

The formula is $C_2H_6CO$ or $C_3H_6O$.

**(d)** $CH_3CH_2CHO$ — propanal; $CH_3COCH_3$ — propanone

**(e)** Propanal forms a fragment ion, $CH_3CH_2^+$, at $m/z$ = 29 and propanone does not have a fragment peak at $m/z$ = 29. The fragmentation pattern confirms that compound A is propanone.

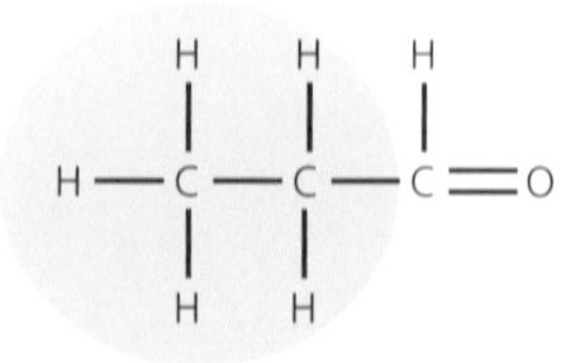


Gives fragment $CH_3CH_2^+$ which has $m/z$ = 29

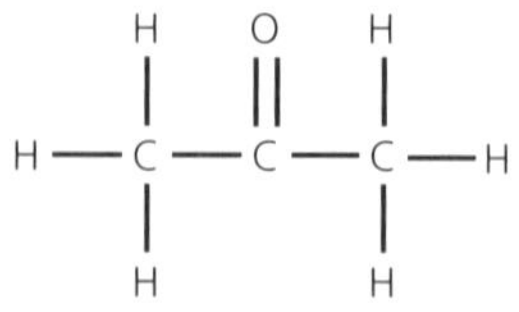


Does not give fragment with $m/z$ = 29

## Chapter 8

**1** **(a)** Fourth order; units of $k$ = $mol^{-3}\,dm^{12}\,s^{-1}$ (or $dm^{12}\,mol^{-3}\,s^{-1}$)

**(b)** **(i)** The rate is three times as fast.

**(ii)** The rate is $(½)^2 = ¼$.

**(iii)** The rate increases by $2 \times 2^2 \times 2 = 16$.

**2** **(a)** Use a colorimeter to monitor change in colour as the $Br_2$ is decolorised.

**(b)** Collect the gas evolved at fixed intervals of time.

**(c)** Use a pH meter to monitor changes in acidity.

**(d)** Observe precipitation of sulfur either by using a colorimeter or observing disappearance of a 'cross'.

**3** **(a)** Experiments 1 and 3: when the $BrO_3^-$ concentration is doubled, the rate doubles, showing that the reaction is first order with respect to $BrO_3^-$.

Experiments 2 and 3: when the $Br^-$ concentration is doubled, the rate doubles showing that the reaction is first order with respect to $Br^-$.

Experiments 2 and 4: when the concentration of $H^+$ is doubled, the rate increases fourfold, showing that the reaction is second order with respect to $H^+$.

The rate equation for the reaction is:

rate = $k[BrO_3^-][Br^-][H^+]^2$

**(b)** Using the rate equation and substituting the values from Experiment 1:

$1.64 \times 10^{-3} = k \times 0.1 \times 0.2 \times (0.1)^2$

$$k = \frac{1.64 \times 10^{-3}}{0.1 \times 0.2 \times (0.1)^2}$$

$$= \frac{1.64 \times 10^{-3}}{2 \times 10^{-4}} = 8.2\,dm^9\,mol^{-3}\,s^{-1}$$

**(c)** rate = $8.2 \times 0.25 \times 0.25 \times (0.25)^2$

$= 3.2 \times 10^{-2}\,mol\,dm^{-3}\,s^{-1}$

**4** slow step $ICl + H_2 \rightarrow HCl + HI$

fast step $ICl + HI \rightarrow HCl + I_2$

**5** **(a)** $K_c = \dfrac{[NO_2(g)]^2}{[N_2O_4(g)]}$ Units: $mol\,dm^{-3}$

**(b)** $K_c = \dfrac{[N_2(g)]^2[O_2(g)]}{[N_2O(g)]^2}$ Units: $mol\,dm^{-3}$

(c) $K_c = \frac{[CO(g)]^2}{[O_2(g)]}$ Units: $mol\,dm^{-3}$

Remember that as carbon is a solid, it has no concentration and therefore does not appear in the equilibrium constant.

(d) $K_c = \frac{[CO_2(g)]^2}{[CO(g)]^2[O_2(g)]}$ Units: $mol^{-1}\,dm^3$ or $dm^3\,mol^{-1}$

6 (a) It is helpful to tabulate initial and equilibrium amounts:

| | Units | $N_2O$ | $N_2$ | $O_2$ |
|---|---|---|---|---|
| Initial moles | mol | 1.00 | 0 | 0 |
| Equilibium moles | mol | 0.10 | 0.90 | 0.45 |
| Equilibrium concentrations | $mol\,dm^{-3}$ | 0.10 | 0.90 | 0.45 |

Remember: when calculating $K_c$, you *must* use concentrations, *not* moles.

(b) $K_c = \frac{[N_2(g)]^2[O_2(g)]}{[N_2O(g)]^2}$

$= \frac{(0.90)^2 \times 0.45}{(0.10)^2} = 36.45\,mol\,dm^{-3}$

(c) The value of $K_c$ will not change. $K_c$ only changes if temperature changes.

It is easy to be trapped into redoing the calculation, changing the concentrations to half their previous values and obtaining a new value for $K_c$. However, changing the volume of the container results in a change in the number of moles of each of the components so that the value of $K_c$ remains the same. Remember, only a change in temperature causes a change in the value of $K_c$.

7 (a) $K_p = \frac{P_{N_2O_4}}{P_{NO_2}^{\ 2}}$ units = $kPa^{-1}$

(b) $K_p = \frac{P_{O_2}^{\ 3}}{P_{O_3}^{\ 2}}$ units = kPa

(c) $K_p = \frac{P_{H_2} \times P_{CO}}{P_{H_2O}}$ units = kPa

8 (a) $K_p = \frac{P_{CO_2} \times P_{H_2}}{P_{H_2O} \times P_{CO}}$

Therefore:

$\frac{K_p \times P_{H_2O} \times P_{CO}}{P_{H_2}} = P_{CO_2}$

$= \frac{8.1 \times 10^{-2} \times 35 \times 35}{18} = 5.5125\,kPa$

(b) total pressure = 35 + 35 + 18 + 5.5 = 93.5 kPa

9 $PCl_5 \rightleftharpoons PCl_3 + Cl_2$

| | | | |
|---|---|---|---|
| Initial amounts | 0.3 | 0 | 0 |
| Equilibrium amounts | 0.08 | 0.22 | 0.22 |
| Mole fraction at $\rightleftharpoons$ | 0.154 | 0.423 | 0.423 |
| Partial pressure at $\rightleftharpoons$ (the total pressure) | 34.2 | 93.9 | 93.9 = 222 |

$K_p = \frac{93.9 \times 93.9}{34.2} = 257.8\,kPa$ (258 to 3 sig figs)

10 (a) $HCO_3^- + H_2O \rightleftharpoons H_2CO_3 + OH^-$

Acid 1 Base 2 Acid 2 Base 1

(b) $HCO_3^- + OH^- \rightleftharpoons H_2O + CO_3^{2-}$

Acid 1 Base 2 Acid 2 Base 1

11 (a) pH = −log(0.15) = 0.82

(b) $pH = -\log\sqrt{(0.15)(6.02 \times 10^{-10})} = -\log\sqrt{9.03 \times 10^{-11}}$

$= -\log 9.5 \times 10^{-6} = 5.02$

(c) $pH = -\log\frac{1.0 \times 10^{-14}}{0.15} = -\log(6.67 \times 10^{-14}) = 13.2$

12 When $20.0\,cm^3$ of $1.00\,mol\,dm^{-3}$ HCl is added to $10.0\,cm^3$ of $1.00\,mol\,dm^{-3}$ NaOH a reaction occurs and the NaOH is neutralised, producing neutral NaCl.

$10.0\,cm^3$ of the $1.00\,mol\,dm^{-3}$ HCl remains un-neutralised. However, this has been diluted to the total volume of the mixture, which is $30.0\,cm^3$. This means the concentration of the HCl is now $(10.0/30.0) \times 1.00 = 0.333\,mol\,dm^{-3}$. Therefore, pH = −log(0.333) = 0.48.

13 (a) If the pH of the acid is 2.70, $[H^+] = 10^{-2.7}$

$= 2.0 \times 10^{-3}\,mol\,dm^{-3}$

In the solution of ethanoic acid,

$[H^+(aq)] = [CH_3COO^-(aq)]$

$K_a = \frac{[H^+(aq)]^2}{[CH_3COOH(aq)]}$

Hence, $[CH_3COOH(aq)] = \frac{[H^+(aq)]^2}{K_a} = \frac{(2.0 \times 10^{-3})^2}{1.7 \times 10^{-5}}$

$= 0.23(52) = 0.24\,mol\,dm^{-3}$

(b) For a buffer at pH 4.0, the concentration of $[H^+(aq)]$ is $1.0 \times 10^{-4}\,mol\,dm^{-3}$.

The concentration of the ethanoic acid stays the same so, use the expression:

$K_a = \frac{[H^+(aq)][CH_3COO^-(aq)]}{[CH_3COOH(aq)]}$

Rearranging gives:

$\frac{K_a[CH_3COOH]}{[H^+]} = [CH_3COO^-]$

$\frac{1.7 \times 10^{-5} \times 0.235}{1.0 \times 10^{-4}} = [CH_3COO^-] = 0.040\,mol\,dm^{-3}$

molar mass of sodium ethanoate = $82.0\,g\,mol^{-1}$

Therefore:

mass required = 82.0 × 0.040

= 3.28 = 3.3 g

14 (a) Indicators, HIn, are weak acids:

$HIn \rightleftharpoons H^+ + In^-$

$K_{in} = \frac{[H^+][In^-]}{[HIn]}$

At the mid-point, $[In^-] = [HIn]$

Hence, $K_{in} = [H^+]$

Therefore, $pK_{in} = pH$

$pH = -\log(6.31 \times 10^{-7}) = 6.20$

(b) $HIn \rightleftharpoons H^+ + In^-$

Yellow Red

In acid solution, the added $H^+$ pushes this equilibrium to the left and therefore the indicator changes colour to yellow.

In alkaline solution, the added $OH^-$ reacts with the $H^+$ from the indicator to produce water. This causes the indicator to adjust by creating more $In^-$ and, therefore, it changes colour to red.

At the end point, the colour of the indicator is orange.

(c) (i) 0.0001 mol dm$^{-3}$ has a pH of 4, so the indicator appears yellow.

(ii) Pure water has a pH of 7, so the indicator will be turning red. However, to the eye it will probably appear orange because conversion to the HIn form will be incomplete.

15 (a) If the acid equilibrium for aspirin is written as:

$HA(aq) \rightleftharpoons H^+(aq) + A^-(aq)$

$$\frac{[H^+(aq)][A^-(aq)]}{[HA(aq)]} = 3.0 \times 10^{-4}\,\text{mol dm}^{-3}$$

pH of the stomach is equal to 1, so $[H^+(aq)] = 0.1\,\text{mol dm}^{-3}$

The ratio of the dissociated salt of aspirin: undissociated aspirin is:

$$\frac{[A^-(aq)]}{[HA(aq)]} = \frac{3.0 \times 10^{-4}}{0.1} = 3 \times 10^{-3}$$

This means the aspirin is largely in its molecular (undissociated) form, HA. This would be likely to dissolve in the lipids on the stomach lining, so bleeding might be a problem.

(b) At pH 7.4, $[H^+(aq)] = 4 \times 10^{-8}\,\text{mol dm}^{-3}$

$$\text{So, } \frac{[A^-(aq)]}{[HA(aq)]} = \frac{3 \times 10^{-4}}{4 \times 10^{-8}} = 7.5 \times 10^3$$

The aspirin is now largely ionised and is mostly present as the anion.

(c) The relative formula mass of $Ca(OH)_2$ is 74.1. Hence, the concentration of $Ca(OH)_2$ is 0.0100 mol dm$^{-3}$.

Calcium hydroxide is a strong base, so it will be ionised fully. The concentration of hydroxide ions present is 0.0200 mol dm$^{-3}$.

If $[OH^-(aq)] = 0.0200$, then $\dfrac{[H^+(aq)] = 10^{-14}}{0.0200 = 5.0 \times 10^{-13}}$

pH = 12.30

At this pH, there would be substantial hydrolysis of the aspirin.

(d) $C_6H_4(OCOCH_3)CO_2H + H_2O \rightleftharpoons C_6H_4(OH)CO_2H + CH_3COOH$

At equilibrium, 0.117 g of $CH_3COOH$ is present.

amount, in moles, of aspirin hydrolysed

$$= \frac{0.117}{60.0} = 1.95 \times 10^{-3}\,\text{mol}$$

initial amount, in moles, of aspirin

$$= \frac{0.900}{180.0} = 5.0 \times 10^{-3}\,\text{mol}$$

percentage of aspirin hydrolysed

$$= \frac{1.95 \times 10^{-3}}{5.0 \times 10^{-3}} \times 100 = 39.0\%$$

## Chapter 9

1 (a)

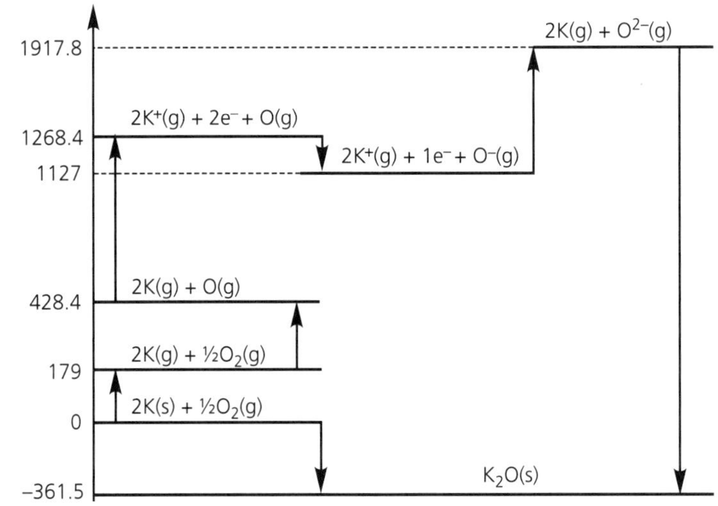


(b) Lattice enthalpy = –2279.3 kJ mol$^{-1}$

2 (a)

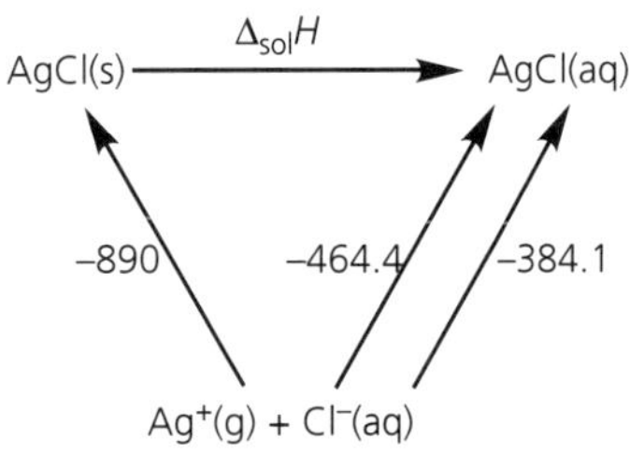


$\Delta_{sol}H = (-464.4) + (-384.1) - (-890) = +41.5\,\text{kJ mol}^{-1}$

(b)

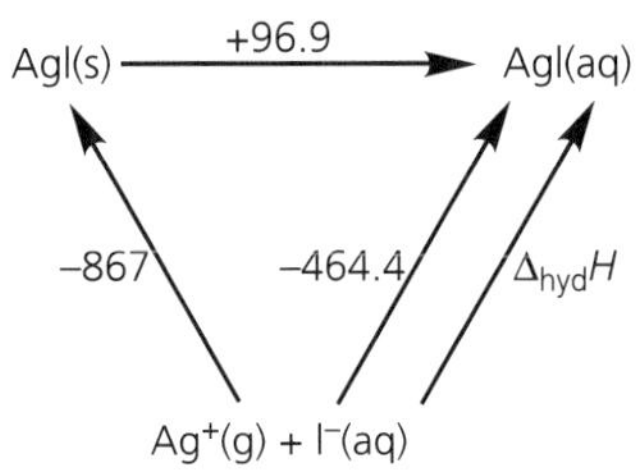


$\Delta_{hyd}H = (-867) + (96.9) - (-464.4) = -305.7\,\text{kJ mol}^{-1}$

(c) Enthalpies of hydration of $Cl^-$ and $I^-$ are = −384.1 kJ mol$^{-1}$ and −305.7 kJ mol$^{-1}$, respectively. The enthalpy of hydration of $I^-$ is less negative than the enthalpy of hydration of $Cl^-$ because the ionic radius of $I^-$ is greater than that of $Cl^-$. This means that the attraction between $I^-$ and the dipoles in $H_2O$ is less than the attraction between $Cl^-$ and the dipoles in $H_2O$.

(d) $\Delta_{sol}H$ for both AgCl(aq) and AgI(aq) are endothermic. This indicates that neither substance will be soluble in water at standard temperature. $\Delta_{sol}H$ for AgI is more endothermic than that for AgCl, indicating that AgI is less soluble than AgCl.

3 (a) *S* will be negative (movement of particles in ice is more restricted).

(b) $\Delta S$ will be positive (the particles in an aqueous solution have more freedom than those in a solid).

(c) $\Delta S$ will be negative (the oxygen atoms from $O_2$ lose their freedom to move).

(d) $\Delta S$ will be negative (the reduction in overall volume as the reaction takes place reduces freedom of movement).

4 Substances with particles with the least freedom of movement tend to have the lowest entropy values. Of the three substances here, iodine is a solid and has particles with the least freedom to move. This identifies iodine as substance B with the entropy value 58.4 J mol$^{-1}$ K$^{-1}$.

Methanol is a liquid and will have the next highest entropy value. Methanol is substance C with the entropy value 127.2 J mol$^{-1}$ K$^{-1}$.

Ammonia is a gas and has particles with the greatest freedom to move. Ammonia is substance A with the entropy value 192.5 J mol$^{-1}$ K$^{-1}$.

5 The equation for the reaction is:

$2Na(s) + \frac{1}{2}O_2(g) \rightarrow Na_2O(s)$

The entropy change, $\Delta S$, is:

$72.8 - (2 \times 51.0 + \frac{1}{2} \times 102.5) = -80.5$ J mol$^{-1}$ K$^{-1}$

6 (a) $CO_3^{2-}(aq) + 2H^+(aq) \rightarrow H_2O(l) + CO_2(g)$

(b) $CaCO_3(s) + 2H^+(aq) \rightarrow Ca^{2+}(aq) + H_2O(l) + CO_2(g)$

(c) $Ca^{2+}(aq) + CO_3^{2-}(aq) \rightarrow CaCO_3(s)$

(d) $OH^-(aq) + H^+(aq) \rightarrow H_2O(l)$

(e) $Cu^{2+}(aq) + 2OH^-(aq) \rightarrow Cu(OH)_2(s)$

(f) $ZnO(s) + 2H^+(aq) \rightarrow Zn^{2+}(aq) + H_2O(l)$

7 (a) Balance symbols and charge:

$MnO_4^-(aq) + 8H^+(aq) + 5e^- \rightarrow Mn^{2+}(aq) + 4H_2O(l)$

Balance charge:

$V^{2+}(aq) \rightarrow V^{3+}(aq) + e^-$

Multiply the second equation by 5 and add the equations together so that the electrons cancel:

$MnO_4^-(aq) + 8H^+(aq) + 5V^{2+}(aq) \rightarrow 5V^{3+}(aq) + Mn^{2+}(aq) + 4H_2O(l)$

(b) Balance symbols and charge:

$MnO_4^-(aq) + 8H^+(aq) + 5e^- \rightarrow Mn^{2+}(aq) + 4H_2O(l)$

Balance symbols and charge:

$V^{2+}(aq) + 3H_2O(l) \rightarrow VO_3^-(aq) + 6H^+(aq) + 3e^-$

Multiply the first equation by 3 and the second equation by 5, so that each has 15 electrons. Add together to give:

$3MnO_4^-(aq) + 24H^+(aq) + 5V^{2+}(aq) + 15H_2O(l) \rightarrow 5VO_3^-(aq) + 30H^+(aq) + 3Mn_2^+(aq) + 12H_2O(l)$

Simplify by cancelling the $H^+$ and $H_2O$ that appear on both sides of the equation:

$3MnO_4^-(aq) + 5V^{2+}(aq) + 3H_2O(l) \rightarrow 5VO_3^-(aq) + 6H^+(aq) + 3Mn^{2+}(aq)$

(c) Balance symbols and charge:

$Cr_2O_7^{2-}(aq) + 14H^+(aq) + 6e^- \rightarrow 2Cr^{3+}(aq) + 7H_2O(l)$

Balance symbols and charge:

$SO_2(aq) + 2H_2O(l) \rightarrow SO_4^{2-}(aq) + 4H^+(aq) + 2e-$

Multiply the second equation by 3, then add together and simplify:

$Cr_2O_7^{2-}(aq) + 14H^+(aq) + 3SO_2(aq) + 6H_2O(l) \rightarrow 3SO_4^{2-}(aq) + 12H^+(aq) + 2Cr^{3+}(aq) + 7H_2O(l)$

This can be further simplified to:

$Cr_2O_7^{2-}(aq) + 2H^+(aq) + 3SO_2(aq) \rightarrow 3SO_4^{2-}(aq) + 2Cr^{3+}(aq) + H_2O(l)$

(d) Balance symbols and charge:

$NO_3^-(aq) + 4H^+(aq) + 3e^- \rightarrow NO(g) + 2H_2O(l)$

Balance charge:

$Cu(s) \rightarrow Cu^{2+}(aq) + 2e^-$

Multiply the first equation by 2 and the second equation by 3, so that each has six electrons. Add together to give:

$8H^+(aq) + 2NO_3^-(aq) + 3Cu(s) \rightarrow 3Cu^{2+}(aq) + 2NO(g) + 4H_2O(l)$

8 (a) $Mg(s) \rightarrow Mg^{2+}(aq) + 2e^-$ $E^\ominus = +2.37$ V

$Zn^{2+}(aq) + 2e^- \rightarrow Zn(s)$ $E^\ominus = -0.76$ V

Therefore, the overall cell potential is 1.61 V.

(b) $Fe^{3+}(aq) + e^- \rightarrow Fe^{2+}(aq)$ $E^\ominus = +0.77$ V

$Sn^{2+}(aq) \rightarrow Sn^{4+}(aq) + 2e^-$ $E^\ominus = -0.15$ V

Therefore, the overall cell potential is 0.62 V.

(c) $Br_2(aq) + 2e^- \rightarrow 2Br^-(aq)$ $E^\ominus = +1.09$ V

$2I^-(aq) \rightarrow I_2(aq) + 2e^-$ $E^\ominus = -0.54$ V

Therefore, the overall cell potential is 0.55 V.

(d) $Zn(s) \rightarrow Zn^{2+}(aq) + 2e^-$ $E^\ominus = +0.76$ V

$I_2(aq) + 2e^- \rightarrow 2I^-(aq)$ $E^\ominus = +0.54$ V

Therefore, the overall cell potential is 1.30 V.

(e) $Br_2(aq) + 2e^- \rightarrow 2Br^-(aq)$ $E^\ominus = +1.09$ V

$Sn^{2+}(aq) \rightarrow Sn^{4+}(aq) + 2e^-$ $E^\ominus = -0.15$ V

Therefore, the overall cell potential is 0.94 V.

9 The aluminum foil sets up an electrical cell with the amalgam:

$Al(s) \rightarrow Al^{3+}(aq) + 3e^-$ +1.66 V

With saliva as the electrolyte, either of the two components of the amalgam is able to receive electrons. The cell potentials under standard conditions are as follows:

$Al(s) \rightarrow Al^{3+}(aq) + 3e^-$ +1.66 V

$Hg^+ + e^- \rightarrow Ag/Hg$ (amalgam) +0.85 V

This has an overall potential of 2.51 V.

$Al(s) \rightarrow Al^{3+}(aq) + 3e^-$ +1.66 V

$Sn^{2+} + 2e^- \rightarrow Sn/Hg$ (amalgam) −0.13 V

This has an overall potential of 1.53 V.

Although the conditions in the mouth are, of course, not standard conditions these electric cells are enough to cause a current to flow, resulting in a nasty shock.

## Chapter 10

1 (a) The change in colour suggests that a ligand exchange has taken place. The aqueous copper sulfate solution is light blue because of the presence of the $[Cu(H_2O)_6]^{2+}$ ion. 1,2-diaminoethane is a stronger ligand than water and the change in colour to a darker blue is due to the formation of the copper-1,2-diaminoethane complex ion.

(b) When HCl is added, the hydrogen ions form a stronger bond with 1,2-diaminoethane than does the $Cu^{2+}$ ion:

$H_2NCH_2CH_2NH_2 + 2H^+ \rightarrow {}^+H_3NCH_2CH_2NH_3{}^+$

The copper(II)-1,2-diaminoethane complex ion is broken down and the 1,2-diaminoethane is replaced by water molecules, restoring the original light-blue colour.

2 (a) The aqueous cobalt ion is pink due to the presence of $[Co(H_2O)_6]^{2+}$ ions. However, at high concentration, chloride ions replace the water molecules, forming the blue cobalt chloride complex ion, $[CoCl_4]^{2-}$.

(b) In the presence of larger amounts of water, the process in part (a) is reversed and pink $[Co(H_2O)_6]^{2+}$ ions are reformed.

The equilibrium:

$[Co(H_2O)_6]^{2+} + 4Cl^- \rightleftharpoons [CoCl_4]^{2-} + 6H_2O$

moves readily from side-to-side depending on the concentration of chloride ions present (water is in vast excess).

(c) When aqueous silver nitrate is added, the silver ions react with chloride ions to produce a precipitate of silver chloride. The blue cobalt chloride complex ion, $[CoCl_4]^{2-}$, is destroyed and the pink $[Co(H_2O)_6]^{2+}$ ions are formed once again.

The $Ag^+$ ion removes the $Cl^-$ ion from the equilibrium:

$[Co(H_2O)_6]^{2+} + 4Cl^- \rightleftharpoons [CoCl_4]^{2-} + 6H_2O$

Pink Blue

The equilibrium moves to the left, hence the solution turns pink. AgCl(s) is also formed.

3 (a) Compound A $[Co(NH_3)_6]Cl_3$ can release three $Cl^-$ ions, which will form a precipitate with added $Ag^+(aq)$ ions. Salt B $[Co(NH_3)_5Cl]Cl_2$ can only release two $Cl^-$ ions because the third $Cl^-$ ion is part of the complex ion. Compound A has three $Cl^-$; compound B has 2 $Cl^-$. Therefore compound A produces 3/2 times as much precipitate of silver chloride as compound B does.

(b) The compounds C and D must have only one $Cl^-$ available as an anion and the other two $Cl^-$ must be present in a complex cation with the four ammonia ligands. This suggests that C and D are *cis–trans* isomers:

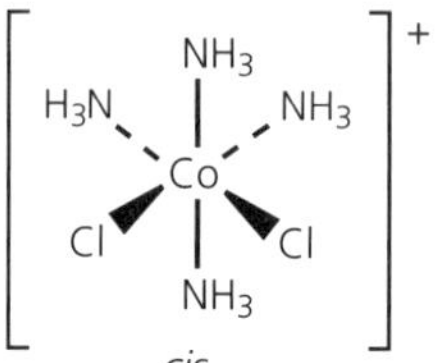


*cis*

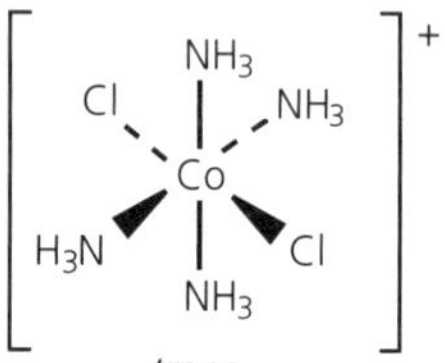


*trans*

4 (a) oxidation number of Zn: +2

(b) oxidation number of Fe: +2

(c) oxidation number of Co: +3

(d) oxidation number of Co: +2

(e) oxidation number of Cr: +3

5 The half-equation for the reduction of $MnO_4^-(aq)$ is:

$MnO_4^-(aq) + 8H^+(aq) + 5e^- \rightarrow Mn^{2+}(aq) + 4H_2O(l)$

The half-equation for the oxidation of $VO^{2+}(aq)$ is:

$VO^{2+}(aq) + 2H_2O(l) \rightarrow VO_3^-(aq) + 4H^+(aq) + e^-$

Multiplying the second half-equation by 5, the overall equation for the reaction simplifies to:

$MnO_4^-(aq) + 5VO^{2+}(aq) + 6H_2O(l) \rightarrow 5VO_3^-(aq) + 12H^+(aq) + Mn^{2+}$

amount, in moles, of $MnO_4^-$ in 23.30 cm$^3$ =

$\frac{23.30}{1000} \times 0.0150 = 3.495 \times 10^{-4}$ mol

Using the equation:

amount, in moles, of $VO^{2+}$ used in the titration = 5 × 3.495 × $10^{-4}$ = 1.7475 × $10^{-3}$ mol

concentration of $VO^{2+} = \frac{1000}{25.0} \times 1.7475 \times 10^{-3}$

= 0.0699 mol dm$^{-3}$

6 (a) $Cr_2O_7^{2-}(aq) + 14H^+(aq) + 6e^- \rightarrow 2Cr^{3+}(aq) + 7H_2O(l)$

$Sn^{2+}(aq) \rightarrow Sn^{4+}(aq) + 2e^-$

The overall equation is obtained by multiplying the second half-equation by 3:

$Cr_2O_7^{2-}(aq) + 14H^+(aq) + 3Sn^{2+}(aq) \rightarrow 3Sn^{4+}(aq) + 2Cr^{3+}(aq) + 7H_2O(l)$

(b) amount, in moles, of $Cr_2O_7^{2-}$ in 20.0 cm$^3$ =

$\frac{20.0}{1000} \times 0.0175 = 3.50 \times 10^{-4}$ mol

Using the equation:
amount, in moles, of $Sn^{2+}$ used in the titration = $3 \times 3.50 \times 10^{-4} = 1.05 \times 10^{-3}$ mol

concentration of $Sn^{2+}(aq) = \frac{1000}{25.0} \times 1.05 \times 10^{-3}$
$= 0.0420\, mol\, dm^{-3}$

(c) The relative atomic mass of tin is 118.7.

mass of 0.0420 mol of tin = $0.0420 \times 118.7$
$= 4.985$ g

percentage by mass of tin in the solder
$= \frac{4.985}{10.00} \times 100 = 49.9\%$

4 (a)

| | Benzene | Phenol | Cyclohexene |
|---|---|---|---|
| Type of reaction | Electrophilic substitution | Electrophilic substitution | Electrophilic addition |
| Reagents and conditions (if any) | $Br_2$ + halogen carrier, such as $AlBr_3$ or Fe | $Br_2$<br>No special conditions | |
| Organic product and observations | Bromobenzene, $C_6H_5Br$<br>$Br_2$ is decolorised | 2,4,6-tribromophenol<br>White precipitate; $Br_2$ is decolorised | 1,2-dibromocyclohexane<br>$Br_2$ is decolorised |

(b) (i) Bromine reacts faster with phenol because one of the lone pairs of electrons on the oxygen in the OH group is delocalised into the ring. This increases the electron density, which in turn polarises the Br–Br bond, so that an electrophile is generated. This then attacks the ring. (Accept the reverse argument for why the reaction with benzene is slower.)

(ii) Bromine reacts faster with cyclohexene because the C=C double bond has a high electron density, which polarises the Br–Br bond, so that an electrophile is generated. This then attacks the C=C double bond. (Accept the reverse argument for why the reaction with benzene is slower.)

## Chapter 11

1

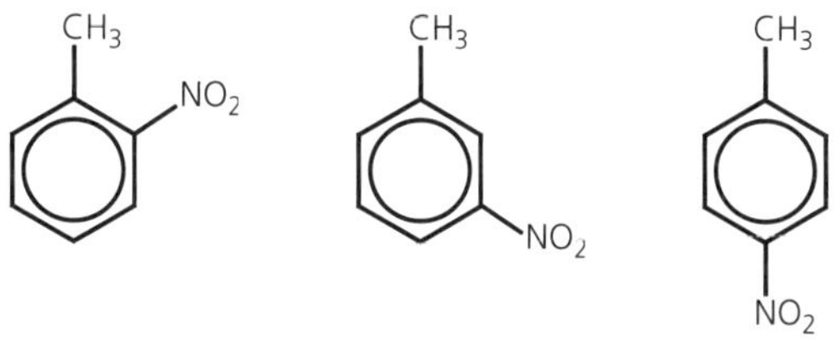


2-Nitromethylbenzene 3-Nitromethylbenzene 4-Nitromethylbenzene

2 $C_6H_5CH_3 + 3HNO_3 \rightarrow CH_3C_6H_2(NO_2)_3 + 3H_2O$

3 $C_7H_8O$

5 Methyl groups are 2,4-directing; nitro groups are 3-directing.

To produce 3-nitromethylbenzene starting with benzene:

step 1 — nitration using concentrated $HNO_3/H_2SO_4$

step 2 — alkylation of nitrobenzene

6 Carbonyl compound used: butanone, $CH_3COCH_2CH_3$

Balanced equation:
$CH_3COCH_2CH_3 + 2[H] \rightarrow CH_3CH(OH)CH_2CH_3$

Reagents and conditions: $NaBH_4$; water as solvent

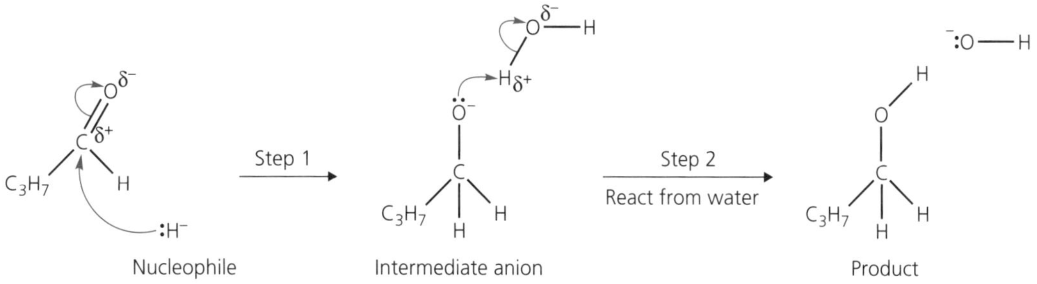

7 (a) propanenitrile

(b) 2-hydroxypentanenitrile

(c) 2-hydroxy-2-methylpentanenitrile

8 $C_6H_5COCH_3 + 2[H] \rightarrow C_6H_5CH(OH)CH$

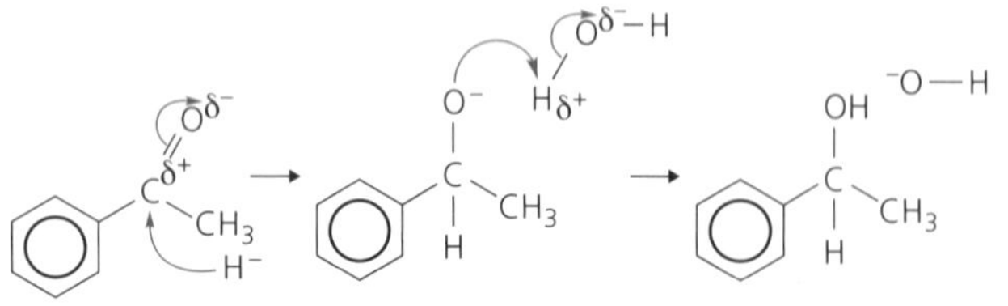


9 (a) A = 2-methylpropanal

B = 3-methylbutan-2-one

C = phenylethanal

D = phenylethanone

E = 2,2-dimethylpropanal

F = cyclohexane-1,4-dione

(b) A, C and E are aldehydes; B, D and F are ketones.

(c) $C_6H_8O_2$

(d) C could be prepared from 2-phenylethanol; D could be prepared from 1-phenylethanol.

(e) Any three from:

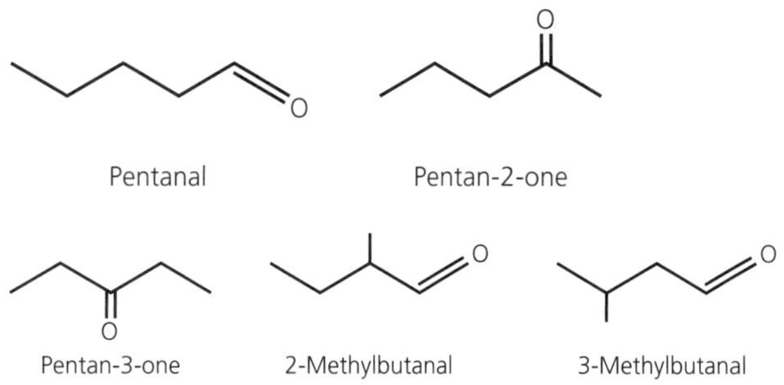


10 (a) $CH_3COOH + CH_3OH \rightarrow CH_3COOCH_3 + H_2O$

$H_2SO_4$ is a catalyst.

(b) molar mass $CH_3COOH = 60.0\,g\,mol^{-1}$

$CH_3COOCH_3 = 74.0\,g\,mol^{-1}$

moles of $CH_3COOH$ used $= \frac{12.0}{60.0} = 0.200$

moles of $CH_3COOCH_3$ produced $= \frac{3.70}{74.0} = 0.0500$

% yield $= \frac{0.0500}{0.200} \times 100 = 25.0\%$

(c) atom economy $= \frac{\text{mass of desired product}}{\text{sum of masses of all products}} \times 100$

$= \frac{74.0}{92.0} \times 100 = 80.4\%$

(d) The reaction is reversible/equilibrium may have not been reached.

11 (a) Reaction with Na(s):

$HCOOH(aq) + Na(s) \rightarrow HCOONa(aq) + ½H_2(g)$

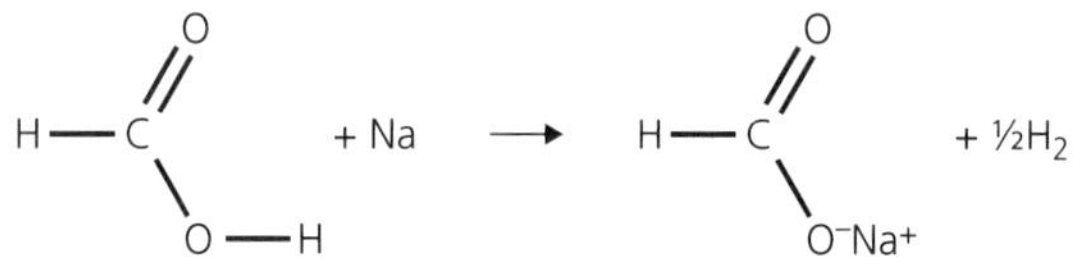

(b) Reaction with $NaHCO_3(aq)$:

$HCOOH(aq) + NaHCO_3(aq) \rightarrow HCOONa(aq) + H_2O(l) + CO_2(g)$

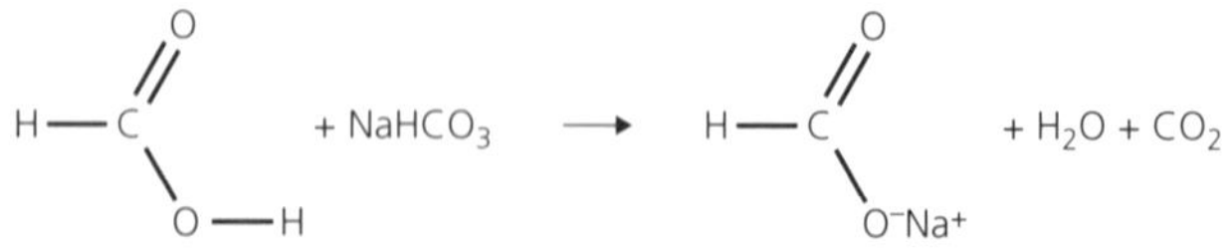

12 (a) Refluxing is continuous evaporation and condensation on heating so that volatile components do not escape.

(b)

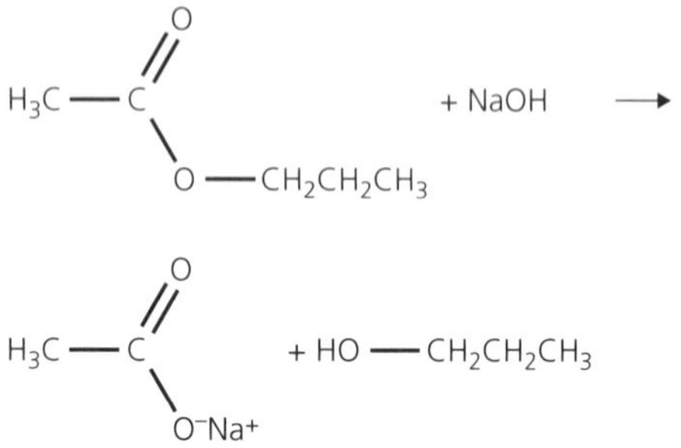

Sodium ethanoate    Propan-1-ol

## Chapter 12

1 (a) $CH_3Cl + NH_3 \rightarrow CH_3NH_2 + HCl$

$CH_3Cl + CH_3NH_2 \rightarrow (CH_3)_2NH + HCl$

$CH_3Cl + (CH_3)_2NH \rightarrow (CH_3)_3N + HCl$

(b) To get maximum yield of $CH_3NH_2$ there must be a large excess of $NH_3$.

2 (a)

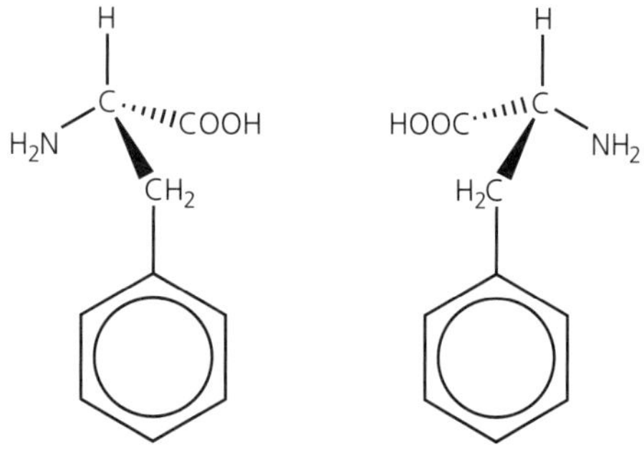

(b) (i) $C_6H_5CH_2CH(NH_2)COOH + HCl \rightarrow C_6H_5CH_2CH(NH_3^+Cl^-)COOH$

(ii) $C_6H_5CH_2CH(NH_2)COOH + CH_3OH \rightarrow C_6H_5CH_2CH(NH_2)COOCH_3 + H_2O$

(iii) $C_6H_5CH_2CH(NH_2)COOH + SOCl_2 \rightarrow C_6H_5CH_2CH(NH_2)COOCl + SO_2 + HCl$

3 (a) $C_{13}H_{10}N_2O_4$

(b)

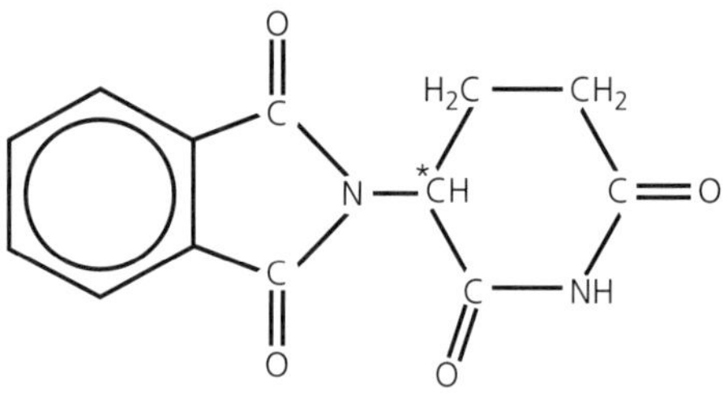

4 (a)

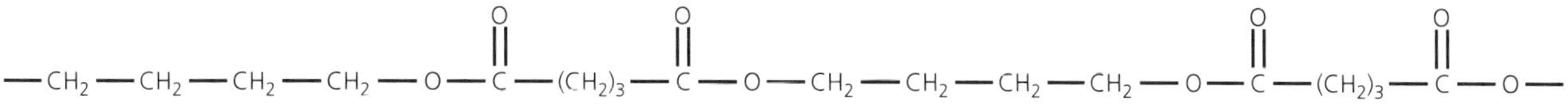

$$—CH_2—CH_2—CH_2—CH_2—O—\overset{\overset{\displaystyle O}{\|}}{C}—(CH_2)_3—\overset{\overset{\displaystyle O}{\|}}{C}—O—CH_2—CH_2—CH_2—CH_2—O—\overset{\overset{\displaystyle O}{\|}}{C}—(CH_2)_3—\overset{\overset{\displaystyle O}{\|}}{C}—O—$$

(b)

$$—O—\overset{\overset{\displaystyle O}{\|}}{C}—CH_2—\underset{\underset{\displaystyle CH_3}{|}}{CH}—\overset{\overset{\displaystyle H}{|}}{N}—\overset{\overset{\displaystyle O}{\|}}{C}—CH_2—\underset{\underset{\displaystyle CH_3}{|}}{CH}—\overset{\overset{\displaystyle H}{|}}{N}—$$

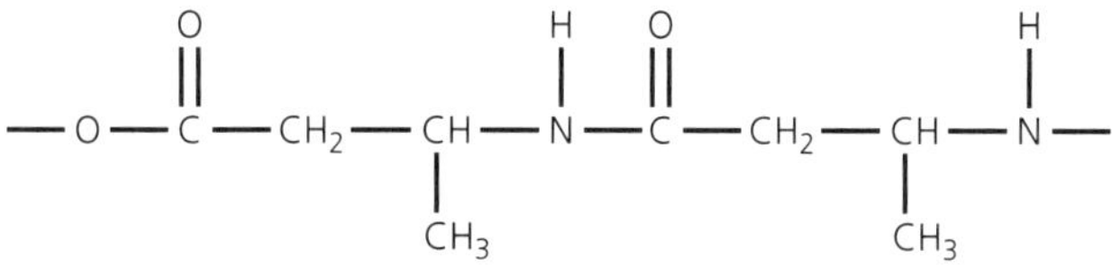

5 (a) (i) **Nylon-4, 6** 1,4-diaminobutane and hexane-1,6-dioic acid (or hexane-1,6-dioyl chloride)

**Nylon-6, 4** 1,6-diaminohexane and butane-1,4-dioic acid (or butane-1,4-dioyl chloride)

**nylon-6,10** 1,6-diaminohexane and decane-1,10-dioic acid (or decane-1,10-dioyl chloride)

(ii) Melting point depends on the strength and amount of intermolecular forces. Nylon-4,6 and nylon-6,10 have an amide link that enables them to form hydrogen bonds with adjacent strands of nylon. There are also van der Waals forces. Nylon-6,10 has more electrons than nylon-4,1, so nylon-6,10 has more van der Waals forces and, therefore, has a higher melting point.

(b) (i)

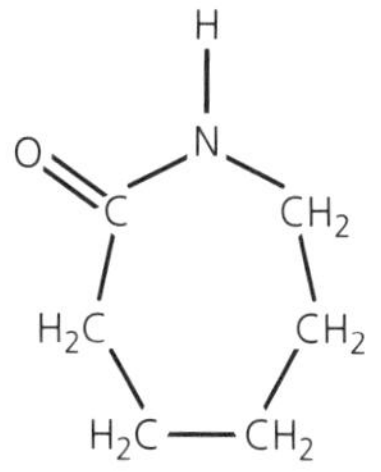

(ii)

$$—\overset{\overset{\displaystyle O}{\|}}{C}—CH_2—CH_2—CH_2—CH_2—CH_2—\overset{\overset{\displaystyle H}{|}}{N}—\overset{\overset{\displaystyle O}{\|}}{C}—CH_2—CH_2—CH_2—CH_2—CH_2—\overset{\overset{\displaystyle H}{|}}{N}—$$

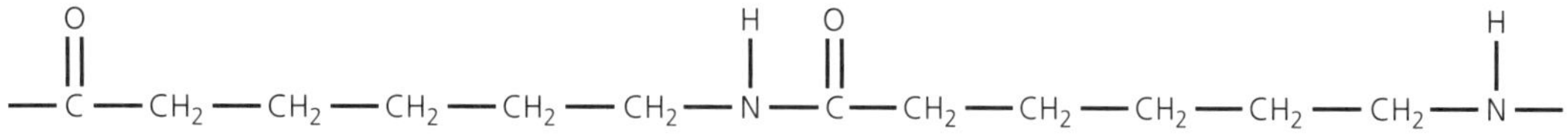

6

Acid hydrolysis gives:

[structure: HO–C(=O)–CH(CH₃)–CH(CH₃)–C(=O)–OH] and [structure: HO–(CH₂)₄–OH]

Base hydrolysis gives:

[structure: ⁻O–C(=O)–CH(CH₃)–CH(CH₃)–C(=O)–O⁻] and [structure: HO–(CH₂)₄–OH]

7

Reduction with NaBH₄
Reaction with HCN

Reduction with NaBH₄
Reaction with HCN
Oxidation to carboxylic acid

Oxidation to an aldehyde or carboxylic acid
React with carboxylic acid to get ester
Dehydrate to form alkene
React with NaBr/H₂SO₄ to get haloalkane

Oxidation to ketone
React with carbxylic acid to get ester
Dehydrate to form alkene
React with NaBr/H₂SO₄ to get haloalkane

**Aldosterone**

Ketone

Primary alcohol

Aldehyde

Secondary alcohol

HO

Ketone

Alkene

Reaction with either H₂ or Br₂ or HBr or H₂O

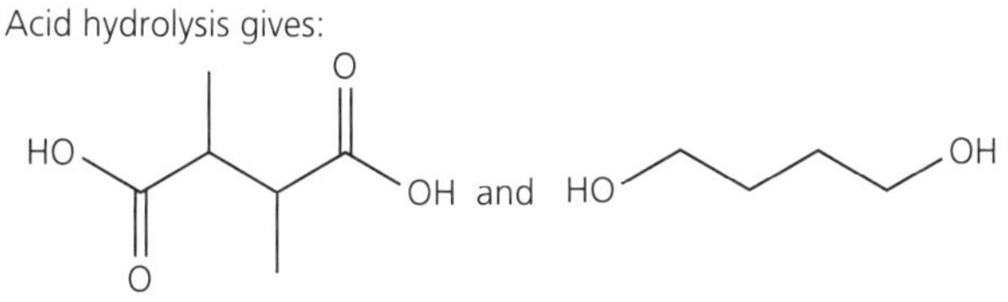

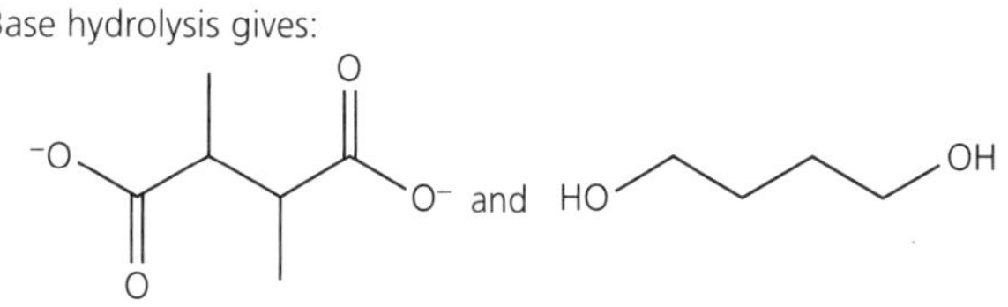

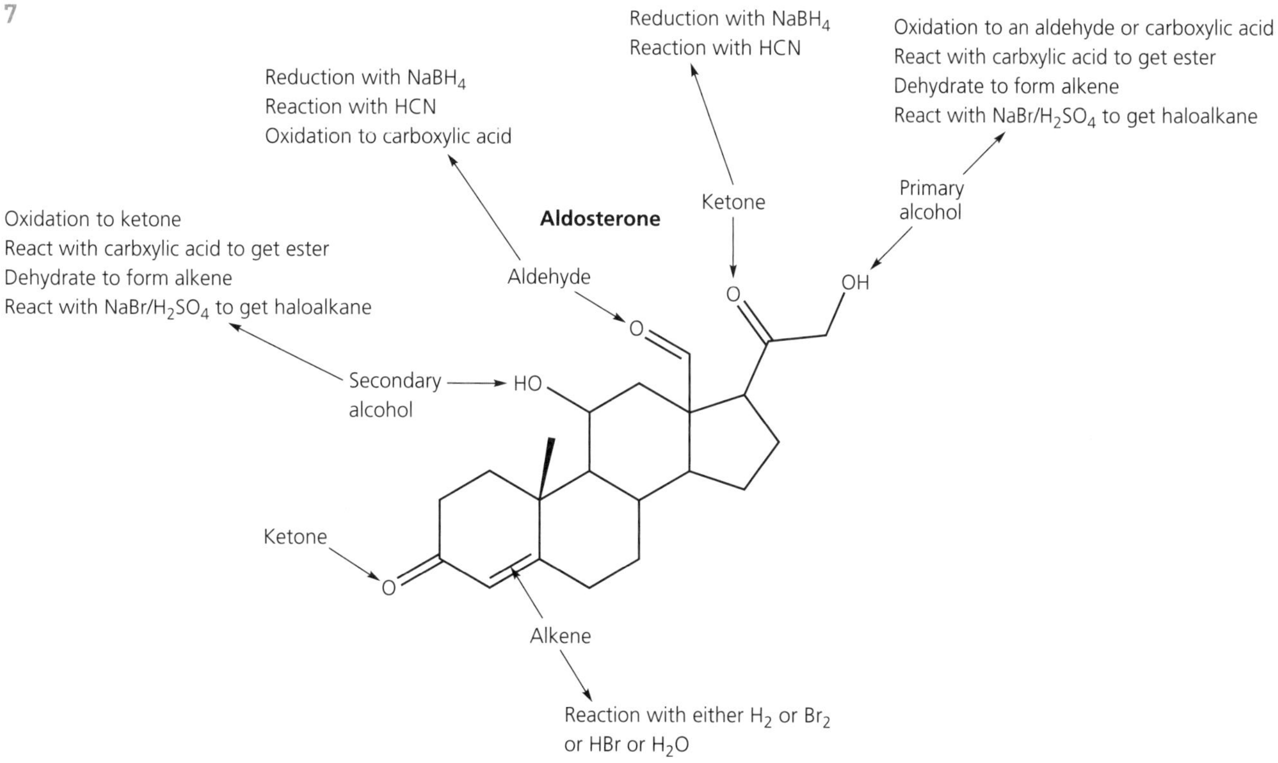

8 (a) 1 mark for each step.
The simplest way is:

**Step 1**

$$H_3C-C=CH_2 + H_2O \xrightarrow[\text{6MPa}]{300°C} H_3C-\overset{OH}{\underset{H}{C}}-CH_3$$

**Step 2**

$$H_3C-\overset{OH}{\underset{H}{C}}-CH_3 + [O] \xrightarrow[\text{Heat}]{H^+/Cr_2O_7^{2-}} H_3C-\overset{O}{C}-CH_3 + H_2O$$

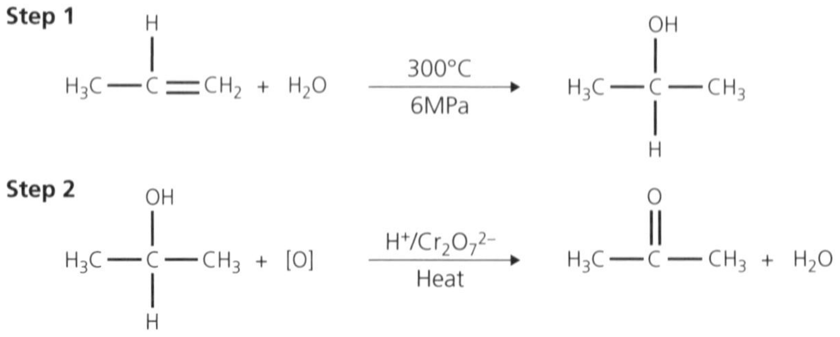

(b) 1 mark for each step.
The simplest way is:

**Step 1**

Loss of water

$$\xrightarrow[\text{Heat}]{\text{Acid catalyst}}$$

+ H_2O

**Step 2**

$$\xrightarrow[\text{catalyst}]{\text{NaOH as}}$$

+ HCl

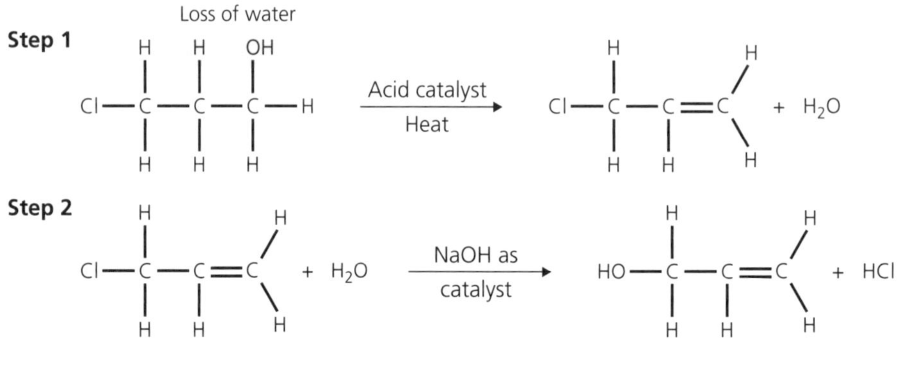

(c) 1 mark for each step.

**Step 1**

+ 2[H]

$$\xrightarrow[\text{NaBH}_4\text{(aq)}]{\text{Reducing agent =}}$$

**Step 2**

$$\xrightarrow{\text{Dehydration by heating}}$$
with an acid catalyst

+ H_2O

**Step 3**

$$\xrightarrow{\text{Polymerisation}}$$

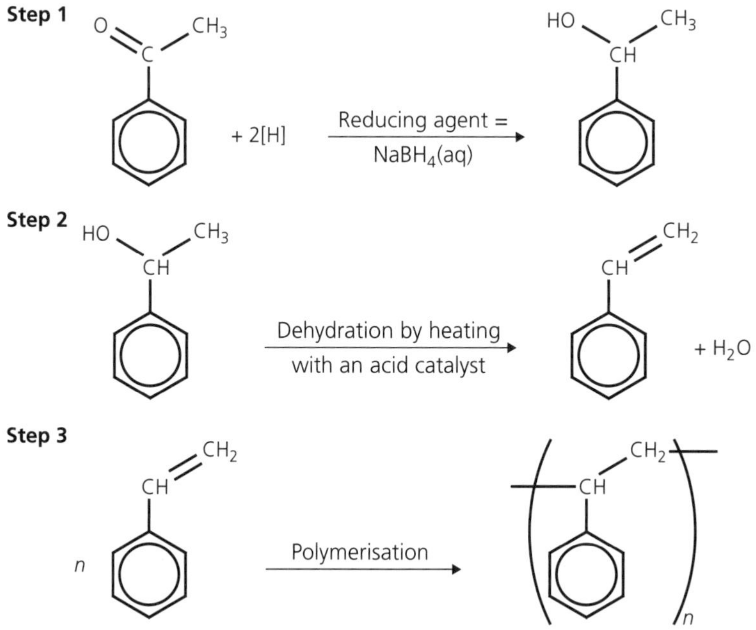

# Chapter 13

1 (a) (i) 5
  (ii) 4
  (iii) 3
  (iv) 5

(b) The two $CH_3$ on the left will be a singlet.
The $CH_3$ on the right will be split into a doublet.

The H on the second C from the right will be split into a quartet.

(c) (i) 3    (iv) 2
  (ii) 5    (v) 3
  (iii) 4

(d) The $CH_3$ on the left is next to a $CH_2$ and will be split into a triplet. The $CH_3$ on the right is next to a $C=O$ and will be a singlet. The $CH_2$ is bonded to a $CH_3$ and to the $C=O$, so will split into a quartet.

2 (a–c)

| | (i) | (ii) | (iii) |
|---|---|---|---|
| | 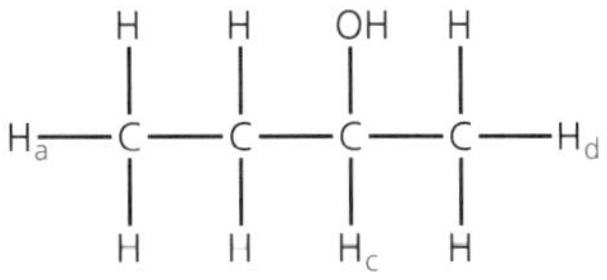 | 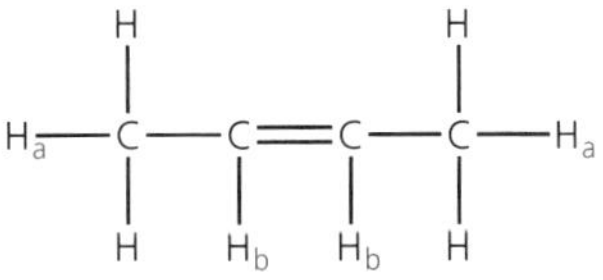 | 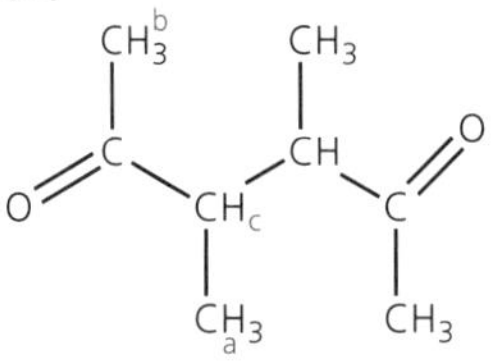 |
| Number of peaks | 5 | 2 | 3 |
| Chem shift range | $H_a$, $H_b$ and $H_c$ 0.5–2.0 ppm<br>$H_c$ 3.0–4.2 ppm<br>$H_d$ 0.8–12.0 ppm | $H_a$ 0.5–2.0 ppm<br>$H_b$ 4.5–6.0 ppm | $H_a$ 0.5–2.0 ppm<br>$H_b$ 2.0–3.0 ppm<br>$H_c$ 2.0–3.0 ppm |
| Number of peaks with $D_2O$ | 4 | 2 | 3 |

| | (iv) | (v) | (vi) |
|---|---|---|---|
| | 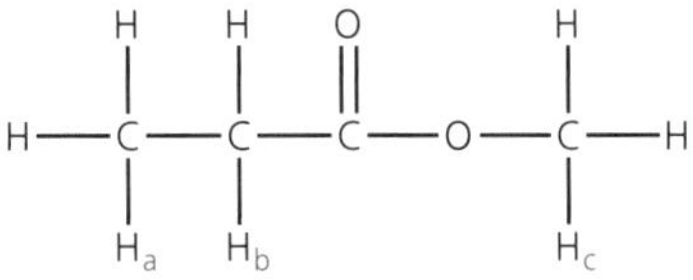 | 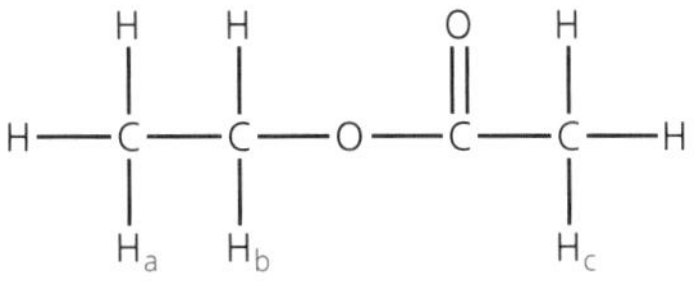 | 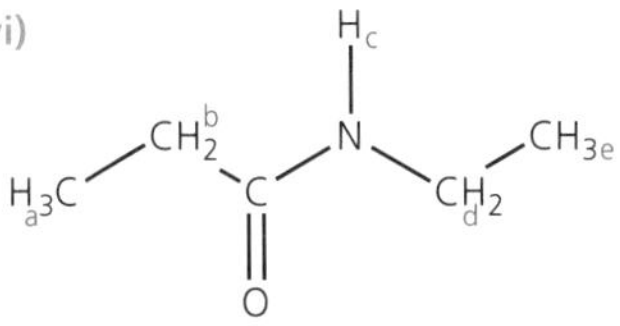 |
| Number of peaks | 3 | 3 | 5 |
| Chemical shift range | $H_a$ 0.5–2.0 ppm<br>$H_b$ 2.0–3.0 ppm<br>$H_c$ 3.0–4.2 ppm | $H_a$ 0.5–2.0 ppm<br>$H_b$ 3.0–4.2 ppm<br>$H_c$ 2.0–3.0 ppm | $H_a$ 0.5–2.0 ppm $H_b$ 2.0–3.0 ppm<br>$H_c$ 0.8–12.0 ppm $H_d$ 2.0–3.0 ppm<br>$H_d$ 0.5–2.0 ppm |
| Number of peaks with $D_2O$ | 3 | 3 | 4 |

3 (a) (i) 4
(ii) 5
(iii) 4
(iv) 5

(b) (i) 3
(ii) 5
(iii) 4
(iv) 2
(v) 4

4

| | (i) | (ii) | (iii) |
|---|---|---|---|
| | 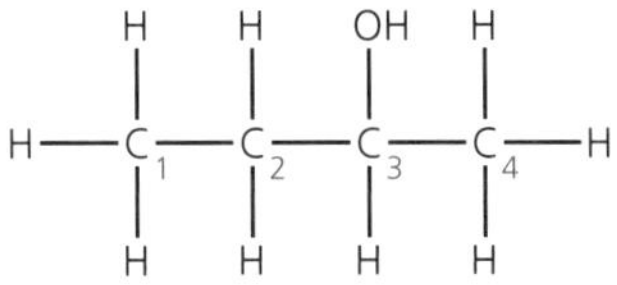 | 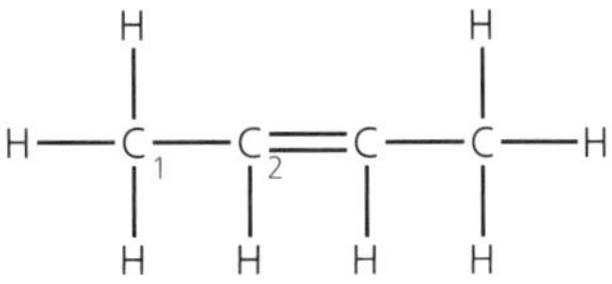 | 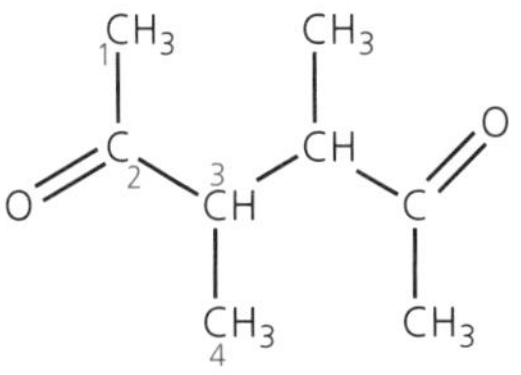 |
| Number of peaks | 4 | 2 | 4 |
| Chemical shift range | $C_1$ $C_2$ and $C_3$ 0–50 ppm<br>$C_3$ 50–90 ppm | $C_1$ 0–50 ppm<br>$C_2$ 110–160 ppm | $C_1$ $C_3$ and $C_4$ 0–50 ppm<br>$C_2$ 160–220 ppm |

| | (iv) | (v) | (vi) |
|---|---|---|---|
| | 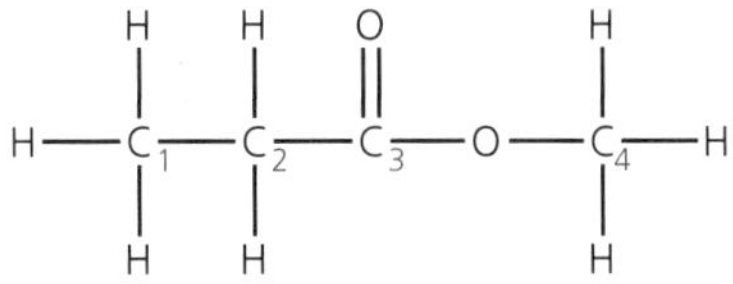 | 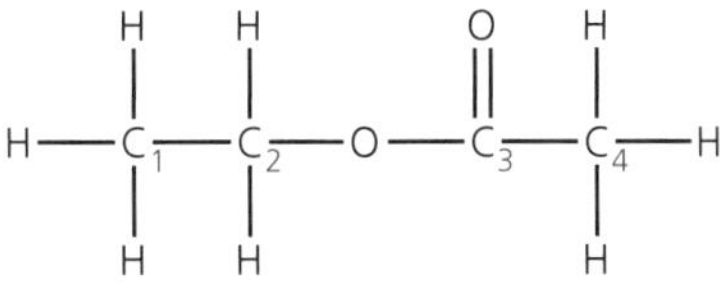 | 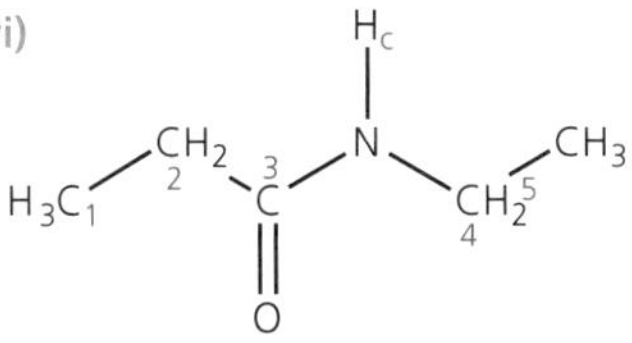 |
| Number of peaks | 4 | 4 | 5 |
| Chemical shift range | $C_1$ and $C_2$ 0–50 ppm<br>$C_3$ 160–220 ppm<br>$C_4$ 50–90 ppm | $C_1$ and $C_4$ 0–50 ppm<br>$C_2$ 50–90 ppm<br>$C_3$ 160–220 ppm | $C_1$, $C_2$, and $C_5$ 0–50 ppm<br>$C_3$ 160–220 ppm<br>$C_4$ 30–75 ppm |

5 (a) $^1$H-NMR detects the two proton environments labelled $H_a$ and $H_b$ in the diagram on the left; $^{13}$C NMR detects the three carbon environments labelled $C_1$, $C_2$ and $C_3$ on the right.

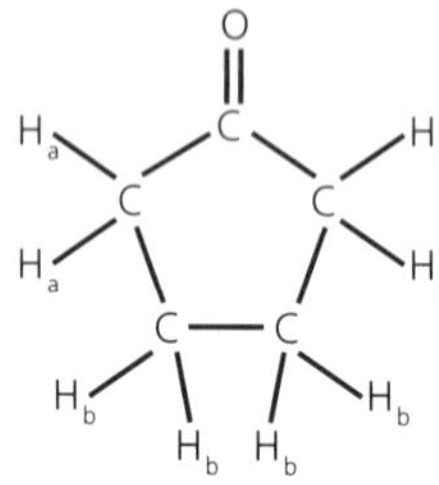

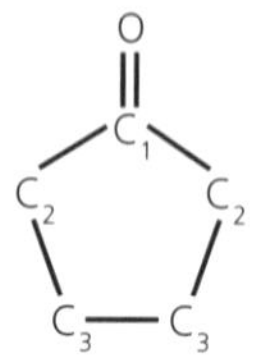

(b) $C_1$ in the range 190–220 ppm

$C_2$ in the range 20–30 ppm (5–55 ppm allowed)

$C_3$ in the range 5–55 ppm

(c) Chemical shifts: $H_a$ in the range 2.0–2.9 ppm; $H_b$ in the range 0.7–1.6 ppm.

Splitting patterns: $H_a$ and $H_b$ would both be split into a triplets as in each case the adjacent carbon has two hydrogens.

Relative peak area: 1:1 as there are four hydrogens in environment $H_a$ and four hydrogens in environment $H_b$.

6 Compound X is butan-2-one, $CH_3CH_2COCH_3$.

**Infrared spectrum**

Infrared spectrum confirms the presence of a carbonyl group.

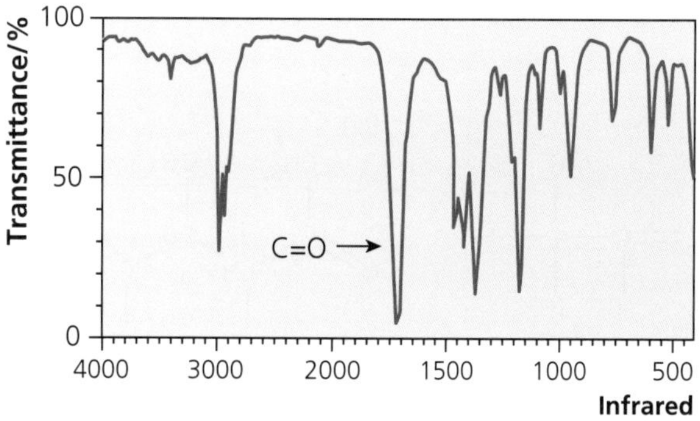


**Mass spectrum**

Mass spectrum indicates the presence of two fragments: $CH_3CO^+(g)$ and $CH_3CH_2^+(g)$. These add up to the molecular ion.

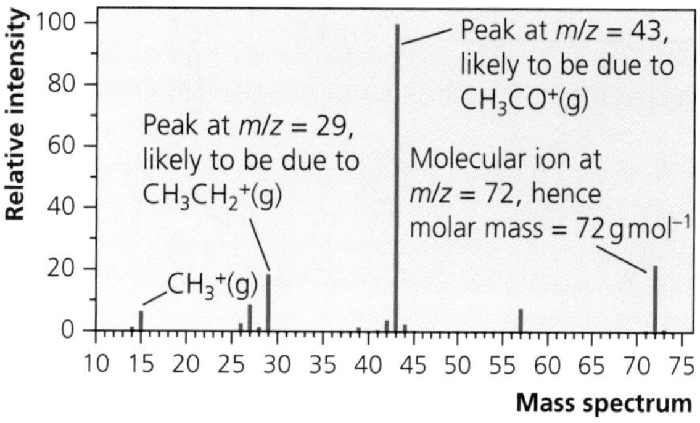


**$^{13}$C-NMR**

$^{13}$C-NMR confirms the presence of four different carbon environments, one of which is a C=O.

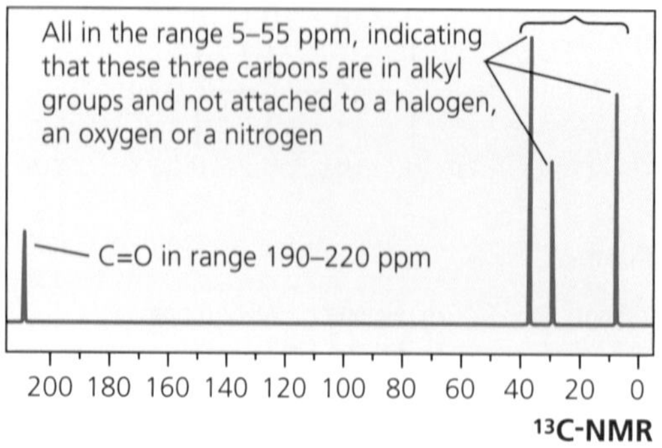


**$^1$H-NMR**

$^1$H-NMR confirms the presence of three different hydrogen environments.

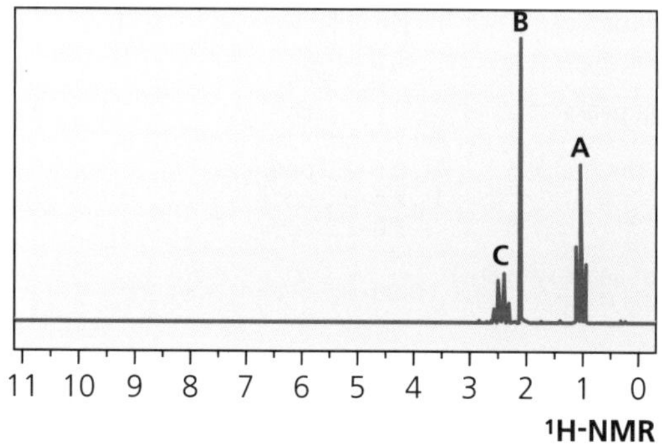


Peaks **A** and **C** show classic triplet and quartet splitting confirming the presence of a $CH_3$ group next to a $CH_2$ group. This also confirms that the carbon on the other side of the $CH_2$ has no hydrogens attached. Peak **B** is a singlet, which confirms that it is bonded to a carbon that has no hydrogens attached.

7

**A**

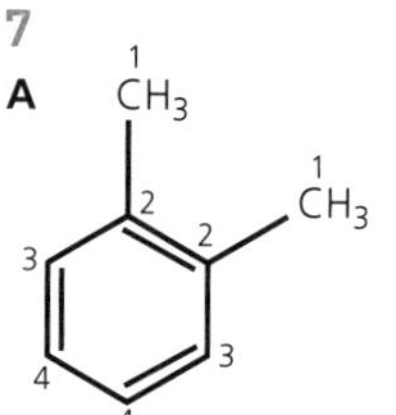

4 peaks

**B**

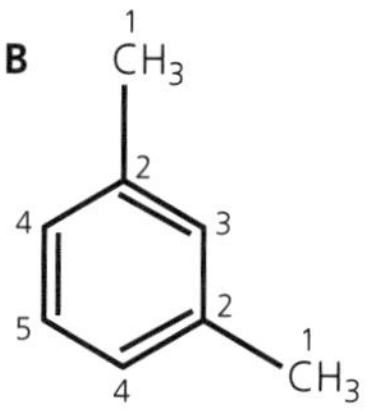

5 peaks

**C**

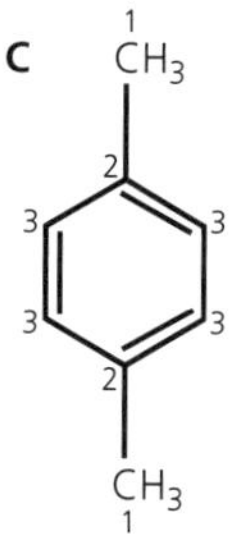

3 peaks

**D**

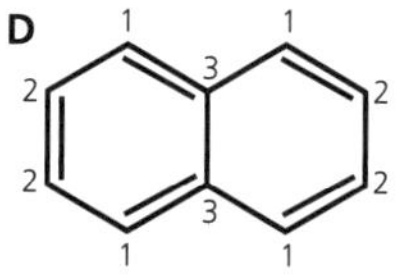

3 peaks

**E**

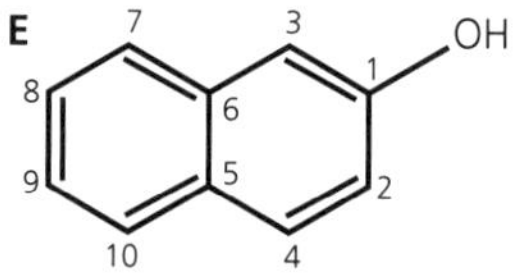

10 peaks

**F**

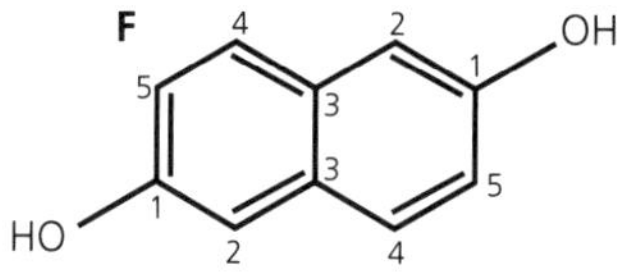

5 peaks

# Synoptic assessment answers

1 $(COOH)_2$ forms $(COO)_2^{2-}$ ions, which are oxidised to $CO_2$.

Hence:

$(COO)_2^{2-}(aq) \rightarrow 2CO_2(g) + 2e^-$

$MnO_4^-(aq) + 8H^+(aq) + 5e^- \rightarrow Mn^{2+}(aq) + 4H_2O(l)$

Multiplying the first half-equation by 5 and the second half-equation by 2 gives the overall equation:

$2MnO_4^-(aq) + 16H^+(aq) + 5(COO)_2^{2-}(aq) \rightarrow 10CO_2(g) + 2Mn^{2+}(aq) + 8H_2O(l)$

moles of $MnO_4^-$ in 23.90 cm$^3$ = $\frac{23.9}{1000} \times 0.0200$ = $4.78 \times 10^{-4}$ mol

moles of $(COO)_2^{2-}$ used in the titration = $\frac{5}{2} \times 4.78 \times 10^{-4}$ = $1.195 \times 10^{-3}$ mol

moles of $(COO)_2^{2-}$ in 250 cm$^3$ = $\frac{25.0}{25.0} \times 1.195 \times 10^{-3}$ = 0.0120 mol

The relative molecular mass of ethanedioic acid is 90.0.

mass of ethanedioic acid in four rhubarb leaves = 90.0 × 0.0120 = 1.08 g

If 24 g is a fatal dose, the number of rhubarb leaves needed = $\frac{24}{1.08} \times 4$ = 89 leaves.

2 25.0 cm$^3$ of $NaXO_3$ contains $\frac{25.0}{1000} \times 0.0500$ = $1.25 \times 10^{-3}$ mol

The overall equation for the titration is:

$2S_2O_3^{2-}(aq) + I_2(aq) \rightarrow S_4O_6^{2-}(aq) + 2I^-(aq)$

relative formula mass of sodium thiosulfate = 158.2

concentration of sodium thiosulfate = $\frac{13.63}{158.2}$ = 0.08616 mol dm$^{-3}$

amount, in moles, of $S_2O_3^{2-}(aq)$ in 29.0 cm$^3$ = $\frac{29.0}{1000} \times 0.08616 = 2.50 \times 10^{-3}$ mol

amount, in moles, of iodine produced = $1.25 \times 10^{-3}$ mol

So, in the reaction, 1 mol of $XO_3^-$ produces 1 mol of $I_2$

Since $2I^-(aq) \rightarrow I_2(aq) + 2e^-$, the oxidation number of X in $XO_3^-$ must reduce by 2 from +5 to +3.

3 (a)

The product is 2-phenylpropane:

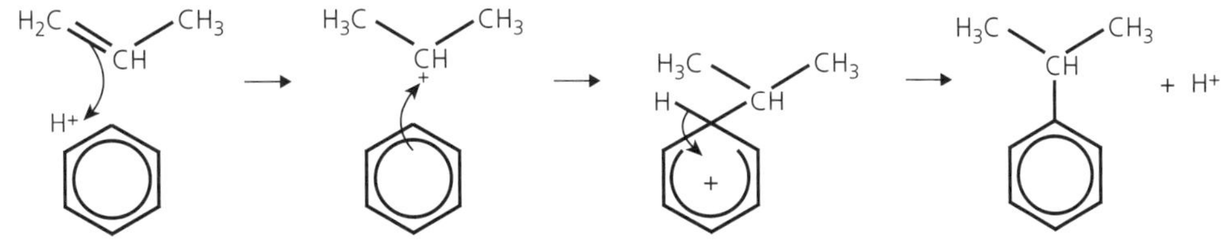

*or*

The product is 1-phenylpropane:

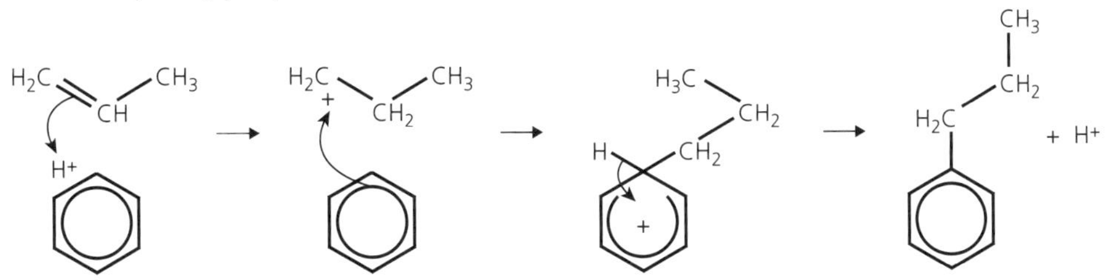

(b) The two possible products are 2-phenylpropane and 1-phenylpropane, as shown above. The product obtained depends on which carbonium ion (carbocation) is formed initially.

(c) Carbonium ions are unstable. They may not exist long enough to collide and react. Anything that stabilises the carbonium ion increases the chance of it existing long enough for collision and reaction to occur.

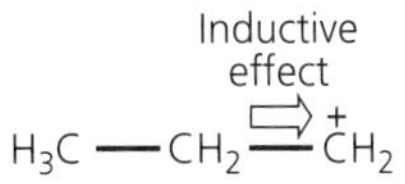


Primary carbonium ion

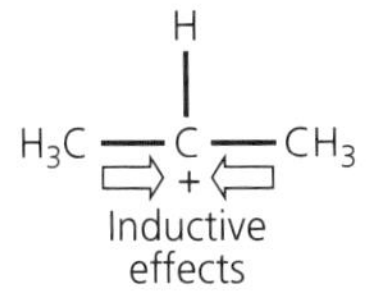


Secondary carbonium ion

Carbonium ions are stabilised by the inductive effect of adjacent alkyl groups, which release electrons along the σ-bond. The primary carbonium ion is stabilised by the adjacent ethyl group, $C_2H_5$; the secondary carbonium ion is stabilised by both adjacent methyl groups. This makes the secondary carbonium ion more stable and, therefore, more likely to exist long enough to collide and react. Hence the major product is 2-phenylpropane.

4

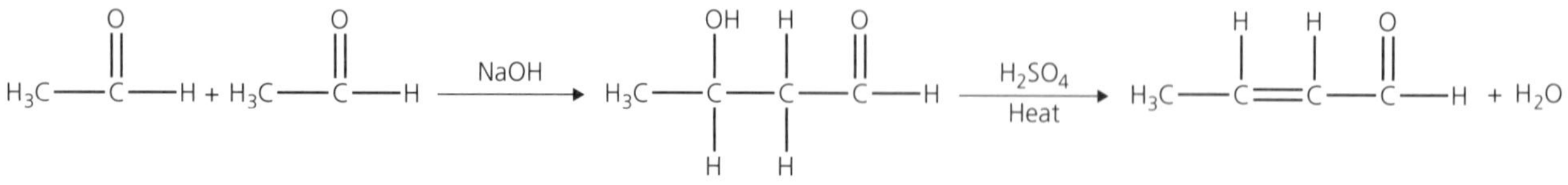


5 atom economy =

$$\frac{\text{molar mass of desired product (i.e. the ester)}}{\text{molar mass of all products}} \times 100$$

$M$ = molar mass of the ester. Therefore:

$$\frac{M}{M+18} \times 100 = 86.57. \text{ Hence } \frac{M}{M+18}$$

$$= \frac{86.57}{100} = 0.8657$$

$$M = 0.8657\,(M + 18) = 0.8657M + 15.5826$$

$$M - 0.8657M = 0.1343M = 15.5826$$

$$M = \frac{15.5826}{0.01343} = 116$$

The molar mass of the ester is 116 g mol$^{-1}$. Ethanol was used for making the ester so the general formula of the ester is $RCOOC_2H_5$. $COOC_2H_5$ has a mass = (12 + 16 + 16 + 24 + 5) = 73, hence the alkyl group R = 116 − 73 = 43 = $C_3H_7$.

The formula of the ester, compound X, is $C_3H_7COOC_2H_5$ and the carboxylic acid, compound Y, is $C_3H_7COOH$.

Compound Y could be:

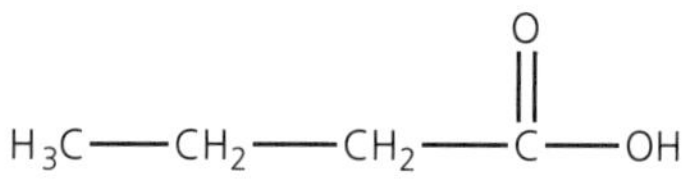

or

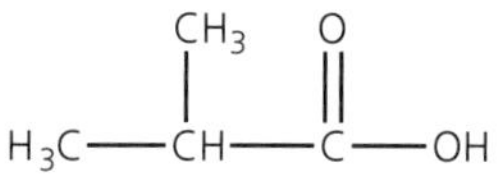

But the $^{13}C$ only has three peaks:

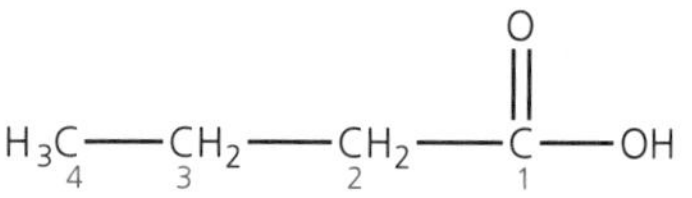

or

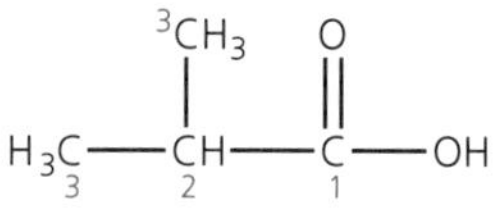

So compound Y is 2-methylpropanoic acid. Identify each peak using chemical shifts: $C_1$ at 185 ppm, $C_2$ at 35 ppm and $C_3$ at 19 ppm.

You should use all of the information in the question—the $^1H$-NMR shows:

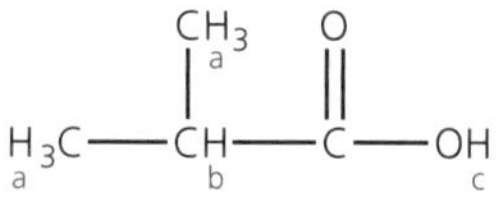

$H_a$ is a doublet and can be assigned to the peak at ~1.00 ppm, $H_b$ is a multiplet (split into 7 by the two adjacent/equivalent $CH_3$) at about 2.5 ppm. $H_c$ is the OH at 12 ppm and could be confirmed by adding $D_2O$ and the peak would disappear.

Compound X, the ester, is therefore:

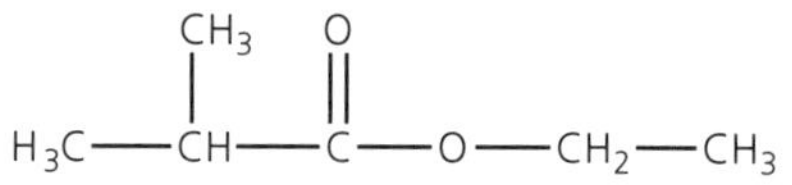

6 The final product has one more carbon than the initial aliphatic reagent. So a nitrile has to be formed. In order to form a nitrile a haloalkane must first be made.

Step 1: $CH_3CH{=}CH_2 + HBr \rightarrow CH_3CHBrCH_3$ (also get a small amount of $CH_3CH_2CH_2Br$)

Step 2: $CH_3CHBrCH_3 + C{\equiv}N^- \rightarrow CH_3CH(C{\equiv}N)CH_3 + Br^-$

($CH_3CH(C{\equiv}N)CH_3$ can be written as $(CH_3)_2CHC{\equiv}N$.)

Step 3: $(CH_3)_2CHC{\equiv}N + 2H_2O + H^+ \rightarrow (CH_3)_2CHCOOH + NH_4^+$

Hydrolysis in the presence of an acid catalyst.

Percentage yield calculation:

$$CH_3CH{=}CH_2 \xrightarrow[\text{40\% yield}]{\text{Step 1}} CH_3CHBrCH_3 \xrightarrow[\text{40\% yield}]{\text{Step 2}}$$

$$(CH_3)_2CHCN \xrightarrow[\text{40\% yield}]{\text{Step 3}} (CH_3)_2CHCOOH$$

It is possible to calculate the moles of $(CH_3)_2CHCOOH$ and then deduce the moles of the other products:

moles of $(CH_3)_2CHCOOH = m/M = \frac{7.04}{88} = 0.08\,\text{mol}$

In step 3, must have started with $\frac{0.08}{4} \times 10 = 0.20\,\text{mol}$.

In step 2, must have started with $\frac{0.20}{4} \times 10 = 0.50\,\text{mol}$.

In step 1, must have started with $\frac{0.50}{4} \times 10 = 1.25\,\text{mol}$.

Need to start with 1.25 mol propene, which at RTP = $1.25 \times 24 = 30\,\text{dm}^3$.